THE UPANIṢADS

A Study of the Original Texts

THE UPANIṢADS

A Study of the Original Texts

N. JAYASHANMUGAM

MOTILAL BANARSIDASS PUBLISHERS
PRIVATE LIMITED • DELHI

*First Edition : Delhi, **2016***

ISBN: 978-81-208-4066-9

MOTILAL BANARSIDASS
41 U.A., Bungalow Road, Jawahar Nagar, Delhi 110 007
8 Mahalaxmi Chamber, 22 Bhulabhai Desai Road, Mumbai 400 026
203 Royapettah High Road, Mylapore, Chennai 600 004
236, 9th Main III Block, Jayanagar, Bangalore 560 011
8 Camac Street, Kolkata 700 017
Ashok Rajpath, Patna 800 004
Chowk, Varanasi 221 001

MLBD Cataloging-in-Publication Data
The Upaniṣads : *A Study of the Original Texts*
by N. Jayashanmugam
ISBN : 978-81-208-4066-9
Includes —Appendix, Bibliography and Index
I. Hinduism II. Upaniṣads
III. Jayashanmugam, N.

Printed in India
by Ajanta Offset, Faridabad.
Published by Motilal Banarsidass Publishers Private Limited
www.mlbd.com • mlbd@mlbd.com

THE UPANIṢADS

A Study of the Original Texts

THE UPANIṢADS

A Study of the Original Texts

N. Jayashanmugam

To

Sri Aurobindo

(1872 – 1950)

Preface

The style of the Upaniṣads is very peculiar. But still it was quite intelligible to the great scholars of the Vedas (*mahāśrotriyāḥ*) about whom we hear from the Chāndogya Upaniṣad. We live in an age far removed from the age of these great scholars. As a result, we find the texts of the Upaniṣads to be very difficult to comprehend. Now commentators come to our help. They elucidate the texts and make them intelligible to us.

A good commentator should have three essential qualities. First, he should be well versed in all the original texts of the Upaniṣads. Second, he should have the skill to logically analyse the texts and successfully bring out their true import through the analysis. Third, he should be absolutely sincere in interpreting the texts. Generally speaking, the commentator is learned and skilful but not sincere in the work undertaken by him. Instead of elucidating the texts for the sake of making them intelligible he often uses elucidation as a means for getting support for his preconceived notions. As a result, he gives up the primary senses of the original words and puts into them his own personal ideas. His elucidation is really unfaithful to the original texts. In such cases he does not help us. However, we wrongly think that we are helped by him to understand the original teachings of the Upaniṣads. There are plenty of instances to prove that an innocent reader of the Upaniṣads is not really helped by the commentator whose work is a right elucidation of the original texts.

In the circumstance what is needed is this: We must use the power of discrimination and reject the wrong readings of the Upaniṣads through the authority of the original texts. By doing so we must try to arrive at the right readings of these texts. For destruction without construction serves no useful purpose.

There are twelve authoritative Upaniṣads. My book covers eight out of the twelve — Īśa, Kena, Kaṭha, Muṇḍaka, Māṇḍūkya, Śvetāśvatara, Chāndogya and Bṛhadāraṇyaka. It is a record of my long association with the Upaniṣads, my sustained attempt at reaching the right readings. My aim is to prove how discrimination and reliance on the original texts are the real sources of help in reading the Upaniṣads. The help given by the commentator is acceptable to the extent he is faithful to the original texts. Otherwise it is not indispensable. Trustworthiness of a commentary is determined not by the large support received from scholars but solely by the measure of its fidelity to the original scripture. There should be no doubt about it.

This book is intended to offer a new perspective to the study of the Upaniṣads. It will be surely helpful to all students of Indian Philosophy, particularly those studying the texts of the Upaniṣads. It contains valuable information and insights not obtainable from the current literature on the subject.

I take this opportunity to thank the *Indian Council of Philosophical Research*, New Delhi, which granted me a Senior Fellowship for studying the Upaniṣads.

NOVEMBER, 2015 N. JAYASHANMUGAM

Contents

Preface vii

Īśa Upaniṣad

Chapter 1 The Unique Possession 1
Chapter 2 The Dark Worlds 6
Chapter 3 Anti-Asceticism 25
Chapter 4 The Law of the Lord 39
Chapter 5 The Rule for Enjoyment 57
Chapter 6 Ātmahan 68

Kena Upaniṣad

Chapter 7 The Īśa and the Kena 82
Chapter 8 The Kena and the Vedic Ideal of Fulfilment 89

Kaṭha Upaniṣad

Chapter 9 The Yoga of Birth and Dissolution 108

Muṇḍaka Upaniṣad

Chapter 10 The Īśa and the Muṇḍaka 115
Chapter 11 The Two Vidyās 127
Chapter 12 Veda and Vedānta-Vyākhyāna 137
Chapter 13 Works and Immortality 151

Māṇḍūkya Upaniṣad

Chapter 14 The World and the Māṇḍūkya Upaniṣad 164
Chapter 15 Gauḍapāda's Kārikā: Two Aspects 172
Chapter 16 Catuṣpādātma-Siddhi 180

Chāndogya Upaniṣad

Chapter 17 The Example of Clay 202
Chapter 18 Scripture, Knowledge, and Delusion 216

Bṛhadāraṇyaka Upaniṣad

Chapter 19 Therefore That Became the World 228
Chapter 20 Death and Immortality 241
Chapter 21 Ātma Vidyā and Madhu Vidyā: Two Expositions 254

General Topics

Chapter 22 Textual Evidence for the Theory of Māyā 293
Chapter 23 The Mortal and the Immortal 302
Chapter 24 Two Forms of Synthesis of Yoga 312
Chapter 25 The Upaniṣads : A Survey of their Teachings 337
Chapter 26 Yoga: A Means to Fulfilment 359

Allied Topics

Chapter 27 Two Types of Devotees 370
Chapter 28 The Śāstra and the Brahmasūtra 380
Chapter 29 Philosophy of the Upaniṣads: A Study by Sri Aurobindo 390

Conclusion

Chapter 30 An Answer to the Critics 403

Appendix 407
Bibliography 408
Index 410

The word of Scripture is infallible; it is in the interpretation the heart and reason put upon the Scripture that error has her portion.

— *Sri Aurobindo*

1

The Unique Possession

GOD'S WORKER

If we give the fullest possible extension to the sense of the word *īśa*, it must be understood as referring to the Lord who is absolutely superior to all that exists here. He is limited neither by the world nor by that which transcends the world. He is in the world as its Inhabitant, but not limited by the forms and names of the world; He is one with the essence that transcends the world, but not limited by that essence. Hence He is the all-exceeding Master and by virtue of this mastery dwells everywhere (*īśāvāsyam idaṃ sarvaṃ*).[1] Since mastery without enjoyment is inconceivable, He is also the All-Enjoyer of the world. His true Law is that of all-mastery and all-enjoyment, a Law by which He is known (*satyadharmā*).[2]

Since He is our supreme Self, we are in possession of His Law in that Self. Owing to the ignorance of that Self we have abandoned our true Law and live in the ego. The ego tries to be the master and enjoyer of all without being the supreme Self. All desires are expressions of its ignorance and all grief and all misery (*śoka*)[3] are products of its desires. Our ideal is therefore to reject the ego and ignorance by rejecting the desires (*māgṛdhaḥ*),[4] get back to the true Law we have abandoned in our ignorance, and through that Law attain all-mastery and all-enjoyment in the supreme Self (*tena tyaktena bhuñjīthā*)[5] of the world.

Of all possessions the greatest is the true Law of the divine Self. By possessing this we arrive at fulfilment in the Self and a divine use of all other possessions — physical, vital, mental and psychic. But who is eligible for seeking the Law, the unique possession (*dhanam*)?[6] It is God's worker who performs all works for the sake of God, for the sake of fulfilling His Will in the world, without shrinking from them (*na vijugupsate*).[7] He is indeed a possessor of supreme knowledge (*vijānataḥ*).[8] For he knows that since the world is a becoming of

God, all works, done for the sake of God in oneself and God in others, culminate in knowledge.

BIRTH AND WORK IN THE WORLD

There are two wrong notions about work and birth in the world. First of all, all works are a source of misery and grief; if they are renounced, the seeds of misery and grief cease to be sown by them. This will bring the miseries to an end, because they cannot sprout from nothing. Secondly, birth is not only an opportunity for undertaking fresh works now but provides an effective link with the works of previous lives. So, even if one refrains from doing work, one will be forced into work by the momentum of past impressions which are beginningless and obstinate (*balavatī vāsanā 'nādiḥ*).[9] As a result, renunciation of work naturally culminates in the renunciation of physical life in the body (*dehatyāgam*).[10] Under no circumstance should a God's worker entertain these notions. On the contrary, he must accept and perform all works without refraining from them (*kurvann eveha karmāṇi*). [11] He must also accept his full term of physical life and complete it most willingly without trying to shorten it by any means (*jijīviṣet śataṃ samāḥ*).[12] For a seeker of the true Law of God it has been ordained thus (*evaṃ tvayi*)[13] — he must win the Law through works done for the sake of God. There is no other way than this (*nānyatheto'sti*).[14] Renunciation of life and work is not a means of attaining that end.

God's worker believes in his oneness with God (*so'ham*)[15] and does all work for Him. He knows that birth and work bind and are inseparably connected with each other. He also knows that their character is unalterable as long as one condition obtains — as long as the doer lives in the ego, considers himself to be an ego and does all work for the satisfaction of the ego. Therefore he refuses to fulfil this condition and tries to change the character of both by his determined refusal. If the ego is eliminated from the scheme of man's life, if the Lord is installed in its place and all works are done for the sake of the Lord, man's will disappears into the will of the Lord. And the Lord's will begins to express itself more and more in all works done by man. Now work can no longer bind the doer of work; nor can it produce misery for him. For it is not done for the sake of ego which separates him from the Lord and keeps him under the delusion that he is a mortal who exists for himself. Birth also changes like work. For works informed by God's consciousness and will take advantage of the connection that exists between birth and past works and acts gradually and steadily on the inherited impressions of man's subconscious being. This eventually wipes out all sins that make his life crooked and miserable (*juhurāṇam enaḥ*).[16] This backward operation of the liberated works of the individual on the obscure past of his birth is referred to as the extension of consciousness to the works of the past (*kṛtaṃ smara*).[17] As a result, he attains a new birth which makes enjoyment of immortality possible (*sambhūtyā amṛtam aśnute*).[18] A God-worker is one who is completely free from ego. He is faultless in his whole being, conscious as well as subconscious. Therefore he will not be tainted by works, even if he appears to act in the same way as an ignorant man acts (*na karma lipyate nare*).[19] Works done for God not only liberate the doer of works from sin and bondage but are a means of winning the Law of God, the greatest possession that he can ever have. Hence his prayer — *naya supathā rāye*.[20]

GOD'S WORKER AND THE SELF-SLAYER

The ancient sages of the Veda are doers of perfect and faultless works (*sukarmāṇaḥ*),[21] works without the taint of ego. With these works as the means they reached the world of Sūrya, the native home of the Sun-God, and attained immortality. This is referred to as the winning of the Sun (*sūryaṃ sanat*).[22] The sages of Vedānta also speak of reaching the Puruṣa, immortal and imperishable in nature, through the gate leading to the Sun (*sūryadvāreṇa*).[23] The same Sun-World is the goal of God's worker. Hence he is praying to the Sun-God to remove the obstruction and grant him the vision of Satyadharma: "O Pushan, do thou remove that for the law of the Truth, for sight (*tat tvam pūṣannapāvṛṇu satyadharmāya dṛṣṭaye*)".[24] In other words, Sun-World symbolises for the Vedāntin the original aspiration and destination of the sages of the Veda.

Those who consider birth and work to be twin sources of bondage and twin obstacles to freedom try to realise the unmoving One (*anejadekam*)[25] by renouncing both (*sannyāsena*).[26] The Vedānta refers to them by the term *ātmahanaḥ* (self-slayers). It does not take them to be really wise, for they miss the significance of the Lord who has taken residence in the world with the object of enjoying world-existence. Fulfilment in world-existence is not possible by rejecting birth and work, for without them world-existence is inconceivable. So far as the Lord's purpose is concerned, both birth and work are necessary. The self-slayers fail to see the true purpose of world-existence, for they live in utter ignorance of the Lord (*andhenatamasāvṛtāḥ*).[27] Being what they are, when they pass out of the body, they cannot go to the highest worlds of freedom and delight referred to as the Sun-Worlds by the Veda. The worlds they go to cannot be compared with the Sun-Worlds. If compared, they can only be labelled as other than the Sun-Worlds (*asūryā nāma te lokā*).[28] In other words, the goal of the Ātmahan is un-Vedic, not conforming to the teachings of the Vedic Ṛṣis.

The reference to the self-slayers is made with a view to suggest through comparison that by accepting God in the world, as also birth and work as the necessary terms of fulfilment in God, the doers of God's work have accepted a means and a goal acceptable to the ancient sages of the Veda.

NOTES

1. Īśa Upaniṣad (hereafter Īś.Up.), Mantra 1.
2. Ibid., Mantra 15.
3. Ibid., Mantra 7.
4. Ibid., Mantra 1.
5. Ibid.
6. Ibid.
7. Ibid., Mantra 6.
8. Ibid., Mantra 7.
9. Vivekacūḍāmaṇi, Verse 267.
10. Jābāla Upaniṣad (hereafter J. Up.), Mantra 6.
11. Īś. Up., Mantra 2.
12. Ibid.
13. Ibid.
14. Ibid.
15. Ibid., Mantra 16.
16. Ibid., Mantra 18.
17. Ibid., Mantra 17.

18. Ibid., Mantra 14.
19. Ibid., Mantra 2.
20. Ibid., Mantra 18.
21. Ṛg Veda, 4-2-17.
22. Ibid., 1-100-6.
23. Muṇḍaka Upaniṣad, 1-2-11.
24. Īś. Up., Mantra 15.
25. Ibid., Mantra 4.
26. J. Up., Mantra 6.
27. Īś. Up., Mantra 3.
28. Ibid.

2

The Dark Worlds*

THE WORD NĀMA IN THE TEXT

The Sun in the Veda represents the light of divine Knowledge. It is therefore appropriate to take the word to stand for Brahman who is the supreme light and knowledge. If the Sun signifies Brahman, then the Sun-worlds must signify the Brahman-worlds. This helps us to understand the true sense of the phrase *asūryā nāma te lokāḥ* [1] in the Īśa. If we drop *nāma* for the time being, it means "the worlds without the Sun, without the light of Brahman." The word *nāma* suggests that the worlds are Sunless only in name (*nāma mātra*) otherwise they are the Sun-worlds (*sūryā lokāḥ*). We have to identify what these strange worlds are — the Sunless worlds yet not really without the Sun, the worlds without Brahman yet not really without Brahman. *Asūryā nāma te lokāḥ* is a characteristic expression of the Īśa Upaniṣad whose style is to combine the opposites as typified in *atyeti tiṣṭhat, taddūre tadvantike, avidyayā mṛtyum tīrtvā*,[2] etc. Generally, the commentaries on the Upaniṣad have not given the word *nāma* the attention it really deserves. Sometimes it is interpreted to mean the notorious; sometimes it is understood as a particle aimed at placing emphasis on *asūryā*; but very often it is dropped and receives no comments. In extreme cases, as in Śaṅkara Bhāṣya, it is rejected as a meaningless particle (*nāmaśabdo'narthako nipātaḥ*).[3] If it is taken in the sense of a mere name, then *asūryā nāma te lokāḥ* means both dark and bright worlds.

THE WORLDS AFTER DEATH

When men die and depart from here, they go to other worlds (*tāṃste pretyābhigacchanti*). [4] There the individual formations of terrestrial existence get enlarged and objectified into independent powers and principles. Such an other-world process is necessary for determining the future course of evolution in the world. Our scriptures speak of three kinds of other worlds: (i) the dark worlds; (ii) the bright worlds; and (iii) the worlds of freedom.

(i) In these worlds there is an overwhelming obscurity. Those who go there are most unfortunate, for they have to live in gloom and suffering. They have no strength to oppose or escape the dark things that have fallen upon them. They struggle with these obscurities without hope or help. In these domains miseries are endless. As the Kaṭha puts it, they are verily joyless worlds (*anandā nāma te lokāḥ*).[5]

(ii) To the second belong the happy and cheerful worlds. Here all is bright and beautiful. Men who go there do not have to struggle and suffer, for they are blessed with a larger life of felicity. Hence they are called the dwellers of the heavenly worlds (*svarga lokāḥ*).[6] All here expand and grow into endless joys. Everything is full and without obstructions. In these worlds of larger existence (*lokaṃ viśālaṃ*) miseries do not exist but misery can arise beyond a particular point. As soon as the cycle of enjoyment is completed by the dwellers here, they are sent back to their earthly abode or plunged into a world much inferior to that (*imaṃ lokaṃ hīnataraṃ vā*),[7] making their ascent to the original level of consciousness a more difficult and a more painful process. In a sense neither the joyless worlds nor the heavenly worlds contribute to the progress of the souls that enter them. Both obstruct their advancement, the former by their adverse conditions and the latter by their law of larger enjoyment.

(iii) The third consists of the worlds of imperishable light and joy, immortal freedom and perfection. All here are suffused with pure consciousness and bliss. All delight in perfect knowledge and mastery. There is no darkness or decay, obstruction or misery. The immortals here, as in the heavenly worlds, are not subject to decay (*ajīryatām amṛtānām*).[8] Men who come here possess mastery over all worlds and realise all desires at their will (*saṃkalpādeva*). As the Chāndogya Upaniṣad puts it, whatever world they become desirous of, whatever objects they desire to have, these arise by their mere will.[9] They are free in every respect because they are perfectly moulded in their soul (*kṛtātmānaḥ*).[10] There is nothing in them which compels re-entry into the world (*na punar āvartante*).[11] In the Bṛhadāraṇyaka Upaniṣad, one of the oldest Upaniṣads, these worlds are referred to as Brahman-worlds (*brahmalokān*).[12]

THE THREE TYPES OF MEN

Thus there are three kinds of worlds beyond the world of mortals, the joyless worlds, the heavenly worlds and the worlds of Brahman. Certainly they are destinations of all who depart from here, but who goes to which destination depends upon the conduct by which one's soul is moulded here.

(i) As the Bṛhadāraṇyaka Upaniṣad puts it, men shape their souls by their works and conduct (*yathākārī yathācārī tathā bhavati*). [13]They become good by good works, bad by bad works. Bad works are works done under delusion without understanding and without taking into account the right rules of action. When works are done against the prescribed methods (*vidhihīnam*) [14] by taking the wrong to be the true law (*adharmaṃ dharmaṃ*),[15] they are deluded and bring grief and suffering, damage and destruction. He who embraces *adharma* makes himself miserable and gloomy.

(ii) Good works fall into two categories, those that bring perishable good and those that lead to imperishable good, Preyas and Śreyas. As against the bad works, the good works done according to *dharma* are superior, for they bring happiness and freedom, Preyas. But far superior are the good works done according to a higher *dharma* which brings imperishable happiness and freedom, Śreyas. Those who aim at the Preyas are ignorant and do not possess the discrimination to see clearly the difference between the two forms of *dharma*. They see the difference between *adharma* and *dharma* and therefore choose the good. But at the same time they do not see the difference between *dharma* and *paramodharma*. They are not subject to the delusive perception by which men resort to bad works. However, they cannot get out of the perverse perception which shows the lower to be the higher law (*ayathāvat prajānāti*).[16] Their system of choice is based upon the feelings of like and dislike rather than upon dispassion and discrimination. They dislike *adharma* and escape the evils of bad works; likewise, they like *dharma* and enjoy the pleasant results of good works. As their enjoyment arises out of attachment for the fruits of good works (*rāgāt*),[17] the freedom and happiness they possess are not true and everlasting. For whatever comes out of attachment is subject to destruction. Hence the doers of good deeds, even if they avoid bad ones, are declared to be men living in the depths of ignorance (*avidyāyām antare vartamānāḥ*).[18]

(iii) The higher law is of two types, the law of renunciation (*sannyāsadharma*) and the law of fulfilment (*satyadharma*). Both of them aim at the Śreyas because both hold that the aim is to be achieved by going beyond ignorance and egoism, desires and attachments. According to the former, the highest good consists in attaining the supreme Person, formless and nameless, by delivering oneself from the bondage of name and form (*nāmarūpād vimuktaḥ parātparaṃ puruṣam upaiti divyam*).[19] As long as the ego binds us to the instruments of cognition and action and makes us into a doer of works, deliverance is not possible. Once we give up the works and the body to which we are bound, the ego and its desires disappear. With their disappearance we are delivered and the highest good is achieved. All renouncers in the hour of their physical dissolution pass beyond death and are released into the worlds of Brahman. Therefore the best that can come out of works comes not when they are done according to the right law (*dharma*) but when they are completely dropped according to the higher law of renunciation (*sannyāsadharma*). As for the other law of fulfilment, the highest good consists not in withdrawing into the formless Person but in getting self-fulfilment in the Lord of the world, Īśvara, who is beyond the former. He is the master of works and enjoyer of world-existence. He is bound neither by the works of Nature nor by the world of which He is the Indweller. As man is one with Him in essence of being and consciousness, his highest aim is to attain absolute likeness to His law of being and becoming (*paramaṃ sāmyam*).[20] Man's aim cannot be otherwise than this (*nānyatheto'sti*). When he lives and works for God in the world, he is freed from ego and attachment and his personal will is completely merged in God's will. Works bring self-fulfilment in God when done according to the law of God (*satyadharma*). This is the highest that we can get out of them. Therefore we are asked to live a hundred years here performing works without bondage.

Thus we have three types of men, the deluded, the ignorant and the liberated. The first are without the benefits of the awakened mind. Hence they go to the joyless worlds. The second are devoid of the discriminating intelligence which helps one to see the inherent defects in the enjoyments obtained through *dharma*. Hence they go to the heavenly worlds where the joys are larger but not imperishable. The third type are free from ignorance and egoism and hence go to the worlds of Brahman, the abodes of imperishable happiness and perfection.

THE THREE CLASSES OF SELF-SLAYERS

In the *sūktas* of the Ṛg Veda there is no direct reference to the phenomenon of suicide. On the contrary, the constant theme of the Vedic poets is that they must live a full life here (*dīrghāyu*).[21] The same desire is found in the Brāhmaṇas and the Upaniṣads also. However, we may not be wrong if we think that suicide was not unknown to the Vedic society, for the Śatapatha Brāhmaṇa speaks to this effect: *na purāyuṣaḥ svaḥkāmī preyāt.*[22]

The Mahābhārata contains many references to suicide and in one place it specifically says that one who commits suicide does not reach the blissful worlds.[23] In the Dharma-Śāstras the consequence of suicide is more vividly brought out than elsewhere. The Parāśarasmṛti says that he who hangs himself out of pride or rage or affection or fear (*atimānād atikrodhāt snehād vā yadi vā bhayāt*)[24] sinks into blind darkness (*andhe tamasi majjati*) and remains trapped in hell (*narakaṃ pratipadyate*).[25] The Viṣnusmṛti looks upon suicides with contempt and says that they are degraded men (*patitā*). Even the thought of suicide is considered to be harmful and must be atoned for by the purificatory rites which wipe out the harm.[26]

In later Upaniṣads and the Smṛtis we find another attitude towards suicide. It is recognised as an ascetic phenomenon and encouraged as such. There seem to be two types of ascetics. To the first belong those who put on orange robes and are shaven and live on alms. They subject themselves to a rigorous self-discipline. They have no possessions, no enmity towards others and are pure in their heart. This gives them the competence necessary for liberating their Self. They have the option of renouncing the body in one of the ways prescribed for them: (i) the hero's method, the method of killing oneself with a sharp weapon; (ii) fasting unto death; (iii) entering into water; (iv) walking into fire; and (v) long journey unto death. The body is found to be an obstruction which does not allow the soul to unite itself with Brahman. When it is destroyed by competent ascetics, the obstruction is removed and the soul becomes one with Brahman (*brahmabhūyāya bhavati*).[27] As for the other ascetics, they tread the path of Brahman by assuming the form they had at birth and living without bonds and possessions. They live on alms and are pure at heart (*śuddhamānasaḥ*) and equal-minded in both gain and loss (*samobhūtvā*). Håving freed themselves from effort and egoism (*aprayatno nirmamaḥ*) they attain the supreme Self (*adhyātman*). But the body proves to be an obstruction if they try to be ever-established in the Self (*adhyātmaniṣṭhaḥ*) for the *aśubha karma* still left in the body acts as an adverse force which steadily thwarts their aim. With the competence conferred upon them by their awakening to the Self they easily dissolve the adversary (*aśubhakarmanirmūlanaparaḥ*) by dissolving the body and become united with the Self. The body is dissolved by the same method of renunciation as the one prescribed for the previous type of ascetics (*sannyāsena dehatyāgaṃ karoti*). [28] Thus body-renunciation is used for two purposes — either for liberating the Self or for uniting oneself with the liberated Self.

In the Manusmṛti also self-slaying for purposes of *mokṣa* is permitted. It refers to the various physical methods of doing away with the body such as *mahāprasthāna yātrā* (death by extended journey), etc. In the case of competent persons it is a means of overcoming the last obstacle to *mokṣa*. Just as the bird on the tree is free to leave the tree at its will, so does the renouncer leave his body (*tyajannimaṃ dehaṃ*).[29] Manu says that when a Vipra, freed from sorrow and fear, discards his body in accordance with the methods adopted by the great sages, he grows great in the world of Brahman:

> *āsāṃ maharṣicaryāṇāṃ tyaktvā'nyatamayā tanum;*
> *vītaśokabhayo vipro brahmaloke mahīyate*.[30]

The word Vipra has two meanings: (i) a Brāhmaṇa; (ii) a wise person. We may, therefore, take the word to stand for a person who is a Brāhmaṇa not only by *varṇa* but also by Brahman-consciousness. Taken in this broad sense, the above verse (6-32) may be understood as referring to a Brāhmaṇa who having reached Brahman discards his body. The qualifying phrase *vītaśokabhayaḥ* clearly indicates that the subject of the verse is a knower of Brahman who has become free from sorrow and fear. It is evident that here Manu speaks of a liberated Brāhmaṇa who resorts to body-renunciation in order to overcome the obstructions of the body. The words *brahmaloke mahīyate* emphasise the exalted position the Brāhmaṇa attains when the above obstructions fall away from him.

We have seen that in the later Upaniṣads and the Manusmṛti self-destruction is recommended as a means of either getting *mokṣa* or making *mokṣa* a perfect state to those who have trod the path of renunciation and attained the necessary competence. But in the Purāṇas such competence is not considered to be essential for getting *mokṣa*. The Padmapurāṇa declares that a man who knowingly or unknowingly, with or without desire dies in the Ganges secures after death both heaven and *mokṣa*.

> *jñānato'jñānato vāpi kāmato'kāmato'pi vā;*
> *gaṅgāyāṃ ca mṛto martyaḥ svargaṃ mokṣaṃ ca vindati.*[31]

Even an idea of *mokṣa* or a desire for *mokṣa* is not necessary for one to become free from *saṃsāra*. It means that whatever be the idea or desire of a person, his suicide will bring him *mokṣa* if it is committed in the Ganges. What is important is the place of death, not the competence of the individual, nor even his motive.

THE IDENTIFICATION OF THE SELF-SLAYERS

There are three types of people who resort to self-willed death: (i) men who have seen the Self but can possess it only at the time of death; (ii) men who both see and win the Self at the fall of the body; (iii) men who rely solely on the power of holy places or rivers to bring them some good in other worlds, or *mokṣa*. In principle the expression *ātmahano janāḥ* stands for all the three types of people. But which one among them is intended by the Īśa Upaniṣad is the point in question.

Before we try to fix the intended sense of *ātmahano janāḥ* we shall work out the correlation between the three types of men referred to in section 3 and the three classes of self-slayers mentioned in section 4. For that will help us to find out the worlds to which these self-slayers are destined to go when they die.

As we have mentioned in section 3, there are three types of men: the deluded, the ignorant and the liberated. In each type the soul is moulded in a particular way and this decides the worlds into which the departed go. In the case of the first the soul is ruined and lost in the abyss of disorder and ignorance. By following the path of *adharma* the deluded invite misery and grief upon their souls. So they find themselves in the joyless worlds when they leave this world. In the case of the second the soul receives a positive mould. It has a power and strength by which it keeps itself away from disorder and destruction. It is capable of a determined effort and growth, a right mode of living and enjoyment. By choosing the path of *dharma* the ignorant are attached to things that are pleasant and beneficial and averse to things that bring misery and grief. When they die, they pass into the heavenly worlds. In the case of the third the soul gets an ideal mould by which it is eternally free and perfect, self-possessed and self-ruled. Its true nature (*svabhāva*) is no longer veiled by ignorance, passions, desires and the dualities. By living according to the supreme *dharma* the liberated win immortal felicity and infinite knowledge. When they depart from this world, they enter the worlds of Brahman. No one can go to these worlds if his soul is not moulded to be a *mukta*. Neither *adharma* nor even *dharma*, except the supreme *dharma*, can bestow upon one this ideal mould. This is the declaration of the sages of the Veda and Vedānta. Any pronouncement on *mokṣa* by other authorities is acceptable only if it agrees with the authority of these ancient sages, otherwise we are not obliged to give serious thought to the teachings given by the former.

The Purāṇas promise *mokṣa* to all who kill themselves in a sacred river or place, without insisting on the possession of the necessary competence. What these people will really get after death is not at all our concern. Our concern is to show how they will be viewed by the highest authority in the country, Veda and Vedānta. According to this authority, they cannot get freedom from *saṃsāra*, for they are not moulded to be *muktas*. They may be classified either as the deluded or as the ignorant. As the deluded, they may be giving allegiance to *adharma* in their life and hence their destination after death will be the joyless worlds. No earthly power can alter the destination, much less the alleged power of their place of death. If, on the contrary, they happen to be the ignorant, they cannot be lured by the promise of *mokṣa* by the Purāṇas. For, without asking them to undergo the painful process of suicide, their law of *dharma* assures them of good things in this world and larger enjoyments in the worlds of heaven. To them the Preyas is all and *mokṣa* is its heavenly version.

Turning now to the Manusmṛti and the later Upaniṣads, the renouncers uphold the supreme law (*paramodharma*) and aim at the

Śreyas by the strength of their competence. They have renounced all —possessions, desires, attachments, delusions, ego and ignorance; they have transcended not only the evils of *adharma* but the good things of *dharma* also. They have acquired the competence necessary for becoming *muktas*. When they do away with the body according to the methods of *sannyāsa*, they succeed in removing the obstacle to *mokṣa* regardless of whether the obstacle is to get *mokṣa* or to make *mokṣa* a steady realisation. They are liberated from *saṃsāra* and reach the worlds of Brahman, for they are moulded to be *muktas* by the law of renunciation prescribed by the ancient sages.

Of the three classes of men mentioned in section 4, the renouncers alone are found to be eligible for everlasting habitation in the worlds of Brahman. In other words, *ātmahanaḥ* evidently stands for the renouncers. Others are excluded from this category because they cannot win the worlds of Brahman on the strength of the alleged capacity of sacred places or rivers to grant freedom from *saṃsāra*. *Mokṣa* is an ideal soul-state which alone makes entry into the worlds of Brahman possible. Neither a stationary nor a moving physical object in the world can produce that soul-state.

As for the competence necessary for *mokṣa* as also for going to the worlds of Brahman after death, one may cite the authority of the Gītā and argue that such qualification is not always necessary. In chapter 8 the author of the Gītā declares that "whoever leaves his body and departs remembering Me even at that time, he attains My status of being, *sa madbhāvaṃ yāti*."[32] He also emphatically says that there is no doubt about this promised attainment (*nāstyatra samśayaḥ*).[33] If we leave aside the fact that here the Gītā is speaking about one whose death is natural and not self-willed, there is a *prima facie* evidence in favour of the above argument. Also, we cannot brush aside the argument saying that it is based on a smṛti text, for the Gītā holds an exceptional position as one of the three foundational texts on Vedānta, a position equal to that of the Upaniṣads. However, the argument loses its force and becomes pointless when we carefully read verses 5 and 6 together. In verse 6 the Gītā says:

> *yaṃ yaṃ vāpi smaranbhāvaṃ tyajatyante kalevaram;*
> *taṃ tamevaiti kaunteya sadā tadbhāva bhāvitaḥ.*[34]

We cannot bring out the full significance of this verse better than Sri Aurobindo. He writes:

> In the critical moment of passing from the mortal plane of living, ... it is not a death-bed remembrance at variance with or insufficiently prepared by the whole tenor of our life and our past subjectivity that can have this saving power. The thought of the Gita here is not on a par with the indulgences and facilities of popular religion; it has nothing in common with the crude fancies that make ... the precaution or accident of a death in sacred Benaras or holy Ganges a sufficient machinery of salvation. The divine subjective becoming on which the mind has to be fixed firmly in the moment of the physical death, *yam smaran bhāvam tyajati ante kalevaram*, must have been one into which the soul was at each moment growing inwardly during the physical life (*sadā tadbhāva bhāvitaḥ*).[35]

As Sri Aurobindo makes it clear, if one imagines that *mokṣa* can be easily attained by a manipulation of the last moment of one's life without making oneself eligible for that ideal in the life one lived, this must be dismissed as one of "the crude fancies" of human mind.

THE ANTI-ASCETIC STANDPOINT

In the hymns of the Ṛg Veda asceticism has no place. The Vedic poets were householders who knew nothing of the *sannyāsāśrama*. Originally, with a few exceptions, the Vedic knowledge passed through a long succession of fathers and sons and flourished within the framework of the family. The poets did not consider life to be an obstacle either to possess God-knowledge or to work out the consequences of this great possession in the world. To them all that belong to the higher planes of existence are here in the embodied being; therefore, either to possess or to enjoy them one does not have to renounce one's life and works. All subsequent developments in the country are either a departure from or a return to this original positive attitude exhibited in the hymns of the Veda.

At the time of composing the Īśa Upaniṣad the departure from the Vedic way of life must have reached a point at which men came to be swayed by ascetic aspirations and ideals which tilted the balance away from the world and placed an exclusive emphasis upon God, thus bringing into human life a lopsided outlook and an undue exaggeration of the limitations of life. And the sage of the Upaniṣad seems to be determined to right the imbalance by reaffirming the ideals of the Veda. Each word, each sentence, each couplet in the Upaniṣad has been deliberately chosen to deliver the message pointedly. The obvious aim of the sage is not made obvious through explicit expressions; but nevertheless this is made good by the chosen style of the Upaniṣad. At each step we see clearly the two sides of his teaching, his tacit opposition to asceticism and trenchant affirmation of the Vedic positivism.

To the ascetics the world, of which we are part, with which we are in constant touch through works, and in which we live, is not the right place of living if our aim is to realise God. For it is a product of Prakṛti. As the Prakṛti is essentially a power of discriminating intelligence (*buddhi rūpaḥ*), it is found to be a consciousness which diversifies and operates as a principle of separation; it is not a consciousness of oneness working out the potentialities of the being in accordance with its own laws of development. In other words, it is not a consciousness self-possessed and self-determined. As this cosmic Buddhi is without a secure basis or support, all its workings and consequences, processes and formations are governed by a necessity and a control both of which are inscrutable and lie beyond the limits of its consciousness and power. Therefore the world is not a place where God, absolutely free and indeterminable, can live and have His divine kingdom. The call of the ascetics is therefore to sever all connections with world, to withdraw completely into the deepest part of one's being untouched and unimpaired by the influences of the world and unite oneself with God who is beyond Time and Space, Name and Form, Birth and Death. The ascetic ideal is accomplished in two stages: first, by renouncing works; secondly, by renouncing the body where the seeds of works are stored up in the form of subtle impressions (*vāsanās*).

The Īśa Upaniṣad does not share the view of the ascetic. It does not view the world either as a product of Nature of which the Buddhi is the highest principle or as a domain of necessity where freedom is inconceivable. It upholds the view that all here are the becomings of God (*ātmaivābhūt*), even that which appears to be other than or devoid of God. The world is indeed the work of Prakṛti which is of the nature of the Buddhi. But this is not the whole truth, for there is the divine Mind (*vijñāna*) which is one with God and not divorced from Him and of which the Buddhi is an instrument and a lower modification. The divine Mind, unlike the Buddhi, is the real source of the world. It is founded upon the One and manifests the world out of the One through a process of triple becoming [36] — Kavi (seer), Manīṣī (thinker) and Paribhū (realiser). From the point of view of this superior Mind, God is indeed beyond Nature (*tannaijati*), beyond the world (*taddūre*) and beyond all existences (*tadu sarvasyāsya bhāhyataḥ*); [37] but He is not limited by His transcendence. He is everywhere, in Nature (*tadejati*), in the world (*tadvantike*) and in all existences (*tadantarasya sarvasya*).[38] He is not limited either by transcendence or by immanence, for He is higher than both. His form is most blessed (*rūpaṃ kalyāṇatamaṃ*)[39] and can be known in that way only when we see both the transcendence and the immanence together (*vedobhyaṃ saha*).[40] Therefore the necessity we see in the world disappears if we understand that the world is basically a work of God's Mind and not of the Buddhi which is ignorant of God and bound by the consciousness of the Many. If God and the world are not opposites, then the first three verses not only set forth the positivist position of the Vedic sages but also reject the views of the ascetics.

(i) The ascetic affirms that the world is Godless (*anīśvaram*) and hence a worthy object of disgust. The Upaniṣad, on the contrary, declares that the world has been created not in accordance with an inscrutable necessity but in obedience to the will of God. It has been created for the sole purpose of habitation by the Lord (*īśavāsyam idaṃ sarvaṃ*), for His enjoyment and delight. Hence to abandon the world out of ascetic disgust is wrong and contrary to God's will. "By seeing the divine law according to which God lives in the world you should wholeheartedly accept the world you have abandoned out of disgust. As you are one in essence of being and consciousness with God, you should, like Him, enjoy the world (*tena tyaktena bhuñjīthāḥ*). In doing so you should eliminate the desires of the heart (*mā gṛdhaḥ*), for God enjoys without ego and desire."

(ii) The second affirmation of the ascetic is that God is to be attained by the renunciation of works and physical life. In an emphatic denial aimed at the ascetics the Upaniṣad says: "You should do all works here without abandoning them (*kurvanneveha karmāṇi*) and wish to live a hundred years without trying to shorten your physical life." With a view to make its position abundantly clear the Upaniṣad adds: "You are a man (*nare*), an embodied being; so the way to God is laid out in you through life and works and not otherwise (*evaṃtvayi nānyatheto'sti*)[41] i.e. not through their renunciation."

(iii) The third affirmation of the ascetic is that as long as one is engaged in works and for this purpose holds on to his physical life, he cannot get away from the world or from the grief and suffering imposed on him by the world, even if he is disgusted with it. The way to get rid of it is to renounce works, become a competent renouncer, and then make the final renunciation of physical life. This also the Upaniṣad rejects and says: "If, as an embodied individual, your active life is modelled on God in the world, the supreme Jiva, you will not be bound by works (*na karma lipyate nare*). God is the master of works, for His Nature from which works are born is without ego and desire. If you remove ego and desire from your *svabhāva*, you will also not fall into the bondage of works but become a master in all that you do in the world."

A further extension of this anti-ascetic standpoint has given rise to the third verse of the Īśa and the verse must be understood as such.

THE SUNLESS WORLDS AND THE SUN-WORLDS

The Īśa is acclaimed by Sri Aurobindo as one of the best scriptures of the world. According to him, it is "a statement of inspired thought each part of which has been perfectly seen by the revelatory faculty and perfectly stated by inspired expression in itself, in relation to the others and in its place in the whole. Not only every S[h]loka but every word in each S[h]loka has been perfectly chosen and perfectly placed."[42] Therefore, if we unveil the full significance of the third verse it may help us to understand how it has been "chosen" and "placed" in the Upaniṣad.

From the anti-ascetic standpoint of the Īśa and also from the dictionary sense (*rūḍhi*) of the word *ātmahan* (one who commits suicide), it is but appropriate to take the words *ātmahano janāḥ* to signify the ascetics who seek God through renunciation which culminates in the destruction of their physical self. Other categories of self-slayers stand excluded from the purview of the Upaniṣad, for its universe of discourse is limited to competent individuals whose aim is the realisation of God. The other self-slayers are either unrelated to the aim of attaining God or, if they are related to the aim, do not possess the right psychological mould.

If we take the first three verses, we find that as the Upaniṣad passes from verse to verse, the anti-ascetic standpoint becomes more and more pronounced. In the first it asks us to abandon world-disgust and make the abandoned world — the world abandoned out of disgust — an object of enjoyment (*bhuñjīthāḥ*); in the second it says that for an embodied individual life and works are the way and not their renunciation (*nānyatheto'sti*); in the third its reference to the ascetics is almost direct — *ātmahanaḥ*, men who resort to body-renunciation for the sake of getting freedom from *saṃsāra*. Two significant expressions are used here to show that the ascetics are not favourably viewed by the Upaniṣad — (i) *janāḥ*, men who are concerned with themselves and their personal good; (ii) *andhena tamasāvṛtāḥ*, men who are obstructed by their blindness and ignorance.

(i) Though the Śreyas is to be attained by the highest law, the Īśa does not find that law in the *sannyāsa dharma*, the law of physical renunciation. It seeks to realise the aim by another law, the law of psychological renunciation *(satyadharma)*. Its insistence is on the renunciation of the ego and desires and not on that of works and embodied life in the world. God's will is to fulfil Himself through works and enjoy self-fulfilment in the world. It is for this purpose that He has taken residence here. Man's aim must therefore be to fulfil God in himself and God in others through works done for Him. He should not envisage a personal aim and pursue it (*nānyatheto'sti*) for that will not be according to the will of God. The ascetic's goal is to abandon the world, abandon life and works and withdraw into the formless and nameless Brahman, the transcendent beyond the world. To him birth is a bondage and this bondage is broken by his personal liberation. However lofty his aim may be, he is very much like an ordinary man (*janaḥ*) who thinks about himself and his personal good. *Mokṣa* is great but it is greater (*saṃsiddhi*) when attained according to God's Will. In God's view *mokṣa* is not an end in itself but a means, a right condition for seeing clearly His will in the world and fulfilling that will in the right way. It is not enough if we possess immortality, but it is necessary that its possession must make faultless works possible (*na karma lipyate*), works informed by God's consciousness. It is for this reason that Sri Krishna declares that those who are united with the supreme Lord are superior (*yuktatamā*) to those who have attained exclusive union with the unmanifest immutable Brahman.[43]

(ii) To work for God in the world is to work for the good of all, for the promotion of unity in mankind (*lokasaṃgraham*).[44] If works are to be done without ego and desire, then there is only one motive for them i.e. the motive of fulfilling God in oneself and God in others, of leading the world to the aim with which God has created it and taken residence in the heart of all creatures. A worshipper of the supreme Lord is therefore a true helper of humanity, a true friend of the world who works for the sake of all.

They who worship the Lord, who is extended equally in the world and in Brahman, do so with *satyadharma*. They are unique and cannot be classed with others who worship either the Avidyā (*avidyām upāsate*) or the Vidyā (*vidyāyāṃ ratāḥ*), either the world of which the Buddhi-driven Nature is the highest cause or the transcendent Brahman beyond the world of names and forms. To worship the world to the exclusion of Brahman is the aim of the ignorant. Hence they follow the law of right enjoyment (*dharma*). To worship Brahman to the exclusion of the world is the aim of the ascetics. Hence they follow the law of renunciation (*sannyāsa dharma*). Thus we have three types of worshippers: (i) the wise who worship the Lord of the world; (ii) the ignorant who worship the world; and (iii) the ascetic who worship Brahman. Among them the wise win the highest merit, because their aim is not their personal good but the good of the world, the fulfilment of God's will in the world. The other two, the ignorant and the ascetic, are inferior to the wise, because both of them aim at personal good (*tamaḥ praviśanti*) — right enjoyment of one's desires, in the case of the first, and deliverance of one's own Self, in the case of the second. Of the two, the ignorant are much closer to the wise than the ascetic. The ignorant seek personal good because they have no choice in the matter. As long as they live in the ego, they are not free to seek any other good. But when they cease to be bound by the ego, they have a chance to choose the good of the world. In the case of the ascetic there is no such chance. For, when they destroy the ego, they choose personal deliverance from *saṃsāra* as the highest good. Once the choice is made their face is eternally turned away from the world and God's will in the world. If the ignorant are inferior to the wise by their attachment to the world (*andhaṃ tamaḥ praviśanti*), the ascetic are far inferior to the latter by their attachment to Brahman (*tato bhūya iva te tamaḥ praviśanti*). The spiritual mould of a person is best known from the destination to which his soul goes. So the Upaniṣad tries to indicate the kind of spiritual mould the ascetics possess by speaking of the dark worlds they enter (*asūryā nāma te lokāḥ*). In other words, the aim of the Upaniṣad is to bring home the point in a manner most appropriate to the Āryan poet, namely, the lesser perfection a soul attains through the ascetic ideal in comparison with the one attainable through the ideal of the wise (*dhīrāḥ*).

The Upaniṣad speaks of the Sunless worlds. This, as we have seen just now, helps us to understand the limitation of the ascetic ideal, but more important than this is a question it raises — is it right to say that the ascetics go to the gloomy worlds after their death rather than to the worlds illumined by the light of Brahman? All facts connected with the question do not permit us to answer in the affirmative. First, the dark worlds are known to be natural destinations of the deluded and not of the ascetics who are freed from *saṃsāra*; second, the ascetics by their soul's mould are destined to go to the worlds of Brahman; third, according to Manu, the self-slaying Vipra (knower of Brahman) goes to the world of Brahman and grows great there; fourth, the Brahman-worlds are known to be not dark but ever-illumined (*sakṛd vibhātaḥ*);[45] and fifth, the Chāndogya clearly says that as is one here, so becomes one on departing hence.[46] In other words, one who has attained liberation here will become a dweller in the world of the liberated on departing from here. Or a knower of Brahman will find his dwelling, after his departure, in the world of Brahman. It is therefore inconceivable that the ascetics, after their death, enter the worlds of gloom, the worlds without the light of Brahman (*asūryā lokāḥ*).

The followers of *satyadharma* are possessors of perfect knowledge (*vijānataḥ*) and have attained *mokṣa* according to the will of God, whereas the ascetics, by following *sannyāsa dharma*, arrive at an exclusive knowledge and a *mokṣa* at variance with God's Will. On account of this deficiency the ascetics are declared to be the dwellers of the Sunless worlds (*asūryā lokāḥ*). However, it does not mean that their worlds are really devoid of the light of Brahman. As the ever-illumined Brahman-worlds are not identically the same, the purity and the concentration of light vary from world to world. In the higher worlds the light has a greater purity and concentration; whereas in the lower worlds, there is a diminution of light on account of lesser purity and concentration. Relatively speaking, the higher worlds are brighter and the lower ones are darker. If the sense of light is to be conveyed by the word "sun," then the higher become the Sun-worlds and the lower the Sunless worlds. It is significant to note that the Kaṭha Upaniṣad speaks of light and shade in the world of Brahman (*chāyātapayoriva brahmaloke*) (in the world of Brahman the abode looks like shade and light).[47] Therefore the worlds of the ascetics called the Sunless are not without the light of Brahman, though their light is not as pure and concentrated as the light of the higher worlds. In other words, the lower worlds of Brahman, the worlds far removed from the brilliance of the Sun, are the destinations of the ascetics who slay themselves.

The poet of the Īśa Upaniṣad has a many-sided perception to be expressed by a phrase which carries multiple significance (*viśvatomukham*). His perception of the worlds of the ascetics is quite complex, containing many elements which do not usually come together — they are inferior worlds, but they are also Brahman-worlds; they are dark worlds, but they are not the dark worlds of the deluded which are without the light of Brahman; they are not the higher worlds where the worshippers of the supreme Lord live, but yet they are Brahman-worlds. He has compressed all these into a single phrase and makes it deliver its multiple senses simultaneously — this is *asūryā nāma te lokāḥ*. The other words — *andhena tamasāvṛtāḥ* — are intended to tell us that the worlds into which the ascetics pass are a direct result of their twin deficiencies, blindness (non-perception) and ignorance (wrong perception) — blindness, in respect of the supreme Lord whose reality and habitation in the world lie beyond their ken; ignorance, in respect of Brahman which they have declared to be the highest object of worship without realising that It is but a means to a greater perfection (*saṃsiddhi*). The peace of Brahman, says the Gītā, is not the culmination but the cause of further ascension and achievement (*śamaḥ kāraṇam*).[48] The words *ye ke ca* specify that only the ascetics find their abodes in the Sunless worlds and not the wise.

Such is the significance of the third mantra of the Īśa Upaniṣad as expounded in our study.

NOTES

*

asūryā nāma te lokā andhenatamasāvṛtāḥ;
tāṃste pretyābhigacchanti ye ke cātmahano janāḥ.
construction:
asūryā nāma te lokā / tāṃste pretyābhigacchanti
ye ke cātmahano janāḥ / andhenatamasāvṛtāḥ.

1. Īśa Upaniṣad (hereafter Īś. Up.), Mantra 3.
2. Ibid., Mantras 4, 5, 11.
3. Śaṅkara, *Īśa Upaniṣad Bhāṣya*, Mantra 3.
4. Īś. Up., Mantra 3.
5. Kaṭha Upaniṣad (hereafter K. Up.), 1-1-3.
6. Ibid., 1-1-13.
7. Muṇḍaka Upaniṣad (hereafter M. Up.), 1-2-10.
8. K. Up., 1-1-28.
9. Chāndogya Upaniṣad (hereafter Ch. Up.), 8-2-10.
10. M. Up., 3-2-5.
11. Praśna Upaniṣad, 1-10.
12. Bṛhadāraṇyaka Upaniṣad, 6-2-15.
13. Ibid., 4-4-5.
14. Gītā, 17-13.
15. Ibid., 18-32.
16. Ibid., 18-31.
17. M. Up. 1-2-9.
18. Ibid., 1-2-8.
19. Ibid., 3-2-8.
20. Ibid., 3-1-3.
21. Ṛg Veda, 6-13-6.
22. Śatapatha Brāhmaṇa, 10-2-6-7.
23. Mahābhārata, Adi., 179-20.
24. Parāśarasmṛti, 4-1, 2.
25. Viṣṇusmṛti, 22-56.
26. Vasiṣṭhadharmaśāstra, 23-18.
27. Jābāla Upaniṣad, Mantra 5.
28. Ibid., Mantra 6.
29. Manusmṛti, 6-78.
30. Ibid., 6-32.
31. Padmapurāṇa, 5-60-55.
32. Gītā, 8-5.
33. Ibid.
34. Ibid., 8-6.
35. Sri Aurobindo, *Essays on the Gita* (1970), pp. 281-282.
36. Īś. Up., Mantra 8.
37. Ibid., Mantra 5.
38. Ibid.
39. Ibid., Mantra 16.
40. Ibid., Mantra 11.
41. Ibid., Mantra 2.
42. Sri Aurobindo, *Supplement* (1972) p. 30.
43. Gītā, 12-2.

44. Ibid., 3-25.
45. Ch. Up., 8-4-2.
46. Ibid., 1-9-4.
47. K. Up., 2-3-5.
48. Gītā, 6-3.

3

Anti-Asceticism

A HIDDEN SIDE

Sri Aurobindo speaks of the epic massiveness of the Īśa Upaniṣad. We realise how profoundly true and meaningful are his words when we see that the teaching of the second verse, which is evidently anti-ascetic, is woven into the whole structure of the Upaniṣad, from the beginning to the end. Its words and phrases, which otherwise do not disclose its anti-ascetic implications, begin to drop their veils and speak in a tone at once startling and firm when viewed in the light of the second couplet. A study based upon this approach brings into the open a hidden side of this ancient Upaniṣad.

When this side of the Īśa is thus brought out, we understand why it is given pride of place among the twelve authoritative Upaniṣads. It is quite conceivable that the object of giving the first place to it is that it should give a lead in the matter of understanding the teachings of other authoritative Upaniṣads in the true perspective. There are numerous passages, couplets, lines, and even phrases in these Upaniṣads which can be interpreted in the light of some of the later Upaniṣads which give prominence to the transcendental Brahman and make the Brahman the supreme goal of asceticism. To interpret them in this way is to miss the synthetic spirit of the original Vedānta as expounded in the concluding chapter of the Vājasaneyi Saṃhitā i.e. in the Īśa Upaniṣad and to lay emphasis on an ideal which is purely transcendental and, therefore, exclusive in its implications. In fact, this is how the later school of the Brahmavāda seeks to interpret the Vedānta, a school whose origin goes back to the time when the twelve Upaniṣads were identified and recognised as the major ones. It is with a determined view to preserve the synthetic spirit characteristic of the original Vedānta and prevent the other authoritative Upaniṣads from being interpreted in the light of those later Upaniṣads that the Īśa seems to have been chosen as the leading text of the twelve major texts.

THE DIVINE INHABITANT

īśāvāsyam idaṃ sarvaṃ yat kiñca jagatyāṃ jagat;
tena tyaktena bhuñjīthā mā gṛdhaḥ kasyasvid dhanam. (1)

All this is for habitation by the Lord, whatsoever is the moving object in the universal movement of Nature.[a] By that you should enjoy the world you have abandoned.[b] Do not desire.[c] Whose is the wealth?[d]

COMMENTS

[a] Do not think that the Lord limits Himself to the spaceless, timeless and motionless order and does not live here. This is an exclusive view of the ascetics. But in reality He lives here also, using all this as His habitation. He is present everywhere.

Though the received sense of *jagatī* is the world, here it is appropriate to insist on its etymological sense — Nature which is the ultimate source (*gati*) of all that are born (*ja*).

[b] By seeing the divine law (*satyadharmāya dṛṣṭaye*) according to which the Lord has taken residence here you should accept the world you have abandoned as an object of ascetic disgust. The disgust for the world arises in the heart as a result of two things: one, the wrong view that God does not exist in the world; two, the ignorance of how the world is regarded by Him. The heart becomes free of the disgust when one sees that the world is not only a habitation of the Lord but used by Him as an object of enjoyment.

[c] You should enjoy the world like the Lord. But on no account should you desire to enjoy out of the ego. For the Lord is not only without disgust but also enjoys without ego and desire.

[d] To enjoy the world like the Lord is a wealth attainable only by the qualified individual. Who is then qualified to win this spiritual wealth? It is he whose heart is free from both ascetic disgust and egoistic desire. Without this freedom nobody can attain the wealth.

kurvann eveha karmāṇi jijīviṣet śataṃ samāḥ;
evaṃ tvayi nānyatheto'sti na karma lipyate nare.(2)

Doing verily works one should desire to live a hundred years here.[a] Thus in you, not otherwise than this.[b] The result of action does not taint the soul in you.[c]

COMMENTS

[a] The ascetics renounce life and works in the belief that the Lord does not exist in the world. But you should desire to live and do works for a hundred years for the sake of God, for He lives here with a view to enjoy world-existence and the works of Nature.

[b] Thus is the law of fulfilment in you — fulfilment through life and works. Self-fulfilment is not, as is held by the ascetics, through renunciation of life and works.

[c] The soul in you is not bound either by living in the body or by doing works through the body, for you live and act not for the sake of the ego but for the sake of God in the world.

asūryā nāma te lokā andhena tamasāvṛtāḥ;
tāṃste pretyābhigacchanti ye ke cātmahano janāḥ.(3)

Those are worlds called the Sunless.[a] To them go after death all people who kill themselves[b], all who are enveloped in blindness and ignorance.[c]

COMMENTS

[a] The Sun in the Veda represents the Light of Divine Knowledge.[1] So the Sunless worlds stand for the worlds devoid of that Light. In the subsequent verses (9 and 12) the word *andhamtamaḥ* is used to refer not to a total blindness but to a limited perception. In verse 9 the worshipper of the Vidyā is blind to the Avidyā; in verse 12 the worshipper of the Asambhūti is blind to the Sambhūti; in neither case is he blind to his object of worship. In the same way *asūryā nāma te lokāḥ* must be understood as speaking not of the worlds where the Light is totally absent but of the worlds where the Light is limited and has not attained its full brilliance and concentration. In other words, the Sunless worlds are not worlds without the consciousness of Brahman but the worlds of Brahman belonging to a lower category. They are not really Sunless worlds but are Sunless only in name (*nāmamātra*).

[b] Who are the self-slayers who, after death, go to the other worlds? Broadly speaking, there are two categories of people who commit suicide and go to the other worlds: (1) those who cannot face ordinary challenging situations in the world; (2) those who believe that God is beyond the world and are therefore disgusted with the world. As the foregoing verses (1 and 2) deal with the spiritual and not the mundane issues, it is most appropriate to take *ātmahano janāḥ* to signify the second category, namely, the people whose aim is to leave the world and find God in the spaceless and timeless order. In olden days ascetics are known to kill themselves and use physical death as a means of reaching Brahman or fixing the liberated soul firmly in Brahman. In later Upaniṣads self-slaying for ascetic purpose is referred to as body-renunciation (*dehatyāgaṃ*).[2]

As violence is tamasic in character, the ascetics who violently remove their bodies fall low and reach corresponding levels of Brahman-knowledge. The worlds they enter are far removed from the concentrated Light of the Sun and hence called the Sunless worlds.

[c] Here the aim of the Upaniṣad is to prohibit the ascetic practice of body-renunciation resorted to by those who are blind and ignorant (*andhena tamasāvṛtāḥ*).

THE OMNIPRESENT BRAHMAN

anejadekaṃ manasojavīyo nainad devā āpnuvan pūrvamarṣat;
tad dhāvato 'nyānatyeti tiṣṭhat tasminnapo mātariśvā dadhāti.(4)

That is unmoving and one.[a] That is swifter than Mind.[b] The Gods cannot reach That, for That always moves ahead.[c] Remaining stable,[d] That outstrips all others in motion.[e] In That, Mātariśvan establishes work.[f]

COMMENTS

[a,d] The words *anejat* (unmoving), *ekam* (one) and *tiṣṭhat* (stable) are to be treated as definitions that bring out the nature of Brahman as the highest form of reality.

[b,c,e] The words *javīyaḥ* (swifter), *pūrvamarṣat* (moves ahead) and *atyeti* (outstrips) have two aspects in common. First, they signify movement; secondly, they are predicates of a common subject — That which

is unmoving and one. As words signifying movement, they suggest the mighty movement of Nature which surpasses all — Mind, the Gods and others. As the predicates of That, they further suggest that this Nature is Brahman itself, working out Brahman's will in the world. This is made perfectly clear by 4 and 5 where the expressions *tiṣṭhat* and *atyeti* are simultaneously applied to Brahman. Precisely speaking, the aim of the predicates is to deny the ascetic position that Nature is opposed to Brahman and, therefore, not-Brahman.

[f] In that Brahman — Brahman seated in its own Nature — Mātariśvan, a form assumed by the Brahman, establishes the work of manifesting the world of names and forms.

tadejati tannaijati taddūre tadvantike;
tadantarasya sarvasya tadu sarvasyāsya bāhyataḥ.(5)

That moves,[a] That does not move;[b] That is far,[c] That is near;[d] That is inside all,[e] That is outside all.[f]

COMMENTS

[b,c,f] Brahman is transcendent; therefore, It is beyond the movement of Nature, beyond the world conditioned by Time and Space, and beyond all Names and Forms.

[a,d,e] Though Brahman transcends all, It is not, as is maintained by the ascetics, limited by Its transcendence. It exists in all — in Nature, in the world and in each name and form — and enjoys habitation as their Indwelling Lord (*antaryāmin*).

THE TRIPLE ASCENT

yastu sarvāṇi bhūtāni ātmany evānupaśyati;
sarvabhūteṣu cātmānaṃ tato na vijugupsate.(6)

He who sees all existences in the Self[a] and the Self in all existences[b] does not, on account of this perception, shrink.[c]

yasmin sarvāṇi bhūtāni ātmaivābhūd vijānataḥ;
tatra ko mohaḥ kaḥ śokaḥ ekatvam anupaśyataḥ.(7)

He in whom the very Self has become all existences[d] is a possessor of perfect knowledge.[e] What delusion, what sorrow is there for one who sees Oneness by this knowledge?[f]

COMMENTS

[a,b,d] To be beyond all, to be inside all and to be one with all (*sarvāṇi bhūtāni*) — they are the three sides of the law of existence of the Lord (*satyadharma*). To the same Law we should ascend in order to be perfect as He is perfect. To see all in the Self, to see the Self in all and to see all as the becomings of the Self — they are the triple step by which one assumes the Law of the Lord.

[e] To see all as the becomings of the Self is the completing vision of the other two. He who sees thus sees like the Lord. Hence he is the possessor of perfect knowledge.

[c] He who sees all in the Self is aloof from all and does not see the indwelling Self. As long as he persists in this vision, he tends to adopt the ascetic position, uphold the law of exclusiveness (*kevaladharma*) and withdraw from the world in accordance with that law. But when his vision extends itself to the Self in all, he sees the necessity of accepting the world and of helping and leading it towards the goal of fulfilment in the Self. Hence he does not shrink from life and works.

[f] Till the rise of the completing vision the possibility of delusion and sorrow persists, for the Self and the all are not yet perfectly united. Where separation exists, there the possibility of delusion and sorrow also exists. Once the completing vision opens up, the vision of Oneness, there is no place for separation or for delusion and sorrow.

THE SVAYAMBHŪ

saparyagāt chukram akāyam avraṇam asnāviraṃ
śuddham apāpaviddham;
kavirmanīṣī paribhūḥ svayambhūḥ
yāthātathyataḥ arthān
vyadadhāt śāśvatībhyaḥ samābhyaḥ.(8)

He is that which has extended in all directions.[a] He is that which is bright, bodiless, woundless, sinewless, pure and unpenetrated by evil.[b] He is the Seer,[c] the Thinker,[d] and the Person who becomes everywhere.[e] Thus He exists by Himself and becomes by Himself.[f] He has arranged all objects according as they are from eternal years.[g]

COMMENTS

[a] He is extended not only in the spaceless and timeless Existence but also in Space and Time.

[b] These six neuter adjectives aim at laying emphasis on the spaceless and timeless Existence i.e. the immutable aspect of the Lord.

[c,d,e] These masculine epithets suggest two things: (a) that all objects (*arthān*) in the world are the self-becomings of the immutable Brahman; (b) that there is no break or discontinuity between Brahman and the world. The ascetics reject the world because they do not see any continuity between Brahman and the world or they find the world to be not-Brahman. The epithets seem to aim at denying the very premises from which the ascetics draw negative conclusions about the reality of the world.

The Lord unrolls the world from his eternal being by a triple process of seeing, conceiving and realising. As the Kavi, He sees the Truth of things in his immutable existence; as the Manīṣī, He thinks out their possibilities and conceives the world to be manifested; finally, as the Paribhū, He brings his conception to the level of eventualities and perceives it as the objectively realised world.[3] Thus the world arises directly from Brahman; and at no stage of manifestation does its material cease to be Brahman and become other than or the opposite of Brahman.

[f] The word *svayambhūḥ* is very significant. Its intended sense is that the Lord who becomes by Himself is the same Lord who exists by Himself. In other words, He is one without a second.

[g] He has arranged the objects not according to what they are in their outward appearance but according to what they are in their original nature, the divine Nature of which they are becomings. The object of arranging them in this way is to put them in a harmonious order, use them as His habitations and enjoy world-existence.

PHYSICAL DEATH AND IMMORTALITY

andhaṃ tamaḥ praviśanti ye'vidyām upāsate;
tatobhūya iva te tamo ya u vidyāyāṃ ratāḥ.(9)

Into a blind darkness[a] enter they who worship the Avidyā;[b] into a greater darkness, as it were,[c] they who devote themselves exclusively to the Vidyā.[d]

anyadevāhur vidyayā anyadāhur avidyayā;
iti śuśruma dhīrāṇāṃ ye nastad vicacakṣire.(10)

One result,[e] indeed, is obtained by the Vidyā and quite another[f] by the Avidyā. Thus we have heard from the wise who have explained that to us.[g]

COMMENTS

[b,d] Nature is the Avidyā, because Nature is not rightly known if it is viewed apart from Brahman. Brahman is the Vidyā, for without It a true knowledge of Nature is not possible.

[a,c] By worshipping only Nature or only Brahman one goes to a blind darkness, because exclusive worship is an ignorance. But a worshipper of Brahman goes to a greater darkness because that which removes ignorance is itself made into an object of ignorant worship. Though the darkness is said to be greater on account of the effect of exclusiveness, the particle *iva* is used with a view to suggest that it is not really greater because in terms of exclusiveness Brahman-worship occupies the same position as Nature-worship.

[e,f] There are two other results corresponding to the two forms of exclusive worship. By Brahman-worship one gets the strength and competence to kill the body and use physical death as a means of liberating the soul from bondage to Nature. By Nature-worship one becomes a master of the secret laws of Nature and increases, through this mastery, one's material prosperity and happiness in the world.

[g] The object of quoting the authority is that the results are too well known for us to mention what they are.

vidyāṃ cāvidyāṃ ca yastad vedobhayaṃ saha;
avidyayā mṛtyuṃ tīrtvā vidyayāmṛtam aśnute.(11)

He who knows That as both and inseparably together,[a] the Vidyā and the Avidyā, crosses beyond death by the Avidyā[b] and enjoys immortality by the Vidyā.[c]

COMMENTS

[a] He who knows Brahman and Nature as the two inseparable aspects of the Lord and worships Him accordingly becomes as perfect as He.

[b] By Nature, in which is seated Brahman, he sees that the body, when rightly used, is an aid and not an obstacle to reaching Brahman. Hence he does not resort to killing the body and using physical death as a means for removing the obstacle. Thus he passes beyond death, beyond body-renunciation, and lives a full life here (*śataṃ samāḥ*).
[c] By Brahman, the ultimate source and support of Nature, he liberates the soul from the bonds of Nature and enjoys immortality without renouncing the body.

> *andhaṃ tamaḥ praviśanti ye'sambhūtim upāsate;*
> *tatobhūya iva te tamo ya u sambhūtyāṃ ratāḥ.*(12)

> Into a blind darkness[a] enter they who worship the Asambhūti;[b] into a greater darkness, as it were,[c] they who devote themselves exclusively to the Sambhūti.[d]

> *anyadevāhuḥ sambhavād anyadāhur asambhavāt;*
> *iti śuśruma dhīrāṇāṃ ye nastad vicacakṣire.*(13)

> One result,[e] indeed, is obtained by the Sambhūti and quite another[f] by the Asambhūti. Thus we have heard from the wise who have explained that to us.[g]

COMMENTS

[b,d] The Non-Birth and the Birth are the two aspects of the Lord. He is the Non-Birth because He is eternally bodiless and unborn. He is the Birth because He is free to take birth and live in the bodies as the enjoyer of world-existence.
[a,c] Both the worshippers of the Non-Birth and those of the Birth go to darkness, for their worship is directed to an exclusive object. But the latter go to a greater darkness, because they miss two things — not only the Non-Birth but a greater opportunity of being born into the divine nature of the Lord and enjoying world-existence like the Lord. Though the darkness is said to be greater in view of the effect of exclusiveness, the particle *iva* suggests that it is not really greater because the worship of Birth is exclusive like that of Non-Birth.
[e,f] Exclusive worship has other results also. A worshipper of Non-Birth liberates the soul from the necessity of rebirth. At the same time he finds his body to be an obstacle to keep the liberated soul exclusively

fixed in the Unborn. As a result, he renounces the body and allows the soul to plunge itself in the Unborn. If the worshipper of Non-Birth has to destroy his body for achieving his goal, the worshipper of Birth uses his body as a good instrument for enjoying the objects of physical birth and attaining the heavenly birth hereafter.
[g] See the comment 'g' on verse 10.

> *sambhūtiṃ ca vināśaṃ ca yastad vedobhayaṃ saha;*
> *vināśena mṛtyuṃ tīrtvā sambhūtyā amṛtam aśnute.*(14)

> He who knows That as both and inseparably together,[a] the Sambhūti and the Vināśa, crosses beyond death by the Vināśa[b] and enjoys immortality by the Sambhūti.[c]

COMMENTS

[a] He who worships the Birth and the dissolution of Birth as the two aspects of the Lord, becomes absolutely free like Him.
[b] By the dissolution of Birth, which is the Non-Birth dissolving the bonds of Birth, he dissolves the necessity of rebirth and sees the unborn Brahman to be the ultimate source and support of the body. As a result of this vision, he sees that the body is not an impediment to be renounced but a good instrument to be preserved and used by the liberated soul for the purpose of fulfilling the will of the Lord in the world. Therefore he rejects the idea of killing the body and using physical death as a means of uniting the liberated soul exclusively with the unborn Brahman. Thus he crosses beyond death, beyond body-renunciation, and lives a full life here (*śataṃ samāḥ*).
[c] By the Birth, the limiting conditions of which are destroyed by the Non-Birth, he enjoys immortality. By using the body as an instrument of true action (*satyadharma*) he passes from the guṇas of the lower Nature to the higher Nature of the Lord hidden behind the guṇas (*devātmaśaktiṃ svaguṇair nigūḍhām*).[4] Again, by using the body as a faultless instrument he expresses the divine Nature in all works done for the sake of the Lord.

THE TRUE LAW

> *hiraṇmayena pātreṇa satyasyāpihitaṃ mukham;*
> *tat tvaṃ pūṣann apāvṛṇu satyadharmāya dṛṣṭaye.*(15)

With the golden lid the entrance to Truth is concealed;[a] that do Thou open, O Nourisher, for the true Law, for sight.[b]

COMMENTS

[a] By pursuing the immutable Brahman as an exclusive truth the *sādhaka* now tends towards the ascetic law of exclusiveness and is not able to see the higher truth of the Lord on whom the true Law (*satyadharma*) is founded, the law by which He holds Brahman and Nature together and lives in Nature and enjoys the works of Nature without ceasing to be Brahman. Since one truth hides another truth (*ṛtena ṛtamapihitam*),[5] the truth that hides is said to be a lid, a barrier; however, it is not a dark veil that hides, but a light that hides another light. Hence it is significantly called the golden lid (*hiraṇmayena pātreṇa*).

[b] If the golden lid is removed and the entrance opened, the *sādhaka* can have a vision of the Lord and, through the vision, put on His divine Law, the true law of existence and of action. Hence the *sādhaka* is asking Sūrya to open the lid.

pūṣann ekarṣe yama sūrya prājāpatya vyūha raśmīn
samūha tejaḥ;
yat te rūpaṃ kalyāṇatamaṃ tat te paśyāmi
yo'sāvasau puruṣaḥ so'ham asmi.(16)

O Nourisher, O Sole Seer, O Controller, O Sun, O Power of the Father of beings,[a] do spread out the rays, do bring together the light.[b] Thy form is most blessed, that form I see in Thee.[c] Who is this and this Puruṣa, that Puruṣa am I.[d]

COMMENTS

[a] All epithets applied to god Sūrya reflect the conditions of the *sādhaka*— his spiritual strength needs to be nourished and increased; his vision to be made indivisible; his will to be developed into a higher will that controls; his soul to be born as a son of God who manifests in the world the Power that belongs to the Father of beings.

[b] The *sādhaka* sees two lights in him, one concentrated in Brahman and the other diffused in the workings of Nature. He sees that for his exclusiveness to go the two lights must become one. Hence he is asking god Sūrya to spread out the light in Brahman and merge it

with the light diffused in Nature, and to bring together the light in Nature and unite it with the light concentrated in Brahman (*vyūha raśmīn samūha tejaḥ*).
[c,d] When the two lights become one, the *sādhaka*'s prayer is granted. Now he gets the vision of the most beautiful form of the Lord who by the true Law is extended in Brahman and in Nature (*asau asau puruṣaḥ*). He further sees that he is indeed a son of God, a divine soul who is one in essence of being and consciousness with the Lord (*so'ham asmi*).

THE CONSCIOUS WILL

vāyur anilam amṛtam athedaṃ bhasmāntaṃ śarīram;
om krato smara kṛtaṃ smara krato smara kṛtaṃ smara.(17)

Let Vāyu become Anilam.[a] Then let this mortal life be immortalized.[b] And let the body reach the end signified by ashes.[c] O Will, remember the Lord,[d] remember all deeds done in ignorance of the Lord.[e] O Will, remember His Will, remember all deeds done in ignorance of His Will.[f]

COMMENTS

[a] To mould his life according to the true law of action the life-force in his body must be transformed into a divine principle. To be so transformed it must be merged with the higher Life-Force not based in the body but in the divine Nature of the Lord (*vāyur anilam*).
[b] His life-force must give up its mortal characteristics, take on those which belong to the immortal Life and become a movement of the divine Nature (*amṛtam atha idaṃ*).
[c] The end signified by ashes (*bhasmena sūcitam antam*) may mean a final state after a full utilisation. For example, the firewood, when fully consumed by the fire, reaches the ultimate state of ashes beyond which it cannot be used as a fuel. Even so, the body, when fully utilised by the life-force of which it is an abode and an instrument, wears out and passes into the final state of death. In other words, the body is capable of living a hundred years (*śataṃ samāḥ*) and so it must arrive at its final state after a long-extended utilisation (*bhasmāntaṃ śarīram*).
[d,e,f] The letter OM signifies the imperishable Lord, for that is the name of the Nameless.[6]

If the life-force is to be transformed and divinized it must be done only through will which is its most natural expression. The human will is ignorant of its true nature and acts according to the dictates of the ego. It must awaken and remember that it belongs to the Lord and is one with His will. It must remember all deeds done in ignorance so that it may sever its connections with the crooked-going sins begotten by those deeds. In proportion as the human will is freed from its bondage to the past ways of life, it becomes conscious of the Lord and participates in the works that fulfil His will in the world. Hence the *sādhaka* calls upon the mental will in him to come out of its forgetfulness and become a conscious principle.

agne naya supathā rāye asmān
viśvāni deva vayunāni vidvān;
yuyodhyasmajjuhurāṇam eno
bhūyiṣṭhāṃ te nama uktiṃ vidhema.(18)

O god Agni, knower of all deeds,[a] lead us by the good path to the riches,[b] remove from us the crooked action of sin.[c] We offer to Thee completest prayer of submission.[d]

COMMENTS

[a,b,c] God Agni is the knower of all deeds, deeds done for the sake of the ego and deeds done for the sake of the Lord in the world. Hence he is most competent to free the *sādhaka* from the many-branching sins of egoistic life and take him by the awakened path to the riches of a divinized life in the world.

[d] The *sādhaka*'s prayer will be meaningful only when he puts himself in the hands of Agni and allows Him to shape his life according to the true law of action. Therefore he closes his prayer with the words of submission, words saturated with devotion and surrender. A will surrendered to Agni and shaped according to the true law is a will that fulfils God in oneself and God in others.

THE VEDIC IDEAL

Though we have fully worked out the anti-ascetic implications of the Upaniṣad, we must bear in mind that it is equally antimaterialistic and tries to set aside the materialistic notions of man and the world. Materialism, like asceticism, is one-sided and does not agree with the synthetic view of the Īśa Upaniṣad. Though the Upaniṣad is opposed to both asceticism and materialism, its predominant aim is always to reaffirm the original Vedic ideal of living in the world as an immortal whose ways of existence and action are according to the true Law (*satyadharmā*). The Vedic poets say that in our real nature we are not human but divine (*dhāmāni divyāni tasthuḥ*).[7] For God is our true Father (*pitṛtamaḥ pitṛṇām*).[8] Our aim is, therefore, to be born as the sons of God (*amṛtasya putrāḥ*),[9] and enjoy divine liberty like Him — an aim to be achieved not elsewhere but here and now (*yannūnam asyāṃ gatim*).[10]

NOTES

1. Ṛg Veda (hereafter RV), 1-50-10.
2. Jābāla Upaniṣad, Mantra 6.
3. Sri Aurobindo, *The Upanishads* (1972), p. 103.
4. Śvetāśvatara Upaniṣad, 1-3.
5. RV, 5-62-1.
6. Kaṭha Upaniṣad, 1-2-16.
7. RV, 10-13-1.
8. Ibid., 4-17-17.
9. Ibid., 10-13-1.
10. Ibid., 5-64-3.

4

The Law of the Lord

THE TRUE MESSAGE

Two things stand out as the prominent features of the Īśa Upaniṣad. First of all, it looks upon the human urge for enjoyment as a legitimate expression of the soul and sets forth the conditions under which it may be elevated and possessed as a divine principle of life. Its aim is to affirm and divinize rather than to reject it as undivine. Secondly, its ideas and arguments are stated with the utmost brevity and worked out in an ordered sequence without omission. On account of these two features the Upaniṣad is considered to be a very important text of Vedānta.

However, the Upaniṣad has been a sealed book to many of us because its expressions are not only terse but very often paradoxical. To us the sage of the Upaniṣad seems to pass from idea to idea like a giant who leaps from mountain to mountain. For we miss the connecting steps of thought between words, verses and passages. We are unable to make out what the sage precisely intends to teach. We manage to explain the meaning of the separate verses, but fail to discover the true message of the Upaniṣad.

The key to discover the true message is to view the Upaniṣad as a unified whole and accordingly apply all exegetical devices to its verses. When this condition is fulfilled, the true message of the Upaniṣad reveals itself to us. As a matter of fact, the whole exegesis is guided by this principle.

THE GOAL OF HUMAN LIFE

īśāvāsyam idaṃ sarvaṃ yat kiñca jagatyāṃ jagat;
tena tyaktena bhuñjīthā mā gṛdhaḥ kasyasvid dhanam.(1)

All this is to be inhabited by the Lord, whatsoever is the moving object in the moving world. Therefore thou shouldst enjoy the

> world through the renunciation of the outer view of things. Do not desire to enjoy the mere form, for whose is the wealth of true enjoyment?

The world falls into two broad divisions, individual objects and universal Nature. To us all objects are forms of matter and the universal Nature is a material force from which all appear and into which all disappear. To see the world in this way is not according to the law of Truth (*satyadharma*). Hence we are asked to see the world as the dwelling place of the Lord, for indeed He lives everywhere, in the objects and in the universal Nature. To see thus is to see that the Lord is both the essence and form of things.

As we see so we enjoy. To see only the form and not the Lord in it is a false view. To enjoy the world on account of the importance of form is to enjoy wrongly and suffer the evil consequences of wrong enjoyment. On the contrary, if we give up the false view and see the Lord in all forms, we will be able to enjoy the world truly and without any fault (*tyaktena bhuñjīthāḥ*).

How do we effect this change in our perception of the world? How do we move from the perception of mere form to the perception of the Lord ensouling each form in the world? It is by renouncing the desire for the world (*mā gṛdhaḥ*) that we can see and enjoy the forms without any fault. No one who has not given up the desire is entitled to the wealth of true enjoyment of forms (*dhanam*).

> *kurvann eveha karmāṇi jijīviṣet śataṃ samāḥ;*
> *evaṃ tvayi nānyatheto'sti na karma lipyate nare.*(2)

> Doing verily all works one should desire to live a hundred years here. Thus is the law of being in thee, not otherwise than this. Action does not attach itself to the soul in thee.

Enjoyment of the world cannot exclude life and works for they are part of the world in which the Lord lives and enjoys all works. It is therefore necessary to bring out the implications of *bhuñjīthāḥ* in terms of life and works.

When desire and attachment fall away from us, we live in the freedom of the immutable Self and look upon the works of Nature as something foreign to our true Self. We may use this freedom as an escape from life and works and arrive at a supreme state of negation.

As a result, life and works may come to an abrupt end. But this is against the will of the Lord in the world. For He has taken residence here neither to flee from the world nor to reject Nature's works, but to enjoy both. Further, to give up life and works is to go against one's own law of being which is not other than the law of the Lord (*so'ham asmi*). Since our law of being is constituted in this way and not otherwise, we should accept the full term of human life as well as the full measure of human activity among our fellow beings in the world (*jijīviṣet śataṃ samāḥ*).

If the liberated individual lives here doing works, works for the sake of the Lord in the world, they do not bind him, because they are done without desire and attachment (*na karma lipyate*). It is the desire that binds the soul and not the works.

asūryā nāma te lokā andhena tamasāvṛtāḥ;
tāṃste pretyābhigacchanti ye ke cātmahano janāḥ.(3)

To the worlds without light and enveloped by a blind darkness depart after death they who slay their souls.

There are two forms of violence which adversely affect the soul, one is psychological and the other is physical. To keep the soul within the bounds of the ego and not to let it discover the Lord seated in the heart is psychological violence, for the mental will in us is on the side of the ego and refuses to give up its allegiance to it in favour of the soul. Likewise, to do away with the body and thus deprive the soul of its instrument by which it seeks to open itself to the indwelling Lord is physical violence, for the mental will listens to the perverse suggestion of the ego and forces the soul to quit its natural field of action and growth. Either way the mental will brings disaster to the soul and obstructs its law of being. In the Vedāntic parlance those who thus allow the mental will to obstruct the soul's law of being and its fulfilment are self-slayers (*ātmahano janāḥ*).

The worlds into which the self-slayers go after death are dark and sunless. These are not worlds favourable to them, for here they have to face a greater obstruction and hostility. To them self-fulfilment is a far-off goal and unattainable till they are released from these lower worlds. The aim of the Upaniṣad is therefore to teach that none can reach self-fulfilment by committing violence upon the soul.

THE KNOWLEDGE OF BRAHMAN

anejadekaṃ manasojavīyo nainad devā
āpnuvan pūrvamarṣat;
tad dhāvato 'nyānatyeti tiṣṭhat tasminnapo
mātariśvā dadhāti.(4)

It is unmoving and one. It is swifter than Mind. The gods do not reach It, because It moves ahead of them. Ever fixed in this position, It outstrips all others in motion. In It Mātariśvan establishes the work of vivifying all forms of Matter.

In the following two verses, the fourth and fifth, two of the connecting steps of thought not explicitly stated in the first verse are set forth and fully developed.

The definition that Brahman is Immutable and One helps us to understand the essential condition under which He and His aim in the world can be truly known. Brahman manifest in Nature lives in the forms and works out His aim in the world. His aim is possession and enjoyment of all that are here.

Mind is a powerful instrument evolved by Nature; the gods increase the powers of Mind by their help and influence. But neither Mind nor the gods are in a position to know the true significance of the manifestation of Brahman (*na āpnuvan*). Mātariśvan, the mightiest of the gods, does the work of manifesting all forms of Matter in Brahman. Even this god cannot understand the real aim of Brahman's manifestation in the world.

As long as we live in the movement and diversity of Nature and depend on things conditioned by her, we can never know God's aim in the world. It can be truly known only when we totally transcend Nature and know Brahman which is immutable and one (*anejadekaṃ*). For it is by knowing Brahman that all else is known (*anena hyetatsarvaṃ veda*).[1]

tadejati tannaijati taddūre tadvantike;
tadantarasya sarvasya tadu sarvasyāsya bāhyataḥ.(5)

That moves, That does not move. That is far, That is near. That is inside all, That is outside all.

The second idea that is implied in the first verse is developed here. Though the Lord is in all and supports all, He goes beyond all. At the same time His transcendence does not exclude the all but informs them without ceasing to be the transcendent. In other words, the Lord is at once in Nature (*tadejati*) and beyond Nature (*tannaijati*), in the world (*tadvantike*) and beyond the world (*taddūre*), in all individuals (*tadantarasya sarvasya*) and beyond all individuals (*tadu sarvasyāsya bhāhyataḥ*). He is free to be all, to go beyond all, and to be both at once. He is absolutely free and not bound by any condition, transcendence or immanence.

THE KNOWLEDGE OF ONENESS

yastu sarvāṇi bhūtāni ātmany evānupaśyati;
sarvabhūteṣu cātmānaṃ tato na vijugupsate.(6)

> He who sees all existences in the Self and the Self in all existences does not, on account of this perception, shrink.

The second verse says that the liberated individual should lead an active life among his fellow beings in the world. It is this idea that becomes the subject-matter of the sixth and seventh verses.

When the individual is freed from ego and desire, he becomes one with the impersonal Self that supports all existences (*sarvāṇi bhūtāni*). He may prefer to live exclusively in the Self and refrain from doing anything that would disturb his exclusive life, particularly from taking active interest in helping other existences who live in ignorance and suffering. But this shrinking disappears when he sees that the Self he loves is also lodged in the heart of all existences. Now more than ever before, he realises his closer affinity to them and is moved by their helplessness and misery. He undertakes all works for their sake without repulsion or fear (*na vijugupsate*). He spends his whole life in working for their deliverance.

yasmin sarvāṇi bhūtāni ātmaivābhūd vijānataḥ;
tatra ko mohaḥ kaḥ śokaḥ ekatvam anupaśyataḥ.(7)

> He in whom the very Self has become all existences is a possessor of perfect knowledge. What delusion, what sorrow can there be for one who sees Oneness by this knowledge?

Personally he is satisfied with the peace and freedom of the Self. Beyond this there is no object for him to be achieved. Living in the

Self he is always detached from works and Nature. So neither delusion nor grief can ever touch him. If they touch him, it is on account of his commitment to his fellow beings in the world. In his effort to deliver them from their miseries he has to deal with the perversities of Nature and willingly let delusion and grief fall on him. For without making this sacrifice he cannot work for their deliverance.

However, it does not mean that there are only two alternatives for him — to be entirely detached from Nature and live in the Self with an attitude of indifference to the sufferings of others or to forgo his personal joy of peace and freedom of the Self for the sake of others and submit calmly to the perversities of Nature. There is a third alternative too — to descend into Nature and use this opportunity to impose the law of the Self and acquire a complete mastery over her operations, so that works become not only an effective means of helping others but also a true expression of inner freedom.

To see all existences in the Self and the Self in all existences is a true but not a complete knowledge. To see the Self and the existences as one i.e. to see the existences as the becomings of the Self (*ātmaivābhūd*) is a knowledge that is both true and complete. He who sees thus is a possessor of perfect knowledge (*vijānataḥ*) and a seer of oneness (*ekatvam anupaśyataḥ*). He understands the true principles and workings of the becomings of the Self in all existences. With this knowledge the whole basis of delusion is removed. Given the knowledge, he finds in grief not a movement of suffering but a necessity for awakening the soul to its divine nature. Therefore if he finds himself in the heart of Nature (*tatra*) while helping others, he removes both of them — delusion by right understanding and grief by right progress.

THE PRINCIPLE AND PROCESS OF BECOMING

saparyagāt chukram akāyam avraṇam asnāviraṃ
suddham apāpaviddham;
kavirmanīṣī paribhūḥ svayambhūḥ yāthātathyataḥ arthān
vyadadhāt śāśvatībhyaḥ samābhyaḥ.(8)

He is verily that which has extended in all directions, that which is bright, bodiless, woundless, without sinews, pure, and unpenetrated by evil. The Seer, the Thinker, the Person who

> becomes everywhere, the Self-Existent has arranged all objects according to their nature from eternal years.

Here *ātmaivābhūd* of the last verse is developed from the point of view of the Lord in order to show how all existences are one with Him in both essence and form. This justifies the teaching of the fifth verse that the Lord is not only in the Self but also in the becomings of Nature (*tadejati tannaijati*).

The Self and Nature are the two terms of cosmic existence of the Lord (*saparyagāt*). In the Self He is bright, bodiless, woundless, without sinews, pure and without evil; in Nature He looses forth his preexistent potentialities by a threefold process of seeing, selecting, and becoming in Name and Form. In seeing the potentialities of his eternal self He is Kavi, in selecting out of them those that are to be manifested He is Manīṣī, and in transforming them into his becomings in Name and Form He is Paribhū. Though the Lord is in the Self and in Nature (*asau asau puruṣaḥ*) He is indivisibly one (*ekam*).

This is the process by which the immutable Self becomes all existences in the world (*arthān*). Having manifested all, the Lord creates a harmonious order by arranging them according to their inner law of being (*yāthātathyataḥ*).

All things preexist in the immutable self of the Lord; they take name and form when He manifests them by his power of Becoming. In other words, all manifestation is a self-manifestation of the Lord (*svayambhūḥ*). This is the principle of creation.[2]

FREEDOM FROM DEATH AND ENJOYMENT OF IMMORTALITY

> *andhaṃ tamaḥ praviśanti ye'vidyām upāsate;*
> *tatobhūya iva te tamo ya u vidyāyāṃ ratāḥ.*(9)
>
> Into a blind darkness enter they who worship Nature, as though into a greater darkness they who devote themselves exclusively to Brahman.

Though the eighth verse is concerned to develop the ideas of the fifth and seventh verses, its main aim is to lay a solid foundation for a crowning achievement i.e. to set forth the indivisible knowledge of the Lord as the basis for conquering death and enjoying immortality here. It is this achievement that becomes the theme of the next six verses, from the ninth to the fourteenth.

From the point of view of universal existence, the Lord manifests himself as both Brahman and Nature (*vidyā avidyā*). Accordingly, He may be worshipped in three ways: as Brahman, as Nature, and as both Brahman and Nature.

In her original form Nature is the power of self-becoming of Brahman. Since we live on the surface of Nature and are conditioned by her surface workings, we only see Nature and not Brahman. To view Nature as if she were independent and not possessed by Brahman is ignorance (*avidyā*). Hence Nature is called Avidyā. He who worships Nature in this way enters into a blind darkness, because he is ignorant of Brahman and sees nothing but movement and diversity.

Brahman is the immutable foundation which originates and supports the becomings of Nature. It is by knowing Brahman that the becomings of Nature are truly known. Hence Brahman is the object of true knowledge (*vidyā*). It is for this reason that Brahman is termed Vidyā. To worship Brahman as if it were exclusive of Nature is to enter into a greater darkness. For the exclusive seeker errs on two sides — on one side, he does not know that Brahman is the very foundation of Nature; on the other side, he does not see that the Will expressed in Nature is really the Will of Brahman.

anyadevāhur vidyayā anyadāhur avidyayā;
iti śuśruma dhīrāṇāṃ ye nastad vicacakṣire.(10)

One result, indeed, is obtained by Brahman and quite another by Nature. Thus we have heard from the wise who have revealed That to us.

Exclusive worship has its own consequence. By worshipping Brahman the soul rises out of the action of Nature. All confusions, evils and sufferings come to an end; all sense of division and limitation falls away from the soul. It always lives in the eternal peace and bliss of Brahman and rejects Nature as something other than Brahman.

By worshipping Nature the soul immersed in ignorance and suffering learns of the secret laws that govern the world and control the forces of life. A systematic application of these laws helps the soul to overcome its material limitations and enjoy prosperity and happiness in the world. There is nothing greater than Nature, for Nature is the ultimate source and support of all. Therefore Brahman-worship is dismissed as an absurdity.

But these results are incomplete and do not bring self-fulfilment to the soul because the full flowering of its law of being comes only when it ascends to the absolute liberty of the Lord and embraces both Brahman and Nature through the law of His indivisible existence.

> *vidyāṃ cāvidyāṃ ca yastad vedobhayaṃ saha;*
> *avidyayā mṛtyuṃ tīrtvā vidyayāmṛtam aśnute.*(11)

> He who knows That as both and inseparably together, Brahman and Nature, crosses beyond death by Nature and attains immortality by Brahman.

To worship the Lord as the omnipresent reality of the world is to worship Him as both Brahman and Nature without bifurcating his indivisible unity of cosmic existence. He who worships thus is not satisfied with the results of the exclusive seeking.

He sees Nature, in whose heart is seated Brahman, to be the source of all instruments, external as well as internal. Of them the highest is the Buddhi. When the Buddhi is impure and carried away by the many-branching works of the sense-organs, Nature is not conscious of the indwelling Brahman and binds us by the law of *saṃsāra*, the law of the duality also called the law of death. When the same Buddhi is pure, withdrawn from the undisciplined operations of the sense-organs, and one-pointed, Nature sees the Brahman as the Lord who enjoys her works. So seeing, Nature ceases to bind and sets free all who are established in the pure Buddhi. Nature is therefore a source of bondage as well as an instrument of freedom: if She binds through the Buddhi, She also liberates through the same Buddhi; this depends on how the condition of Buddhi is (*mana eva manuṣyāṇāṃ kāraṇam bandhamokṣayoḥ*).[3] He who thus sees and worships Nature i.e. lodges himself in the pure Buddhi, is freed by Nature from the law of death (*avidyayā mṛtyuṃ tīrtvā*).

Not only does he go beyond death through the pure Buddhi but also he delivers his soul into Brahman by worshipping Brahman. By doing so he attains the very form of Brahman — Brahman whose *svabhāva* is Nature and who enjoys Nature and the works of Nature without ceasing to be Brahman — and becomes immortal (*vidyayā amṛtam aśnute*) like Brahman.

Though the devotee crosses beyond death by withdrawing from Nature, he does not renounce the world. He finds Nature to be not necessarily binding him to the law of death. For Nature binds only the unawakened, not the awakened one. Therefore, even after the attainment of immortality, his desire for living a hundred years here (*śataṃ samāḥ*) does not diminish but finds a good justification for its fulfilment. Fulfilment consists in attaining immortality and also living a full life.

> *andhaṃ tamaḥ praviśanti ye'sambhūtim upāsate;*
> *tatobhūya iva te tamo ya u sambhūtyāṃ ratāḥ.*(12)
>
> Into a blind darkness enter they who worship the Non-Birth, as though into a greater darkness they who devote themselves exclusively to the Birth.

From the point of view of formative Nature, the Lord manifests himself as both the Non-Birth and the Birth of existences. He is eternally unborn, but yet in his absolute freedom He descends into the forms of the world. Here too He may be worshipped in three ways: as the Non-Birth (*asambhūti*), as the Birth (*sambhūti*), and as both the Non-Birth (Dissolution) and the Birth.

To worship the Non-Birth as if it were the whole truth is to enter into a blind darkness, because we miss the truth of Birth. Likewise, to look upon the Birth as if it were all is to enter into a greater darkness, because we miss not only the truth of Non-Birth but the truth of free Birth as well.

> *anyadevāhuḥ sambhavād anyadāhur asambhavāt;*
> *iti śuśruma dhīrāṇāṃ ye nastad vicacakṣire.*(13)
>
> One result, indeed, is obtained by the Birth and quite another by the Non-Birth. Thus we have heard from the wise who have revealed That to us.

Exclusive worship, whether of Non-Birth or Birth, has its own result. Worship of Non-Birth takes the soul to the eternally Unborn, and in contrast to the freedom of living in the Bodiless (*akāyam*) the other worship keeps the soul bound to the law of death. Therefore the worshipper of Non-Birth rejects the worship of Birth and protects his soul by renouncing the body which alone makes birth in the world possible or inevitable.

The worshipper of Birth considers that the soul is helpless without the body, for it is the body which makes birth in the world possible and without which the soul cannot enjoy the good things of the world or win the heavenly body necessary for living in the world of the gods (*svarga*). Hence he does not favour the worship of Non-Birth which destroys the Birth by destroying the body.

However, neither the Birth nor the Non-Birth can be the true goal of human life, for in both the soul is bound by attachment, in the Birth by the attachment to the joy of embodiment and in the Non-Birth by the attachment to the joy of freedom, in the one by an iron chain and in the other by a chain made of bright gold (*hiraṇmaya*). This is inevitable because all exclusive pursuits originate from attachment and finally end in bondage. The true goal of human life consists in rising into the infinite consciousness of the Lord and enjoying absolute freedom by possessing both the Birth and the Non-Birth as the two inseparable aspects of divine existence in the world.

> *sambhūtiṃ ca vināśaṃ ca yastad vedobhayaṃ saha;*
> *vināśena mṛtyuṃ tīrtvā sambhūtyā amṛtam aśnute.*(14)

> He who knows That as both and inseparably together, the Birth and the Dissolution, crosses beyond death by the Dissolution and enjoys immortality by the Birth.

A worshipper of the Lord in His completeness looks upon Him as both the Non-Birth and the Birth of existences. On account of this he is entitled to a greater liberty and enjoyment not accessible to an exclusive seeker of Non-Birth or Birth.

We live in bondage to the law of death as long as we are bound by the impure Buddhi. If we rise from the impure to the pure Buddhi, we are withdrawn and detached from the inner and outer instruments which impose on us the law of death. But the final conquest over the impure Buddhi comes only when the soul is delivered into the unborn Brahman by the worship of Non-Birth, otherwise the impure Buddhi may assert itself again and reestablish the law of death. As the Non-Birth destroys completely the rule of the impure Buddhi on the one hand and the bondage of death on the other, it is also called the Dissolution (*vināśa*). In other words, the best way to conquer death is to deliver the soul by the Non-Birth or the Dissolution (*vināśena mṛtyuṃ tīrtvā*).

The conquest over death by the Non-Birth culminates in the attainment of immortality. Attainment of immortality is important, but more important than this is enjoyment of immortality. It is not enough if the soul becomes immortal, but its instruments too must come out of their old ways of working, i.e. out of the ways of working according to the law of death, and aid the immortal soul. This is done through the worship of Birth. When the instruments are thus won back for the immortal soul, they begin to express immortality. All works done in the world through them are the works of God, works that fulfil God's will in oneself and in others. To win the instruments for the awakened soul and use them for God's work in the world is to enjoy immortality by the Birth (*sambhūtyā amṛtam aśnute*). To be here for the full term allotted to the devotee and do liberated works for God is the goal ordained for him by God (*evaṃtvayi nānyatheto'sti*).

THE PROCESS OF WINNING IMMORTALITY

> *hiraṇmayena pātreṇa satyasyāpihitaṃ mukham;*
> *tat tvaṃ pūṣann apāvṛṇu satyadharmāya dṛṣṭaye.*(15)

> With a golden lid the face of the Truth is concealed; that do Thou open, O Nourisher, for the vision of the law of the Truth.

Now come two prayers addressed successively to the gods Sūrya and Agni. The gods are none other than the supreme Īśa self-represented in two positive forms. In his aspect of knowledge the Lord is Sūrya; similarly, in his aspect of will the same Lord is Agni.

The object of these two prayers is to describe the process by which immortality is both attained and enjoyed. In fact the last four verses of the Upaniṣad take up the theme of the preceding verses, particularly the eleventh and the fourteenth, and develop it from the practical point of view in the fifteenth to the eighteenth.

It may be noticed that in the first two verses of the Upaniṣad the sage gives practical instructions to a student who waits for the master's word on the lines upon which he should proceed. The expressions *bhuñjīthāḥ, mā gṛdhaḥ*, and *jijīviṣet* are obviously instructions meant to be put into practice by the student. Therefore, after explaining the implications of these instructions fully in the next twelve verses, from the third to the fourteenth, the sage comes back to his practical teaching and describes in the four concluding verses the steps by which the *sādhaka* has to move towards the goal of *bhuñjīthāḥ*.

It is now clear that the closing verses form a sequel to the Upaniṣad not only in thought but in form as well. As is held by some, there is nothing illogical or inappropriate in them, for all of them are in perfect order. The prayer to Sūrya is offered by a *sādhaka* already sufficiently advanced on the path of spiritual life. His prayer goes out at a critical point at which he has seen the Lord but has not seen Him according to the true law of existence (*satyadharma*). For the law remains hidden from his vision (*satyadharmasya mukham apihitam*).

The *sādhaka* has come out of the darkness of ignorance and the necessities of mortal life. He lives in the eternal light and freedom of the immortal Self. Now he finds that this blessed condition, this state of immortality itself has become a golden barrier (*hiraṇmayena pātreṇa*) that sets a limit to his spiritual strength. Living in the state of immortality is a joy of incomparable freedom and peace; but when attached to this joy, it becomes a golden fetter that binds and does not let the soul pass out of it and see the true form of the Lord.

On one side, he sees the immutable Self seated in the eternal silence and stillness; on the other side, he sees Nature ceaselessly working in his body and in the world around and imposing the law of death on all existences. The Self and Nature thus stand divided; yet he sees a hidden link that connects them together. For the silent Self secretly enjoys the workings of Nature; and Nature too does her works in secret obedience to the Self. He can embrace them together and see them as one (*vedobhayaṃ saha*) only when he is able to understand their secret oneness (*ekatvam*). He cannot get hold of this secret as long as he is bound by the joy of the immutable Self and does not enter into the law of the Truth, the true law of the Lord's existence by which the Self and Nature are held together in an indivisible oneness. His prayer therefore begins with an appeal to lift the golden barrier (*tat tvaṃ pūṣannapāvṛṇu*) and allow him to see and enter by this seeing, into the true law of the Lord (*satyadharmāya dṛṣṭaye*).

pūṣann ekarṣe yama sūrya prājāpatya vyūha raśmīn
samūha tejaḥ;
yat te rūpaṃ kalyāṇatamaṃ tat te paśyāmi
yo'sāvasau puruṣaḥ so'ham asmi.(16)

O Nourisher, O sole Seer, O Controller, O Sun, O power of the Lord of beings do spread out the rays, do bring together the

> light. Thy form is most blessed, that form I see in Thee. Who is this and this *puruṣa*, that *puruṣa* am I.

The *sādhaka* appeals to Sūrya for increasing his spiritual strength, for granting the vision of oneness of the Self and Nature, and for checking the exclusive tendency that separates these two principles so that he may enter into the higher law of existence and possess the power of the Lord of beings.

In him the Self and Nature stand apart because the consciousness in each is markedly different. In the Self the consciousness is extremely concentrated, whereas in Nature it is extremely dispersed. If these two principles are to be harmonised, it can be done only by reversing in each its characteristic mode of operation of consciousness. When reversed, the consciousness in the Self spreads out, goes into the confused workings of Nature and arranges them in the right order (*vyūha*); in consequence, the consciousness in Nature pulls itself out of its confused workings and moves towards the concentrated oneness in the Self (*samūha*). When they shed their inherent limitations and begin to fuse with each other, the Self and Nature, the *sādhaka* gains entry into the divine law of the Truth and lives in the inner sanctum of the Lord. He is blessed with the vision of the Lord's most beautiful form constituted according to His true law of existence (*rūpaṃ kalyāṇatamaṃ*). He becomes one with the divine Person who is at once this immutable Self and this mutable Nature (*yaḥ asau asau puruṣaḥ saḥ aham asmi*). He sees Nature as the very becoming of the divine Self (*devātmaśakti*).[4] Not only has he realised immortality in the soul but also he is in possession of the key to an immortal life in the body, a life of divine thoughts and emotions, divine impulses and actions in all circumstances.

THE PROCESS OF ENJOYING IMMORTALITY

> *vāyur anilam amṛtam athedaṃ bhasmāntaṃ śarīram;*
> *om krato smara kṛtaṃ smara krato smara kṛtaṃ smara.*(17)

> Vāyu is Anilam. Therefore this life-force must be made immortal. Ashes are the body's end. Om, O Will bear in mind that the world has been made for the Lord's habitation, bear in mind the world thus made. O Will bear in mind that the body too has been made for His habitation, bear in mind the body thus made.

The *sādhaka* is blessed with the vision that his soul is one with the supreme Puruṣa who is extended not only in the Self but also in Nature. But this vision is to be realised as an effective power in life. In other words, he must now establish an immortal life in the body, a life which expresses immortality in all its movements — mental, vital, and physical. This is clearly the subject of the closing verses, the seventeenth and eighteenth.

Anilam is the original divine force not based in the body but in the Self, whereas Vāyu is based in the body and operates as the life-force in all parts of the body. While Anilam is conscious and not separated from the Self, Vāyu not being conscious is separated from that Self. But in essential fact they are one (*vāyur anilam*) and not opposed to each other, for Vāyu is Anilam obscured and deformed by the obscurities of the body. Therefore the life-force, which works primarily as Will in us, must detach itself from the body, drop its mortal characteristics and become immortal in all its movements — physical, vital, and mental (*atha idaṃ amṛtam*).

Indeed the body is obscure, and, like the inevitable end of all obscure forms, its end is destruction (*bhasmāntaṃ*). But that is no reason for abandoning it before the appointed time. The obscurities of the body can darken the Will and distort its original divine nature only when the Will is attached to the body and considers itself to be an inherent force of the body. When the Will is detached and awakened to its immortal nature, the body becomes a harmless instrument. A Will so detached and awakened must clearly look at the body from the point of view of the Lord and refrain from abandoning it as unusable for any divine purpose. All this (*idaṃ sarvaṃ*) has been made for the Lord's habitation and enjoyment; even so, the Will has to admit, the body must be regarded as having been made (*kṛtaṃ*) for the Lord and allowed to go on for a hundred years (*śataṃ samāḥ*) and serve as a habitation of the Lord.

agne naya supathā rāye asmān
viśvāni deva vayunāni vidvān;
yuyodhyasmajjuhurāṇam eno
bhūyiṣṭhāṃ te nama uktiṃ vidhema.(18)

O god Agni, knower of all ways, lead us by the good path to the riches; remove from us the crooked action of sin. We offer to Thee completest prayer of submission.

To awaken the life-force in the body to its original divine nature and to use the body as an instrument for God's work in the world are the twin ideals now proposed to the *sādhaka*. To progress towards them by one's own strength is very difficult, for it is beset with dangers owing to the crooked action of the sins lodged in the darkest parts of the life-force. The best way to progress without dangers is to call in the grace of Agni who is the Lord himself in his aspect of Will. If the *sādhaka* takes refuge in god Agni who knows all ways of protecting his devotee, he is sure to walk safely in the good path and possess eventually the spiritual riches hidden behind the obscure layers of the life-force (*agne naya supathā rāye*). Hence he takes shelter in Agni with a prayer of completest submission.

THE TRUE ENJOYMENT: ITS BASIS, PRINCIPLE AND PROCESS

In conclusion we may state that the aim of the Upaniṣad is to place before us the ideal of True Enjoyment in all its aspects — its basis, principle and process.

The True Enjoyment: The world may be enjoyed in two ways: it may be enjoyed for its own sake or for the sake of the indwelling Lord. To enjoy the world for its own sake is a false enjoyment, for it brings bondage and suffering. It binds the soul to the dualities of life, exposes it to fear, sorrow and delusion, and compels it to pass from death to death. On the contrary, to enjoy the world for the sake of the indwelling Lord is a true enjoyment, for it brings freedom and bliss. It delivers the soul from the dualities, from fear, sorrow and delusion, and from the necessity of death. If we learn to see the world as the habitation of the Lord, we learn the secret of true enjoyment and of true living in the world.

The Basis: Two things distinguish themselves as the fundamental truths of the Lord — Immutability and Oneness. He is immutable, but it does not mean that He cannot move out of his immutability and create the world; nor does it mean that the world is created out of something other than the Lord but not independent of Him. On the contrary, He is not bound by his immutability; He is free to manifest the world out of Himself. By commissioning his power of Becoming He becomes all existences in the world (*sarvāṇi bhūtāni*). He lives in them as the Lord of creatures (*prajāpati*) because they are his own becomings. Even when He becomes all existences, he is always immutable, because he is One and in virtue of his Oneness he exceeds all limitations associated with the world.

The soul is forgetful of the Lord. Because it lives in the movement and the multiplicity of the world as if it is bound by them; and also because it dwells in the ego as if it is bound by the law of the ego. When the soul learns to detach itself from the movement and multiplicity as also from the ego and its law of existence, it becomes aware of the indwelling Lord and realises its identity with Him (*so'ham asmi*). Like the Lord, it lives in the world but is not bound by its movement and multiplicity. Like Him, it enjoys the world but is not conditioned by the law of death. It becomes a divine soul manifesting the divine law of existence in the world (*satyadharma*).

The Principle: True enjoyment is ensured when inner freedom culminates in outer freedom. By annihilating the ego the soul realises its oneness with the Lord who embraces both Brahman and Nature, the Non-Birth and the Birth; by eliminating the law of death from the inner and outer instruments the liberated soul expresses immortality in all works done in the world (*na karma lipyate*).

The Process: First comes the realisation of the Self. Then comes the passage from the Self to the supreme Self, the Lord who is the Truth and whose law is the true Law. If we are overcome by the joy of freedom that comes by the conquest of the Self, we face a division in consciousness — a consciousness gathered in the silent Self as opposed to a consciousness scattered in the active Nature. This proves to be a barrier in the passage to the Lord. When the grace of Sūrya intervenes and saves the soul from its attachment to the joy of freedom, the barrier is removed and the divided consciousness becomes unified. Once the passage is cleared the vision of the most beautiful form of the Lord and that of the soul's oneness with Him simultaneously arise. We see now that we are a master unbound by the world and also an enjoyer of all this, like the Lord who is superior to the world and by this superiority enjoys habitation in the world.

Though this is a unique vision and knowledge, it must translate itself into a power of life and an effective principle of living in the world. For knowledge must fulfil itself in life. When this takes place through the grace of Agni, the passage to the supreme Lord is completed and the life-force in us is transformed into a divine force which enjoys using the body for God's work in the world.

Thus there are three steps in the process of true enjoyment: first, the realisation of the Self; second, the vision of the true form of the Lord and of the soul's identity with Him; and third, the transformation of the life-force into a principle of divine living in the world.

It is no exaggeration if we say that the Īśa is the greatest among the twelve major Upaniṣads, for in it we find the supreme statement of the entire Vedānta.

NOTES

1. Bṛhadāraṇyaka Upaniṣad, 1-4-7.
2. Sri Aurobindo, *The Upanishads* (1972), pp. 98-104.
3. Maitrī Upaniṣad, 6-34.
4. Śvetāśvatara Upaniṣad, 1-3.

5

The Rule for Enjoyment

GOD AND THE WORLD

All this, whatever there is (*idaṃ sarvaṃ yatkiñca*),[1] is determined by the action of the three *guṇas* of *sattva, rajas* and *tamas*. Not only *rajas* and *tamas* but even *sattva* binds; all three bind through ignorance and ego. One may therefore conclude that God, who is absolutely free and of the nature of knowledge, cannot reside in a world subject to the action of the *guṇas* and that the abode of God must be somewhere beyond names and forms (*nāma rūpa*).

But there is a higher principle hidden behind the *guṇas* of Prakṛti (*devātmaśaktiṃ svaguṇair nigūḍhām*).[2] As self-power of God, the higher Prakṛti is one with God or God himself in universal Movement. Though it is hidden by the play of the *guṇas*, the *guṇas* are not entirely opposed to it. Somehow they arise from the higher Prakṛti (*svaguṇāḥ*).[3] Thus there are two kinds of Prakṛti, a lower one and a higher one. As the lower rises from the higher Prakṛti, the world, superficially determined by the *guṇas*, is really a manifestation of God's Nature (*ātmaśakti*).[4] Therefore the world is a fit abode of God and it must be considered as such (*īśāvāsyam idaṃ sarvaṃ*).[5] All habitation is for enjoyment. Hence God's habitation is for the sake of enjoyment.

God is one and immutable (*tad anejadekaṃ*).[6] Mātariśvan is Nature. And Nature is God himself in universal Movement. In God (*tasmin*)[7] Mātariśvan establishes all moving objects (*apaḥ*).[8] Remaining in God (*tiṣṭhat*), he outstrips the moving objects (*dhāvato 'nyānatyeti*).[9] He overtakes even Mind and the Gods (*pūrvamarṣat*).[10] For Mātariśvan is always greater than all he has brought into existence.

God is absolutely free — free not only in immutable existence but also in mutable nature,[11] not only beyond space and time but also in the world conditioned by space and time,[12] not only beyond forms and names but also in things possessing forms and names.[13] In a word, He is gone everywhere (*saparyagāt*).[14]

Basically, God is of the nature of immutable existence. And this is brought out by six neuter adjectives — *śukram, akāyam, avraṇam, asnāviram, śuddham,* and *apāpaviddham.*[15] Though He is immutable, he is the cause of the world and creates all by self-becoming (*svayambhū*).[16] There are three steps in the self-becoming of God — Kavi, Manīṣī and Paribhū.[17] As Kavi, He sees the truth of things in his immutable existence; as Manīṣī, He conceives the world he has chosen to manifest; as Paribhū, He objectifies the conception and, through this, brings the world into existence. In the three steps God alone is the material of creation. Having created the objects, he preserves their inherent laws (*yāthātathyato'rthān*)[18] and arranges them according to their laws. Otherwise the world will be chaotic and unfit for enjoyment.

God's Nature is absolutely free like God. The lower Nature of the three *guṇas* is a lower action of God's Nature. Though the world is pervaded by the *guṇas*, it is derived from and supported by His Nature. In other words, it is a self-becoming of God. A true knowledge culminating in a true enjoyment of the world is possible only when we pass from the lower to the higher Nature, from the false to the true law of action (*satyadharma*).[19]

THE DEVOTEE: HIS MEANS AND ENDS

Since God dwells everywhere and since objects arise from his supreme Nature, there is a good justification for accepting the world abandoned out of a wrong conclusion (*tena tyaktena*)[20] and for enjoying the world like Him (*bhuñjīthā*).[21] But likeness to God is possible only when we give up our sense of separate existence from God and the resultant habit of enjoying the world for the sake of our separate self. As long as desires persist in us, we are conditioned by them and live as a separate self. So they are to be renounced (*mā gṛdhaḥ*).[22] But how to renounce them? By enquiry, "Whose possession is this world (*kasyasvid dhanam*)?"[23] It reveals that the whole world is God's creation and, therefore, God's possession. Nothing belongs to us — neither our soul nor our body nor even things said to be "our" possessions. A persistent enquiry (*vicāra*) leads to the conviction that the sense of personal possessions is utterly false and without any foundation. A right conviction alone is not sufficient, for it can show the falsity of the wrong conviction but cannot destroy the habits of conduct which preserve the wrong one.

As desire and attachment for possessions are due to both wrong conviction and wrong conduct, right conviction is to be followed by right conduct. When the two are combined, desire gradually gives way and one realises God as his *svarūpa* and enjoys all things like Him. Hence one has to perform all actions with right conviction without refraining from them (*kurvanneveha karmāṇi*).[24] As the body is a possession of God, one has to retain it for the full term as ordained by Him (*jijīviṣet śataṃ samāḥ*)[25] and use it for His sake. The seeker of God has to live and do works like this (*evaṃ tvayi*)[26] and not otherwise than this (*nānyatheto'sti*).[27] As his life and works are free from the fault of desire, *karma* does not taint him (*na karma lipyate nare*).[28]

We have heard from the wise that there are two means, knowledge (*vidyā*)[29] and works (*avidyā*),[30] each having its own result. He who is devoted to works goes to a blind darkness (*andhaṃ tamaḥ*),[31] for he faces grave difficulties by trying to enjoy like God with the mere strength of will. Will without the light of knowledge is blind and not free from the fault of desire. It is therefore the cause of ineradicable miseries. He who is devoted to knowledge goes to a greater darkness (*tato bhūya tamaḥ*),[32] for he falls into an error of thinking that by the mere strength of knowledge he can enjoy like God. Knowledge without an effectuating will can only produce delusion and not enjoyment. As the error of knowledge is greater than the error of will, the devotee is said to enter into a greater darkness. But he who combines both knowledge and works (*ubhayaṃ saha*)[33] really enjoys like God. He overcomes the evil of desire (*mṛtyuṃ tīrtvā*)[34] through works enlightened by knowledge of God's will and realises the immortal Inhabitant of the world (*amṛtam aśnute*)[35] through knowledge strengthened by works fulfilling His will.

Again, we have heard from the wise that there are two goals, a right one (*sambhūti*)[36] and a wrong one (*asambhūti*),[37] each having its own result. The wrong one is enjoyment and the right one is renunciation. He who is devoted to enjoyment goes to a blind darkness (*andhaṃ tamaḥ*),[38] for he is immersed in ignorance and misery. Enjoyment tainted by desire is oblivious of God's example and produces only evil results. On account of this, it is aptly called destruction (*vināśa*).[39] He who is devoted to renunciation goes to a greater darkness (*tato bhūya tamaḥ*),[40] for he has neglected the example set by God himself, the example of enjoying the world without desire. As neglect by deliberate decision is more powerful than enjoyment by natural desire, the devotee is said to enter into a greater darkness. But he who combines both enjoyment and renunciation (*ubhayaṃ saha*)[41] truly follows God's example. He overcomes the evil of desire (*mṛtyuṃ tīrtvā*)[42] through enjoyment (*vināśena*)[43] transformed by renunciation and realises the immortal Inhabitant of the world (*amṛtam aśnute*)[44] through renunciation (*sambhūtyā*)[44] upgraded by enjoyment. A transformed enjoyment is an enjoyment of the world not for the sake of desire but for the sake of God; an upgraded renunciation is a renunciation not of the world but of desire for the world.

The devotee's aim is not only to mould himself according to God's example but also to propagate the glory and greatness of the ideal among his fellow men and shape them through his works. In fact this is the real justification for his desire to live a hundred years doing works in the world. He sees all beings to be unmanifest in Ātman (*sarvāṇibhūtanyātmanyeva*)[45] and Ātman to be residing in all manifested beings (*sarvabhūteṣu cātmānaṃ*).[46] As a result, he does not shrink from extending the ideal of divine enjoyment to the entire human race (*tato na vijugupsate*).[47] As his work for humanity is founded upon the supreme knowledge of oneness (*ekatvam*),[48] it does not bring him delusion and grief which, under the conditions of ignorance and ego, are its inevitable results.[49] In other words, he incurs no bondage through works performed by him.

In olden days ascetics viewed the world to be an evil, and birth and works to be two forms of the evil, because they saw only the play of the three *guṇas* everywhere. As a result, they sought God through renunciation of birth and works (*dehatyāgam*). In the Īśa they are called *ātmahano janāḥ*.[50] In the Ṛg Veda the sages are doers of divine works (*sukarmāṇaḥ*)[51] and constantly pray for a life of hundred years (*śataṃ himāḥ*).[52] To them the Sun is the symbol of Brahman and Sun-Worlds symbolise Brahman-Worlds. They reach Sun-Worlds through divine works. From the first line of the second verse and that of the third it is evident that the Īśa not only subscribes to the Vedic tradition but is certainly opposed to the ascetics. It is opposed to them because their attitude towards God and renunciation are evidently un-Vedic (*aśrauta*). We notice its displeasure towards them from the remark that after their death the ascetics go to worlds *other than* the Sun-Worlds (*asūryā nāma te lokāḥ*).[53] The word *ātmahan* is closely connected with *tyaktena* in the first verse which refers to the world abandoned by the seeker of God. Even if the *ātmahan* happens to be a seeker of God, he errs — errs by destroying God's possessions (for his soul and body are really God's) and deliberately doing violence to the example God himself has set by living in the world and enjoying his habitation (*īśāvāsyam idaṃ sarvaṃ*).[54] In view of the offence committed by the ascetics they are called men enveloped in blindness and ignorance (*andhena tamasāvṛtāḥ*).[55]

The devotee of God follows God's example. He lives and works for the sake of leading all men to that example. He incurs no bondage from works. In him knowledge and works, enjoyment and renunciation are inseparably and harmoniously united together. As he seeks God through harmony and oneness and follows, by doing so, in the footsteps of his Vedic forefathers, he sets aside the exclusive and un-Vedic views of the ascetics.

PRAYERS FOR GOD'S GRACE

Generally the last four mantras of the Īśa are considered to be very obscure and not related to the other mantras in an intelligible manner. As a result, scholars try to remove the obscurity through two explanations. The first is that Sūrya and Agni are objects of worship for an Agnihotrin. The second is that the four mantras are prayers offered by him when he is on his death-bed on account of old age. If we keep in mind that many of the key words in the prayers reveal an intimate connection with the mantras of the Ṛg Veda, we may note that Sūrya and Agni, as in the Veda, are really symbols of psychological phenomena[56] and not objects of external worship. As the Agnihotrin is confined to his death-bed, he is depicted as a helpless person with no strength for active life. This hardly agrees with what we witness in the beginning of the Īśa where the command is for a ceaseless active life (*kurvanneveha karmāṇi*),[57] a life of action and enjoyment (*bhuñjīthāḥ*).[58] It is quite unnatural that the Upaniṣad should close with a picture of a person incapable of moving out of his bed. No scholar who reads the Upaniṣad properly will support these explanations. Therefore they must be dismissed as of no significance.

It is true that the Upaniṣad is obscure in many places. But a right attitude towards it is that the obscurity is in us rather than in the mind of the seer of the Upaniṣad. A careful study reveals that the mantras really develop an idea of the opening mantra which closes with the word *dhanam*.[59] There are two vital clues in them which confirm our view. The words *hiraṇmaya*[60] and *rāye*[61] in them go back to the word *dhanam* and suggest that the last four mantras are a logical extension of the first. If we accept the suggestion and read the four mantras in this light, they cease to be obscure and become quite intelligible.

With the help of knowledge and works the seeker of God overcomes the evil of desire (*mṛtyuṃ tīrtvā*) and moulds himself and others according to God's example. But he cannot shape himself into an absolute image of God. So whenever his effort (*prayatna*) diminishes and aspiration (*utsāḥ*) dwindles there is an upsurge of desires from the subconscient self which destroys his accumulated gains in one stroke. Since his visions and experiences, in spite of their overwhelming effect, have not yet matured into steady realisations and become his *svabhāva*, he has to maintain his aspiration only through effort. When there is a slackening of the effort, the subconscient comes to the surface and begins to dominate him. On one such occasion the seeker invokes the grace and help of Sūrya and Agni, the two symbolising the original powers of Knowledge and Will, for absolutely removing the obstacle.

Hiraṇyam refers to possessions and *hiraṇmaya pātram*[62] to a vessel with an abundance of possessions. The seeker images his own subconscient self to be a vessel with an abundance of *desires* for possessions. The desires are of different sorts — some ordinary, some powerful, some bright with the light of *sattva*, some compelling with the force of *rajas*, some obscure with the darkness of *tamas*, and so on. Among them sins are desires which fulfil themselves through crooked methods (*duryuktibhiḥ*). Such desires are generally violent and obscure and rarely come to light. But they are always productive of worst evils. As long as these desires survive, they do not allow the seeker to be securely lodged in his true self and possessed of steady realisations. On account of the obstruction by "the vessel", the seeker's direct vision of God and God's example has disappeared; he is no longer in possession of the true law of action by which he followed the example. Hence his prayer, "O Sun, remove that obstruction (*tat tvaṃ pūṣann apāvṛṇu*)".[63] The aim of this prayer is to get back the direct vision and the true law of action (*satyadharmāya dṛṣṭaye*).[64]

God's form is most beautiful (*kalyāṇatamaṃ*).[65] For He is the all-pervading Person (*asau asau puruṣaḥ*)[66] who reveals himself to be the true Self of the perceiver of God's form (*so'ham*). In ignorance he thinks that he is the indweller and possessor of his body and also the enjoyer of objects through the body. But when he sees that God is his true Self, the whole conception changes. He now sees God to be the indweller, the body to be God's instrument and all objects to be God's objects of enjoyment. This was the original vision of the seeker of God and is now lost on account of obstruction. How has the loss occurred? The light of his consciousness has been broken into a thousand rays and scattered among the desires — this is how it has occurred. So the recovery of the vision depends upon the recovery of his original consciousness. How is the consciousness to be recovered? First the rays must be withdrawn and then the light in them must be gathered into the original light of his unified consciousness (*vyūha raśmīn samūha tejaḥ*).[67] God Sūrya alone can accomplish it, pull him out of his deplorable condition and take him back to his original vision of God. For Sūrya is verily a power of the Lord of beings (*prājāpatya*).[68]

The body is the most exterior part of one's being and bound inextricably by the *guṇas*. Like the mental and vital parts, it cannot be shaped into an image of God. Hence it is fit to be ultimately consumed by fire (*bhasmāntaṃ śarīram*).[69] Till then it can serve as a good instrument lasting for a hundred years (*śataṃ samāḥ*).[70] Pervaded by Vāyu, all in us — soul, mind, life and senses — appear to be mortal and cannot put on the image of God. In essence Vāyu is the immortal Anilam, the original Life-Force of God (*vāyur anilam amṛtam*).[71] Therefore, when the seeker of God acts according to the true law, Vāyu disappears into Anilam and Anilam pervades his whole being and shapes his soul, mind, life and senses into an image of God, without the mortal characteristics by which they are usually bound. As a result, desires disappear and the seeker enjoys the world like God. Such were the gains that came to him through the true law. Now, on account of obstruction, he is dispossessed of the law. Though the law is not there, the memory of its possession is still there. Sometimes it is better to remember the past, for it gives a certain strength to act even in a hopeless circumstance. So he tells himself, "O Will, remember God (OM), remember all deeds done in accordance with the true Law; O Will, remember God, remember all deeds done for the sake of manifesting the immortal Anilam".[72] With the strength derived from the remembrance the seeker now prays to Agni.

Agni is the knower of all things that are manifested (*viśvāni deva vayunāni vidvān*).[73] He knows both Vāyu and Anilam: Vāyu to be a distortion of Anilam and Anilam to be free of the mortal characteristics of Vāyu; Anilam to be one that removes desires, shapes the soul, mind, life, and senses according to the true Law and makes them into an image of God. He knows that when Vāyu is fully transformed into Anilam, no sin can survive in spite of its crookedness (*juhurāṇamenaḥ*).[74] In him Knowledge and Will are one and indivisible. Hence the seeker offers a complete prayer of submission and calls upon Agni to remove the crooked-going sin through a complete transformation of Vāyu and lead him back to the enjoyment of possessions by the good path, the path laid out in God's example (*supathā rāye*).[75] The true law consists in acting according to God's example. To act thus is to be on the good path.

It is significant that the prayer is uttered not only for the seeker's sake but also for the sake of others for whose good he works (*asmān*).[76] Though the loss is incurred by him, it is indirectly a loss for others also. For in his personal loss is included the loss of the work done for others' good. Apart from this, there is a direct sense in which the loss concerns both the seeker and the other people simultaneously. For both are dispossessed of the direct vision of God's example and the true Law: in the case of the seeker the loss is of recent origin, whereas in the case of the other people it is there from time immemorial. This seems to be the justification for offering the prayer on behalf of all.

With knowledge and works the seeker passes from the lower to the higher Nature. But when he is obstructed by "the vessel", he again falls into the lower Nature. Hence he tries to overcome the obstruction and rise to the higher Nature through the help and grace of Sūrya and Agni.

KNOWLEDGE, WORKS, AND DEVOTION

Knowledge and works are indeed helpful in winning the vision of God's example and the true Law. But they are helpless against the subconscient self, the vessel of obstruction (*pātram*). For it is crooked-going. It is a formidable task for a human being to deal with the subconscient stuff. Only God's grace can do that successfully. Hence devotion to God intervenes as the sovereign means of eliminating the subconscient over which the seeker has no control whatsoever. Thus knowledge and works find their fulfilment in devotion. This is the true significance of the word *namas*.[77] Sri Aurobindo explains that the word symbolises "submission to the divine Being".[78]

Generally knowledge, works and devotion are said to be Vedāntic in origin. Most of the Upaniṣads emphasise knowledge. Occasionally, as in the Śvetāśvatara, knowledge and devotion or, as in the Muṇḍaka, knowledge and works, are spoken of. But none of them except one lays emphasis on all — knowledge, works, and devotion, the exception being the Īśa Upaniṣad. This is its uniqueness. Therefore there seems to be a good justification for the Īśa to be placed at the head of the twelve Upaniṣads.

NOTES

1. Īśa Upaniṣad(hereafter Īś. Up.), Mantra 1.
2. Śvetāśvatara Upaniṣad, 1-3.
3. Ibid.
4. Ibid.
5. Īś. Up., Mantra 1.
6. Ibid., Mantra 4.
7. Ibid.
8. Ibid.
9. Ibid.
10. Ibid.
11. Ibid., Mantra 5.
12. Ibid.
13. Ibid.
14. Ibid., Mantra 8.
15. Ibid.
16. Ibid.
17. Ibid.
18. Ibid.
19. Ibid., Mantra 15.
20. Ibid., Mantra 1.
21. Ibid.
22. Ibid.
23. Ibid.
24. Ibid., Mantra 2.
25. Ibid.
26. Ibid.
27. Ibid.
28. Ibid.
29. Ibid., Mantra 9.
30. Ibid.
31. Ibid.
32. Ibid.
33. Ibid., Mantra 11.
34. Ibid.
35. Ibid.
36. Ibid., Mantra 12.
37. Ibid.
38. Ibid.
39. Ibid., Mantra 14.
40. Ibid., Mantra 12.
41. Ibid., Mantra 14.

42. Ibid.
43. Ibid.
44. Ibid.
45. Ibid., Mantra 7.
46. Ibid.
47. Ibid.
48. Ibid.
49. Ibid.
50. Ibid., Mantra 3.
51. Ṛg Veda, 4-2-17.
52. Ibid., 6-13-6.
53. Īś. Up., Mantra 3.
54. Ibid., Mantra 1.
55. Ibid., Mantra 3.
56. Sri Aurobindo, *The Secret of the Veda* (Dec. 1971), pp. 265, 274.
57. Īś. Up., Mantra 2.
58. Ibid., Mantra 1.
59. Ibid.
60. Ibid., Mantra 15.
61. Ibid., Mantra 18.
62. Ibid., Mantra 15.
63. Ibid.
64. Ibid.
65. Ibid., Mantra 16.
66. Ibid.
67. Ibid.
68. Ibid.
69. Ibid., Mantra 17.
70. Ibid., Mantra 2.
71. Ibid., Mantra 17.
72. Ibid.
73. Ibid., Mantra 18.
74. Ibid.
75. Ibid.
76. Ibid.
77. Ibid.
78. Sri Aurobindo, *The Upanishads*(1972), p. 133.

6

Ātmahan

THE INTERPRETATION OF THE PHRASE

The Īśa Upaniṣad, which forms the concluding portion of the Vājasaneya Saṃhitā, is known for its terse but very highly flexible expressions. On account of these expressions it lends itself to be interpreted in so many different ways, unlike any other Upaniṣad. There is a phrase in the third verse of the Upaniṣad, namely, *ātmahano janāḥ*, which has received a good deal of attention from the commentators, both Indian and Western, for it is capable of giving at least two different senses — one is physical and another metaphysical.

The conventional sense of the word *ātmahan* is very clear and unambiguous — it means one who commits suicide. Yet this sense is not taken into account while interpreting *ātmahano janāḥ*. Śaṅkara's rendering of the phrase is: the people who kill the eternal Self in themselves (*ātmānaṃ nityaṃ hiṃsanti*). Obviously the word *ātmahan* is forced to give up its conventional sense and yield an unconventional one. We learn from Swāmī Satyānanda Saraswatī's commentary that the phrase was originally understood in the sense of the people who kill themselves.[1] But he has not disclosed the source from which he came to know about this "orthodox interpretation" of *ātmahano janāḥ*.

In Bhavabhūti's *Uttararāmacarita*, a well-known Sānskṛt drama, there is a clear allusion to the third verse of the Īśa Upaniṣad.[2] It depicts King Janaka as contemplating suicide. But he changes his mind with the reflection that according to the sages, those who commit suicide reach, after death, the worlds enveloped in blind darkness. Bhavabhūti writes thus (Fourth Act):

> *andhatāmiśrā hy asuryā nāma te lokāstebhyaḥ pratividhīyante ya ātmaghātina ity evam ṛṣayo manyante.*

This clearly shows that the third verse of the Īśa Upaniṣad was originally understood as prohibiting suicide. This also corroborates the view of Swāmī Satyānanda Saraswatī.

A general rule in the Vedāntic exegesis is that the received sense of a word carries greater authority and validity than the one which deviates from it. Therefore it is necessary to study all the ramifications of the phrase *ātmahano janāḥ* and determine how far the conventional sense of *ātmahan* contributes to a right understanding of the phrase as well as the verse in which the phrase occurs. We must also bear in mind that while fixing the precise sense of *ātmahano janāḥ,* we have to take into account not only the whole verse of which the phrase is a part, but also the two other verses that precede this verse. As the phrase is a part of the third verse, so is the teaching of this verse inseparably related to the teachings of the preceding verses. In other words, the phrase is best understood when it is viewed in the light of all the three verses, — verses 3, 2 and 1.

ŚAṄKARA'S INTERPRETATION

We shall now see how Śaṅkara analyses the three verses and note why he prefers an unconventional to a conventional interpretation. The first verse teaches that the Self is to be protected by renouncing the world (*sannyāsena*). Keeping in view those who are incapable of renouncing the world, the second verse calls upon them to enjoy a long life in the world by doing works enjoined by the Veda and escape the evil that prohibited works bring (*aśubha karma*). The third verse says that *ātmahanaḥ*, when they die, take *asuric* births characterised by blind darkness (*andhena tamasāvṛtāḥ*).

Now the question is this: who are these people called *ātmahanaḥ*? If we adhere to the conventional sense of the word *ātmahanaḥ*, we may say that it stands for the people who kill themselves, who violently remove their bodies. It agrees with the teaching of the verse that when these people die, they take *asuric* births, for, by committing suicide, they have done a wrong deed (*aśubha karma*). Though the conventional sense of the word fits in with the verse of which it is a component, we have to see how the teaching of the verse is related to the teachings of the other two verses, verses 2 and 1. The third verse may be related to verses 2 and 1 if we accept that committing suicide is an *aśubha karma* and that those who resort to this wrong deed stand excluded not only from those who protect the Self through renunciation but also from those who are engaged in the Vedic works and take care to protect their human self from the evil associated with *aśubha karma*. As far as this goes, it makes complete sense. But beyond this we face a difficulty. The expression *aśubha karma* stands for the whole class of wrong deeds, not only for the act of killing oneself. Hence it does not make sense why the Upaniṣad should choose the self-slayers, exclude the other wrong doers and say that the former alone take *asuric* births when they die. Are not the latter also entitled to the same fate when they depart from the world? As a result, Śaṅkara has surrendered the conventional sense of *ātmahano janāḥ* i.e. the people who commit suicide.

In his effort to find a more suitable sense to *ātmahano janāḥ* Śaṅkara, as has been already pointed out, takes the expression to mean the people who kill the eternal Self by veiling it through the fault of ignorance (*ātmānaṃ nityaṃ hiṃsanti avidyādoṣeṇa*). In other words, those who kill the Self are the ignorant people (*avidvāṃsaḥ*). Precisely speaking, they are men who are attached to the world and wish to live a hundred years here performing works ordained by the Veda, men who imagine themselves to be mere mortals (*naramātra*). But then why do they take *asuric* births when they die? That is because they are not free from the fault of ignorance, the fault of not renouncing the world and of living under the notion that they are mere mortals.

This raises two questions, rather a single question in two forms: (i) Is it not a contradiction that they who are engaged in prescribed works should attain *asuric* instead of *deva* births promised by the Veda? (ii) Does it make sense that they who escape *aśubha karma* by the performance of works ordained by the Veda should fall into *asuric* births which are the results of *aśubha karma*? To these questions Śaṅkara has one answer — since the *deva* births are far inferior to the brilliance of the unborn Ātman, they are said to be *asuric*. Here he makes "*asuric* births" stand for "*deva* births", an antonym to do duty for a synonym. This, as Sri Aurobindo says, is a "misuse" of word.[3]

If the physical sense of *ātmahano janāḥ* is too narrow to include all who resort to wrong deeds, the metaphysical sense of the same expression is too broad to exclude the whole class of wrongdoers. As the sense is either too narrow or too broad, Śaṅkara cannot give the right interpretation of the phrase.

SRI AUROBINDO'S INTERPRETATION: AN EARLY VERSION

Sri Aurobindo has written several commentaries on the Īśa Upaniṣad of which one alone covers the entire Upaniṣad. In one of his early commentaries (written before 1914) he has explained the sense of the first three verses of the Īśa.

According to Sri Aurobindo, the first verse tells us that we must "enjoy by abandonment", i.e. we must abandon the desires of the heart and enjoy leading the world, leading "men upwards to the Divine."[4] "We must not", says the second verse, "turn our backs on life, must not fling it from us untimely or even long for early release from our body but willingly fill out our term, even be most ready to prolong it to the full period of man's ordinary existence so that we may go on doing our deeds in the world," deeds "devoted to God" and, therefore, freed from the binding effects of the ego.[5] The third verse contains a warning to those who kill themselves: "it is no use taking refuge in suicide or the shortening of ... life, because those who kill themselves instead of finding freedom, plunge by death into a worse prison of darkness — the Asuric worlds enveloped in blind gloom."[6]

Sri Aurobindo, it is obvious, accepts the conventional sense of *ātmahano janāḥ*. So he renders the phrase as "those who slay themselves."[7] He finds Śaṅkara's interpretation of the phrase to be "startlingly unnatural and paradoxical," for the eternal Self (*ātmānaṃ nityaṃ*) "neither slays nor is slain," as is clearly affirmed by the Upaniṣads.[8] According to him, to take *ātmahanaḥ* "in the sense of suicides"[9] is natural. But then who are these self-slayers and what is the occasion for the Upaniṣad to talk about them in the third verse?

The verse itself contains a clue which, when fully developed, tells us who the self-slayers are. It says that the people who kill themselves go to other worlds enveloped in blind darkness. From the Bṛhadāraṇyaka we know these dark worlds to be worlds into which the unawakened and ignorant sink after death (*avidvāṃso-'budho janāḥ*).[10] It is therefore clear that *ātmahano janāḥ* are the ignorant people who kill themselves, the people who take their bodies to be the real self. The next question to be answered is: Why does the Upaniṣad bring in the subject of self-slayers and the dark worlds to which they depart after death? As this question is related to the sequence of the three verses — verses 1, 2 and 3, we shall see how it is understood by Sri Aurobindo. "Enjoy by abandonment," says Sri Aurobindo, is the formula of the first verse. It declares that our aim is to enjoy working for God in the world by abandoning all that separate us from Him — desires and attachments, ego and ignorance. The aim is therefore to abandon the human self, know God to be our true Self (*so'ham*) and offer devoted service to Him. From this is derived the next formula of spiritual life — "Complete the full term of human existence and do all works without bondage." Works continue even after the realisation of God, for they do not bind God's worker and are necessary for fulfilling Him in humanity. This is the teaching of the second verse, a natural extension of the first. Together the two verses give a complete account of the spiritual ideal to be pursued by us. Now we shall see which aspect of this ideal is further developed in the third verse. If we do this, we shall have found out the reason for the third verse to talk about self-slayers. Sri Aurobindo seems to hold the view that the third verse develops the idea of freedom common to the two preceding verses. He writes:

> The Śruti says ... that those who slay themselves go down into the nether world of gloom, for they have associated the self with the body and fancied that by getting rid of this body, they will be free, but they have died full of impressions of grief, impatience, disgust and pain.[11]

According to him, the verse teaches that the ignorant who try to be free from grief etc. by removing their bodies, attain the very opposite of what they desire. We may agree with him that the verse invites our attention to the consequences of viewing freedom in a physical as against a spiritual perspective. But what we do not understand is this: Why does the sage of the Upaniṣad, after expounding the spiritual ideal of the awakened, pass on to the physical ideal of the ignorant and its consequences? This has no relevance to the awakened, for they have already gone beyond the level of the ignorant and seen the futilities of getting freedom through physical means. Thus the third verse is entirely unrelated to the sense of the previous verses. This perhaps is the reason why Sri Aurobindo himself gave up the physical sense of *ātmahanaḥ* in his final commentary on the Īśa Upaniṣad (written in 1914-15).

TWO WESTERN INTERPRETATIONS: P. THIEME

P. Thieme has written a commentary on the Īśa Upaniṣad according to the Kāṇva recension. It covers the first fourteen verses. His work is scholarly, but at the same time misses at many places the subtleties of the Vedānta. His aim is to show that the verses of the Īśa "form a consistent, meaningful whole."[12] According to him, the whole Upaniṣad must be viewed as a discussion moving from *pūrvapakṣa* to *siddhānta* through *uttarapakṣa*. He tries to connect all apparently disconnected statements in the text through this approach. As we are mainly interested in the interpretation of *ātmahano janāḥ*, we shall confine ourselves to his exposition of the first three verses of the Upaniṣad and leave the rest.

In the first verse is stated a *pūrvapakṣa* view. It says that since the Lord (the supreme Self) is seated in the heart of all living beings, a sage should nourish himself (*bhuñjīthāḥ*) with what is abandoned i.e. with what is voluntarily ceded to him (*tyaktena*). Therefore he should not rob or kill another living being (*māgṛdhaḥ kasya sviddhanam*). Then in the second comes an *uttarapakṣa* — a sage who acts without attachment (*evaṃ tvayi*) is not soiled by his action i.e. by killing (*na karma lipyate nare*). Finally, the original position is maintained in the third in the form of a *siddhānta*. It goes back to the view of the first and says that the sages who resort to killing (*ātmahano janāḥ*) are guilty of *hiṃsā* and hence go to the demoniac worlds of gloom after death. We shall quote from his article:

> It looks as if the three verses contain a little discussion: the first speaker (A) maintains that you shall not rob or kill a living being, giving an ethical reason for it. The second speaker (B) rebuts this with the principle that action without "attachment" does not "soil" a man. Thereupon "speaker A" upholds his view, adding that killing is not only wrong, but will be punished in hell.[13]

The sense Thieme gives to *ātmahano janāḥ* is neither conventional like Sri Aurobindo's nor metaphysical like Śaṅkara's, but artificial, for it takes away the reflexive sense of *ātmahanaḥ* and imports into it the demonstrative sense of *ātman* so as to make that term mean "slayers of other beings".

Apart from this violence, Thieme's interpretation makes the third verse irrelevant. To see how he has driven the verse to this position we have to review his interpretations verse by verse. He tries to connect the three verses by showing that they represent three steps in a discussion on the conduct of a sage. The first verse says: "You should not rob or kill a living being, for every living being is a dwelling place of the Lord, that is, the Self."[14] The sage is to maintain his devotion to other living beings in the matter of food also; even for the sake of physical nourishment he should not kill another living being. Thus "enjoinment of *ahiṃsā*"[15] upon the sage is the first step (verse 1) in the discussion.

In the next step (verse 2) another aspect of the sage's conduct is taken up. The second verse says: "You may do anything (even rob or kill a living being), provided you are acting without 'attachment' (passion, fear, hope, desire): for thus sin will not soil you."[16] So the sage does not become guilty of *hiṃsā* if he kills for food and this killing is without attachment. This contradicts the positions taken by the first verse.

In the final step (verse 3) the Upaniṣad is expected to restate in the light of the rebuttal its original position that the sage who is devoted to all living beings should not only practise *ahiṃsā* but be also unattached in his actions. It is an error to think that unattached actions are dry and devoid of the noble emotions of the heart. They are indeed devoid of personal motives and interests, but not of the boundless emotional concern for the good of other living beings in the world. In fact unattached actions and *ahiṃsā* are not alternatives between which the sage has to make a choice. So the Upaniṣad ought to show that unattached actions support and not exclude *ahiṃsā* under any circumstance. But, contrary to this, the Upaniṣad comes to an irrelevant conclusion that the sages who kill go to the worlds of gloom after death.

Apart from this, there is another difficulty. Thieme thinks that the first three verses of the Upaniṣad are concerned with the conduct of a sage. Accordingly, he takes *ātmahano janāḥ* to be the sages who kill or do *hiṃsā*. But if we take the clue provided by the word *janāḥ*, we will be forced to conclude that the third verse is concerned with the ordinary ignorant people who kill other living beings, not the sages who see the Lord in all and are devoted to them as His habitations.

TWO WESTERN INTERPRETATIONS: SHARMA AND YOUNG

Arvind Sharma and Katherine K. Young make out a case for the literal interpretation of the phrase *ātmahano janāḥ* in the Īśa, as distinguished from the metaphorical interpretation put on it since the time of Śaṅkara. They show that though the metaphorical interpretation of the phrase — "the people who kill the Self in themselves" — has won wide acceptance among many Indian scholars, it cannot be ignored that there is enough evidence to the contrary in the history of Hinduism itself i.e. evidence in support of its literal interpretation — "the people who commit suicide." Speaking of the third verse where the phrase occurs, they write:

> An examination of the evidence on the point, however, suggests that the verse has been understood in a literal sense within the history of Hinduism more often than is recognised, that this understanding of the verse makes much more sense in the context of the Upaniṣad itself than has been generally acknowledged, and that, therefore, much greater credence should be accorded to this particular literal interpretation as disapproving of suicide than has hitherto been the case.[17]

As we are interested in the exegetical rather than in the historical aspect of the phrase, we shall examine how successfully Sharma and Young build their argument on the basis of exegesis.

They rightly point out that by going into the historical aspect of *ātmahano janāḥ* one cannot conclusively establish that it should be understood in the literal and not in the metaphorical sense. They write: "The fact that a particular interpretation was demonstrably common during a significant period of the history of Hinduism does not by itself render it correct or even plausible as a valid option, unless it can be established that it is consistent with the text and the context in which it is found".[18] Therefore they try to explain the sense of *ātmahano janāḥ* in the context of the first three verses as follows:

> The first line of the first verse of *Īśa* ... portrays the universe as pervaded (and therefore possessed) by God. The second line draws the conclusion that as it is enveloped/possessed by God it should be enjoyed through renunciation and nothing in it should be coveted, because it belongs to God.
>
> The second verse discusses the consequences of such a world-view of the universe in relation to the idea of *karma*, which is a major concern of the Upaniṣads ... The second verse seems to carry with it the assurance that if a person were to perform action, either ritual or otherwise, in the spirit of the first verse, then the person will not be tainted or smeared by *karma*. In this context the third verse seems to be designed to prevent the reader of the Upaniṣad from drawing the mistaken conclusion that since action is invariably associated with one's body, it might be possible to get rid of *karma* by getting rid of one's body, that is, by committing suicide.[19]

From this explanation emerge three points relevant to our purpose: first of all, the phrase *ātmahano janāḥ* is used in the third verse in the sense of the people who commit suicide; secondly, the *ātmahanaḥ* are those who try to escape the bondage of *karma* by destroying the body with which alone performance of actions is possible; thirdly, the aim of the verse is to prohibit suicide as a means of escape from the bondage of *karma*.

Sharma and Young hold that the third verse arises in the sequence in order to remove a "mistaken conclusion" from a premise we have accepted by accepting the teaching of the second verse. According to them, the mistaken conclusion — "to get rid of *karma* by getting rid of one's body" — follows from the premise supplied by the second verse — "action is invariably associated with a body". Given the premise, the conclusion will be mistaken only under one condition, namely, only when one fails to grasp its implied sense that though action is invariably associated with the body, the removal of *karma* does not depend upon removing one's body. Now the question is this: Is it really possible to put this sense into the premise? Except by a wild imagination it is impossible. Further, the premise, as stated by Sharma and Young, does not contain the whole teaching of the second verse which says that one should live a hundred years in the world and do works without bondage i.e. do works "in the spirit of the first verse" which tells us that all are God's possessions (including all that one has and does). In this form the premise is very clear and allows no room for any kind of misunderstanding, much less any wrong conclusion. Therefore there is no point in the assertion of Sharma and Young that the aim of the third verse is to prevent us from drawing a "mistaken conclusion" from the second verse.

Sharma and Young, like Thieme, fail to demonstrate the relevance of the third verse to the preceding verses of the Īśa Upaniṣad. By failing to do so, they have not exegetically justified the literal sense of the phrase *ātmahano janāḥ*, a sense considered to be most appropriate and most natural by them.

SRI AUROBINDO'S INTERPRETATION: THE FINAL VERSION

Sri Aurobindo's is the best among the extant commentaries on the Īśa Upaniṣad. It is a complete work which appeared in the Ārya series in 1914-15. In it is found the substance of the whole Vedānta. It is worth recalling what Sri Aurobindo has to say about the phrases of the inspired writings such as the Īśa: "each phrase in Veda, as in the motion of the universe itself, lives not to itself but goes back to all that has gone before and reaches out to all that is coming; all moreover obey an unexpressed central unity which once grasped, illumines the whole text, but without which these writings break up into a mass of disconnected thoughts."[20] His commentary on the Īśa is an admirable substantiation of this pronouncement made by him.

The Lord, *Īśa*, who is one and free, "does not desire, but inalienably contains, possesses and enjoys." So too our soul, who is one with Him, must give up desire, possess and enjoy all (*tena tyaktena bhuñjīthāḥ*).[21] This is the teaching of the first verse. The next verse expands the ideas of the first. As the freedom from desire is not due to inaction or its possession is "limited to the enjoyment of the inactive Soul that only witnesses without taking part in the movement," its completeness includes "the doing of works in this material world and a full acceptance of the term of physical life." The Lord fulfils himself in the world by works and "man also is in the body for self-fulfilment by action." The human soul by becoming one with the Lord is not "bound by the result of its works"[22] (*na karma lipyate nare*). Now comes the third verse and speaks about *ātmahano janāḥ*. After death, it says, they enter into other worlds, sunless and dark (*asūryā nāma te lokāḥ*).

Before we know who the *ātmahanaḥ* are and why they go to the gloomy worlds after death, let us take the word *ātmahan* and analyse it. When we add the suffix *han* (to obstruct, to kill) to *ātman*, we get *ātmahan*. Ātman is used in three distinct senses:[23] (i) physical body (*śarīra*); (ii) the individual self or soul living in the body (*śārīrātmā*); and (iii) the eternal Self beyond the body (*aśarīrasyātmā*). As the second verse of the Upaniṣad is concerned with the individual soul who dwells in the body and uses the body as its instrument, it is but appropriate to take the *ātman* in *ātmahan*, which occurs in the very next verse, in the second sense mentioned above i.e. in the sense of the soul living in the body. In this sense *ātman* can be more justifiably combined with the suffix *han* than when it is taken to mean the eternal Self. For just as an individual soul is nourished and protected by right living and right works, so also it may be made to wither away and die without nourishment and protection by wrong living and wrong works not conducive to its natural development or brought to a sudden end by wrongly removing it from the body which is its field of life and works and throwing it irretrievably into violent states of fear, grief and horror. In so far as wrong living and wrong works submerge a person in desires and attachments and wrong or self-willed dissolution of the body sinks him inescapably into violent passions, they represent themselves as two forms of obstruction to his self-fulfilment, more appropriately, as two forms of killing the soul in him (*ātmahananam*). This is the significance of Sri Aurobindo's rendering of *ātmahano janāḥ* as those "who are slayers of their souls".[24]

Though Sri Aurobindo has not dealt with the process by which he has arrived at his interpretation of *ātmahano janāḥ*, it can be surmised if we take a look at the passage where he has given his comments on the third verse of the Īśa:

> By persisting in gross forms of ignorance, by coercing perversely the soul in its self-fulfilment or by a wrong dissolution of its becoming in the Movement, one enters into states of blind darkness, not into the worlds of light and of liberated and blissful being.[25]

Here he mentions two things about the soul: (i) to coerce it perversely by persisting in the gross forms of ignorance; (ii) to wrongly dissolve its becoming in the Movement. They refer to the two forms of killing the soul mentioned above. Further, he has excluded the two interpretations of *ātmahano janāḥ* with which we are already familiar — (i) "those who kill the eternal Self"; and (ii) "those who commit suicide". He does not favour the first, because killing of the eternal Self, as was mentioned before, is inconceivable. The Kaṭha Upaniṣad clearly affirms that the Self neither kills nor is killed. Nor does he accept the second, because its emphasis is on the body rather than on the soul whose prospects of self-fulfilment have become utterly gloomy.

Before we proceed further we shall refer to an adverse comment made by a scholar on Sri Aurobindo's rendering of *ātmahano janāḥ*. He first says that Sri Aurobindo has not accepted Śaṅkara's interpretation of the above phrase as slayers of the Self. Then he points out that "through oversight, Sri Aurobindo himself has adopted the translation of *ātmahano janāḥ* as slayers of their own souls".[26] There is no oversight at all in respect of Sri Aurobindo's translation, for he has translated the phrase with an eye on the distinctive significance of the word "soul". As one well-versed in the writings of the Vedānta, he uses the words 'soul' and 'Self' not as synonyms. For they have two different senses. While the soul refers to a consciousness intimately connected with the body (*śārīrātmā*), the Self stands for a higher consciousness completely detached and without any such connection (*aśarīrasyātmā*). This explains, as we have already shown, why killing of the soul is conceivable and killing of the Self is not. The scholar's comment issues out of a mistaken view that 'soul' and 'Self' are synonymous terms.

Now we know who the *ātmahanaḥ* are — they are killers of their souls, they who obstruct the progress of their souls by plunging them in desires and attachments or in states of violent passions from which escape is hardly possible. But then why does the Upaniṣad speak of them and their entry into the worlds of blind darkness? The answer to this question is to be found in the whole sequence of verses 1, 2 and 3. The central idea of the three verses is self-fulfilment through liberation: while the first two speak of it affirmatively, the third negatively by denying self-fulfilment and liberation.

In the first two verses the Upaniṣad tells us that the way to self-fulfilment lies through renunciation and liberated works. It means, as Sri Aurobindo says, that the liberated soul, by doing works without the ego, possesses the worlds beyond "as it possesses the material birth, accepting in them a means towards the divine manifestation in which they form a condition of its fullness".[27] It is by protecting and nourishing itself that the soul conquers death and wins the worlds of Light. In the third verse the Upaniṣad says that those who destroy their souls are bound by death and after death go to dark worlds where such people live in grief and suffering. Unlike these ordinary people (*janāḥ*) who destroy their souls and go to the dark worlds, those who reach self-fulfilment and conquer the other worlds are heroes (*narāḥ*).[28] The phrase *ātmahano janāḥ* is intended to suggest by contrast that those who fulfil themselves are *ātmavanto narāḥ*. This gives a suitable answer to the question why the subject of *ātmahanaḥ* is introduced in the third verse of the Upaniṣad.[29]

The conventional sense of a word is generally desirable. However, it does not mean that it should be favoured in all circumstances. As the conventional sense of *ātmahano janāḥ* is not consistent with its context, Sri Aurobindo has ignored it and insisted on its etymological sense. He is perfectly justified in giving the sense of the slayers of their souls to the words *ātmahano janāḥ*, for it brings out very clearly its relevance to the third verse.

NOTES

1. Swāmī Satyānanda Saraswatī, *Isavasya Upanishad* (1973), Monghyr: Bihar School of Yoga, p.23.
2. The date of Bhavabhūti is the eighth century A.D.Śaṅkara is believed to have lived about a hundred years before him.
3. Sri Aurobindo, *The Upanishads* (hereafter TU) (1972), p.465.
4. Ibid., p.455.
5. Ibid., pp.455 and 458.
6. Ibid., p.466.
7. Ibid., p.468.
8. *Sri Aurobindo Archives and Research* (1977), Vol.1, No.2, p.76.
9. Ibid., p.76.
10. Bṛhadāraṇyaka Upaniṣad (hereafter Bṛ. Up.), 4-4-11.
11. TU, p.468.
12. P. Thieme, *Īśopaniṣad*, JAOS 85 (1965), p.97.
13. Ibid., p.93.
14. Ibid., p.92.
15. Ibid., p.90.
16. Ibid., p.92.
17. Arvind Sharma and Katherine K. Young, *The Meaning of Ātmahano Janāḥ in Īśa Upaniṣad* (3), JAOS 110 (1990), p.596.
18. Ibid., p.598.
19. Ibid., p.601.
20. Sri Aurobindo, *The Life Divine: A Commentary on the Isha Upanishad* (1981), p.35.
21. TU, p.75.
22. Ibid., pp.76-77.
23. (i) Chāndogya Upaniṣad (hereafter Ch. Up.), 8-8-1; (ii) Bṛ.Up.,4-3-35; (iii) Ch. Up., 8-12-1.
24. TU, p.64.
25. Ibid., p.77.
26. P.B.Gajendragadkar, Ed., *The Ten Classical Upanishads* (Bombay: Bharatiya Vidya Bhavan), 1981, Vol. I, p.97.
27. TU, p.120.
28. The word *naraḥ* is also used in the sense of a hero. See Monier Williams, *Sanskrit-English Dictionary*, Indian Edition, 1987.
29. See the passage on the inspired writings in the opening paragraph of this section.

7

The Īśa and the Kena

THE SECRET CONNECTIONS

At the head of the authoritative Upaniṣads stands the Īśa. If we leave aside questions concerning the style, language and date of the Upaniṣads and lay emphasis on their substance, we understand why the Īśa is given pride of place among them. There are many reasons for its unique position, but one appears to be very important and most relevant.

If we read the Īśa in a proper manner, get into the heart of each word and each phrase, see how the whole Upaniṣad is a progressive unfolding of a single theme and finally allow the text with its richness and harmony to sink into the deepest layer of our consciousness, then little by little it opens its secret chambers by entering which we enter all the other Upaniṣads, with an unparalleled insight and understanding. Not only do we see the secret connections by which the Upaniṣads are tied together but we realise that all their ideas and perceptions belong to the same family and possess the same significance. In other words, if we learn to see through the eye of the Īśa, we shall see all the twelve Upaniṣads to be parts of a single unified whole. This explains why the enumeration of these Upaniṣads begins with the Īśa.

THE THREE MAIN SUBJECTS

We shall take the Kena as an example. The Īśa is concerned with three main subjects: (i) Brahman, (ii) immortality and (iii) works. And in all of them the Īśa and the Kena are identical and speak with one voice though their words are different.

(i) In the Īśa Upaniṣad the supreme Lord is seen in two ways: as one who is beyond all limitations and as one who is everywhere.

The Lord is higher than all — Nature, the world and the individual. He is higher than even the Immutable that supports Nature, and the formless and nameless essence from which arise both the world and the individual. Though He is absolutely higher than all, He is extended everywhere (*saparyagāt*).[1] He is in Nature and in the Immutable beyond Nature (*tadejati tannaijati*);[2] in the world and in that which is beyond the world (*taddūre tadvantike*);[3] in the individual and in that which is beyond the individual (*tadantarasya sarvasya tadu sarvasyāsya bāhyataḥ*).[4] He is known in his completeness when we know him to be extended everywhere in these two fundamental terms, — here and beyond (*ubhayaṃ saha*).[5]

The Lord's extension in the immutable and the essential is quite conceivable, because He is by definition the all-exceeding Puruṣa. But it is unintelligible that He is extended in Nature, the world and the individual, because to be extended in them is to admit the limitations with which they are associated. He certainly exceeds all, but it does not imply that the all are other than and opposed to Him. When the Lord is defined to be all-exceeding, the purpose is to distinguish Him from the all. But if the distinction is turned into an opposition, then the Lord's extension in the all is found to be a contradiction and an impossibility. Just as it is an error to think that there is no Lord except the all, so it is an error to hold that there is nothing except the Lord. Both are there — the Lord and the all. Since He is one without a second (*ekaṃ*),[6] all are Himself, multiple results of His own becomings (*ātmaivābhūt*).[7] If the all are his own becomings (*paribhūḥ*), then the Lord's extension in them is as conceivable as the other.

(ii) Man is not merely a soul but a body as well. His divine significance is shared by both. A right use of all instruments lodged in his body enables him to live in the pure Buddhi and overcome the dualities referred to as Death by the Upaniṣads. Buddhi is an instrument of Nature (*avidyā*). Nature binds if the Buddhi is impure and dominated by the senses; the same Nature frees if the Buddhi is pure and withdrawn from the senses. If we are awakened and live in the pure Buddhi, we cross over the dualities through Nature (*avidyayā mṛtyuṃ tīrtvā*).[8] Once we are freed from *mṛtyu* we realise that our true Self is not even the pure Buddhi but Brahman which is eternal and imperishable, not touched by the action of Nature. With the knowledge of Brahman we become immortal (*vidyayā amṛtam aśnute*).[9]

To arrive at immortality through knowledge (*vidyayā*) is a great achievement. However, it is not the greatest. For we have to enjoy immortality by expressing it in the world through our instruments. We have overcome *mṛtyu* by withdrawing from the instruments, but we have not removed it from them. Hence immortality cannot be expressed through the instruments bound by Death. Freedom from Death is not the same as eradication of Death. When it is eradicated from the instruments, they begin to express immortality in the world (*sambhūtyā amṛtam aśnute*).[10] When the soul is born in Brahman, it is a new birth; when the whole being is born in Him, it is a perfect birth (*sambhūti*) which expresses immortality through all instruments and the works performed by them.

(iii) Birth and works are considered to be twin sources of bondage. Works bind, because they are always done for the satisfaction of ego; birth also binds, because the subconscient in us is made up of the impressions of past works done for the sake of ego. As a matter of fact, the ego that now expresses itself in works is lodged very securely in the subconscient part of our being. Ascetics try to get rid of the ego by renouncing works. But there is the danger of being pushed into works without their conscious consent. For the subconscious source of ego is left intact and not touched by *karmasannyāsa*. It is for this reason that the ascetic is advised to be extremely alert and avoid all chances of being overtaken by the subconscient. He is told that inadvertence is destruction (*pramādo mṛtyuḥ*).[11] He is also warned that if he falls, he can never rise again (*patitasya vinā nāśaṃ punarnāroha īkṣyate*).[12] In view of the risk involved in dealing with the subconscient the ascetic generally renounces his very birth (*dehatyāgam karoti*)[13] and attains *mokṣa*.

The ascetic solution to the problem of birth and works is alien to the original Vedānta. Hence the Īśa Upaniṣad rejects it and says that one should desire to live a hundred years doing all works here (*kurvanneveha karmāṇi jijīviṣet śataṃ samāḥ*).[14] It further says that those who renounce their birth (*ātmahanaḥ*)[15] do not go to the Sun-worlds of the Veda but to the worlds that are merely known as other than the Sun-worlds (*asūryā nāma te lokāḥ*).[16]

Though birth and works are not inherently faulty, they appear to be so owing to their association with ego. Therefore it must be possible to remove the fault without doing harm to them. If works are done not for one's own sake but for the sake of God, they do not bind (*na karma lipyate*).[17] They begin to express His will and ultimately culminate in knowledge and freedom. Birth too does not bind when the conscious being filled with God invades the subconscious being and purges it of all impressions of past works till it ceases to be a dark region of crooked-going sins (*juhurāṇam enaḥ*)[18] and becomes conscious like itself. This is referred to as the extension of consciousness to the works of the past (*kṛtaṃ smara*).[19] When the whole being becomes a conscious instrument, one attains perfect birth and becomes a faultless doer of God's work. This is the Vedāntic solution to the problem of birth and works.

THE HARMONY BETWEEN THE ĪŚA AND THE KENA

If we now turn to the Kena, all the teachings of the Īśa reappear here, making it obvious that we are not strangers to it. However, it has its own characteristic differences. While expounding the nature of Brahman (*brahmaṇo rūpam*)[20] it insists that it must be known in the way in which the ancients had known of it. The attainment of immortality by the instrumental self is described through a highly suggestive story of the gods. And finally, it makes a very brief comment about works, leaving all the ideas connected with them to be worked out from relevant passages in the text.

(i) Just as the Lord of the Īśa Upaniṣad exceeds all and is also extended in all, so the Deva of the Kena Upaniṣad is beyond all definable terms and yet pervades both the known and the unknown in the world.

There are two aspects of the world, the known (*viditāt*)[21] and the unknown (*aviditāt*),[22] the forms grasped by our faculties and the formless Self beyond their grasp. But Brahman is superior to both, for It is not definable either by the first (*anyadeva tadviditāt*)[23] or by the second (*aviditādadhi*).[24] Though It surpasses both, It is not external to them. It appears here as that which is not expressed by the word and also as that by which the word is expressed, as that which thinks not with mind and also that by which the mind is thought, as that which sees not with the eye and also as that by which one sees the eye's seeings, as that which hears not with the ear and also as that by which the ear's hearing is heard, as that which breathes not with the breath and also as that by which the life-breath is led forward in its path. Brahman must be known as the highest which manifests itself simultaneously in these two aspects of the world (*tadeva brahma tvaṃ viddhi*)[25], the known and the unknown.

(ii) Just as immortality in the Īśa is to be attained by the Vidyā and enjoyed by the Sambhūti, so in the Kena it must be possessed by both the Vidyā and the Pratibodha.

There are two selves, the eternal Self (*ātmā*) and the instrumental self consisting of Mind, Life and Senses (*adhyātmā*). The eternal Self is usually confused with and obscured by the instrumental self. Therefore we are not conscious of the eternal Self. Since the instrumental self is bound by Death, we think we are mortals subject to pain and grief. When this self is purified and the light of sattva sufficiently increases in it, the eternal Self is seen as a distinct entity. With the knowledge of the Self one enters into the supreme Self and Lord, the highest form of Brahman (*brahmaṇo rūpam*)[26] , and becomes immortal (*vidyayā vindate 'mṛtam*).[27]

Like the eternal Self, the instruments of Mind, Life and Senses can attain immortality. If they cease to express Death and begin to reflect the Lord, they shape themselves into His image and express immortality in the world. This is possible only when immortality was already possessed through the eternal Self. Knowledge by oneness (*vidyā*)[28] is the first and primary means; knowledge by reflection (*pratibodha viditaṃ*) is the next and resultant means. By the first immortality is attained in the eternal Self; by the second the instruments get their share of immortality and discover their divine significance — Mind becoming the Mind of the Lord, Life becoming the Life of the Lord and Senses becoming the Senses of the Lord. This is fulfilment of the instrumental self in the Lord (*amṛtatvam hi vindate ātmanā*).[29] With the fulfilment it attains a glory and strength never to be tainted by Death (*ātmanā vindate vīryaṃ*).[30]

Immortality is to be gained not only by the Self, eternal and imperishable, but also by the whole being, *ātmā* as well as *adhyātmā*. To be one with the supreme Self through the Self is the basic attainment (*amṛtam*)[31] but to be a true image of the supreme Lord through the instrumental self is the ultimate and highest attainment (*amṛtatvam*).[32] With the ultimate attainment alone one truly exists (*satyamasti*).[33]

(iii) Just as the Īśa speaks of works not generating bondage, so the Kena says that knowledge of Brahman has works as its foundation.

Mind, Life and Senses are the three instruments, the whole significance of which lies in the works they do. The character of their works is determined by the condition under which they operate. If the instruments work for the ego, works are a source of bondage and death; if they work for God, works are a source of freedom and immortality. Therefore, to found Brahman in works is to do works for God and eliminate the ego originally founded in them.

If works are the foundation of Brahman, such works eventually culminate in converting this birth itself into a perfect birth with Brahman as its sole possessor and enjoyer. For birth and works are interdependent, one influencing and modifying the other.

Given the instruments and their divine significance, works cannot be renounced. They are always necessary. It is through works that the instruments fulfil themselves in God. Again, it is through works that the instruments express God in the world. In both cases God's foundation in works is an absolute necessity.

A study of the two texts clearly vindicates the traditional view that the Upaniṣads are one and homogeneous in substance irrespective of the different names they have and the different branches of Veda to which they belong. The modern pronouncement that they are heterogeneous and contradictory is ill-founded and contrary to facts.

NOTES

1. Īśa Upaniṣad (hereafter Īś. Up.), Mantra 8.
2. Ibid., Mantra 4.
3. Ibid.
4. Ibid.
5. Ibid., Mantra 11.
6. Ibid., Mantra 7.
7. Ibid., Mantra 8.
8. Ibid., Mantra 11.
9. Ibid.
10. Ibid., Mantra 14.
11. Vivekacūḍāmaṇi, Verse 321.
12. Ibid., Verse 328.
13. Jābāla Upaniṣad, Mantra 6.
14. Īś. Up., Mantra 2.
15. Ibid., Mantra 3.

16. Ibid.
17. Ibid., Mantra 2.
18. Ibid., Mantra 18.
19. Ibid., Mantra 17.
20. Kena Upaniṣad, 2-2.
21. Ibid., 1-4.
22. Ibid.
23. Ibid.
24. Ibid.
25. Ibid., 1-5.
26. Ibid., 2-2.
27. Ibid., 2-4.
28. Ibid.
29. Ibid.
30. Ibid.
31. Ibid.
32. Ibid.
33. Ibid., 2-5.

8

The Kena and the Vedic Ideal of Fulfilment

BRAHMAN AND LIFE

Life is a principle by which man is in contact with outside world and enters into various relations with it. He establishes right contacts and maintains right relations with the world in proportion to the right contact and relation he has with that which exceeds Life and of which Life is an instrument of manifestation and enjoyment, — the all-constituting and all-exceeding Brahman.

Life manifests itself in three successive forms — physical, vital and mental. Through the first it acts upon the objects of sense; through the second it seeks to possess and enjoy them; through the third it cognises them and gives appropriate directions to the physical and vital faculties to fulfil the will arising out of its cognition. Of the three the mental is most important, for the physical and the vital exist for it and accomplish what it knows and wills to be.

Life, as it exists now, is subject to the action of the lower Nature and its three *guṇas*. Therefore it does not express Brahman; nor does it exist as the instrument of Brahman. It looks as if Life exists for the lower Nature and can express only the God who represents this Nature — the god of Death. Bound inextricably with Death, Life is a source of delusions and miseries, wrong relations and wrong results. Hence it is viewed as the opposite of Brahman, as the dark veil that conceals the Immortal and deludes the soul into a mortal being subject to pain and grief.

If the soul is to realise Brahman, it is possible only by rejecting the lower Nature. In this process Life itself may be rejected, as is done by many who consider it to be inherently evil (*sadoṣa*) and incapable of existing apart from the lower Nature. In that case the realisation of Brahman becomes exclusive, for they ignore the important fact that Life is originally a manifestation of Brahman, a means used by Brahman for the enjoyment of world-existence. This paves the way for the advent of asceticism which regards the indeterminate and unmanifest Brahman as the supreme goal to be realised through renunciation of works and world-existence (*sannyāsena*).

But the Kena's aim is to precisely reject this asceticism with its twin aspects – (i) the indeterminate Brahman which denies the world; (ii) renunciation of works which is the means of attaining the Brahman. For asceticism is un-Vedic and opposed to the knowledge of which the Vedas are all limbs (*vedāḥ sarvāṅgāni*).[1] In this respect the Kena and the Īśa are identical. The opening verses of the Īśa strike at the very root of asceticism. The disciple in the Upaniṣad has rejected the world to be a place of bondage and misery and has known the Lord to be beyond Time, Space and Causality. At this point he approaches his master and the master asks him to reject his exclusive ascetic attitude and embrace and enjoy the world like the Lord: "By seeing the Law according to which the Lord dwells in all forms (*tena*)[2] you should accept and enjoy the world you have now abandoned (*tyaktena bhuñjīthā*),[3] and be free from the desires of the heart (*māgṛdhaḥ*).[4] You should live a hundred years here doing all works (*kurvanneveha karmāṇi*).[5] For the Law is thus ordained in you (*evamtvayi*) and not otherwise (*nānyatheto'sti*).[6] You will not be bound by works if you perform them not for your sake but for the sake of God (*na karma lipyate nare*)."[7] In fact, in its opposition to asceticism the Īśa is more outspoken than the Kena Upaniṣad.

Though both the Kena and the Īśa aim at showing the harmonious relation that exists between the Lord and the world, the former restricts the scope to one but a most important aspect, namely, the relation of Life in the world to the Lord of the world.

THE SUPREME DEVA

There is a God (*devaḥ*) by whom mind missioned and shot to its mark falls; by whom the first life-breath is yoked and moves forward on its path; by whom this word that men speak is impelled; and by whom eye and ear are set to their workings. Who is that God? Who is the Master of all these – Mind, Life and Senses? The Upaniṣad answers that that God is "hearing of our hearing, mind of our mind, speech of our speech, life of our life-breath and sight of our sight." In other words, that is the Absolute exceeding all and at the same time supporting all workings we find in our instrumental being.

The instrumental being is our outer self; behind it is our inner Self, our eternal and true Self which cannot be known in terms of the functions of sight or speech or mind. For "there sight travels not, nor speech nor mind." As it cannot be grasped by these faculties, there is no way to know or teach of it (*na vidmo na vijānīmo yathaitadanuśiṣyāt*).[8] All that can be said of it is that it is unknown (*aviditāt*).[9] If the Deva exceeding the instrumental self is other than the known (*anyadeva tadviditāt*),[10] the same in relation to the eternal Self is above the unknown (*aviditādadhi*).[11] In other words, the Deva is at once the supreme Self and Master. In the expression *anyadeva tadviditād atho aviditādadhi*[12] the word *atho* (again) clearly indicates that He is both, not merely the supreme Self or the Master. In the same manner the Gītā speaks of Him as *paramātmā avyayaīśvaraḥ*.[13] That He must be understood in this comprehensive sense is the teaching of the Vedic sages; it is so we have heard from them (*itiśuśruma pūrveṣām*).[14] So He must be worshipped in this form and not otherwise. The wise (*dhīrāḥ*)[15] who worship Him in this form (*brahmaṇo rūpam*)[16] — as the Lord of our active self and also as the higher Self beyond our eternal Self, — attain double freedom, freedom in the eternal Self that is no longer obscured by the active self (*amṛtam*)[17] and freedom in the active self which is no longer bound by death (*amṛtatvam*).[18] To free the eternal Self from its subjection to the active self is *atimucya*;[19] to free mind, life and senses from their bondage to the law of death is *pretya asmāllokāt*,[20] departure from the domain of death usually referred to as our domain. This corresponds to the two forms of immortality mentioned in the Īśa Upaniṣad — *vidyayā* (by the knowledge of the Self) *amṛtam aśnute*[21] and *sambhūtyā* (by birth or physical self) *amṛtam aśnute*.[22] This is the ancient doctrine of immortality.

As Life is bound by Death, i.e., by the action of the lower Nature, it may be considered as inherently evil. Then liberation of the eternal Self is possible only by renouncing Life, otherwise Death cannot be crossed over. The seeker of the Self naturally becomes a seeker of the indeterminate Brahman who excludes the world and Life as the two forms of Death. This is the view of the ascetics (*sannyāsins*). But the Kena does not subscribe to this view, because it is contrary to the teachings of the ancient sages. Therefore it is determined to reject the exclusive view of Brahman favoured by the ascetics.

In the human being Brahman manifests itself in two forms — (i) as the eternal Self beyond the grasp of our faculties; (ii) as the self active in mind, life and senses. That alone, that having the two forms, one should know to be Brahman (*tadeva brahma tvaṃ viddhi*)[23] and not this eternal Self which is exclusive of the active self and which is worshipped by the ascetics as Brahman (*nedaṃ yadidam upāsate*).[24] The Upaniṣad devotes five verses 1-5 to 1-9 to drive home this point.

In each of the five verses the first line mentions the two forms to be taken into account in order to know Brahman as the ancient sages knew of It; in the second line is used a refrain to put the seal of approval on the knowledge received from the ancients and reject the one offered by the ascetics. For example, let us take verse 5. The first line mentions the two forms thus: that which is unexpressed by the word and that by which the word is expressed. The second line says, "That alone (That having the two forms) one should know to be Brahman, not this currently worshipped as Brahman by the ascetics (not the unknown, not the Self outside the grasp of our faculties). The rest of the verses repeat the same idea with the same intention to preserve the original view of the ancients.

THE TWO GATEWAYS TO IMMORTALITY

The first two mantras of the second chapter of the Upaniṣad deal with a discussion between the disciple and others who are his co-disciples. The rest of the mantras are the words of the master.

As in the Īśa, the disciple is sufficiently advanced in his spiritual practice, for he is acknowledged to have known the two manifestations of Brahman — the Self (*tvaṃ*) and the gods (*deveṣu*), the eternal Self untouched by activity and the instrumental self in which the gods have become active and established their rule. A co-disciple tells him: "You have known a little of the form of Brahman, the little in you and the little in the gods (*brahmaṇo rūpam yadasya tvaṃ yadasya deveṣu*).[25] I think that It is known well when the clues provided by the two manifestations are carefully followed up by you (*mīmāmsyaṃeva*)."[26] This implies that as long as the clues are not rightly used and rightly developed, the form of Brahman cannot be known well. Disagreeing with this view the disciple says: "I do think I do not know Brahman well provided I see merely the two manifestations. But I do not so see them. For their clues have been taken and rightly used. So Brahman is not unknown to me. Any of us who knows It like me knows that, i.e., he knows that It is not unknown to him".[27] From this reply it is evident that the disciple knows Brahman very well (*suveda*).[28] The whole discussion will be absolutely clear only if we know what it is to know Brahman well by following up the clues.

Now the teacher intervenes and supplies the needed light. First of all, he speaks of a form of knowledge referred to as knowledge by reflection (*pratibodham*).[29] "He by whom It is not thought out with mental ideas, has the thought of It; he by whom It is thought out with these ideas, knows It not."[30] Our mind is accustomed to the process of analysis and synthesis. It knows by analysing the data provided by the senses and synthesising the results of analysis. In other words, mind knows through artificial construction. As the real Existence is the origin of all forms and as all images created by the senses are obscure, no construction, however carefully developed, can give us a faultless insight into It. As long as we rely on mental constructions we can never know the Truth. But when we dispense with them and try to be in direct contact with It, true knowledge arises. So there are two kinds of thought — (i) a thought arising out of construction; (ii) a thought arising out of reflection. We have already found that a thought resulting from mental construction cannot reveal That. When the mind ceases to analyse and construct upon obscure images, it becomes a passive instrument that can faithfully reflect and be in direct contact with That. A thought born of such reflection gives a true knowledge of That. It is called *pratibodhaviditaṃ*.[31] In this process the mind gradually gives up its old habit and becomes a more and more perfect instrument of reflection. When it is absolutely free of its old habit and faultlessly reflects That, it arrives at its divine fulfilment, its divine nature and its divine utility as the instrument of the Lord (*amṛtatvaṃ hi vindate*).[32]

For mind to arrive at its divine fulfilment in the Lord of mind is indeed a unique glory and power. The other instruments, life and senses, cannot get it except through mind. Mind is the chief instrument of our active self and so no part of the self can change or rise to a new level independent of it. Once it gets the power of being a divine instrument (*vīryaṃ*) [33] it leads the other instruments also to the same goal. When the whole active self finds its fulfilment in the Lord, the mind knows and thinks of nothing except the Lord; the life seeks and enjoys nothing except the Lord; the senses grasp nothing except the Lord. This is one gateway to immortality, a gateway originally found out by the Vedic Ṛṣis and subsequently rediscovered and reaffirmed by the sages of the Upaniṣads. With the rise of asceticism which denies life and birth it became a forgotten way and remained so for a long stretch of time till Sri Aurobindo retrieved it from obscurity in his monumental commentaries on the Veda and the Vedānta.

There is another gateway of immortality too, more important and more fundamental than the other. As long as the eternal Self is confused with the active self, one is in bondage to the lower Nature. One lives in the ego and is subjected to the dualities of good and bad, pleasure and pain, ignorance and knowledge. In reality we are not the active self controlled by the ego nor the ego which imposes the dualities on the soul. If we learn to separate the soul from the active self, it is freed from the ego and the dualities, stands aloof and becomes one with the real Self, eternal and inactive, without form and without name, birthless and deathless. Unattached and unbound, the Self supports and remains a witness of the active self. It is absolutely free but not at all the master of that from which it is freed. Freedom is complete only when the Self is free to possess and enjoy the other self. As long as the Self is aloof and divided from the active self, it can neither possess nor enjoy mind, life and senses. It cannot be otherwise, because it is but a representation (*dabhram*)[34] and not yet that which it represents, the supreme Self, the imperishable Brahman. The right way for the Self to be the master is to ascend into the supreme Self which is eternally and inalienably the Master of the world of forms, the Lord of mind, life and senses. It is by the knowledge of the supreme Self that ascension into It becomes possible (*vidyayā vindate'mṛtam*).[35] If the Self enters into the supreme Self and Master through *vidyā*, the active self is freed from the ego and finds its true relation to the Lord of mind, life and senses through *pratibodha*. Just as mastery is a result of freedom, so too is knowledge by reflection a result of knowledge by oneness. To know Brahman as the supreme Self as well as the Lord of all creatures is to know the form of Brahman in its completeness (*suveda*).[36] This is the light the teacher sheds upon the discussion concerning the complete knowledge of Brahman to be possessed by the disciples.

Having stated the nature of complete knowledge the teacher proceeds to bring out its practical significance. He says that if one knows Brahman here in this body, one exists as the true image of Brahman (*satyamasti*).[37] If one has not known Brahman in this body i.e. in the becomings of mind, life and senses, then there is great loss. One may have attained Brahman through the eternal Self, but if one fails to shape the active self into a divine image through forging a right relation to the Lord of mind, life and senses, the loss is indeed immense. For a great opportunity is lost.

The expression *pretya asmāllokāt amṛtā bhavanti*[38] is significant. It occurs twice in the Upaniṣad. Literally, it means "having gone forward from this world they become immortal." The word *pretya* generally gives the sense of departure after death. But we cannot put this sense into the word, because the Upaniṣad speaks of knowing Brahman here and now. From *pret* to go forward, the word means a forward movement without implying physical death. Hence the above expression means "having gone forward from this world, i.e. from a life organised around ego, they become immortal, i.e. they enter into another form of life organised around the Lord." In other words, though one goes forward, one does not leave the order of becomings (*bhūteṣu bhūteṣu*), becomings with reference to the individual (*adhyātmam*)[39] and becomings with reference to the gods (*adhidaivatam*).[40] Wise men go forward from the world of ego and by doing so they discover the divine significance of the world of names and forms.

FREEDOM FROM DEATH

The central theme of the Upaniṣad is to determine the right relation between the Lord and the instruments of our active self – mind, life and senses. It has four aspects: (i) the form of Brahman (*brahmaṇo rūpam*); (ii) the Self (*tvaṃ*); (iii) the subjective (*adhyātmam* mentioned as *ātmanā*) and (iv) the objective (*adhidaivatam* mentioned as *deveṣu*) sides of the active self. While (i) is elaborated in the first, and (ii) and (iii) in the second, (iv) is dealt with partly in the third and partly in the fourth chapter. All other things not included in these four appear in the last six verses of the fourth chapter.

In 15 mantras (twelve in chapter 3 and three in chapter 4) a highly suggestive story of the gods is told with a view to unfold the *adhidaivata* aspect of the active self. According to the story, Brahman, the supreme Deva, won a victory for the gods who represent Him in the world and do His work here. Though they represent Brahman, they know not Him. Owing to this ignorance the victory won for them by Brahman is wrongly considered by them to be their personal victory and a cause of their personal greatness. Therefore Brahman desires to remove this false notion of the gods. He appears before them in the form of a Yakṣa. But they cannot identify him. So three of them — Agni, Vāyu and Indra — approach him in order to find out who he is. Not only do they fail to know him but the power each one has fails to work in his presence — Agni's power to burn, Vāyu's power to move and Indra's power to grasp. When Indra's turn comes, he cannot exercise his power, for the Yakṣa disappears from his view. Not being able to succeed in his attempt, Indra approaches Umā Haimavati who is in the same space where the Yakṣa was, and learns from Her that it was Brahman who appeared as a Yakṣa. Though he fails in one sense, he succeeds in another sense by knowing the fact from the Woman who "shines out in many forms" (*striyam bahuśobhamānām*).[41] Hence he is greater than all the gods, even Agni and Vāyu.

Before we proceed further, it will be helpful to analyse the story and note the points that emerge from it. For this will help us to understand the relevance of the story to the central theme of the Upaniṣad.

The gods have a work. In that they are victorious and by that victory they have grown great. Among the gods involved in the work three are important: Agni, Vāyu and Indra. Of the three Indra is preeminent. In real fact the work they do is not their work. Hence victory and greatness are results that belong to the real doer of the work, namely, Brahman. The gods know one another and beyond this they know not who they really are or what they are really doing. Nor do they know who the real doer is. From ignorance arises egoism, from egoism false notions. They think they are independent. So they take the work to be theirs, the results to be theirs, the doer to be themselves and the enjoyer to be themselves. When the work is done out of ignorance and egoism it is not rightly done. Owing to the fault introduced by the gods the work does not reach its original goal. It not only misses its true goal but moves towards a wrong goal. A direct intervention by the real doer becomes necessary to put the work on the right track. The intervention takes place first as a challenge through a Yakṣa and then as a help and advice through Umā Haimavati. As a result, the gods come out of their ignorance and egoism and become fit for doing the work rightly. When the work is done rightly, it progresses towards its original goal.

As these points are closely knit together, we shall try to bring them under three major heads and see how they are related to the main teaching of the Upaniṣad: (i) the work of the gods; (ii) the work of Brahman; (iii) the right way of doing the work.

(i) The gods Indra, Vāyu and Agni and the instruments mind, life and senses correspond to each other, for they are the two sides of the same active self. While the gods (*adhidaivatam*) are the objective expressions of mind, life and senses, the instruments (*adhyātmam*) are the subjective expressions of Indra, Vāyu and Agni. The condition of one determines the condition of another. If the instruments operate in a condition of obscurity, the gods are dormant and do not affirm themselves; likewise, if the gods are active and uphold their rule in the active self, the instruments become pure and operate in a condition of light. On both the sides the same order of eminence prevails: if Indra leads Vāyu and Agni on the objective side, mind gives the lead to life and senses on the subjective side. Thus there is an intimate connection between the gods and the instruments, a kind of causal connection by which one influences and modifies the other.

As they are now, mind, life and senses are subject to the action of the lower Nature and her three *guṇas*. The *guṇas* are involved in an endless conflict and confusion. When the Sattva predominates, there is elimination of darkness and growth of light; when the Tamas gains supremacy, there is elimination of light and growth of darkness. On the objective side, this ceaseless conflict is represented as a battle between Devas and Asuras, the gods and the demons. When the gods are victorious, they grow great, help man's advancement and manifest godly qualities in him such as good, right, joy, freedom, knowledge, etc. When the rule of the demons prevails, they protect themselves with all that destroy light. They hinder man's progress and promote ungodly qualities in him, qualities that deny godly ones. To vanquish the demons, assist man in his progress and establish godly qualities in him are the threefold work of the gods. This is how the gods understand their work.

(ii) Brahman is the supreme Ātman and Deva in the world of whom the gods are "positive self-representations." Brahman's will in the world is to fulfil itself through the liberated Self and the instruments freed from the action of the lower Nature. Accordingly, there are two steps in the process of self-fulfilment.

(a) To raise the instruments of mind, life and senses by the purity and light of Sattva and liberate the Self, eternal and inactive, from bondage to the active self is the first step.

Liberation of the Self through the purified instruments is an indispensable condition without which self-fulfilment is not possible. If Brahman were to stop here and pursue the line of exclusive identification with the supreme Self without taking cognisance of its other and inseparable aspect, namely, the Lord, then the liberated Self would arrive at extinction and not fulfilment. But this cannot be Brahman's will in the world. For, as the Lord of the world, Brahman's will must be for fulfilment and not extinction.

Though extinction in the supreme Self is a possibility for an ascending soul in the world, the Upaniṣads throw their emphasis on the ideal of fulfilment which is referred to as attainment of *sāṃrājya.*[42] The Īśa Upaniṣad is opposed to the ideal of extinction. It says that to enter into Brahman by taking it to be exclusively the supreme Self is to enter as if into a supreme darkness (*bhūya iva tamaḥ*).[43] In like manner the Kena asks us not to take Brahman to be exclusively the Self which is unexpressed by the word and worshipped by the ascetics as the supreme object of attainment (*nedam yadidam upāsate*).[44] Therefore liberation of the Self must be a condition for fulfilment, not a final goal to be pursued for its own sake.

(b) If the supreme Self which is indivisible from the supreme Lord is reached through the Self, it makes fulfilment possible (*vidyayā vindate'mṛtam*). As a result, the purified instruments are liberated from the action of lower Nature and turned into divine instruments — mind into the divine Mind of the Lord, life into the divine Life of the Lord and senses into the divine Senses of the Lord. With this fulfilment in the Lord the instrumental self possesses a divine power and glory not subject to the corrupting influence of the lower Nature (*ātmanā vindate vīryaṃ*). This is the twofold work of Brahman in the world, the work which the gods have not properly understood.

(iii) Ignorance and egoism are the two major faults of the lower Nature. No principle operating within the domain of this Nature can be free from these faults, whether they are human instruments or the gods. The gods do not know that they represent Brahman; nor do they know that they are doing Brahman's work. According to their understanding, their work is to battle against the demons, vanquish them and bring about the rule of light and the birth of godly qualities in man. With this they become active and increase themselves in him. They take this work and its result to belong to themselves (*vijaye devā amahīyanta*).[45] They think they are responsible for the two.

When the gods increase themselves, light and purity increase abundantly in mind, life and senses. As a result, man's true Self emerges as a distinct entity and is no longer confused with the instruments of the active self. But at the same time his instruments, though pure and bright, are conditioned by Death, the god of the lower Nature. The gods have conquered the demons that represent *tāmasic* and *rājasic* egoism, but they have not conquered themselves. For they have not outgrown the fault of *sāttvic* egoism on account of which they do Brahman's work without knowing that it is Brahman's. They delight in their victory thinking that they have saved man from Death and helped him eliminate Death from his active self, though in fact his active self is still bound by it. It is too subtle for them to realise that they too, like demons, serve the god of Death, for the latter cannot be banished as long as ego survives in them in the form of *sāttvic* attachment to work and its results. The gods have done the work to the point of purifying the instruments and freeing the true Self. Beyond this the work has not progressed and reached the goal of self-fulfilment in Brahman. The progress is obstructed by the *sāttvic* attachment.

Not only have the gods failed to carry the work of perfecting the instruments to its natural end but they allow the work to take a wrong turn and reach a wrong end. Man develops an ascetic attitude towards life and views life to be inextricably bound up with Death. His goal, therefore, becomes self-extinction in the supreme Self. If the work is to be carried forward to its natural goal, the gods must be awakened to their faults and made to see that the final freedom from Death comes only when the *sāttvic* egoism is removed and that their work is not merely to liberate man but also to lead him towards fulfilment by a total eradication of Death from his instrumental self. It is to awaken them to these faults and teach them of these right perceptions that Brahman appeared as a Yakṣa.

The right way of doing the work is therefore to lead man to self-fulfilment in Brahman.

THE GODS AND THE INSTRUMENTS

Sāttvic egoism comes in the way and obstructs the work of the gods; hence Brahman intervenes to remove the obstruction and carry forward the work through the awakened gods. The Upaniṣad gives us a few illuminating hints and with these we have to work out the process of removing the obstruction and awakening the gods.

The fault of the gods is twofold, ignorance and egoism. This is removed in two stages. First, in the form of a Yakṣa who challenges the gods and proves that by themselves they are nonentities. They are made to understand that the powers they have are not their possessions but belong to someone else over whom they have absolutely no control. Second, in the form of Umā Haimavati who teaches that not only the works they do but the victory they have gained in the works do not belong to them. To this effect she speaks: "In the victory of Brahman you shall grow to greatness."[46] While the first removes their ignorance, the second dissolves their egoism. But then who is this woman? Why does the Upaniṣad suddenly bring her in?

There are three clues from which it is easy to understand who the woman is. First, she is said to be found in the same space where the Yakṣa stood and challenged the gods (*tasminnev ākāse striyam*).[47] This indicates that the Yakṣa and Umā are one, though they have two different forms and functions. The word *eva* is intended to affirm their identity. Second, the Upaniṣad further says that the Yakṣa is Brahman (*sā brahma*).[48] Now we clearly understand the true form of Umā. If Umā is the Yakṣa and if the Yakṣa is Brahman, then Umā is none other than Brahman. It is Brahman who first appeared as a Yakṣa and then as Umā. We now know that Umā is Brahman, but do not know why Brahman should appear as Umā in order to help Indra. Third, the Upaniṣad uses two significant epithets — *striyam* (woman) and *bahuśobhamānām* (who shines out in many forms)[49] — to refer to Umā Haimavati. Superficially speaking, Umā's role in the story is to simply tell Indra who the Yakṣa was. Considering the insignificant role given to Umā, the Upaniṣad does not seem to gain anything in substance by adding the two epithets to her. In actual fact, the aim of the Upaniṣad is to precisely tell us that the role she plays is very significant. Umā is Brahman in its feminine aspect, the aspect of Śakti or Nature (*striyam*). She is the supreme Nature (*parā prakṛti*) of Brahman, the ultimate source of all forms we find in the world (*bahuśobhamānām*). Sri Aurobindo, whose commentaries on the Upaniṣads disclose to us the original Vedānta as it flourished in the prehistoric ages, has taken Umā to be the divine Nature of Brahman. "Uma," says he, "is the supreme Nature from whom the whole cosmic action takes its birth; she is the pure summit and highest power of the One who here shines out in many forms."[50] In other words, Umā represents the original divine Nature in which all conditioned and deformed here by the lower Nature including the gods, are released from their limitations and arrive at their divine form and fulfilment. This is the significance of Umā Haimavati.

The way for the gods to get rid of their ignorance and egoism is to rise into the divine Nature from the lower Nature of the three *guṇas* and become conscious and perfect instruments by which Brahman's work is truly and completely accomplished — this is the message the Upaniṣad seeks to deliver through the help given by Umā Haimavati to god Indra.

When the gods become perfect and conscious, having freed themselves from the action of the lower Nature, they help man to raise his instrumental self beyond the whole system of the dualities and conquer Death. The Upaniṣad tries to describe the process by which the passage from the lower to the higher Nature is effected. It takes for granted that the condition necessary for this transition has already been fulfilled — the liberation of the Self and the subsequent ascent by the liberated Self into the supreme Self and Lord (*vidyayā vindate'mṛtam*).[51]

The passage from the lower to the higher Nature is initially a slow and gradual process. Accustomed as they are to the light of *sattva* and the joy and satisfaction that come from the *sāttvic* freedom, the gods cannot easily open themselves to the immortal light of Brahman except on occasions when they are able to suspend in them the action of the lower Nature. Till the gods are completely free of the influence of the lower Nature the higher Nature uses these occasions and acts on them through momentary reflections. The phenomenon of short-lived reflections of the divine Nature is like the flash of lightning (*vidyuto vyadyutat*).[52] Since the gods cannot maintain their receptivity beyond a few moments, they frequently go back to their original condition and close themselves to the higher influence. This is like the falling of the eyelid (*nyamīmiṣat*).[53] It is by these momentary openings and reflections that the substance of the gods is gradually liberated and perfected (*iti adhidaivatam*).[54]

The transfiguration of the gods is a prelude to that of man's instrumental self. Purification of his instruments brings freedom from *tāmasic* and *rājasic* egoism, but not from the egoism of *sāttvic* nature. With this freedom he lives in the true Self and realises that his ultimate goal is not complete aloofness from the instrumental self or the world on which this self acts, but self-fulfilment in Brahman as a perfect Self and a perfect image of the Lord. For this the true Self must become one with the supreme Self and Lord and the divine Nature must extricate the instruments from the lower Nature which now binds by its *sāttvic* light and freedom. After entering the supreme Self and Lord, the process of extrication begins. In this process mind comes first, for any change in the instrumental self can come only through mind which is the leader of both life and senses. Hence the Upaniṣad confines itself to mind and its extrication. It is by ceasing to think with its ideas and becoming passive that mind frees itself from the lower Nature. And in proportion as it becomes passive it begins to reflect the divine Mind of the Lord and arrive at its divine fulfilment. The Upaniṣad says that mind seems to move towards the supreme Lord (*gacchatīva ca mano'nena*).[55] As it is passive, mind cannot really move towards the Lord. But yet it seems to move by its very passivity, for the more passive it becomes the more faithful is the image of divine Mind reflected in it. But then how is it possible for mind to arrive at this passivity? By will (*saṇkalpaḥ*)[56] and constant remembrance of that which the will has accepted (*upasmarati abhīkṣnaṃ*),[57] namely, the ideal of becoming an image of the divine Mind through absolute passivity and surrender (*iti adhyātmam*).[58]

Just as man attains Brahman through the knowledge of the Self (*vidyayā vindate'mṛtam*)[59], so through the surrender of the instrumental self he attains the very image of Brahman (*amṛtatvam hi vindate ātmanā*).[60] This is the teaching the ancients have declared to us (*nastadvyācacakṣire*).

THE SECRET TEACHING OF BRAHMAN

The teacher recalls now the disciple's request to tell him the secret teaching of Brahman, though such a request is not found in any of the foregoing chapters or in any of the foregoing mantras of the last chapter. But we have to suppose from the words of the teacher that the teaching is given at the request of the disciple. Having said in great detail all that need be said about Brahman, he now proceeds to put his teaching in the form of a practically useful formula.

Before we deal with this formula we have to briefly state the substance of his teaching. (i) Brahman is the supreme Self and Lord. It is above the unknown and other than the known. It must be understood as such. For it is so that the wise have attained That. They have attained Brahman through the knowledge of the eternal Self (*vidyayā*) as well as the image of Brahman through the instrumental self (*ātmanā*) that passively reflects. By this double attainment they have known Brahman in its completeness (*suveda*). (ii) Unlike the ancient sages, the ascetics here seek Brahman differently. To them Brahman is the unknown (*aviditād*) for It cannot be grasped by the eye or the speech or the mind. It is this Brahman that they worship. But the Kena does not favour the worship of this Brahman (*nedaṃ yadidam upāsate*). For what they know to be Brahman is merely one aspect of the Brahman about which we have heard from the ancients (*dabhramevāpi ... brahmaṇo rūpam*).[61] In a word, his teaching is that we must give credit only to the ideal of the ancients (*pūrveṣām*)[62] and not the one which is currently pursued by the ascetics.

Now we shall try to understand the significance of the teacher's formula. He says that the name of That is Tadvanam and must be worshipped as possessing this name. Śaṅkara and many others take *tadvanaṃ* to mean "that which is adorable."[63] In the context of the Upaniṣad the word *tadvanaṃ* may be taken to mean "that abode." As a matter of fact, there are two abodes, one aimed at and attained by the ancients and another regarded as the object of attainment by the ascetics of the current age. The Upaniṣad says that the Brahman you choose for your goal and realisation should be That which the ancients chose as their abode (*taddha tadvanaṃ nāma*),[64] not This which the ascetics of the current age have chosen (*nedam*).[65] That alone must be your choice. This is brought out forcefully by the imperative *upāsitavyaṃ*.[66] It is clearly an echo of *tadeva brahma tvaṃ viddhi*[67] which occurs in the beginning of the Upaniṣad.

There are two possibilities in life — extinction and fulfilment. But the natural impulse of all creatures is fulfilment, fulfilment by mastery. Therefore, he who fulfils himself in Brahman, following in the footsteps of the sages of the Veda, is sought by all as the standing example of their true aspiration.

THE VEDIC FOUNDATION OF BRAHMAN-KNOWLEDGE

The knowledge of Brahman as expounded here has three parts — practical, scriptural and essential. On the practical side, its foundations are *tapas*, self-control and works.[68] By *tapas*, self-control and works one reaches the supreme Self and Lord; by self-control and works one removes Death and attains the image of the Lord in the instrumental self. As long as the instruments of mind, life and senses have divine significance and divine utility works performed by them have the same significance and utility. Works are necessary to purify and perfect them; having raised them to their divine forms, works are again necessary to express immortality in the world through the operation of the perfected instruments. On the scriptural side, it is founded upon the words of the Vedas, the highest authority of the ancient Ṛṣis. Finally, on the essential side, its abode is in the highest truth, whether it concerns life or scripture. The highest truth consists in the destruction of the evil arising out of the lower Nature and the attainment of the vaster world and infinite heaven (*anante svarge loke jyeye*)[69] where all forms of this world arrive at their divine fulfilment.

The scriptural aspect must be given prominence in view of the fact that the Upaniṣad proclaims the ancients to be the original exponents of Brahman-knowledge (*iti śuśruma pūrveṣāṃ ye nastad vyācacakṣire*).[70] Evidently the reference is to the ancient sages of the Veda, the sages mentioned by the Ṛks.

There are three main parts in the system of knowledge as taught by the Upaniṣad — (i) the Self, (ii) the gods and (iii) Brahman. As they are, neither the Self nor the gods supported by the Self can give us a complete knowledge of the form of Brahman (*brahmaṇo rūpam*).[71] For they are but a representation and a representation can only reveal a little of Brahman (*dabhrameva*).[72] In order to know Brahman in its completeness we have to carefully follow the little light they have in them and discover the right relations by which they emerge into the full light of that which they represent. Though by themselves the representations do not reveal Brahman fully, they are surely the indispensable means of ascending into It and knowing It in its completeness. All of them — the Self, the gods, Brahman and the connections of the first two to the third — are, according to the Upaniṣad, rooted firmly in the sacred words of the Vedas (*vedāḥ sarvāṅgāni*).[73] It is not the case where one part is supported by the Vedic utterances and the rest are not, as in that of the ascetics who deny the representations of Brahman in the world and enter Brahman by dissolving them. He who knows Brahman in its completeness and without excluding its representations in the world knows in accordance with the Vedas (*suvediḥ*).[74] To know Brahman is indeed a great achievement, but to know Brahman completely in accordance with the Vedas is still greater. Hence the Muṇḍaka refers to the Brahman-knower through a significant expression *śrotriyaṃ brahmaniṣṭham*.[75]

NOTES

1. Kena Upaniṣad (hereafter Ke. Up.), 4-8.
2. Īśa Upaniṣad (hereafter Īś. Up.), Mantra 1.
3. Ibid.
4. Ibid., Mantra 2.
5. Ibid.
6. Ibid.
7. Ibid.
8. Ke. Up., 1-3.
9. Ibid., 1-4.
10. Ibid.
11. Ibid.
12. Ibid.
13. Gītā, 15-17.
14. Ke. Up., 1-4.
15. Ibid., 1-2.
16. Ibid., 2-1.
17. Ibid., 2-4.

18. Ibid.
19. Ibid., 1-2.
20. Ibid.
21. Īś. Up., Mantra 11.
22. Ibid., Mantra 14.
23. Ke. Up., 1-5.
24. Ibid.
25. Ibid., 2-1.
26. Ibid.
27. Ibid., 2-2.
28. Ibid.
29. Ibid., 2-4.
30. Ibid., 2-3.
31. Ibid., 2-4.
32. Ibid.
33. Ibid.
34. Ibid., 2-1.
35. Ibid., 2-4.
36. Ibid., 2-2.
37. Ibid., 2-5.
38. Ibid., 1-2.
39. Ibid., 2-5.
40. Ibid., 4-4,5.
41. Ibid., 3-12.
42. Chāndogya Upaniṣad, 2-24-13.
43. Īś. Up., Mantra 9.
44. Ke. Up., 1-5.
45. Ibid., 3-1.
46. Ibid., 4-1.
47. Ibid., 3-12.
48. Ibid., 4-1.
49. Ibid., 3-12.
50. Sri Aurobindo, *The Upanishads* (1972), p. 219.
51. Ke. Up., 2-4.
52. Ibid., 4-4.
53. Ibid.
54. Ibid.
55. Ibid., 4-5.
56. Ibid.
57. Ibid.
58. Ibid.
59. Ibid., 2-4.
60. Ibid., 1-4.
61. Ibid., 2-1.

62. Ibid., 1-4.
63. Śaṅkara , *Kena Upaniṣad Bhāṣya,* 4-6.
64. Ke. Up., 4-6.
65. Ibid., 1-5.
66. Ibid., 4-6.
67. Ibid., 1-5.
68. Ibid., 4-8.
69. Ibid., 4-9.
70. Ibid., 1-4.
71. Ibid., 2-1.
72. Ibid.
73. Ibid., 4-8.
74. Ibid., 2-2.
75. Muṇḍaka Upaniṣad, 1-2-12.

9

The Yoga of Birth and Dissolution

THE MEANS AND END

The word *yoga* means both effort and union. When there is an effort to reach Ātman, it is yoga; when there is union with Ātman, that too is yoga. Thus yoga is both a means and an end. Though we generally think that the means is the sole determinant of the end, the Kaṭha Upaniṣad does not think so. Let us note what it says about the relation between the two.

Ātman is attained through knowledge (*prajñānena enam āpnuyāt*).[1] What are the conditions under which this knowledge arises? According to the Kaṭha, there are four conditions: (i) cessation from bad conduct; (ii) control of the senses; (iii) concentration and (iv) tranquillity of the mind.[2] If the four are not fulfilled, then the knowledge does not arise. But in the previous verse the Upaniṣad says that only he whom Ātman chooses can attain Him (*yam eva eṣa vṛṇute tena labyaḥ*).[3] Now the important question is this: Which is the real determinant of the knowledge of Ātman, individual effort as outlined in 1-2-24 or Ātman's choice as mentioned in 1-2-23?

A careful study of the above two verses shows very clearly that both are necessary in the matter of attaining Ātman — individual effort and Ātman's choice. Through individual effort one becomes fit for the knowledge of Ātman. Without this fitness Ātman cannot be attained. But with this fitness alone one cannot attain Ātman, for He can be attained only when He reveals himself (*ātmā vivṛṇute tanūṃ svām*).[4] Yoga as an effort of reaching Ātman is within the power of man, but yoga as union with Ātman is beyond his power (*apauruṣeya*). Therefore, in yoga the end is not an inevitable outcome of the means, although the means is as important as the end.

THE GREAT ONES

As the law of Ātman is very subtle and, therefore, not easy of knowledge (*na hi suvijñeyamaṇureṣa dharmaḥ*),[5] we begin to know Him when we find out the great ones (*varān*) and learn of them (*nibodhata*).[6] The great ones are those who have attained union with Ātman. By observing their life and conduct we understand, however vaguely, the nature of Ātman that dwells in them.

But this is possible only when we know where Ātman stands self-revealed to individuals. For He is not revealed to all. In this connection a verse in the Kaṭha Upaniṣad is noteworthy. It is one of the well known verses. It runs thus:

> He is Ātman — Ātman for whom both the Brāhmaṇa and Kṣatriya are food (*odanaḥ*) and for whom Death, which is the source of all delusion, attachment and grief, is supplementary food (*upasecanam*). Who in this way knows where He exists (*ka itthā veda yatra saḥ*)?[7]

The question is very significant. It implies that nobody knows where Ātman is revealed to individuals in this manner — as the eater of food — except among the Brāhmaṇas and Kṣatriyas. In other words, wise men who have attained Ātman can be easily found among them rather than among others. For, by temperament and training, they are generally known to be the ardent seekers of Ātman. There are two distinguishing marks by means of which wise men among them are recognised — they who are food for Ātman, they in whom Death has become supplementary food for the same Eater-Ātman.

A distinction is made between food and supplementary food. The aim is to tell us that the latter is taken along with the former. Beyond this point, it is unnecessary to dwell upon it. But an important point to be noted about food is this: when food is eaten, it changes into a refined substance and, eventually, gets the very nature of the eater.

When someone is said to be food for Ātman, it means that all his thoughts, words, feelings, and deeds are given up to Him. When they are thus given up, all mortal features associated with them are also given up. Hence Ātman's food refers to not only the individual with his thoughts etc. (*odanam*) but also all that make him a mortal being (*upasecanam*). We may say that when Ātman eats, two things happen: (i) man's mortality is destroyed; (ii) he becomes pure and attains the very nature of Ātman who is immortal and blissful.

We shall now return to the original question of finding out the great men. How do we recognise them? First, they would be found among the Brāhmaṇas and Kṣatriyas. Second, they would be possessing the two marks mentioned above — absence of mortal features and possession of immortal bliss. This seems to be the method suggested in the verse 1-2-25.

THE TWO WONDERFUL PERSONS

Ordinary men are food for Death. So they suffer the evils of Death. When they meet great men who have conquered Death and attained immortality, they take them to be their examples. They try to overcome Death and become immortal like them. For this purpose they seek the help of the great men themselves.

When the great agree to teach them the secret of immortality, they do so out of compassion and love for the world. As the Upaniṣad[8] says, both of them — the giver and the receiver of the teaching — are wonderful. The former is wonderful, for he brings good to the world. The latter is wonderful, for he attains immortality not for his sake but for the sake of the world.

THE DISSOLUTION OF DELUSIONS

The sense-objects are objects of enjoyment for the senses. Behind the senses are the mind, the intellect, and Ātman. When the mind is not a means of control, when the intellect is not a means of discrimination, and when Ātman remains hidden in the heart (*guhāhitaṃ*),[9] the senses operate for their own separate existence (*pṛthagbhāvam*).[10] This is a delusion. Apart from this, the sense-objects are their separate source of enjoyment (*pṛthagutpatya-mānānāṃ*).[11] This too is a delusion. He in whom the senses operate in this manner and by whom the sense-objects are thus used, is deluded and overcome by the evil of transmigration (*saṃsāraṃ*)[12] which makes repeated births and deaths inevitable.

When the mind and intellect come to the front and impose themselves on the senses, the senses change their mode of operation. From the mind they learn that their separateness is an illusion. From the discriminating power of the intellect they understand that as they are not separate organs, they do not enjoy the sense-objects for their own separate satisfaction. In other words, they understand that they exist for Ātman and enjoy the sense-objects for the sake of Ātman. For He is the real enjoyer (*bhoktetyāhur manīṣinaḥ*).[13] He in whom the senses are liberated from their delusions, he through whose liberated senses Ātman is the enjoyer of objects, is wise and not born again (*na jāyate*).[14] He attains the highest place of Viṣnu (*apnoti tadviṣnoḥ paramaṃ padam*)[15], a notion which is as old as the Vedas.

As the union with Ātman is attained through the dissolution of the delusions caused by the senses, Yoga is defined as the Dissolution (*yogo hi apyayaḥ*).[16]

THE BIRTH OF WISDOM

Ātman is hidden in the hearts of men (*guhāhitaṃ*).[17] But He can be known through the method of successive dissolution — through the dissolution of speech (which represents all organs) into mind, mind into intellect, intellect into the great Ātman (the manifest Ātman), and the great Ātman into the peaceful Ātman (the unmanifest Ātman).[18] But this method stops short of the Puruṣa who is higher than the peaceful or unmanifest Ātman (*avyaktāt tu paraḥ puruṣaḥ*).[19] For this Puruṣa reveals himself by himself.

When Ātman is known, the knower is struck by two things. (i) Ātman is unlike anything that exists in the world (*anirdeśyaṃ*);[20] (ii) Ātman's nature is the nature of supreme bliss which cannot be equated with any in the world (*paramaṃ sukham*).[21] This Ātman is described thus: He is soundless (*aśabdam*), touchless (*asparśam*), formless (*arūpam*), undecaying (*avyayaṃ*), tasteless (*arasaṃ*), eternal (*nityam*), odourless (*agandavat*), without beginning (*anādi*), and without end (*anantam*).[22] The descriptions tell us that He transcends all (*atyeti*) and is not related to the world. One who knows thus hastily concludes that the world is devoid of Ātman. Having concluded thus, he shrinks from all connections with the world (*vijugupsate*).

A knower of Ātman may shrink from the world. But what about Ātman? Does He also shrink from the world? Before we answer this question, we shall note how Ātman's connection with the world is described by the Upaniṣad.[23]

There are two examples — fire[24] and air.[25] Through them three points are made about Ātman. (i) By himself he is without any form (*arūpam*); (ii) he enters the world as its inner Ātman (*sarvabhūtāntarātmā*), assumes all its forms (*rūpam rūpam pratirūpaḥ*) and gets outside (*bahiḥ*), outside his original position; (iii) he is one (*ekaḥ*) and not divided by his self-externalisation. From this it is clear that Ātman is both formless and formed. He is both beyond and within the world. Here two important points are made about the inner Ātman. (a) Though he has modified himself into the world, he is not affected by its misery (*lokaduḥkhena*).[26] How is this possible for him? Though he is united with the world and its misery, he is not affected by the misery because he is essentially beyond the world (*bāhyaḥ*).[27] This becomes clear from the example given by the Upaniṣad. It says that Ātman is not affected in the same way as the sun is not affected by the defects of the world (*na lipyate bāhyadoṣaiḥ*).[28] The sun is not affected by the defects, because its rays alone come into contact with them and not the sun which is beyond the world. (b) He is not only the indweller (*antarātmā*) but also the enjoyer (*bhoktā*)[29] of the world. From this we know that he has entered the world not because he is capable of doing so but because he wants to enjoy living in such a circumstance.

We shall now come to the question whether Ātman shrinks from the world. It is true that he transcends the world, but it is not true that he shrinks from the world. We have found that Ātman beyond the world enters the world, modifies himself as the world and, above all, becomes the enjoyer of the world. If this is the nature of Ātman, how can the knower of Ātman come to shrink from all things in the world and finally abandon them? This is because he has known Ātman in the aspect of transcendence alone and also because he imagines from this aspect that the world is devoid of Ātman. It is now clear why he is compelled to shrink from the world. This is certainly a result of the error of the mind. As soon as the error is eliminated, he does not shrink (*na vijugupsate*).[30] How is the error eliminated? It is eliminated when he knows his living self (*imaṃ jīvam*) to be Ātman himself who has become the lord and enjoyer of the world (*madhvadaṃ īśānaṃ bhūtabhavyasya*).[31] He who knows both the aspects of transcendence and immanence of Ātman has no reason at all to shrink from the world. This world is to be enjoyed by him for the sake of Ātman in him.

This marks the birth of wisdom in him. Hence Yoga is defined as the Birth (*yogo hi prabhavaḥ*).[32]

A UNIQUE TEXT

The Kaṭha is unique among the authoritative Upaniṣads. For it contains many important teachings about Yoga. One of them relates to the definition of Yoga as the Birth and Dissolution — the birth of wisdom, the wisdom of seeing Ātman everywhere; the dissolution of delusions, the delusions created by the senses.

NOTES

1. Kaṭha Upaniṣad, 1-2-24.
2. Ibid.
3. Ibid., 1-2-23.
4. Ibid.
5. Ibid., 1-1-21.
6. Ibid., 1-3-14.
7. Ibid., 1-2-25.
8. Ibid., 1-2-7.
9. Ibid., 1-2-12.
10. Ibid., 2-3-6.
11. Ibid.
12. Ibid., 1-3-7.
13. Ibid., 1-3-4.
14. Ibid., 1-3-8.
15. Ibid., 1-3-9.
16. Ibid., 2-3-11.
17. Ibid., 1-2-12.
18. Ibid., 1-3-13.
19. Ibid., 2-3-8.
20. Ibid., 2-2-14.
21. Ibid.
22. Ibid., 1-3-15.

23. Ibid., 2-2-9, 10.
24. Ibid., 2-2-9.
25. Ibid., 2-2-10.
26. Ibid., 2-2-11.
27. Ibid.
28. Ibid.
29. Ibid., 1-3-4.
30. Ibid., 2-1-5.
31. Ibid.
32. Ibid., 2-3-11.

10

The Īśa and the Muṇḍaka

TWO MOST IMPORTANT UPANIṢADS

Among the twelve authoritative Upaniṣads two are considered to be most important. One gets this importance by position and the other by title. While the Īśa is made to stand at the head of the Upaniṣads, the Muṇḍaka is given the title of the Head Upaniṣad. No one can doubt that the Īśa stands first in the order of enumeration of the Upaniṣads. But it is open to doubt whether the Muṇḍaka is known anywhere by the above title. If it is known by such a title, then it is necessary to clear the doubt by pointing to its exact source.

It will be fruitful to go into the titles of some of the Upaniṣads. For example, Īśa and Kena come from words used by the concerned Upaniṣads themselves. Like these two, Praśna also is traced to a word uttered by a sage in the Upaniṣad. Unlike the three, Śvetāśvatara is based on the name of the teacher of the Upaniṣad. As Muṇḍaka cannot be explained through such methods, Swāmi Nikhilānanda tries to explain it by a different method — by analysing the sense of the word *muṇḍaka* itself in the light of the text.

THE MEANING OF THE TITLE

In a note on the title of the Muṇḍaka Upaniṣad Swāmī Nikhilānanda observes in the following manner :

> The word mundaka means, literally, one with a shaven-head, that is to say, a sannyasin or monk. In obedience to Vedic injunctions, a sannyasin is required to shave his head in order to denote his complete renunciation of the ritualistic activities obligatory for a householder. The tuft of hair which householders belonging to the three higher castes wear is required in the Vedic rites. The Mundaka Upanishad exhorts

> the practice of complete renunciation and is therefore particularly suited to a sannyasin.[1]

If we carefully read this note, we find that the author reaches his point through two steps. First, he connects the shaven-headed with "a sannyasin" who "is required to shave his head in order to denote his complete renunciation of the ritualistic activities obligatory for a householder". Second, he connects the sannyasin with the subject of the Upaniṣad which "exhorts the practice of complete renunciation", renunciation of all types of Vedic works. Given these two premises, his conclusion — the Upaniṣad is "particularly suited to a sannyasin" — is inevitable.

The Upaniṣad's case for renunciation is developed in four important steps. (i) Works are inferior (*avaraṃ karma*)[2] because they are frail rafts and incapable of getting us the highest good (*śreyaḥ*).[3] In other words, they cannot get us the uncreated Brahman (*nāsty akṛtaḥ kṛtena*).[4] (ii) Those who do works go to the worlds of Brahman where resides the lord of the gods and from where, when the fruits of their works are exhausted, they fall again into this world and, in some cases, into a lower world even (*hīnataraṃ vā*).[5] (iii) Those who perform works dwell in the depth of ignorance and are trapped in delusion, because their works proceed out of attachment (*rāgāt*).[6] (iv) The right way to reach the highest good, the uncreated Brahman (*akṛtaḥ*),[7] is to renounce all works (*nirvedamāyāt*),[8] come out of ignorance and delusion, and approach a teacher who has mastered the Vedas and established himself in the Brahman (*śrotriyaṃ brahmaniṣṭham*).[9] And the case thus developed by the Upaniṣad makes Swāmī Nikhilānanda's conclusion about its title really unassailable.

AṄGIRAS AND ŚAUNAKA

In the Upaniṣad Aṅgiras teaches Śaunaka who approaches him with a question — What is that by knowing which the whole world becomes known? The latter's aim is to possess two forms of knowledge — (i) a knowledge which is possessed not for its own sake but for the sake of another knowledge (*kasminnu vijñāte*);[10] (ii) a knowledge without exclusion, that is, a knowledge of both the essence and the form of things (*sarvam idaṃ vijñātaṃ*).[11]

From this it is clear that for Śaunaka the utility of ultimate knowledge consists in getting perfect mastery over the world, the immutable essence expressing itself in names, forms and works (*trayaṃ vā idam*).[12] Therefore his aim is mastery and not renunciation of the world. There are two more internal evidences to show that he is not a renouncer of works and possessions. First of all, he is a householder setting an example to others in the matter of realising the best (*śreyas*) through family institution. Hence he is called the *great* householder (*mahāsālaḥ*).[13] Secondly, he is a doer of works not opposed to knowledge and at the same time a seeker of Brahman. His works are faultless and devoid of ego by which he can fulfil himself in the imperishable Brahman. If he is not thus qualified, Aṅgiras would not have received him and consented to instruct him in Brahmavidyā. We are forced to read *aṅgirasaṃ vidhivad upasannaḥ*[14] in this manner, because the Upaniṣad has clearly laid down that the qualification for those who want to receive instruction in Brahmavidyā is that they should be doers of works, well-versed in the Vedas, and seekers of Brahman (*kriyāvantaḥ śrotriyā brahmaniṣṭhāḥ*)[15]. Since Śaunaka is depicted as a householder approaching the master according to rule, we must decide against Swāmī Nikhilānanda's conclusion that the Upaniṣad is "particularly suited to a sannyasin." For the same reason we cannot take the title Muṇḍaka to mean the shaven-headed sannyasin.

HEAD UPANIṢAD

The word Muṇḍakam means head, the head of a person. Hence the title Muṇḍaka Upaniṣad may be construed as "Head Upaniṣad". In other words, the title suggests that this Upaniṣad must be regarded as the first among the authoritative Upaniṣads. Already the Īśa is considered to be the first and given the first place in the order of enumeration of the Upaniṣads. If the Muṇḍaka also is considered to be the first Upaniṣad, then we have to demonstrate how this is possible, without prejudice to the premier position accorded to the Īśa.

If we carefully read the Īśa and the Muṇḍaka, we may recognise that in certain respects they are unique and easily excel other Upaniṣads. We must remember that the sages of the

Upaniṣads were preoccupied with one work and that was to found Vedānta, the true nature of the Vedic ideal. In the work of founding Vedānta both the Īśa and the Muṇḍaka are the foremost among the authoritative Upaniṣads. A scholar well-versed in these ancient texts may not fail to see that in the above work the two Upaniṣads are identical in spirit but markedly different in detail.

THE BRĀHMAṆAS AND THE ASCETICS

In the prehistoric times the Vedic culture came into existence and flourished for several centuries without interruption. Afterwards it began to decline and finally disappeared. The Mantras of the Ṛg Veda are the only records we now have of this great culture. Though the culture became extinct, the Mantras were carefully preserved and handed down from generation to generation.

During the age of Brāhmaṇas sustained attempts were made to revive the original Vedic culture out of the Mantras. A highly complicated system of *yajñas* and worship of the gods like Agni and Indra was born and the whole nation moulded its life in terms of this new system. The Brāhmaṇas were considered to be the authentic expositions of the original ideal of the Veda.

At some stage, probably when the age of the Brāhmaṇas reached the peak of its growth, doubts about their authenticity began to assail the minds of those who saw that the original ideal embodied in the Mantras differed widely from the one currently upheld by all. To them the new system had failed to reach the Greatest among the gods (*devānāṃ śreṣṭhaṃ*),[16] spoken of as That One by a Mantra (*tadekaṃ*),[17] by not going beyond the duality of good and bad in works. For the system was founded upon the duality of *vidhi* and *niṣedha,* prescribed works and prohibited works. And the attainment of the immortal form of That One is not possible through this oppressive means (*maryati dvena*).[18] So another attempt was made to recover the original ideal of the Mantras by abandoning all action, prohibited as well as prescribed. As the new school stood for a total renunciation of works, the advocates of this school were known as renouncers or ascetics (*parivrājakas*) about whom there is a reference in Yāska's Nirukta.[19]

The ascetics too have their own disadvantage. They are right in holding that the supreme Deva cannot be attained by works conditioned by the duality of good and bad. But they have erred by concluding that the Deva must be reached through abandonment of all works. For the Mantras do not support such a view. According to them, there is another category of works which is not conditioned by the duality and is therefore capable of leading directly to the supreme Deva. These works are perfect and divine (*sukṛta*) not only because they are free from the fault of duality but because they bring about filfilment in the great God. The doers of such works are called *sukarmāṇaḥ*.[20] In other words, the Mantras favour fulfilment through perfect works rather than self-extinction through renunciation of works. Hence the ascetics, like the Brāhmaṇas, have not succeeded in discovering the original ideal of the Mantras.

This paved the way for the appearance of the seers of the Upaniṣads whose one work was to found Vedānta, the true nature of the Veda. Their work was twofold: (i) to expound the original teaching of the Vedic Mantras; (ii) to reject the teachings of the Brāhmaṇas and the ascetics as unauthentic or un-Vedic. In this work, as was already pointed out, two Upaniṣads are prominent. They are the Īśa and the Muṇḍaka.

THE ĪŚA UPANIṢAD

In the Īśa there are two prayers addressed to two of the gods of the Veda, Sūrya and Agni. The first prayer is an expanded version of a Mantra of Ṛṣi Śrutavit Ātreya.[21] Here the Mantra has been modified into two verses, verses 15 and 16. In his introduction to *Hymns to the Mystic Fire* (1972) Sri Aurobindo works out the parallels between the words of the Mantra and those of the Upaniṣad and establishes the close connection between the two. Likewise, in the prayer to Agni verse 18 contains a Mantra bodily taken from a hymn attributed to Ṛṣi Agastya Maitrāvaruṇi[22] and verse 17 is added as a link between verse 16 and verse 18. Thus the two prayers in the Upaniṣad are intended to set forth the original teaching of the Veda as embodied in the Mantras of the two Vedic poets.

As they are, the four verses are difficult to understand. The difficulty is partly due to the Vedic symbols of Sun and Fire and partly due to omissions in the sequence of ideas. If we learn to think in the same manner as the seer of the Upaniṣad thought, then we overcome the difficulty and understand the verses.

(i) There is a veil between us and the true Lord of our being (*satyasyāpihitaṃ mukham*), a veil which is bright like gold (*hiraṇmayena pātreṇa*). It is the ego that acts as a veil between man and the Lord. When the veil is removed, we not only perceive the Lord to be our true self but are in possession of the true Law of action founded upon Him (*satyadharmāya dṛṣṭaye*). Knowledge and the true Law of action are the two things needed for man to become free and perfect.

(ii) Ego is indeed a light but a broken light. Its perceptions are divided, disorderly and conflicting. But when they are rightly ordered into a unified light, we enter into the true light of the Lord (*vyūha raśmīn smūha tejaḥ*) which is harmonious and one. His most blessed form (*rūpaṃ kalyāṇatamaṃ*) unfolds itself. He is found everywhere (*asau asau puruṣaḥ*) and known to be our true self (*so'hamasmi*).

(iii) Having obtained knowledge through the help of god Sūrya who is the Lord himself in his aspect of Knowledge, it must be transformed into a fact of life, a power of active existence in the world. The original life-force in the Lord (*anilam*) and the life-force in us (*vāyu*) are essentially one and the same (*vāyuranilam*). Vāyu appears to be different from Anilam, because it possesses the mortal characteristics of the ego. When it dispossesses them, it becomes one with the immortal Life (*amṛtam athedaṃ*). For this transformation to be fully effected the body must be retained and used for a hundred years (*śataṃ samāḥ*). Ashes signify destruction after a full utilisation, as in the case of a piece of wood completely consumed by fire (*bhasmāntaṃ*). That exactly must be the end of the body (*śarīram*) which Vāyu uses as its abode. To state the process of transformation in practical terms, Vāyu becomes Anilam when the human will remembers all deeds of the past done in obedience to the ego, succeeds in wiping out their crippling effects and becomes one with the divine Will through the grace of god Agni who represents the Lord in his aspect of Will (*krato smara kṛtaṃ smara*).

(iv) Agni, knower of all deeds (*viśvāni deva vayunāni vidvān*), removes the impressions of sinful deeds (*juhurāṇam enaḥ*), perfects the human will and leads it to fulfilment in the divine Will (*naya supathā rāye*).

In short, according to the Īśa, the original Vedic ideal consists in arriving at the knowledge of oneness with the Lord who is everywhere and in possessing, as a result, the true Law of action by which His Will in the world is fulfilled.

As for the second part in founding Vedānta, the Īśa denounces the ascetics. They teach that the Vedic ideal is to be realised through complete renunciation, renunciation of both birth and works. In the Īśa they are known as body-renouncers (*ātmahanaḥ*).[23] It condemns them as men enveloped in blinding darkness (*andhenatamasāvṛtāḥ*).[24] The Sun-Worlds are worlds of fulfilment and perfection in the imperishable Deva through perfect works. As the ascetics insist on realising the Deva through renunciation, the worlds they go to are denounced as other than the Sun-Worlds (*asūryā nāma te lokāḥ*).[25] In other words, the Īśa's aim is to say that renunciation does not bring about self-fulfilment but something quite contrary to that, namely, self-extinction. With a view to reject renunciation as a whole it categorically affirms that one should live a hundred years and perform works in the world (*kurvanneveha karmāṇi jijīviṣet śataṃ samāḥ*),[26] works that do not create bondage (*na karma lipyate*)[27] but culminate in freedom and fulfilment (*naya supathā rāye*).[28]

The Īśa opposes the ascetics for the same reason for which the Brāhmaṇas are opposed by the Muṇḍaka. In the current age the ascetics are considered to be the best authorities on the original teaching of the Veda. So the work of founding Vedānta is not complete unless the ascetics' account of the Veda is completely rejected. The ascetics' view of renunciation is un-Vedic not because they insist on giving up the fault of ego and duality but because their insistence is on giving up birth and works, the two factors necessary for life in the world.

THE MUṆḌAKA UPANIṢAD

There are four verses in chapter 3 of this Upaniṣad — verses 1-1 to 1-4 where the original ideal of the Ṛg Veda as found in Mantra 1-164-20 is developed. This Mantra is from a hymn sung by Ṛṣi Dīrghatamas.

There are two difficulties in comprehending the four verses. First, the sage speaks in images; second, he omits connecting steps in the sequence of his thoughts. If we know how to deal with them, then it is easy to comprehend the verses.

There are two images: bird and tree. A passive being is imaged as a bird that merely watches, while an active being is depicted as a bird that eats. The world where beings live and lead an active life is portrayed as a tree where birds dwell and eat fruits.

(i) There are two beings in the world (*vṛkṣaṃ*), finite and infinite. They are intimately united together (*sayujā sakhāyā*). While the finite being is engaged in works (*pippalaṃ svādvatti*), the infinite Being is not so engaged (*anaśnan*) but silently watches (*abhicākaśīti*) the works done everywhere by Nature.

(ii) As non-lord (*anīśa*), the finite being, even though it exists in the same world where the infinite Being exists (*samāne vṛkṣe*), is lost in works (*nimagnaḥ*). Deluded by works (*muhyamānaḥ*), it grieves (*śocati*). When it sees the other Being (*anyam*), the Lord (*īśam*) who is worshipped (*juṣṭam*) by the wise and whose greatness (*asya mahimānam*) is in not being bound by the works of Nature, it becomes free from grief (*vītaśokaḥ*).

(iii) When the finite being thus sees the golden-coloured infinite Being (*puruṣam*), the Lord (*īśam*) who does works (*kartāram*) through Nature and whose seat is the immutable Brahman beyond Nature (*brahmayoniṃ*), it becomes taintless (*nirañjanaḥ*). Having given up the duality of sin and virtue in works (*puṇyapāpe vidhūya*), it attains absolute likeness to the Lord (*paramaṃ sāmyam upaiti*) in whom the immutable Brahman and the mutable Nature are one and harmonious.

(iv) The life-force in Nature is this Lord himself (*prāṇo hyeṣa yaḥ*). Through this He pervades all beings (*sarvabhūtair vibhāti*). He who knows this (*vidvān*) does not talk of anything else (*bhavate nātivādī*), that is, he does not give credence to the other view that since Nature in the beings is opposed to the Lord and works through confusion and strife, He is to be attained by renouncing all works, the view generally shared by the knowers of Brahman belonging to the ascetic school. He is indeed the greatest knower of Brahman, unlike the ascetics, for he sees no opposition between the Lord and Nature and performs works with his true being firmly seated in Him (*ātmaratiḥ kriyāvān*).

In brief, this is the teaching of the Vedic poet Dīrghatamas. Man has forgotten his oneness with the Lord of the world and regards himself as a non-lord bound by works. As a result, he is in delusion and grief. He overcomes the two when he grows in likeness to the Lord and like Him acts in perfect mastery and freedom.

As regards the second part in the work of founding Vedānta, the Muṇḍaka brings out the un-Vedic character of the Brāhmaṇas. First of all, their works are performed out of attachment for good as embodied in their prescriptions (*vidhi*). Hence they are inferior works (*avaraṃ karma*).[29] Second, those who acclaim these works as the best are deluded men (*pramūḍhāḥ*)[30] and do not know the other type of works which is superior in nature (*nānyat śreyo vedayante*).[31] Third, the worlds of Brahman to which good works take us are not abodes of eternal freedom and joy, for, as soon as the fruits of our works are exhausted, we fall into our old human life or into a life lower than that (*hīnataraṃ*).[32] Fourth, with inferior works no one can reach the Vedic world of the imperishable Person (*nāsty akṛtaḥ kṛtena*),[33] for it can be reached only by the Sun-path (*sūryadvāreṇa*).[34] In the Veda the world of the imperishable Person is imaged as the world of the Sun and the path leading to that world is a path of superior works, works done without desire and attachment or without the fault of duality or of any form of mortality.[35]

According to the Muṇḍaka, the original teaching of the Veda is known not only by going back to the Vedic source but also by seeing very clearly that in the Brāhmaṇas the Veda is not rightly expounded. As long as one believes in the authority of the Brāhmaṇas one can never know the true teaching of the Veda. The works of the Brāhmaṇas are un-Vedic not because they insist on a highly complex system of works but because the works they prescribe are faulty in nature.

THE SPECIAL MERITS OF THE TWO UPANIṢADS

If we place the Īśa and Muṇḍaka by the side of the other Upaniṣads and take a look at the work the two have done in founding Vedānta, we may recognise the special merits they possess.

First, they directly go to the original source and mention the Mantras from which the teaching of the Veda is developed. Second, they not only state the Mantras in their original or modified form but elaborate them in terms of their own insights and observations. Third, they insistently bring out that knowledge and works are not really opposed, for perfect works lead to fulfilment in knowledge and, likewise, knowledge founds the true law of action. Fourth, in the denunciation of the teachings which are opposed to those of the Vedic poets they are complementary to each other. If the Īśa condemns the ascetics, the Muṇḍaka directs its attack at the Brāhmaṇas.

If we take these merits into consideration, we may understand why the Īśa and the Muṇḍaka stand out as the two most prominent and important Upaniṣads.

A NOTE ON THE ŚVETĀŚVATARA UPANIṢAD

A question arises as to why the Śvetāśvatara is not included in the category of the Īśa and Muṇḍaka Upaniṣads. For more Vedic Mantras appear in it than in other Upaniṣads. For instance, in its second chapter alone there are six Mantras taken from the Vājasaneyi Saṃhitā (11-1 to 5, 32-4). Moreover, the question assumes greater importance in view of the fact that both the Muṇḍaka and the Śvetāśvatara have chosen the same Mantra from poet Dīrghatamas (1-164-20) for elucidating the original teaching of the Veda (*vedaguhyam*).[36]

(i) With the help of verse 3-1-2 of the Muṇḍaka the Śvetāśvatara develops in its fourth chapter the teaching of the Veda from Mantra 1-164-20. In this connection it cites another Mantra to emphasise the need for knowing the true sense of the Veda. The abode of the Mantras of the Ṛg Veda and the gods is in the highest and imperishable Heaven, and the Ṛg Veda is of no avail to him who does not know its abiding place. According to the Upaniṣad, the true teaching of the Veda consists (a) in knowing not only the Lord of Māyā to be the supreme God (*māyinaṃ ca maheśvaram*),[37] but Prakṛti, which causes bondage, to be a formation of His Māyā (*māyām tu prakṛtiṃ*),[38] and (b) in attaining infinite peace (*śāntimatyantam*)[39] by this knowledge. If we compare its account of the Veda with that of the Muṇḍaka, it is certainly no less brilliant than the other. We know that the work of founding Vedānta is both an affirmation and a negation — affirmation of the original teaching of the Veda and negation of the teachings of the Brāhmaṇas and the ascetics who fail to give a proper account of the Vedic ideals. In this work the Upaniṣad is concerned with the first and neglects the second. A cursory glance at it will be sufficient to show that it makes no attempt to criticise the position of either the Brāhmaṇas or the ascetics. Here the omission in the original text is very obvious.

(ii) Apart from this, the Śvetāśvatara's main aim is to consolidate and preserve the teachings of the previous seers of the Upaniṣads. It is corroborated by the words of the other Upaniṣads that occur in it and by its own words. As for the first, there are frequent references to the Muṇḍaka and Kaṭha in the Upaniṣad. As for the second, there are two verses where its concern for the true teachings of the ancient Upaniṣads is brought out very clearly — *vedaguhyopaniṣadsu gūḍham*;[40] *vedānte paramam guhyaṃ purākalpe pracoditam.*[41] If we take these two facts (i) and (ii) into account, it is clear why the privilege of being the first Upaniṣad is confined to the Īśa and the Muṇḍaka alone and not extended to the Śvetāśvatara.

NOTES

1. Swāmī Nikhilānanda, *The Upanishads* (Vol.1) (1951), p.256.
2. Muṇḍaka Upaniṣad (hereafter M. Up.), 1-2-7.
3. Ibid.
4. Ibid., 1-2-12.
5. Ibid., 1-2-10.
6. Ibid., 1-2-9.
7. Ibid., 1-2-12.
8. Ibid.
9. Ibid.
10. Ibid., 1-1-3.
11. Ibid.
12. Bṛhadāraṇyaka Upaniṣad, 1-6-1.
13. M. Up., 1-1-3.
14. Ibid.
15. Ibid., 3-2-10.
16. Ṛg Veda (hereafter RV), 5-62-1.
17. Ibid.
18. Ibid., 5-3-7.
19. Nirukta, 2-8.

20. RV, 4-2-17.
21. Ibid., 5-62-1.
22. Ibid., 1-189-1.
23. Īśa Upaniṣad, Mantra 3.
24. Ibid.
25. Ibid.
26. Ibid., Mantra 2.
27. Ibid.
28. Ibid., Mantra 18.
29. M. Up., 1-2-7.
30. Ibid., 1-2-10.
31. Ibid.
32. Ibid.
33. Ibid., 1-2-12.
34. Ibid., 1-2-11.
35. RV, 1-70-1.
36. Śvetāśvatara Upaniṣad, 5-6.
37. Ibid., 4-10.
38. Ibid.
39. Ibid., 4-11.
40. Ibid., 5-6.
41. Ibid., 6-22.

11

The Two Vidyās*

THE TWOFOLD DISTINCTION

In the Muṇḍaka Upaniṣad an important distinction is made between *parā vidyā* and *aparā vidyā,* higher knowledge and lower knowledge. It is a distinction made nowhere else in the Upaniṣads but founded upon an attitude tacitly shared by all knowers of Brahman (*brahmavido vadanti*).[1] According to Aṅgiras, there are two sources. The Vedas—the Ṛg, the Yajur, the Sāma and the Atharva — and other works such as the science of pronunciation, the code of rituals, grammar, etymological interpretation, prosody and astronomy belong to the first source, and the knowledge we get from it is lower (*aparā vidyā*).[2] To the second source belongs that by which That Imperishable (*tad akṣaram*)[3] is known. The knowledge we get from this source is higher (*parā vidyā*).[4] If we carefully read the passage (1-1-5) where the twofold distinction is made, we may find that it gives rise to three important questions. (i) In what sense is the term Vedas used here? Does it include the Upaniṣads or not? (ii) The works such as the science of pronunciation are products of human effort (*pauruṣeya*) and do not teach of the Imperishable. Apart from this, they are combined with the Vedas and then the entire list is brought under the common category of lower knowledge. Can we conclude from this list that the Muṇḍaka aims at denying that the Vedas are impersonal in origin and teach of the Imperishable? (iii) Is it possible to identify from the word *yayā* the means by which the Imperishable is attained (*adhigamyate*)?[5]

(i)The word Vedas is used in two different senses — in the broad sense it includes the Upaniṣads; in the narrow sense it denotes only the Saṃhitās and the Brāhmaṇas. If the Vedas include the Upaniṣads, then the former cannot be brought under the lower knowledge, for the knowledge of the Imperishable is repeatedly enunciated in the latter. If, on the contrary, the Vedas do not include the Upaniṣads and if we agree that the Upaniṣads put forth the knowledge of the Imperishable, then also the Vedas cannot be placed in the category of the lower knowledge, for the Upaniṣads constantly declare that what they state is really the teaching of the Vedas. (ii) If we suppose that the Vedas including the Upaniṣads cannot give us the knowledge of the Imperishable and that they have to be considered as works composed through human effort, then we cannot think of another more authoritative text by which the Imperishable can be known. (iii) In the absence of a text more authoritative than the Vedas we are practically left with nothing to rely upon for the knowledge of the Imperishable. As a result, the expression *yayā* signifies nothing, though it is used by the Upaniṣad to denote something which makes the knowledge of the Imperishable possible.

Now two conclusions impose themselves on us: (i) either the twofold distinction of knowledge is wrong or (ii) if we accept the twofold distinction, we must concede that there is something which is other than the Vedas (including the Upaniṣads) and by which the Imperishable can be known. We cannot give credit to the first because it amounts to undermining the authority of Śruti. Hence we have to accept the twofold distinction and, having done so, try to understand in the light of all other relevant passages why the Muṇḍaka has made that distinction.

ŚAṄKARA'S INTERPRETATION

In his *pūrvapakṣa* Śaṅkara invites our attention to two consequences that arise if we accept the position of the Muṇḍaka. First, if the knowledge of the Imperishable cannot be had through the Vedas, then no other text in the world can give this knowledge. He quotes the Manusmṛti, which says that other texts, texts other than the Vedas are occupied with dark things, and points out that such texts are useless and unacceptable (*niṣphalatvāt anādeyā syāt*).[6] Second, if the Upaniṣads are included in the Vedas, the distinction between the lower and the higher knowledge becomes illogical and meaningless (*anarthaka*).[7]

Then comes Śaṅkara's final view (*siddhānta*). He thinks that the term Vedas is used here in the narrow sense which excludes the Upaniṣads. Further, he thinks that by the term the meaning implied everywhere is the assemblage of words (*vedaśabdena tu sarvatra śabdarāśiḥ vivakṣitaḥ*).[8] As an assemblage of words, the Vedas cannot give us any cogent knowledge, much less a knowledge of the Imperishable. Hence from the mastery of the Vedas can come only lower knowledge i.e. knowledge of the words (*aparā vidyā*). But this is not the case with the Upaniṣads. They cannot be regarded as an assemblage of words (*na upaniṣad śabdarāśiḥ*),[9] for only by them is imparted the knowledge of the Imperishable (*upaniṣad vedyam akṣaraviṣayam hi vijñānam*).[10] As this knowledge is distinctly stated in them (*prādhānyena vivakṣitaṃ*),[11] they must be regarded as the means of the higher knowledge (*parā vidyā*). In Śaṅkara's view it is appropriate to take the expression *yayā* as referring to the Upaniṣads.

In order to meet the two points in the *pūrvapakṣa* — (i) if the knowledge of the Imperishable falls outside the scope of the Vedas, then we can never get this knowledge; (ii) if the Vedas include the Upaniṣads, then the distinction between the lower and the higher knowledge becomes illogical — Śaṅkara takes the word Vedas to exclude the Upaniṣads and shows that the Upaniṣads are the means to the knowledge of the Imperishable. But unfortunately his attempt has proved suicidal. He teaches that though the Vedas cannot give us the knowledge of the Imperishable, we have the Upaniṣads which serve as the means to that knowledge. As we have stated in the beginning, the Upaniṣads frequently refer to the Vedas as their authority and declare that the knowledge they possess is derived from the Vedic hymns. The Muṇḍaka itself is a case in point. It says that its teaching about the Imperishable has been declared by the Ṛg Veda (*tad etad ṛcā abhyuktam*).[12] Therefore the Imperishable is not an exclusive teaching of the Upaniṣads; on the contrary, it is the subject-matter of the Vedas also.

With a view to show why the Vedas are accorded an inferior position or why they are not regarded as the means of higher knowledge Śaṅkara says that they are an assemblage of words (*śabdarāśiḥ*).[13] The word Vedas, he points out, is intended everywhere to convey this sense. What exactly is meant by the expression *śabdarāśiḥ*? We shall see what Śaṅkara himself makes of this expression. Though he has introduced it as a definition of the Vedas, he has not explained his definition. However, we get a clue from his words with which he distinguishes the Upaniṣads from the Vedas. He says two things about the Upaniṣads — (i) they are not an assemblage of words (*na upaniṣad śabdarāśiḥ*);[14] (ii) the knowledge of the Imperishable is distinctly mentioned in them (*prādhānyena vivakṣitam*).[15] We may not be wrong if we conclude that the Upaniṣads are not an assemblage of words because they distinctly talk about the knowledge of the Imperishable. The clue we get here is that in the case of the Vedas the converse of this conclusion must be true i.e. the Vedas are an assemblage of words because they do not distinctly speak of *akṣara viṣayam*. It is now easy to grasp Śaṅkara's definition and also why the Vedas are included in the category of the lower knowledge. But this does not seem to be the view of the Muṇḍaka. It does not use the word Vedas in the sense of a mere assemblage of words but in the sense of an interpreted text whose true import can be clearly comprehended. This is the reason why the Vedas are enumerated along with the six well-known aids with which the Vedic texts are studied and their true import is brought out. As an interpreted text, the Vedas will be found to distinctly deal with (what Śaṅkara calls) *akṣara viṣayam*. In spite of this clear indication and in an apparent contradiction to what it has subsequently said about the higher knowledge the Muṇḍaka deliberately brings the Vedas within the category of the lower knowledge. This is the crux of the problem.

THE KNOWLEDGE OF THE IMPERISHABLE

We have noticed in the beginning that the distinction between the lower and the higher knowledge gives rise to three questions a thorough examination of which leads to the following results.

(i) The Vedas, whether they include the Upaniṣads or not, cannot be put in the category of the lower knowledge. (ii) If we set aside the Vedas including the Upaniṣads as constituting the lower knowledge, we cannot think of another more authoritative source from which the Imperishable can be known. (iii) If we decide to accept the twofold distinction in spite of these grave difficulties, we must concede that there must be something which is other than the Vedas and the Upaniṣads and by which the Imperishable can be known.

We shall now try to re-examine the original questions and see how far these results are inevitable. What we are going to say here was already anticipated to some extent in the previous section. Hence there may be a certain amount of repetition. But that is necessary, because without it we cannot unfold the significance of the expression *yayā* in verse 1-1-5.

(i) As the Upaniṣads form an integral part of the Vedas, the latter may be taken in their broad sense to include the former. That the Upaniṣads are integral to the Vedas is clearly recognised by the Muṇḍaka itself in 3-2-10. However, the whole Śruti, containing both the Vedas and the Upaniṣads, must be viewed as belonging to the lower knowledge.

(ii) The Vedas are not produced through human effort *(apauruṣeya)*. Nor is their true import anything other than the Imperishable *(akṣara)*. The six works beginning with the science of pronunciation are unlike the Vedas. For they are neither impersonal in origin nor aim at teaching the Imperishable. Why then does the Muṇḍaka mention the Vedas along with the six works as if they have the same status as the latter? The underlying aim is to re-affirm the traditional notion about the two types of works and not to deny the uniqueness of the former. The six works are traditionally known to occupy the subordinate position of being the aids necessary for arriving at a right interpretation of the Vedic texts. The question is what justifies their association with the Vedas *here*, especially when the Vedas are said to be lower? This may have a clue as to why they are considered lower. The real intention of the Muṇḍaka is to suggest an important point through their association. The true import of the Vedas is determined to be the Imperishable with the help of the six works. The import thus determined gives merely a knowledge through words and not a knowledge through direct contact or union with the Imperishable. This is the reason why the Vedas fall under the category of the lower Vidyā. We must note that they fall under the lower category not because they are an assemblage of words but because they give us a knowledge of the Imperishable which is merely verbal (*mantramātra*). Śaṅkara has missed this important point, for he is under two wrong notions — the notion that the Vedas do not deal with the Imperishable and the notion that the words *aparā* and *parā* are absolutely exclusive of each other. In fact, the first is a consequence of the second notion. The lower differs from the higher in the method of knowing the Imperishable, otherwise the goal of the two Vidyās is the same. The Imperishable in the Vedas which are studied through the Vedāṅgas, is known from *mere* words. This is the intended significance of the association between the two — the Vedas and the Vedāṅgas.

When the title of Parā Vidyā is denied to the Vedas and the Upaniṣads, it does not necessarily follow that there should be another body of texts in the world which takes the place of these scriptures and deservedly claims that title. It is quite conceivable that the title is denied to them with a view to suggest that the Parā Vidyā stands for a higher source, a source higher than the recognised body of texts, from which arises not the mediate but the immediate knowledge of the Imperishable.[16]

(iii) Śaunaka approaches Aṅgiras and asks him to impart the knowledge of That by which he will be in possession of world-knowledge (*sarvam idaṃ vijñātaṃ*).[17] This involves three important things: (i) the lower knowledge, *aparā vidyā*; (ii) the higher knowledge, *parā vidyā*; and (iii) the Imperishable, *akṣaram*. As we have already noted, the object of both the Vidyās is the Imperishable. Though there is a basic difference between the two Vidyās, the lower helps the higher. By the lower Vidyā the intellect is steadily fixed on the true import of the Vedas i.e. the Imperishable. Eventually, the means necessary for attaining the Imperishable i.e. the higher Vidyā emerges from the discipline imposed on the intellect by the lower Vidyā. Hence the teacher insists that both the Vidyās have to be known (*veditavye*)[18] by the seeker of Brahman. Though both the Vidyās are about the Imperishable, world-knowledge arises only from the higher Vidyā.For from this Vidyā the Imperishable is known not through words but through actual attainment.

Though there are two Vidyās, the higher Vidyā is said to be the means of attaining the Imperishable. From the word *parā vidyā* or *yayā* nothing can be said about the nature of the means.

For we do not know what actually makes that means. The Muṇḍaka 1-1-5 is silent on this point. However, from the relevant verses of the text we note that this point refers to the inner Ātman seated in the cavity of the heart (*antarātmā*).[19] It is by this Ātman, says the Muṇḍaka, that the Imperishable is attained. There are two significant passages in the Muṇḍaka that speak of Ātman as the means: (i) in 2-2-9 the Imperishable is declared to be known by the knowers of Ātman (*tad yad ātmavido viduḥ*); and (ii) in 2-2-5 Ātman is called the bridge to the Immortal (*jānatha ātmānam ... amṛtasyaiṣa setuḥ*). The same idea is found in the Māṇḍūkya also. It says *saṃviśaty ātmanātmānaṃ*[20] (he enters Ātman by Ātman). The reason why the means *yayā* is left undefined by the Upaniṣad is that it is well-known among the seekers of Brahman that Ātman is the direct means of knowing the Imperishable. If Brahmavidyā is the foundation of world-knowledge, then Ātmavidyā is the direct means of Brahmavidyā.

THE SUPREME IMPERISHABLE

If the foundation of world-knowledge is the Imperishable, which Imperishable is to be regarded as the proper foundation? For the Muṇḍaka speaks of three Imperishables in succession — *akṣarāt parataḥ paraḥ*. And the enumeration is clear.

The number of *akṣaras* mentioned by the Muṇḍaka is not the same everywhere. In 1-2-13 it is one; again in 2-2-2 it is one; but in 2-1-2 it is three. The number may vary according to the context, but where three *akṣaras* are mentioned, there the Upaniṣad must be considered as revealing its most authentic side.

Śaṅkara sees two *akṣaras* in the Upaniṣad — the first signifies the unmanifested Māyā (*akṣarāt parataḥ*) and the second the unconditioned Brahman (*paraḥ*). Besides, he considers the second *akṣara* alone to be necessary in the conception of Brahman. This is not proper exegesis.

The Muṇḍaka speaks of three Brahmans. (i) There is a lower Brahman, a Puruṣa who is the Lord (*īśam puruṣam*).[21] He is the golden-coloured maker, the all-knower and the world-knower (*sarvajñaḥ sarvavid*)[22]. He is the leader of the life and the body.

He has put a heart in the material being, and in that being He has taken a firm foundation (*pratiṣṭhito'nne hṛdayam sannidhāya*).[23] He is here close to us; for those who have vision He is even here in this world, hidden in the secret heart (*iha antike ca paśyatsu ihaiva nihitaṃ guhāyām*).[24] (ii) There is a higher Brahman beyond the Lord dwelling in the heart of all beings (*sarvabhūtāntarātmā*).[25] The higher is the source from which the lower gets all — formed existence, mastery, freedom, knowledge, power, bliss, etc., (*īśaṃ puruṣaṃ brahmayonim*).[26] It is vast, effulgent and unthinkable. It is subtler than the subtlest, farther than the farthest. It is without stain and without parts. It is pure and the light of lights. It is invisible, ungraspable, without connections, without colour, without eye and ear, without hands and feet. It is what the wise see as the source of all beings (*bhūtayoniṃ*).[27] (iii) Besides the two, there is also a third, a supreme Brahman. Just as the higher is beyond the lower, so is the supreme Brahman beyond both and therefore known as *paramam brahma*.[28] Though the Highest transcends the two, It is still their foundation (*paramam brahma dhāma*).[29] Not bound by its transcendence, It is extended everywhere (*sarvagataṃ*).[30] It is extended in the higher[31] and in the lower.[32] The sages who have reached this all-pervading Brahman are perfectly moulded in their Ātman (*kṛtātmanaḥ*).[33] For in them the true Law of the supreme Brahman has been fully unveiled and the individual Ātman has attained absolute likeness to the Brahman (*paramaṃ sāmyam upaiti*).[34] They enter into all worlds (*sarvameva āviśanti*)[35] and enjoy the objects of their desires (*jāyate tāṃśca kāmān*).[36]

There is a perfect correlation between the three *akṣaras* and the three Brahmans. The Brahman triad is the key to the other triad. It helps us to understand each of the three *akṣaras* and the relation of each to the others. The Muṇḍaka certainly gives an account of three Brahmans as if each is having an independent existence. But they are one Brahman in three forms. To know each in itself and each in relation to the others does not mean that they exist separately and do not form a unified whole. As a matter of fact, they are one and indivisible and must be known as such. A knowledge that arises out of the unified view of the Brahman is a complete knowledge (*samyagjñāna*).[37]

The One who is close to the world and seated in the secret heart of beings is the all-knowing Lord — He is the lower Brahman. We begin to realise that the Lord is not all when we see that his source is in the higher Brahman. In the language of the Muṇḍaka the two are referred to as the lower (*avara*) and the higher (*para*)[38] or as the interior (*ābhyantara*) and the exterior (*bāhya*).[39] The perceptions of the two alternate as long as they are successive, one about the higher or the exterior and the other about the lower or the interior. If they are held together without conflict or mutual exclusion, then one enters into the highest state and gets the perception of the supreme Brahman. Here the Brahman is not only above the higher and the lower, the higher Brahman and the Lord, but possesses them as the two inseparable aspects of its indivisible oneness. It is the simultaneous possession by the highest Brahman that is indicated by the significant expression *sabhāhyābhyantaraḥ* in 2-1-2 where the prefix *sa* gives the sense of integral possession. The all-inclusive and integral nature of the supreme Brahman is again mentioned in 2-2-8 where the Muṇḍaka says that the higher and the lower Brahmans must be seen in That, the highest Brahman (*tasmin dṛṣṭe parāvare*).[40] Thus we see that the Highest does not leave out the other two but includes them as Its two aspects.

If *akṣara* denotes Brahman, then all that we have said about the three forms of Brahman apply with equal force to the three *akṣaras*. First, there are not three Akṣaras, but three forms of one Akṣara. Second, the supreme Akṣara (*paraḥ*), though surpasses the other two (*akṣaraḥ, akṣarāt parataḥ*), is not external to them but extended equally in each of them and includes both as its own two inseparable aspects. It is the supreme all-inclusive Akṣara that is intended to be the means of world-knowledge (*sarvavidyā*) and not the one which excludes the higher and the lower Akṣaras and exists in isolation.

NOTES

* *tatrāparā ṛgvedo yajurvedaḥ sāmavedo atharvavedaḥ*
śikṣā kalpo vyākarṇaṃ niruktam chando jyotiṣamiti;
atha parā yayā tadakṣaram adhigamyate.

1. Muṇḍaka Upaniṣad (hereafter M. Up.), 1-1-4.
2. Ibid., 1-1-5.
3. Ibid.
4. Ibid.

5. Ibid.
6. Manusmṛti, 12-9.
7. Śaṅkara, *Muṇḍaka Upaniṣad Bhāṣya* (hereafter M. Up. B.), 1-1-5.
8. Ibid.
9. Ibid.
10. Ibid.
11. Ibid.
12. M. Up., 3-2-10.
13. Śaṅkara, M. Up. B., 1-1-5.
14. Ibid.
15. Ibid.
16. M. Up., 1-1-5.
17. Ibid., 1-1-3.
18. Ibid., 1-1-4.
19. Ibid., 2-1-9.
20. Māṇḍūkya Upaniṣad, Mantra 12.
21. M. Up., 3-1-3.
22. Ibid., 1-1-9.
23. Ibid., 2-2-8.
24. Ibid., 3-1-7.
25. Ibid., 2-1-4.
26. Ibid., 3-1-3.
27. Ibid., 1-1-6.
28. Ibid., 3-2-1.
29. Ibid.
30. Ibid., 1-1-6.
31. Ibid.
32. Ibid., 2-2-1.
33. Ibid., 3-2-2.
34. Ibid., 3-1-3.
35. Ibid., 3-2-5.
36. Ibid., 3-1-10.
37. Ibid., 3-1-5.
38. Ibid., 2-2-9.
39. Ibid., 2-1-2.
40. Ibid., 2-2-9.

12

Veda and Vedānta-Vyākhyāna

THE VEDIC ORIGIN

We have heard from scholars that the Upaniṣads represent the essence of the Veda. In substantiation of their view they point out that the word Vedānta is applied to the Upaniṣads only in that sense. They also draw our attention to the fact that the Upaniṣads themselves frequently proclaim that what they teach has already been taught by the Veda (*tad etat ṛcābhyuktam*). Unless we are told where and in what manner the Upaniṣads have developed the original teachings of the Veda the substantiation in terms of their appellation and proclamation hardly proves their Vedic origin. Since a practical proof of their origin is a desideratum, some scholars contend that the word Vedānta should be understood only as signifying the concluding portion of the Veda. But this amounts to closing one's eyes to the implications of the expression *tad etat ṛcābhyuktam* appearing repeatedly in the Upaniṣads. If we give due weight to the above expression and make a serious attempt at finding a satisfactory evidence, we may conclusively establish the Vedic origin of the Upaniṣads.

There are two main factors which explain why the question of the Vedic origin of the Upaniṣads is not given the attention it deserves. One is the obscurity of the Ṛks and the other is the exclusive importance given to the Upaniṣads. Even during the time of the Ṛks there were difficulties in comprehending them. This is evident from the words of one of the Vedic ṛṣis, Dīrghatamas. He says: "For him who does not know the supreme ether, imperishable and immutable, where the Ṛks and all the gods abide, what shall he do with these Ṛks (*yas taṃ na veda kiṃ ṛcā kariṣyati*)"?[1] Here he does not seem to talk about the unqualified who study the Ṛks. For such a thing was inconceivable in ancient times. So he must be talking about the qualified who are however not possessed of the right means of comprehending the Ṛks.

When the Vedavādins became prominent, the Ṛks were considered to be no more than sacred words to be recited in the performance of sacrifices. Now the term Veda came to denote the Brāhmaṇas to which the Ṛks were an important appendage. In course of time the appendage lost its importance and the Veda was equated with the works of the all-powerful Brāhmaṇas. As a result, the Veda became a book of works (*karma*). When the influence of the Brāhmaṇas began to decline, there arose another powerful movement founded by the Brahmavādins whose emphasis fell exclusively on the Upaniṣads. They held that the Veda signified not the works of the Brāhmaṇas but the knowledge of Brahman embodied in the Upaniṣads. In this sense the Veda was referred to as a book of knowledge (*jñāna*).

This led to rival claims as to which part represented best the spirit of the Veda. After the heat subsided the question was finally settled in favour of the Brahmavādins who said that the Veda consisted of two parts, one dealing with works and another with knowledge, and that the works rightly performed brought about the necessary qualification for getting the knowledge of Brahman. In other words, works were subordinated as an external means to knowledge (*bahiraïga-sādhana*).

As was the case with the Brāhmaṇas, so was it with the Upaniṣads: What was originally a higher term in a hierarchy became later the only term with no hierarchy at all. In other words, after sometime the Upaniṣads were given the position of being the all-sufficient source of Brahman-knowledge, because knowledge alone is the direct means of realising Brahman. In this long historical process little by little the Ṛks went into oblivion, first as an important appendage to works and then as one of the many features of sacrificial works not directly connected with knowledge. This is precisely the reason why studies on the Upaniṣads pay scant attention to the problem of their Vedic origin and take their title of Vedānta to mean only the final portion in the compilation of the Vedas.

Though history is useful, the light it gives is not always helpful. Just as the Brahmavādins discarded history and considered the Veda to be a book of knowledge, so also the history of the Brahmavādins has to be set aside in order to understand afresh the teaching of the Ṛks. Undoubtedly, in this new movement Sri Aurobindo has emerged as a pioneer in the field of Vedic studies. According to him, both the Brāhmaṇas and the Upaniṣads represent two different attempts at discovering the sense of Ṛks. While the first conserves the form, the second reveals the soul of Veda. Naturally, the Upaniṣads use the Vedic word as "a seed of thought and vision" for recovering "old truths in new forms". In his view the title of Vedānta is given to the Upaniṣads not only because they form the concluding portion of the Veda but also because they have a direct connection with the Veda and represent its profound teachings.

A careful study of the Upaniṣads from this point of view opens our eyes to two important facts: (i) they are conscious that there is a supreme secret in the Veda not seizable by those who do not possess the right means (*vedānte paramam guhyam*);[2] (ii) they expound what they consider to be of great importance in the Veda, as in the Chāndogya where the word OM, considered to be the essence of the Ṛg Veda, is the subject of elaboration (*aum ity etad akṣaram ... tasyopavyākhyānam*).[3]

MUṆḌAKA UPANIṢAD

There is a well-known mantra from the Ṛg Veda (1-164-20) which talks about two birds sitting on a tree — one eats the fruit and another sees without eating anything. It runs as follows:

dvā suparṇā sayujā sakhāyā samānaṃ vṛkṣam pariṣasvajāte;
tayor anyaḥ pippalaṃ svādvatty anaśnan anyo abhicākaśīti.[4]

Two of the Upaniṣads, Muṇḍaka and Śvetāśvatara, develop the mantra by using it as "a seed of thought and vision". For this is the method by which the Upaniṣads bring out the inner sense of the Ṛks. The above mantra is taken from a hymn sung by Ṛṣi Dīrghatamas, one of the well known poets of the Ṛg Veda.

First let us take up the elucidation of the mantra by the Muṇḍaka Upaniṣad. According to the Upaniṣad, there are two persons in the world (*dvā suparṇā*),[5] finite and infinite. They are one in essence of being and consciousness and possess the same law of action in the world as companions (*sayujā sakhāyā*).[6] The infinite Person is the golden-coloured Lord of the world (*īśaṃ puruṣaṃ*),[7] whose seat is the immutable Brahman beyond Nature (*brahmayonim*)[7] and who is the doer of works through Nature (*kartāram*).[8] As the immutable Brahman beyond Nature, He is not the doer of works (*anaśnan*)[9] but the witness of works done by Nature (*abhicākaśīti*).[10] Thus He is not the doer though He does works through Nature. This is His greatness (*mahimānam*).[11] On account of this greatness He is worshipped by the wise (*juṣṭaṃ*).[12]

The finite person, though he lives in the same world (*samāne vṛkṣe*),[13] where the infinite Person lives unbound by the works of Nature, deludes himself into thinking that he is a non-lord bound by his works (*muhyamānaḥ*).[14] For he has fallen into the ego (*nimagnaḥ*)[15] which obscures his essential oneness with God and deprives him of God's law of action, the law by which one is free from the bondage of works. By being a non-lord, he is bound by works and grieves on account of this bondage (*anīśayā śocati*).[16] When he escapes the ego and sees God and his greatness of being free from the duality of virtuous and sinful works, he no longer grieves (*vītaśokaḥ*).[17] For he overcomes the duality (*puṇyapāpevidhūya*)[18] and becomes stainless (*nirañjanaḥ*).[19] With this he recovers his oneness with God and possesses God's law of action in the world (*paramaṃ sāmyam upaiti*).[20]

There is no opposition between God and Nature, for Prāṇa by which Nature is active is God himself (*prāṇo hy eṣa yaḥ*).[21] Through this He pervades all beings that are born of Nature (*sarvabhūtairvibhāti*).[22] But ascetics hold that God and Nature are mutually opposed. Hence they conclude that God must be realised only by renunciation of works which express the will of Nature. Those who realise God to be all-pervasive through Nature pay no attention to the view of the ascetics (*nātivādi*).[23] They are doers of works who delight in Ātman and bring about the play of Ātman in their life (*ātmakriḍa ātmaratiḥ kriyāvān*).[24] In the broad category of the knowers of Brahman the ascetics form one type. The best of them belong to another type. What makes a person the best knower of Brahman (*variṣṭhaḥ*)[25] is his capacity to express Brahman in his life.

A complete union with Brahman is the true nature of the human soul. Hence in his true nature he is godlike. As a deluded being, he has forgotten his original immortal form and regards himself as a mortal and grieves. When he recovers his true nature, he realises his complete union with Brahman. To be united in essence of being and consciousness is to be a knower of Brahman. But to be united both in essence of being and in nature of being is to be the best among the knowers of Brahman. When he is thus integrally united, there is no grief but the play of Ātman in his life. This, according to the Muṇḍaka, is the teaching of Dīrghatamas, one of the important sages of the Vedas.

ŚVETĀŚVATARA UPANIṢAD

The Śvetāśvatara is perfectly qualified, like the Muṇḍaka, for elucidating the mantra 1-164-20. And to this effect it recalls the words of the poet Dīrghatamas who says that unless one rises to the supreme ether where the gods and the Ṛks reside, one cannot comprehend the true sense of the Veda (1-164-39). It looks as if the whole Śvetāśvatara is an elucidation of 1-164-20. A notable feature of this attempt is that it is guided by the light already thrown on the above mantra by the Muṇḍaka.[26]

For the sake of convenience we shall first set forth the elucidation and then proceed to relate it to the two texts of the Śvetāśvatara, 4-6 and 4-7. The expression Māyī (Lord of Māyā) means two things, an eternal being and an eternal power of being. Of them the being is more fundamental than the power of being. While the power of being exists for the sake of the being, the being exists for its own sake.

As the eternal being, the Lord is one than whom there is nothing else higher.[27] He is all-pervading,[28] tranquil,[29] immortal and imperishable.[30] He is the universal being,[31] the witness,[32] without parts, without activity, without blemish[33] and without the *guṇas*.[34] He is beyond the three divisions of time.[35]

As the eternal power of being, the Lord controls both knowledge and ignorance.[36] He is the all-source,[37] all-creator,[38] all-ruler,[39] all-doer[40] and master of works.[41] He is the lord of the world[42] and ever-seated in the heart of all.[43] He is auspicious,[44] brings good and removes evil.[45] He is the possessor of the *guṇas*[46] and exists in the midst of chaos created by the *guṇas*.[47] He is the lord of the *guṇas*[48] and protector of the world.[49] He is the author of time.[50]

With his Māyā the Lord looses forth all creatures (*māyī sṛjate viśvam etat*).[51] The whole world is filled with them (*bhūtais tu vyāptaṃ sarvam idaṃ*).[52] They are parts of God, because they are godlike and held together as his eternal manifestations (*tasya-avayavabhūtaiḥ*).[53] As Māyā expresses God in the world, it does not separate his creatures from him. They are fully conscious of their origin and absolute likeness to him. They are one with God not only in essence of being and consciousness but also in law of action. Hence they are called lords (*patayaḥ*).[54]

In the process of creation Māyā manifests godlike beings referred to as the sons of God (*amṛtasya putrāḥ*).[55] In this process another Māyā comes into play (*tasmiṃs cānyaḥ*),[56] a Māyā from which all instruments arise and with which all beings are deluded. Even though it deludes them, its power of delusion cannot penetrate into their secret hearts, for there it is obstructed by the Lord's Māyā (*anyo māyayā saṃniruddhaḥ*).[57] In their hearts the Lord is ever-seated (*hṛdaye sanniviṣṭaḥ*),[58] and protects their original forms by his Māyā. Therefore his creatures, while deluded on the surface, are always in their innermost part conscious of their immortal forms and united with him.

But then are there two Māyās? If so, how to distinguish one from the other? If the other Māyā is obstructed by the Lord's Māyā, how does the Lord stand in relation to the former? There are indeed two Māyās, one is the source of the creatures and the other is the source of their instruments conditioned by mortality. While the first is already known as the Māyā of the Lord, the second is to be known as Prakṛti (*māyāṃ tu prakṛtiṃ vidyāt*),[59] the Prakṛti of the three *guṇas* (*triguṇaḥ*).[60] In relation to Māyā God is the Lord of Māyā (*māyī*)[61] and in relation to Prakṛti restrained by Māyā the Lord of Māyā is to be known as the great Lord (*māyinaṃ tu maheśvaraṃ*).[62] For He controls both Māyā and Prakṛti (*yonim yonim adhiṣṭhaty ekaḥ*),[63] elsewhere referred to as knowledge and ignorance (*vidyāvidye*).[64]

From this it is clear that God must be known as the great Lord who binds through Prakṛti and protects and releases through Māyā (*saṃsāra-mokṣa ... hetuḥ*).[65] If through his grace God is known (*dhātuḥ prasādāt*),[66] all fetters fall away and one passes over death and recovers one's original immortal form. There is no other way for removing death and suffering (*nānyaḥ panthāḥ*).[67]

Now we shall look at the two texts of the Śvetāśvatara 4-6 and 4-7 in the light of the above elucidation. There are two types of beings in the world (*dvā suparṇā*),[68] God and godlike creatures. By God is meant both his eternal being and eternal power of being. In the being He is immutable and in the power of being He is the doer of works. Since the creatures are godlike, they are united with God in being as well as in power of being. In point of being they are one in essence (*sayujā*)[69] and in point of power of being they are one in law of action (*sakhāyā*),[70] the law by which they act without the bondage of action.

The one which does not eat the fruit but merely sees (*anaśnan anyo abhicākaśīti*)[71] refers to God who is seated in the immutable Ātman and sees all actions done by Māyā. The one which eats the fruit (*anyaḥ pippalaṃ svādvatti*)[72] stands for man who is bound by the *guṇas* of Prakṛti and acts without possessing his Ātman. Hence he is separated from both God and God's law of action.

Both God and man are in the same world (*sāmane vṛkṣe*).[73] But man comes to misery (*śoka*).[74] From this one may conclude that the misery is inevitable for one who lives in the world and is engaged in works. This is wrong, for God who lives here and is the doer of all works (*viśvakṛt*)[75] is always auspicious (*śivaṃ*)[76] and tranquil (*śāntam*).[77] Misery comes not from the world or works done in the world but from doing works not according to God's law.

Owing to self-subjection to the *guṇas* man has lost sight of his true Self and is caught in the mechanism of Prakṛti (*nimagnaḥ*).[78] As a result, he has fallen into the delusion that he is a mortal conditioned by the duality of works (*muhyamānaḥ*), a non-lord (*anīśa*).[79] He grieves because it is a consequence of his inability to be a master of works (*anīśayā śocati*).[80]

Wise men have renounced their false notion and realised their immortal Self by worshipping the great Lord (*maheśvaraḥ*). When the mortal man sees the other type of life lived by the wise (*anyam*),[81] the Lord worshipped by them (*juṣṭam īśam*)[82] and the

Lord's greatness as taught by them (*asya mahimānam iti*),[83] the greatness arising from His law of action, he becomes freed from grief (*vītaśokaḥ*).[84] In other words, he overcomes grief when he learns to live in the immutable Ātman and act through Māyā without falling into the bondage of action. Positively, in place of grief he begins to express the joy of Ātman in works.

Man is really a son of God. He is one with God not only in his essence of being but also in his nature of being. In short, he is immortal like God who is both the immutable Ātman and the mutable Māyā. But his immortal form is obscured by his wrong identification with the *guṇas* of Prakṛti. On account of this wrong identification he is subject to grief and suffering. When he worships God as the great Lord, God's Māyā frees him from the bonds of the *guṇas* and restores to him his original form untouched by Prakṛti and her imperfections. Living like God, he no more grieves but expresses Ātman in life. According to the Śvetāśvatara, this is what Ṛṣi Dīrghatamas teaches through his Ṛk Mantra 1-164-20.

THE MERITS OF THE TWO VYĀKHYĀNAS

Though the Ṛg Veda abounds in obscure Ṛks, both the Muṇḍaka and Śvetāśvatara have chosen a Ṛk which is relatively simple and easy of comprehension. For they can easily show through this that the secret sense of the Ṛks can be discovered if we carefully grasp the clues supplied by them.

Secondly, in spite of the fact that the two Upaniṣads deal with the same Ṛk of Dīrghatamas, the Śvetāśvatara seems to be a comprehensive exposition of the mantra, from beginning to end. In this respect it is markedly different from the Muṇḍaka whose exposition is very brief and takes no more than three couplets, 3-1-2 to 3-1-4. However, it does not mean that the Muṇḍaka's exposition is less important. On the contrary, the Śvetāśvatara owes a good deal to the Muṇḍaka in so far as it uses one of the Muṇḍaka's couplets on the Ṛk as its base and starting-point.

Thirdly, the two Upaniṣads very clearly establish that for the Vedic sages the unqualified opposition between works and knowledge does not exist, for only works born of the *guṇas* are renounced as the source of misery and bondage. By subscribing to this ancient view of the Veda, the Upaniṣads themselves disprove the myth that they advocate *sarvakarmasannyāsa* as the way to *mokṣa*.

Fourthly, the world is primarily a manifestation of the Lord's Māyā which does not operate through confusion and error. Hence all creatures of the Lord are his real manifestations. Unlike Māyā, Prakṛti works through confusion and error and produces delusions through its *guṇas*. When the delusion is destroyed, all here shine in their original immortal forms. This is the precise significance of the distinction between Prakṛti and Māyā, a distinction manifestly made only in the Śvetāśvatara. Later the Gītā develops this idea and makes it a cornerstone of its yoga of works (7-5) (*karma yoga*).

Fifthly, the Ṛk 1-164-20 refers to God as both a non-doer and a witness who supports the works of Māyā. This idea appears in the Muṇḍaka as the Lord whose seat is the immutable Brahman and who is the doer of works through Māyā.[85] In the Śvetāśvatara it is mentioned as the Lord of Māyā who is both being and power of being, the immutable (*akṣaram*) and the mutable (*kṣaram*).[86] From this it is clear that the Lord is not the immutable Brahman erroneously seen through Māyā but possesses the Brahman as an aspect of his universal existence. To take the Lord to be an erroneous representation of the immutable Brahman is to misunderstand both the Muṇḍaka and the Śvetāśvatara.

Sixthly, there are three parts in the Ṛk (1-164-20). First, the original relationship between God and man, expressed through *sayujā sakhāyā*;[87] second, God's law of action, expressed through *anaśnan anyo abhicākaśīti*;[88] third, man's action which is contrary to God's law, expressed through *anyaḥ pippalaṃ svādvatti*.[89] The Ṛk becomes intelligible only when we know how the three parts form a harmonious whole. The purpose of an exposition is to work out the harmony in explicit terms and make the Ṛk intelligible. This is what the Upaniṣads have done in their expositions of the mantras of the Veda.

In reality man and God are perfectly united. God exemplifies that divine mastery consists in possessing Ātman and in being a witness of works done by Māyā. But somehow man has fallen from his original state of divine mastery and has become a blind doer of works. This is the substance of the Ṛk. The important point here is that the Ṛk does not say how the fall came about and how man can recover the original law of divine mastery. This is the problem to be resolved, the main issue to be discussed and taken to its logical end.

The Muṇḍaka seeks to resolve the problem in this way: first, by attributing man's fall to immersion and delusion; second, by showing that his recovery lies through the knowledge of God's greatness as revealed by the wise; third, by affirming that his knowledge makes him a possessor of Ātman (*ātmaratiḥ*)[90] and a doer of works (*kriyāvān*)[91] who has brought about the play of Ātman in works (*ātmakrīḍaḥ*).[92] In other words, man's fall is due to his immersion in ego and his delusion that he is a non-lord conditioned by works; the way to his recovery is to become Ātman in place of being a non-lord and do works which express Ātman, not ego.

In resolving the problem of the Ṛk the Śvetāśvatara is certainly guided by the Muṇḍaka. The fact that it uses the latter's couplet 3-1-2 is a clear proof that it is in perfect agreement with the latter's exposition. The omission of the other two couplets 3-1-3 and 3-1-4 of the Muṇḍaka does not mean that the Śvetāśvatara considers them to be unimportant. Rather it recognises them too by recognising 3-1-2. For they simply develop the central idea of 3-1-2. However, it is not wholly satisfied with the Muṇḍaka's exposition, for the Muṇḍaka has not shown how man, who is perfectly united with God, can separate himself from God and become a non-lord. Immersion and delusion are the results and not the cause of his fall. Unless there is something in God's Māyā which predisposes to such a fall, the fall can never take place. This seems to be the view of the Śvetāśvatara.

As long as God is the Lord of Māyā, man's fall is really unaccountable, for Māyā works in the conditions of knowledge and harmony. At some stage in the process of creation it must assume an inferior mode of operation not in its original conditions but in the conditions of ignorance and confusion (*kalilasya madhye*).[93] Given this necessity, the inferior Māyā works through the mechanism of ego which is the principle of self-forgetfulness, and the three *guṇas* from which arise all conflicts and confusions, all bonds and miseries. The appearance of this inferior Māyā in the process of creation is referred to as *tasmiṃs cānyaḥ*.[94] In order to differentiate it from the Lord's Māyā it is designated as Prakṛti (*māyāṃ tu prakṛtiṃ vidyāt*).[95] When the immortal beings get into the domain of Prakṛti and assume the conditions of mortal existence, their entry and assumption are referred to as immersion and delusion.[96] Since Prakṛti is the inferior operation of Māyā, the Lord of Māyā is redesignated as the supreme Lord (*maheśvaram*)[97] under whose control operates not only Māyā but Prakṛti as well. Therefore, when Prakṛti binds, its action is not independent but subject to the will of the supreme Lord and implies that the Lord is the real cause of bondage (*bandhahetuḥ*)[98] and none other than him.

Now man's fall becomes intelligible — Prakṛti's appearance is the immediate cause, while the ultimate cause of his fall is the supreme Lord. It is for this reason that in the process of liberation God's grace is given a decisive role to play (*dhātuḥ prasādāt*).[99] With His blessings alone[100] one can overcome the delusion of death and not otherwise. This is the insight the Śvetāśvatara gives us about man's fall from his original divine form and his subsequent recovery from the fall.

The couplet 4-10 of the Śvetāśvatara is most misunderstood. Its first line runs thus:

māyāṃ tu prakṛtiṃ vidyāt māyinaṃ tu maheśvaram.

Generally, the first three words are taken to be an assertion that the Lord's Māyā is the same as Prakṛti. But this is wrong, because it does not agree with the words that follow — *māyinaṃ tu maheśvaram*. The word *maheśvaram* implies that the Lord is raised to another level where His control becomes considerably larger than before. If the Lord's Māyā is redefined as Prakṛti, then the redesignation of Māyī as Maheśvaram is quite uncalled for. For the scope of the Lord's control remains the same as before. The redesignation of Māyī is justifiable only when the Lord's control becomes larger than before and is extended to another principle besides his Māyā. Therefore the first three words of the above line must be taken, as we have already shown, as a definition of the inferior Māyā (*anyaḥ*)[101] as Prakṛti, and not as a redefinition of the Lord's Māyā. This perfectly agrees with the general drift of the Upaniṣad.

NOTES

1. Ṛg Veda (hereafter RV), 1-164-39.
2. Śvetāśvatara Upaniṣad (hereafter S. Up.), 6-22.
3. Chāndogya Upaniṣad, 1-1-1.
4. Muṇḍaka Upaniṣad (hereafter M. Up.), 3-1-1.
5. M. Up., 3-1-1.
6. Ibid.
7. Ibid., 3-1-3.
8. Ibid.
9. Ibid., 3-1-1.
10. Ibid.
11. Ibid., 3-1-2.
12. Ibid.
13. Ibid.
14. Ibid.
15. Ibid.
16. Ibid.
17. Ibid.
18. Ibid., 3-1-3.
19. Ibid.
20. Ibid.
21. Ibid. 3-1-4.
22. Ibid.
23. Ibid.
24. Ibid.
25. Ibid.
26. Ibid., 3-1-2.
27. S. Up., 3-9.
28. Ibid., 3-11.
29. Ibid., 6-19.
30. Ibid., 1-10.
31. Ibid., 3-21.
32. Ibid., 6-11.
33. Ibid., 6-19.
34. Ibid., 6-11.
35. Ibid., 6-5.
36. Ibid., 5-1.

37. Ibid., 5-5.
38. Ibid., 4-14.
39. Ibid., 3-4.
40. Ibid., 6-16.
41. Ibid., 6-11.
42. Ibid., 6-7.
43. Ibid., 4-17.
44. Ibid., 4-14.
45. Ibid., 6-6.
46. Ibid., 6-2.
47. Ibid., 5-13.
48. Ibid., 6-16.
49. Ibid., 6-17.
50. Ibid., 6-2.
51. Ibid., 4-9.
52. Ibid., 4-10.
53. Ibid.
54. Ibid., 5-3.
55. Ibid., 2-5.
56. Ibid., 4-9.
57. Ibid.
58. Ibid., 3-13.
59. Ibid., 4-10.
60. Ibid., 5-7.
61. Ibid., 4-9.
62. Ibid., 4-10.
63. Ibid., 4-11.
64. Ibid., 5-1.
65. Ibid., 6-16.
66. Ibid., 3-20.
67. Ibid., 6-15.
68. Ibid., 4-6.
69. Ibid.
70. Ibid.
71. Ibid.
72. Ibid.
73. Ibid., 4-7.
74. Ibid.
75. Ibid. 6-16.
76. Ibid. 4-14.
77. Ibid. 6-19.
78. Ibid. 4-7.
79. Ibid.
80. Ibid.

81. Ibid.
82. Ibid.
83. Ibid.
84. Ibid.
85. M. Up., 3-1-3.
86. S. Up., 1-8.
87. RV, 1-164-20.
88. Ibid.
89. Ibid.
90. M. Up., 3-1-4.
91. Ibid.
92. Ibid.
93. S. Up., 5-13.
94. Ibid. 4-9.
95. Ibid. 4-10.
96. Ibid. 4-7.
97. Ibid. 4-10.
98. Ibid. 6-16.
99. Ibid. 3-20.
100. Ibid. 4-11.
101. Ibid. 4-9.

13

Works and Immortality

THREE STRANDS OF THOUGHT

From its title it may be understood that the Muṇḍaka is an Upaniṣad of capital importance. For it is known by the title of Head Upaniṣad (*muṇḍakam*). We may note that there are three strands of thought in it. First, it says that those who reach the Brahmaloka through works, return, after sometime, to this world or some other but lower world (*imaṃ lokaṃ hīnataraṃ vā viśanti*).[1] Second, it speaks of the wise taking to the life of a monk who has renounced works and going where the immortal Puruṣa dwells (*vidvāṃso bhaikṣyacaryāṃ carantaḥ... prayānti ... yatrāmṛtaḥ*).[2] Third, it declares that he who knows works, *tapas* and Brahman to be beyond mortality cuts asunder the knot of ignorance in this embodied life (*avidyāgranthiṃ vikiratīha*).[3] Thus one finds works unworthy, because they cannot break the chain of *saṃsāra*; another insists on renouncing them, because they are the sources of *saṃsāra*; a third regards them as lying beyond mortality and serving as a means to immortality. As the three strands of thought lie side by side, each emphasizing its own truth, they have to be reconciled and rightly related through proper interpretation of the relevant texts.

PRESCRIBED WORKS

Works are founded upon the mantras of three Vedas — Ṛg, Yajus and Sāman. Though they are embedded in them, their practical application is made possible by the discoveries of the wise (*kavayaḥ*).[4] Desires are rightly fulfilled through them. Only those who are intent on fulfilling their desires in the right way are qualified for these works (*satyakāmāḥ*).[5]

Agnihotra is the first among the prescribed works. It produces right result only when it is performed at the new moon, the full moon, the four months of autumn, and the harvest time, when guests are invited, oblations are made to Viśvas, animals and birds are fed, and when nothing is done contrary to the Vedic injunctions (*avidhinā*).[6] An Agnihotrin who moulds his whole life according to these injunctions, passes after his death to the Brahmaloka where the lord of the gods is seated (*devānām patiḥ*).[7] Here he gets god-form and enjoys like the gods through the form given to him.

Thus far the Muṇḍaka paints a good picture about the Agnihotrin, his deeds and the world he reaches after death. But the later half of 1-2 changes radically into a strong rebuff and outright condemnation. Agnihotrins are denounced in many ways — *mūḍhā* (fools), *bālā* (immature minds) and *pramūḍhā* (deluded minds). They are compared to the blind led by the blind. Living in ignorance, so goes on the Upaniṣad, they think that they are wise and have attained the goal of life.

Why is the Upaniṣad blowing hot and cold about the Agnihotrins? In one sense they are praiseworthy and in another sense they are fit to be condemned. Praiseworthy, because they are unlike those who disregard the Vedic injunctions and become victims of sinful deeds; fit to be condemned, because their world won through good works and their enjoyments obtained there are both transitory, and the example they thus set is unwise. Good works are helpful to those who want to escape *aśubha karma*; they are unhelpful to those who want to get rid of the cycle of *saṃsāra*. As the Upaniṣad considers *saṃsāra* to be a greater evil than *aśubha karma*, it condemns the Agnihotrins and their path of works. It teaches that prescribed works too must be abandoned, like those prohibited by the Vedas (*niṣedha*).

RENUNCIATION OF WORKS

Good works are indeed incapable of taking the Agnihotrins to an eternal world where they can stay and enjoy without having to face banishment from the world and to be reborn in the world of mortals. In other words, they are incapable of destroying the law of *saṃsāra*. If they are incapable of doing so, what should one do in order to win immortality which is hailed as the supreme good in the Vedas?

Ascetics say that there is a world from which no return to the world of mortals is possible; that there is a path by which one can go to this world. It is the world where the immortal Puruṣa, who is no other than the imperishable Ātman of all creatures, dwells (*yatra amṛtaḥ sa puruṣo hy avyayātmā*);[8] it is the path of knowledge known as the sun-path (*sūryadvāreṇa*).[9] Who are qualified for this sun-path? (i) Those who renounce their domestic life built upon the pillar of works and live in the forest (*upavasanty araṇye*);[10] (ii) those who embrace the life of a monk who has renounced works and possessions (*bhaikṣyacaryāṃ*);[11] (iii) those who live in the faith shifted from the path of works to the sun-path and practise concentration on Ātman (*tapaḥ śraddhe*);[12] and (iv) those who have attained peace of mind and knowledge through renunciation (*śāntā vidvāṃsaḥ*).[13] In other words, this is the teaching of the ascetics — that knowledge is the means of reaching the Immortal (*amṛtaḥ*); that it is of the imperishable Ātman (*avyayātmā*); that it arises only when all works, good and bad, are renounced by renouncing domestic life (*upavasanty araṇye*). They insist on renunciation of works because works are done out of desire and attachment (*rāgāt*),[14] and the desire is the source of *saṃsāra*.

The Muṇḍaka speaks of the yoga of renunciation (*saṃnyāsa yogāt*).[15] The yoga is not only of renunciation of works but of renunciation radical and extreme. In this yoga men established in the Vedāntic knowledge pass beyond mortality (*parāmṛtaḥ*),[16] beyond all that are bound by desire and attachment. At the hour when the withdrawal from desire and attachment comes to the final end (*parāntakāle*),[17] they are liberated on all sides (*parimucyantisarve*).[18] To be liberated thus is to be liberated not only from the law of *saṃsāra* but also from name and form without which the law can never operate. In other words, the ultimate goal of the yoga of renunciation is total absorption into the highest of the high Puruṣa (*parātparaṃ puruṣam*).[19] It is like the rivers that give up their name and form and disappear into the ocean (*samudre astaṃ gacchanti nāmarūpe vihāya*).[20] This is inevitable. We know that works, name and form go together and make a triad.[21] Hence when works are renounced, this logically leads to the renunciation of name and form also.

The sun-path of the ascetics is based initially on renunciation of works and ultimately on that of name and form. For our purpose we shall take renunciation to be of works mainly, because it concerns name and form only at its ultimate level. Therefore, according to the ascetics, the law of *saṃsāra* is broken and immortality attained only when works which are the source of *saṃsāra* are abandoned.

IMMORTALITY AND WORKS

The view of the ascetics is that the imperishable Ātman is known and immortality attained only when works are renounced. If renunciation and immortality go together, then it implies that works are incompatible with immortality. But when we examine the relevant verses in the Muṇḍaka, they teach that there is no such incompatibility. Rather they hold that works culminate in immortality through culmination in the knowledge of the imperishable Ātman (*avyaya ātmā*).

(i) Let us take verse 1-1-6. It says that the imperishable Ātman has two aspects — eternal being (*nityaṃ*) and manifold becoming (*vibhuṃ*). In the eternal being, it is invisible, ungraspable, without family, without caste, without eyes, ears, hands and feet; in the manifold becoming, it is the source of beings associated with family, caste, eyes, ears, hands and feet. In relation to the aspect of becoming, the aspect of being is subtle; in relation to the aspect of being, Ātman is supremely subtle (*susūkṣmaṃ*). In the supremely subtle aspect Ātman is not external to the being and the becoming, for it is extended in both (*sarvagataṃ*). Thus Ātman has not two but three aspects; (i) the eternal being; (ii) the manifold becoming; and (iii) the supremely subtle form which is extended in both. This is how the wise see the supremely subtle Ātman — as both the imperishable being (*tad avyayaṃ*) and the manifold becoming which is the source of beings (*yad bhūtayonim*).

(ii) It follows from 1-1-6 that the same Ātman is both the eternal being and the nature of being from which arises the world. In other words, there is no contradiction between being and nature of being. They are inseparable from each other. In order to bring out the harmony between the two the Upaniṣad speaks sometimes of the world being born from Ātman (*etasmāt jāyate*);[22] sometimes of Ātman being the great support of the world (*mahatpadam*)[23] or being seated in the heart of all (*hṛdayaṃ sannidhāya*)[24] or pervading everywhere (*prasṛtam*).[25] Here, it must be noted, the harmony is worked out from both sides, from the sides of the world and Ātman.

(iii) If Ātman is the material source of the world, how does its material transformation take place? There are two aspects to the transformation, subjective and objective. Subjectively, it is a conceptive Idea; objectively, it is a perceptive Fact. On the subjective side, there is an expansion of the potential hidden in the eternal essence of Brahman through energism of consciousness (*tapasā cīyate brahma*);[26] on the objective side, the expanded potential of Brahman comes out with three things — name, form and material substance which is a source of physical mould for names and forms (*tasmāt etad brahma nāmarūpam annaṃ ca jāyate*).[27] Thus the transformation is originally an expansion through *tapas* and eventually a projection in physical terms through *karma*. As *tapas* and *karma* are the two successive levels of Brahman's transformation, inward and outward, higher and lower, *para* and *apara,* and partake of the nature of Brahman, they are declared to be beyond mortality like Brahman (*karma tapo brahma parāmṛtam*).[28] A point to be borne in mind is that Brahman undergoing transformation is still Brahman. Hence the carefully chosen expression *etad brahma*.[29] This Brahman with name, form and material substance is the world (*nāmarūpam annaṃ*).

As the means of mortals, both *tapas* and *karma* serve the purposes of the ego. Here *karma* is a means for getting objects of desire and *tapas* a means for quickening the results of *karma.* By serving the mortals they cause bondage and transmigration.[30] If a mortal recognizes them to be the original means by which Brahman transforms itself into the world, and uses them for Brahman's own sake, the knot of mortality is broken and he becomes immortal even here. Hence the following verse: "When the higher (*para* i.e. *tapas*) and the lower (*avara* i.e. *karma*) are seen in Brahman (*tasmin*), the knot of the heart is broken (*hṛdayagranthiḥ*), all doubts concerning one's essential identity with Brahman are resolved (*sarvasaṃsayāḥ*) and all *karmas* that make one a mortal creature (*asya karmāṇi*) are destroyed."[29] A right use of *tapas* and *karma* destroys bondage and transmigration and brings about freedom and immortality.

Therefore *karma* is of two types, one is inferior (*avara*)[30] and another is superior (*anyat śreyaḥ*).[31] The inferior *karma* is done out of the desire of the ego (*rāgāt*)[32] and causes *saṃsāra*. And the superior one is done for the sake of Brahman. In this the knowledge of the immortal Brahman is born (*karmasu amṛtam abhijāyate*).[33] And by this the cause of *saṃsāra* is destroyed. It is in the latter sense that the Muṇḍaka suggests compatibility between *karma* and immortality.

ṚṢI DĪRGHATAMAS AND WORKS

The Muṇḍaka seeks the support of Ṛṣi Dīrghatamas for its view of works. His verse beginning with *dvā suparṇā* (two birds) is well-known.[34] It speaks about man and God through the image of two birds. There are three things here: (i) the words *sayujā* and *sakhāyā*[35] express the original relationship between man and God; the latter two are one in essence of being and consciousness (*sayujā*) and possess the same law of action in the world as companions (*sakhāyā*); (ii) the words *anaśnan anyo abhicākaśīti* state God's law of action which consists in possessing the immutable Ātman (*anaśnan*) and in being a detached witness of works done by Nature (*abhicākaśīti*); (iii) the words *anyaḥ pippalaṃ svādvatti* show that man's action is contrary to God's law, for he is not in possession of the immutable Ātman and, in consequence, enjoys through attachment for works.[36]

The Muṇḍaka develops the teachings of Dīrghatamas fully and shows that works done according to God's law put an end to man's *saṃsāra* and make him immortal. Though he lives in the same world where God lives unbound by the works of Nature, he deludes himself and thinks that he is a non-lord bound by works (*muhyamānaḥ*). For he has fallen into the ego (*nimagnaḥ*) which obscures his essential oneness with God and takes away God's law of action from him, the law by which God is free from the bondage of works. By being a non-lord he is bound and on account of the bondage he grieves (*anīśayā śocati*). When he sees God and his greatness which consists in being immutable through Ātman and doing works through Nature without incurring bondage, he becomes a possessor of God's law and no longer grieves (*vītaśokaḥ*)[37] like the mortal.

Here the Muṇḍaka points out to the harmony implicit in the imperishable Lord (*īśaṃ puruṣaṃ*) who is extended in the immutable Brahman beyond Nature as his seat (*brahmayonim*) and in the mutable Nature as the doer of works (*kartāram*). On account of the equal extension in both Brahman and Nature, He is the non-doer and yet the doer of works. By recovering God's law of works man attains absolute likeness with God (*paramaṃ sāmyaṃ upaiti*)[38] and lives like God. He is not bound by works even when he performs them. Like God, he is in possession of the harmony between non-action and action. This, according to the Muṇḍaka, is the true import of the verse of Dīrghatamas.

It becomes clear from the above that works are not necessarily opposed to immortality and, when done according to God's law, culminate in immortality and make a divine life possible for man who lives in the midst of all creatures.

RENUNCIATION AND FULFILMENT

There are no two opinions about the fact that works done out of desire and attachment are incapable of overcoming the law of *saṃsāra*. But from this, two conclusions are possible: (i) they are the source of *saṃsāra*, and *saṃsāra* is to be overcome only by renouncing them (*sannyāsa*); (ii) they are truly the source of *saṃsāra*, but what makes them so is the desire; and *saṃsāra* is to be overcome not by renouncing them but by renouncing the desire and doing them for the sake of Brahman (*brahmārtham*). As a result of these two possibilities, the Muṇḍaka speaks of two powerful means to immortality, renunciation and fulfilment.

Let us take the case of renunciation. The path of renunciation designated as *sannyāsa yoga* [39] begins with a disgust for works (*nirvedam ayāt*) [40] and closes with the declaration that they are not the means to the uncreated Brahman (*nāsty akṛtaḥ kṛtena*).[41] Having said thus, the Upaniṣad points out that they who follow *sannyāsa yoga* do so in accordance with the well-determined import and knowledge of Vedānta (*vedānta-vijñāna-suniścitārthāḥ*).[42] The pronouncement of the Muṇḍaka is that works can never be a means to immortality and that their renunciation is well-founded on the teachings of Vedānta.

Let us now take the case of fulfilment. The path of works, which may be called *parāmṛtakarmayoga*, is founded upon the original work of transformation of Brahman of which *tapas* is the inward or higher aspect. Even if *karma* alone is spoken, it includes *tapas*, for the two are inseparable from each other. When *tapas* and *karma* are used as the original means of Brahman, they cut the knot of mortality in the heart and change the seeker into a godlike individual who possesses the divine law of works and enjoys immortality in this life, individual and collective. Not only works but name and form are informed by immortality and manifest the immortal consciousness and delight here. Such an individual fulfils himself in God, renounces nothing essential in him, and reaches supreme likeness with God (*paramaṃ sāmyaṃ*). Through an analysis of the above mantra of Dīrghatamas (1-164-20) the Muṇḍaka establishes that *parāmṛtakarma* is the true import thereof. With this the Upaniṣad proves that its view of works is supported by the authority of Veda.

Having projected renunciation and fulfilment as equally important means to immortality and as the means equally attested by scripture (the former by the Vedānta and the latter by the Veda), the Muṇḍaka proceeds to give its own verdict on their relative merits. Here the Upaniṣad takes into account the path of the gods by which also Brahman is realized.[43]

Whether a seeker chooses renunciation or fulfilment or the path of the gods, his goal is the realization of Brahman. Hence, when he reaches his goal, he is called a *brahmavid.* Though the realization of Brahman is common to all three paths, the nature of realization is not the same. It varies according to the means adopted by the individual.

In the path of renunciation the seeker attains the imperishable Brahman and merges in it by giving up his name and form. It is a condition of self-extinction in Brahman. On the contrary, in the path of fulfilment he renounces nothing except his ego which conceals his essential oneness with Brahman and imposes on him the false law of action by which he incurs bondage of works and grieves. By renouncing the ego he recovers his original Brahman-like form and shines both inwardly and outwardly, inwardly as one identified with the immortal Brahman and outwardly as one possessing mastery over works through the divine law of action. This is a condition of self-fulfilment in Brahman. In the path of the gods Brahman is realized after departure from the world. Among *brahmavids* who pass beyond *saṃsāra* and realize Brahman the one who reaches self-fulfilment through works is declared to be the best (*brahmavidāṃ variṣṭhaḥ*)[44] by the Muṇḍaka Upaniṣad. The declaration is not found elsewhere in the Upaniṣads.

Now a question arises as to how the Muṇḍaka comes to this conclusion. All knowers of Brahman cross over *saṃsāra* and become immortal, and their attainments are supported by the teachings of Vedānta and Veda. Then on what basis does the Muṇḍaka conclude that one who follows the path of *parāmṛta-karma* and reaches self-fulfilment in Brahman is the best among the knowers of Brahman? The answer to the question is not difficult to find in the Upaniṣad.

In the Muṇḍaka he who uses works for the sake of Brahman and attains self-fulfilment in Brahman is referred to by the word *kriyāvān*. He is fulfilled at two levels, individual and collective. In his individual life he delights in Ātman through works done according to the divine law of action (*ātmaratiḥ*); in his collective life he is at play with Ātman in all other beings through works and help them discover the divine law of action and realize immortality in this world (*ātmakrīḍaḥ*).[45] This contains the clue necessary for answering the above question.

Man escapes the evil of *saṃsāra* and becomes immortal not for his own sake but for the sake of the others, for the sake of helping them to get rid of the evil and realize immortality. If he cares for his own personal liberation from *saṃsāra* and personal enjoyment of immortality, he is indifferent to the world and the obligation he owes to the others who are bound by *saṃsāra* and suffer on account of the bondage. Personal liberation, dissolution of one's own self in Brahman or departure from the world for the sake of living in Brahman, may be a great achievement, but not great enough to be of use to the others and their good. In other words, to care for personal good and neglect the good of the others is, as

Sri Aurobindo rightly says, "an outcome of ego".[46] In the Vedic age immortality was sought not for personal utility but for the utility of the others. Such a view of immortality is aptly described as "spiritual pragmatism"[47] by Sri Aurobindo. Now we understand the significance of why the Muṇḍaka seeks the support of the Veda for its view of fulfilment through works. When it speaks about the Kriyāvān at play with Ātman in the other living beings, it indicates that he is working for the good of the others and excels the *sannyāsin* who seeks self-extinction in Brahman and the seeker who passes through the path of the gods and knows Brahman in another world. It is for this reason that the Kriyāvān is considered to be the best among the Brahmavids (*variṣṭhaḥ*)[48] by the Muṇḍaka Upaniṣad.

MUṆḌAKA AND BṚHADĀRAṆYAKA

According to the Muṇḍaka, works are the means of fulfilment in Brahman, individually as well as collectively. But such a view, it may be contended, is opposed to two important passages in the Bṛhadāraṇyaka Upaniṣad. First, the critic draws our attention to the text 2-4-14 and says that "there is an utter absence of actions and their means for the knower of Brahman".[49] Second, our attention is again drawn to the text 4-4-19 which says that there is no difference whatsoever in Brahman. Prima facie the critic is right in saying that the Bṛhadāraṇyaka goes against the position of the Muṇḍaka. The Muṇḍaka Upaniṣad suggests two things — (i) that the Kriyāvān delighting in Ātman sees the world and its plurality; (ii) that he does works for the sake of leading the others to self-fulfilment in Ātman. And these two suggestions are destroyed by the declarations of the Bṛhadāraṇyaka.

(i) Let us first take the text 4-4-19 which says that there is no difference whatsoever in Brahman (*neha nānāsti kiñcana*). We can understand its true import only when we bear in mind the special sense in which the word difference (*nānā*) is understood by the Bṛhadāraṇyaka. From the text 1-4-10 we may state the sense thus: where two persons are said to be in a relation of other (*anya*) to other (*anya*), a relation where one is considered to be other and one considers himself to be other, there the relation is one of "difference". The relation prevails till one is ignorant that he is a form of Ātman, identified in thoughts, feelings, and deeds with those of another form of Ātman. When the veil of difference is lifted, the relation of otherness is replaced by another relation—a relation which permits the perception of the forms of Ātman and their oneness in thoughts, feelings and deeds. Such an individual is glorified by the Īśa Upaniṣad. It says that he is the supreme knower who sees all beings as the manifestations of the very essence of Ātman (*yasmin sarvāṇi bhūtanyātmaivābhūd vijānataḥ*).[50] Here he sees two things simultaneously — the existence of all and the existence of Ātman which manifests itself as all. Therefore, when the Bṛhadāraṇyaka denies perception of difference in Brahman, its intention is to deny only the difference arising from the other-based relation and not the one based on the relation between the forms of Ātman or between the forms and Ātman.

If the Muṇḍaka view of the Kriyāvān delighting in Ātman implies perception of the world containing a multiplicity of the forms of Ātman, it perfectly agrees with the intended sense of the text of the Bṛhadāraṇyaka Upaniṣad (4-4-19). There is no doubt about the sense of the text.

(ii) We shall now turn to the other text in the Bṛhadāraṇyaka — 2-4-14. The text describes two kinds of interaction with the world of beings. When the world is regarded by an individual as a collectivity where the thoughts, feelings, and deeds of a being are at variance with those of another being and where the beings are not considered to be in possession of Ātman, his interaction with the world proceeds from the sense of otherness: for him "other (*itaraḥ*) smells other (*itaraṃ*), other sees other", and so on. This is the interaction of an unawakened individual with the world, an individual who is bound by the sense of otherness. As the relation of otherness is a falsehood, an outcome of false perception, it is referred to as an apparent duality (*dvaitamiva*).

When the same world is regarded by an individual as a totality where the thoughts, feelings, and deeds of a being are identified with those of another being and where the beings are considered to be in possession of Ātman, his interaction with the world proceeds from the sense of oneness: for him Ātman smells Ātman, Ātman sees Ātman and so forth. Here the subject is Ātman, the object is Ātman, and the interaction is between the two forms of Ātman. This is the interaction of an awakened individual with the world, an individual who sees everything as the manifestation of the very essence of Ātman (*sarvam ātmaivābhūt*).

The change in the manner of interacting with the world, corresponding to the change in the way of looking at it, is brought out in a dramatic manner through a series of interrogations — "What and by what one smells? What and by what one sees?" etc. The aim of these questions is definitely to deny something consequent on the change in the mode of perception, and the point is what exactly is the thing denied. The aim is to clearly deny that now in the act of smelling, seeing, etc., the object, the subject, and their interaction are governed by the sense of otherness. Hence the object is no longer other but Ātman, the subject is no longer other but Ātman, and the interaction is no longer other-based but Ātman-based. What disappears is the wrong perception or the sense of otherness, otherwise the terms and their interaction continue to remain as before. It is improper to conclude otherwise, to conclude that the entire interaction, which includes the subject and the object, disappears when the knowledge of Ātman arises. It accords neither with the words of scripture nor with the demands of reason. The above conclusion is totally untenable.

With regard to the concept of the Kriyāvān delighting in Ātman and doing works for the sake of helping his fellow beings, the Muṇḍaka and the Bṛhadāraṇyaka are not against each other, but have complete concurrence. They teach the same idea, the same principle, and the same philosophy. And about this there is no doubt whatsoever among the wise.

NOTES

1. Muṇḍaka Upaniṣad (hereafter M. Up.), 1-2-10.
2. Ibid., 1-2-11.
3. Ibid., 2-1-10.
4. Ibid., 1-2-1.
5. Ibid.
6. Ibid., 1-2-3.
7. Ibid., 1-2-5.
8. Ibid., 1-2-11.

9. Ibid.
10. Ibid.
11. Ibid.
12. Ibid.
13. Ibid.
14. Ibid., 1-2-9.
15. Ibid., 3-2-6.
16. Ibid.
17. Ibid.
18. Ibid.
19. Ibid., 3-2-8.
20. Ibid.
21. Bṛhadāraṇyaka Upaniṣad, 1-6-3.
22. M. Up., 2-1-3.
23. Ibid., 2-2-1.
24. Ibid., 2-2-7.
25. Ibid., 2-2-11.
26. Ibid., 1-1-8.
27. Ibid., 1-1-9.
28. Ibid., 2-1-10.
29. Ibid., 1-1-9.
30. Ibid., 1-2-7.
31. Ibid., 1-2-10.
32. Ibid., 1-2-9.
33. Ibid., 1-1-8.
34. Ṛg Veda, 1-164-20.
35. M. Up., 3-1-1.
36. Ibid.
37. Ibid., 3-1-2.
38. Ibid., 3-1-3.
39. Ibid., 3-2-6.
40. Ibid., 1-2-12.
41. Ibid.
42. Ibid., 3-2-6.
43. Ibid., 3-1-6.
44. Ibid., 3-1-4.
45. Ibid.
46. Sri Aurobindo, *The Synthesis of Yoga* (1979), p.257.
47. Sri Aurobindo, *The Upanishads* (1972), p.134.
48. M. Up., 3-1-4.
49. Śaṅkara, *Bṛhadāraṇyaka Upaniṣad Bhāṣya*, Tr. Swāmi Mādhavānanda (1965), p.376.
50. Īśa Upaniṣad, Mantra 7.

14

The World and the Māṇḍūkya Upaniṣad

GAUḌAPĀDA AND ŚAṄKARA

The earliest known commentator of the Māṇḍūkya Upaniṣad is the celebrated Advaitin Gauḍapāda. As his Kārikās cover a few of the original mantras, Śaṅkara has extended Gauḍapāda's commentary to the whole text. This is the merit of Śaṅkara's work. Their commentaries are regarded by scholars everywhere as the authentic expositions of the Māṇḍūkya Upaniṣad.

TWO FORMS OF ĀTMAN

The Upaniṣad has defined Ātman as four-footed (*ātmā catuṣpāt*).[1] Actually there are two major forms of Ātman — three-footed and single-footed. When the two forms are put together, they make Ātman four-footed. Let us note how the two forms are related to each other in the Upaniṣad.

There are two kinds of descriptions — positive and negative, corresponding to the two forms of Ātman. First come the positive descriptions of the three-footed Ātman.[2] He is Viśva (*viśvātmā*), the cogniser of the external world and the enjoyer of the gross objects (*bahiṣ-prajñaḥ, sthūlabhuk*). He is Taijasa (*taijasātmā*), the cogniser of the internal world and the enjoyer of the subtle objects (*antaḥ-prajñaḥ, praviviktabhuk*). He is Prājña (*prājñātmā*), the cogniser of the mass of original forms and the enjoyer of the delight which keeps the forms as a mass (*prajñāna-ghanaḥ, ānandabhuk*). Thus the three-footed Ātman stands for the world cognised and enjoyed in three ways.

Next come the negative descriptions of the single-footed Ātman.[3] He is described through a series of negations — not conscious of the internal (*nāntaḥ-prajñam*), not conscious of the external (*na bahiṣ-prajñam*), not conscious of the two (*na ubhayataḥ-prajñam*), and not conscious of the original mass of forms (*na prajñāna-ghanam*). As if to make the series more specific, He is further described in these terms — not seen (*adṛṣṭam*), not involved in any dealings (*avyavahāryam*), not grasped by sense organs (*agrāhyam*), not defined through mark (*alakṣaṇam*), not grasped by mind (*acintyam*), and not possessed of name (*avyapadeśyam*). Thus the single-footed Ātman refers to That which is devoid of all contents of the world.

Prima facie the two descriptions are mutually destructive. For one makes the other impossible. But this does not seem to be the view of the Upaniṣad which has defined Ātman as four-footed (*saḥ ayam ātmā catuṣpāt*). It clearly shows that in some sense the two forms of Ātman are not mutually opposed, for they are the two forms of the same Ātman. The same Ātman is three-footed under one condition and single-footed under another condition. Ātman is indivisible and remains undivided by the two conditions.

GAUḌAPĀDA'S VIEW OF RECONCILIATION

The earliest attempt at the reconciliation of the conflicting descriptions of Ātman is found in the Kārikās of Gauḍapāda. Negatively, the Upaniṣad denies the world by saying that it is (i) neither known by Ātman (*na prajñam*)[4] nor derived from Ātman (*prapañcopaśamam*).[5] In this way the reality of the world is completely denied. Positively, the Upaniṣad speaks about two things — (i) Ātman's internal (*antaḥ-prajñaḥ*) (mantra 4) and external (*bahiṣ-prajñaḥ*) (mantra 3) cognitions of the world; (ii) creation of the world from Ātman (*yoniḥ sarvasya*).[6] In this way the reality of the world is clearly asserted. However, according to Gauḍapāda, this assertion does not contradict the previous view that the world has no reality whatsoever. He suggests that all positive descriptions are to be considered as those of Ātman under self-delusion (*saṃmohitaḥ svayam*),[7] Ātman overcome by his own delusion (*svamāyayā*).[8] Therefore the world created from Ātman and cognised by Ātman is illusory and not real. As long as the positive descriptions deal with illusory creations and illusory cognitions of Ātman, they do not speak about the real world. For in reality the self-deluded Ātman neither creates nor cognises the world. In this manner the negative and the positive descriptions of Ātman give up their mutual opposition and discuss the same point. Their mutual opposition is more a fiction of the unthinking mind than a fact ascertainable by rational enquiry. According to Gauḍapāda, the descriptions, whether negative or positive, have one thing to teach and the teaching is that the world is unreal or illusory (*abhūtam*).

A recapitulation of Gauḍapāda's discussion is helpful. He has formulated his view of reconciliation particularly from two texts — *prapañcopaśamam* (the world does not preexist in Ātman);[9] *yoniḥ sarvasya* (the world preexists in Ātman i.e. Prājñātman).[10] As it stands the second text does not agree with the first text. Gauḍapāda removes the contradiction by pointing out that it speaks about Ātman under self-delusion. Since it speaks about the self-deluded Ātman, its intention is to say that in reality the world does not preexist in Him. In this way the two texts get reconciled.

A close examination of his interpretations discloses that Gauḍapāda faces many difficulties. First, he takes *prapañca-upaśamam* to be a negative text. It is possible for the text to give a positive meaning also — the world is stilled in Ātman i.e. the world preexists in the eternal stillness of Ātman. If we insist on this positive sense, it does not conflict with the other text which also says that the world preexists in Ātman. If reconciliation of the texts is the sole aim, then it is easily achieved without the painful labour of straining the inconvenient text. If the world preexists at two levels, then it is not clear how it can arise from two different sources. This is how the world arises — while Prājñātman arises from the pure Ātman, the world arises from Prājñātman. This is the reason why the world is said to preexist at two levels — the pure Ātman and Prājñātman. Second, his ingenious reading of the second text takes away its original sense and puts into it another sense which was not there. He has thus forced a positive text to give a negative sense not at all intended by it. This is violence and, therefore, impermissible. Third, if Ātman is the source of the world through self-delusion, it means that though the world is nonexistent in Him (*abhūtam*), it is created from Him through his delusion. This sense cannot be put into the word *yoni* which generally means a cause where an effect preexists in an unmanifest state. Therefore to say that *yoni* is a cause of a nonexistent effect is to speak non-sense. Fourth, the view of illusory creation is nowhere set forth in the Upaniṣads. Therefore it is denounced as un-Vedic or opposed to the Veda (*avaidika*) by the Padmapurāṇa.[11]

Another account of Gauḍapāda's view is possible. The positive descriptions of Ātman are not essential but provisional, not real but false attributions. They are given with a view to be rejected subsequently (*adhyāropāpavāda*).[12] In this way they are not opposed to the negative ones; rather they culminate in the latter. Even this version has its own difficulty. The positive descriptions are not intended to be false ascriptions by the original text. No evidence of any kind is discernible in the text in support of such ascriptions, as claimed by the above view.

From the above discussion it is evident that Gauḍapāda's theory of illusory creation or false ascription is untenable. And this makes his reconciliation of the conflicting texts a futile attempt.

A TEXT-BASED VIEW OF RECONCILIATION

Prima facie the negative and the positive descriptions of Ātman are mutually exclusive. A right understanding of them shows clearly that they permit each other and uphold a harmonious and synthetic view of Ātman.

The descriptions of the single-footed Ātman are negative — not conscious of the internal, not conscious of the external, etc. But they are not intended to say that the world thus denied is unreal. On the contrary, they deny limitation by the world. If by the negative the absoluteness of Ātman is asserted, the assertion supposes that the world is a limited but a real phenomenon or expression of the absolute Ātman.

Viewed in this light, the descriptions of the three-footed Ātman deal with the modifications of the single-footed Ātman. First, He modifies himself as Prājñātman, the cogniser of the mass of original forms of the world. Second, He further modifies himself as Taijasātman, the cogniser of the subtle forms of the internal world. Third, He finally modifies himself as Viśvātman, the cogniser of the gross forms of the external world. In this way the single-footed Ātman undergoes three successive transformations and becomes the world.

There is an important textual evidence in the Upaniṣad to prove the above assertion that the world is created through the threefold transformation of the single-footed Ātman. One of the epithets of Prājñātman is *ekībhūtaḥ.*[13] It occurs in an important place in the Upaniṣad. On one side, it is preceded by the descriptions of Viśva-Taijasa-Ātman; on the other side, it is succeeded by the further descriptions of Prājñātman[14] and the negative descriptions of the single-footed Ātman.[15] Thus it looks both forward and backward. If we bear in mind this key position of the epithet, we may not fail to note that it gives two meanings. In relation to the mantras 3 and 4 it means that Taijasa-Viśva-Ātman preexisted in Prājñātman; in relation to the mantra 7 it means that Prājñātman himself preexisted in the single-footed Ātman. The idea of pre-existence of the effect in the cause is generally conveyed by the idea of oneness (*ekatva*) of the effect with the cause. This is the significance of *ekībhūtaḥ*. Literal meanings of the epithet will be helpful to easily grasp its significance — (i) he (Prājñātman) who held Taijasa-Viśva-Ātman in a state of oneness with him; (ii) he (Prājñātman) who was in a state of oneness with Ātman. From these it is clear that the world arises from two causes, Ātman and Prājñātman. We have come to the same conclusion in an earlier discussion held from another point of view. The two conclusions are parellel to each other and, therefore, one confirms the truth of the other through their parallelism arising from internal coherence.

From the epithet *ekībhūtaḥ* we also note two other things. (i) Prājñātman had preexisted in the single-footed Ātman and comes into actual existence through transformation from the latter. (ii) Likewise, Taijasa-Viśva-Ātman had preexisted in Prājñātman and comes into actual existence through transformation from the latter. All preexistent effect comes into actual existence through transformation of the original cause. This is inevitable. Thus it must be admitted that the Māṇḍūkya subscribes definitely to the theory of creation by transformation (*pariṇāmavāda*). In the face of this unassailable evidence Gauḍapāda's theory of creation by Illusion (*māyāvāda*) cannot be attributed to the Māṇḍūkya Upaniṣad by any means, even by means of *adhyāropa-apavāda.*

Having placed the negative and positive descriptions of Ātman in the right perspective, we shall now proceed to demonstrate how they give a unified view of Ātman. He has two inseparable aspects — essential and phenomenal. In his essential aspect He is *niṣprapañca*, for He exceeds the world characterised by limitations. This is the theme of the negative descriptions. In his phenomenal aspect He is *saprapañca*, for He has become the world and assumed all its limitations. The world is real, because it is a manifestation of the very essence of Ātman (*sarvam-ātmaivābhūt*).[16] This is the theme of the positive descriptions. Collectively, the negative and the positive descriptions set forth the complete view of Ātman. One without the other makes the description one-sided and incomplete. This is why Ātman is carefully defined as four-footed by the Māṇḍūkya Upaniṣad. The reconciliation put forward here is offered by the Upaniṣad itself, for it is derived from its own words.

CREATION AND TRANSFORMATION

In the course of our discussion we have pointed out that the Māṇḍūkya subscribes to the theory of creation by transformation. We have reconciled the conflicting texts with the help of this theory. We have established the theory on textual evidence. But it must be established on rational grounds too, otherwise it will be left without a sound basis.

Gauḍapāda is opposed to the theory of transformation. Because the theory contradicts the teaching of the Upaniṣads which repeatedly proclaim Ātman to be immortal (*amṛtaḥ*).[17] As this nature of Ātman is immutable (*na prakṛteranyathābhāvaḥ*),[18] He is never born as the world. Therefore creation by transformation of the immutable Ātman is impossible. If this is the case, how do we understand the presence of so many creation-texts in the Upaniṣads? Gauḍapāda's answer is this — in these texts the view presented by them is that the world is created through Ātman's self-delusion (*svamāyayā*). However, such a view of Ātman is nowhere presented by the Upaniṣads. The word Māyā in the Śvetāśvatara Upaniṣad is used in the sense of Prakṛti, the material cause of the world[19] where all forms really exist in an unmanifest state. As the material cause of the world, Māyā is not a source of illusions but a mother of real creations. If Ātman creates through Māyā i.e. through Prakṛti, then the creation will be through transformation and not through illusion. Hence Gauḍapāda's answer is contrary to the teaching of the Upaniṣad.

A careful study of the Upaniṣads shows that Ātman is absolutely free — He is not only free from limitations but also capable of exceeding this freedom and creating the world from himself. In his absolute freedom He exceeds his immutability and creates the world through self-transformation. Thus immutability and transformation can be attributed to Ātman simultaneously without any difficulty. This is best illustrated by the Muṇḍaka text *akṣarāt sambhavati iha viśvam.*[20] A real world is produced from Ātman without prejudice to his immutability. Gauḍapāda sees Ātman's freedom but not His absolute freedom. This is why Gauḍapāda is unable to understand that for Ātman both immutability and transformation are possible simultaneously. The view presented here may look illogical. But in reality this is the underlying logic of all Upaniṣads which declare the immutable Ātman to be the source of the real world.

Nature provides a suitable example through the clay. The pot is a transformation of the clay. But the clay in the pot is unaffected by the transformation. For the clay transformation and freedom from transformation are simultaneously possible. In proof of transformation the clay always abides in the pot; in proof of freedom from transformation the clay always abides in its own clay-nature. There is no mutual opposition between the clay and the pot. However, Advaitins argue that the immutability of the clay reduces the pot to a mere illusion because the pot comes into existence through the transformation of the clay. Their argument is tenable only when the clay and the pot are opposed to each other. But, as we have already said, such an opposition is not in evidence at all. Hence their argument is untenable. If a clod of clay can perform the miracle of combining immutability with transformation, why can the absolutely free Ātman not accomplish the same miracle in the creation of the world?

In support of their view Advaitins quote a text from the Chāndogya Upaniṣad — *vācārambhaṇaṃ vikāro nāmadheyaṃ mṛttiketyeva satyam* (all change is unreal while the clay alone is real).[21] Precisely stated, the text is construed as saying that while the clay is real, all things made of clay are unreal (*anṛta*). But there is a more acceptable reading of the text. By the clay (*mṛtpiṇḍena*) all things made of clay (*sarvammṛnmayam*) become known. This is possible only when there is no confusion between the word clay and the clay. For confusion can modify the word and produce out of it an illusory clay. But in reality the clay does not arise from the word clay. Therefore this is what the text says. In the confused state of mind an illusory clay is begun by the word clay (*vācārambhaṇaṃ vikāraḥ*). But the fact is that the illusory clay is but the name clay (*nāmadheyaṃ*) and not the clay. In other words, while the word clay is a name, the clay is declared to be a reality (*mṛttiketyeva satyam*). This removes the confusion between the two — the word and the clay. Thus understood, the text ceases to support the Advaitins.

Now that the theory of transformation is established on the basis of both scripture and logic our view of reconciliation of the conflicting texts has a greater claim to validity and trustworthiness.

NOTES

1. Māṇḍūkya Upaniṣad (hereafter Mā. Up.), Mantra 2.
2. Ibid., Mantras 3,4,5,6.
3. Ibid., Mantra 7.
4. Ibid.
5. Ibid.
6. Ibid., Mantras 4,3.
7. Gauḍapāda Kārikā (hereafter GK), 2-19.
8. Ibid.
9. Mā. Up., Mantra 7.
10. Ibid., Mantra 6.
11. Padmapurāṇa, Ch. 263.
12. GK, 3-26.
13. Mā. Up., Mantra 5.
14. Ibid., Mantras 3,4.
15. Ibid., Mantras 6,7.
16. Bṛhadāraṇyaka Upaniṣad, 2-4-14.
17. GK, 3-20.
18. Ibid., 3-21.
19. Śvetāśvatara Upaniṣad, 4-10.
20. Muṇḍaka Upaniṣad, 1-1-7.
21. Chāndogya Upaniṣad, 6-1-4.

15

Gauḍapāda's Kārikā: Two Aspects

The Māṇḍūkya Kārikā is an expository work on the Māṇḍūkya Upaniṣad, a work attributed to Gauḍapāda who is considered to have lived about a hundred years before the advent of Śaṅkara. He is said to be the teacher of Śaṅkara's teacher Govindabhagavatpāda. Besides a commentary on the Māṇḍūkya Upaniṣad, Śaṅkara has also written a commentary on Gauḍapāda's Kārikā which consists of 215 verses.

The Māṇḍūkya Upaniṣad is acclaimed as "*sarva-vedānta-sāriṣṭha*" (the essence of the entire Vedānta). It is one of the twelve authoritative Upaniṣads, containing only twelve mantras. Traditional Advaita teaches that Brahman is real and the world is illusory (*brahmasatyam jaganmithyā*). Gauḍapāda's aim in writing the Kārikā is to win scriptural support for this teaching of Advaita.

THE REALITY OF ĀTMAN

Advaitins point out that there are important clues in the Upaniṣads which Gauḍapāda utilises in order to interpret the Māṇḍūkya passages. They are: description of Ātman through affirmations[1] and negations,[2] condemnation of duality[3] and laudation of non-duality,[4] and *neti neti* statements about Ātman.[5] Their aim is to stress that Gauḍapāda interprets the Māṇḍūkya in the light of the very method used in other Upaniṣads.

(i) Ātman is taught in the Upaniṣads through affirmative and negative descriptions. Affirmative statements connect Ātman with the world, while negative statements declare Ātman to be not connected with the world. Thus Ātman is said to be both connected (*saprapañca*) and not connected with the world (*niṣprapañca*). This is the significance of the two descriptions.

(ii) If Ātman is connected with the world, the seeker of Ātman cannot break the connection with the world and its evils. Therefore duality is condemned. On the other hand, Ātman not connected with the world brings to the knower of Ātman complete freedom from the world and its evils. Hence non-duality is extolled. From the condemnation and praise we must note that the relevant passages have to be interpreted in two different ways — the affirmative in their secondary sense and the negative in their primary sense. This makes the first less important than the second.

(iii) The true import of *neti netyātmā* is that Ātman cannot be grasped except through negations (*apavāda*) which are made possible through earlier superimpositions (*adhyāropa*). In other words, passages connecting Ātman with the world superimpose the world on Ātman and passages denying connection of Ātman with the world reject the superimposed world and reveal Ātman. Here the affirmative passages are not considered to be equal in status to the negative ones. For they speak about Ātmān's connection with a world which is condemned by the Upaniṣads. In view of this position they are interpreted in their secondary sense unlike the negative passages which are interpreted in their primary sense. This makes the second more important than the first.

We shall now explain how Gauḍapāda uses these clues and interprets the Māṇḍūkya Upaniṣad. Broadly speaking, the passages of the Upaniṣad may be brought under two divisions: those speaking about Viśva, Taijasa and Prājña, and those speaking about Ātman. All that follow depend on this classification.

The passages of the first category are about the three conditions of the world — causal, subtle, and gross. Through the three, Ātman appears as Prājña, Taijasa and Viśva. Thus we may speak of three positive descriptions. Gauḍapāda takes them to be statements about the affirmative view of Ātman.

The passages of the second category declare that Ātman is unseen, ungraspable, uninferable, unthinkable, indescribable, non-dual, and a state of destruction of all extension in name and form (*prapañcopaśamam*).[6] Gauḍapāda takes these passages to be descriptions of the negative view of Ātman.

As sleep, dream, and waking are the delusions of Māyā and as Prājña, Taijasa and Viśva are bound by these delusions — the first by sleep, the second by dream, and the third by waking, Ātman's connection with the world is open to the evils of Māyā and hence deserves condemnation. On the other hand, Ātman not connected with the world is free of the evils and therefore extolled as the auspicious (*śivam*)[7] and declared as the object to be known (*vijñeyaḥ*)[8] by all seekers of wisdom.

In keeping with the formula of *neti netyātmā*[9] Gauḍapāda interprets the affirmative passages to be speaking about the superimposition of the world on Ātman and the negative ones to be speaking about the rejection of the superimposed world and causing revelation of Ātman through this method.

THE FALSITY OF THE WORLD

If, according to Gauḍapāda, the world is a superimposition on Ātman (*adhyāropa*), then it must be a false attribution. This gives rise to a question, do we find scriptural evidence for considering the world to be false *(vitathā)*?[10]

Gauḍapāda is at pains to find suitable evidence from the Upaniṣad. He invites our attention to the three states which qualify Ātman in the world — sleep, dream, and waking. Sleep qualifies Prājña (*suṣuptasthānaḥ*),[11] while dream and waking qualify respectively Taijasa(*svapnasthānaḥ*)[12] and Viśva (*jāgaritasthānaḥ*).[13] Gauḍapāda explains that while sleep is a condition of non-perception of the fact of Ātman, dream and waking are conditions of wrong perception of the same fact. Therefore from the erroneous perceptions of Prājña, Taijasa and Viśva arises the world — from the first the causal world, from the second the subtle world, and from the third the gross world. A world thus created through errors cannot but be false. This is how Gauḍapāda analyses the Upaniṣad and concludes that the world it speaks about is false.

Not satisfied with the scriptural argument, Gauḍapāda produces a logical argument also to prove that the world is false. This is an analogical argument. In dream we see things like the mountain and the elephant. Are they real? If they are, then these huge objects must be confined within the confined space of the body of the dreamer. As this is impossible, we are forced to conclude that the mountain and the elephant are not real but illusory objects.[14] We must note that dream-contents have two important characteristics. First, they are perceived; second, they are experienced in dream alone and not in other states. It takes a little reflection to see that waking has both these characteristics. In waking, all objects are invariably objects of perception. Besides this, they are experienced in waking alone. Analogically, therefore, the objects perceived in waking must be declared to be illusory like those perceived in dream.[15] Thus the world of waking, believed to be real by popular thinking, is dismissed as illusory by Gauḍapāda's reasoning.

Thus from Gauḍapāda's Kārikā we understand that the Māṇḍūkya stands for two important views. First, the world is a false creation superimposed on the non-dual Ātman. Second, the Ātman, which is otherwise ungrasped, becomes grasped through the removal of the superimposition. If they are the teaching of the Upaniṣad, there is hardly any difference between this and the teaching of traditional Advaita. This is precisely what the Kārikā is intended to prove.

REFUTATION OF GAUḌAPĀDA'S ARGUMENTS

(i) A survey of the Upaniṣads shows that Ātman is defined through affirmative and negative texts. If the Māṇḍūkya is interpreted in the light of the other Upaniṣads, it is a worthwhile attempt. But the result depends on how the two texts are actually used in arriving at a right definition of Ātman.

(ii) It is said that non-duality is praised (*praśasyate*)[16] and duality is condemned (*nindyate*).[17] But the fact is that praise and condemnation are based on the ideas of approval and disapproval attributed to scriptural authority. For example, the statement 'This Ātman is Brahman'[18] is intended to remove the false view that Ātman is not Brahman. It is far from stating that Ātman is in a commendable position. Likewise, the statement 'He who perceives as if the world of plurality exists by itself goes from death to death'[19] is intended to affirm that an ignorant individual is helplessly bound by mortality. It is far from saying that an ignorant individual passes from one undesirable state to another. To read these metaphysical statements as statements of approbation and disapprobation is to be unfaithful to their original sense. Even if we admit that these readings are permissible, it does not necessarily follow that the affirmative and negative texts are unequal in status and that the former, unlike the latter, are to be interpreted in their secondary sense.[20] Apart from this, such readings go against the view that all scriptural statements are equally important and equally forceful. For they are *apauruṣeya* in nature. The above distinction between the two texts is invented only to explain away the inconvenient one. Therefore Gauḍapāda's method of interpretation is not supported by the authority of scripture i.e. by the authority of Upaniṣads.

(iii) If we accept that *neti netyātmā* means revelation of Ātman through denial of superimposition, this implies that we accept the classification of laudatory and condemnatory statements, as also the distinction of primary and secondary texts, in scripture. As we have already observed, these two — the classification and the distinction — do not exist in the Upaniṣads. If this is so, *neti netyātmā* is to be interpreted in accordance with the view that the negative and the affirmative texts are complementary and define Ātman both negatively and affirmatively.

(iv) Ātman is described in affirmative and negative terms. He is affirmatively described, because he is connected with the world i.e. with Prājña, Taijasa, and Viśva; he is negatively described, because he is not connected with Prājña or Taijasa or Viśva i.e. not connected with the three forms of the world. Thus Ātman is both cosmic (*saprapañca*) and acosmic (*niṣprapañca*). This is conveyed through a short phrase Ātmā Catuṣpāt[21] (Ātman is four-footed). There is actually no opposition between the two — the cosmic (the three-footed) and the acosmic (the single-footed), the world and Ātman. For Ātman does not deny the world except limitation by the world. From this it is clear that Ātman is grasped not by rejecting the world but by rejecting all limitation caused by the world. This is the true significance of *neti netyātmā* where the negative particle *na* is used to convey the idea of limited negation and not absolute negation. Gauḍapāda's mistake is that he has taken the negative particle in the sense of absolute negation.

(v) Gauḍapāda maintains that Prājña, Taijasa and Viśva are bound respectively by sleep, dream and waking. As the three states are equated with erroneous perceptions, the world created under their influence is not real but illusory. But the questions are whether Prājña and the rest are bound and, if so, whether they are characterised by erroneous perceptions. If we closely read the original text, we find that they are not so described. First, Prājña is known by the title *sarveśvaraḥ*.[22] It means that he is absolutely free and not subject to any limitation. If he is free, then Taijasa and Viśva also must be free, for they are verily his own manifestations. Second, he is also known by another title *sarvajñaḥ*.[23] It means that nothing is hidden from him and therefore his perceptions cannot be erroneous. The same may be said about Taijasa and Viśva also, for they develop only the original perception of Prājña. From this it must be concluded that the world created by Prājña and the rest is not illusory but real.

Apart from this, nowhere in the Upaniṣads the world is said to be illusory either indirectly or directly. (a) In none of the Upaniṣads world-creation is illustrated through examples drawn from delusive experiences. (b) The examples given by them like spider etc. suggest only real creation (*sṛṣṭi*).[24] As a result, even the general trend of the Upaniṣads does not support Gauḍapāda's view of the world.

(vi) Let us now turn to Gauḍapāda's logical proof of the falsity of the world. There are two steps in the proof. First, Gauḍapāda tries to prove the illusory character of dream-contents on the ground that objects like mountain and elephant cannot be "confined within the confined space of the body of the dreamer". Here he relies on the evidence of waking state which alone shows that the objects are huge and cannot be located within the body of the dreamer. So the dream-contents are measured by the perceptions of the waking state and declared to be illusory by reference to that measure. We must admit that a measure of this type measures nothing. For dream-contents are like the objects of the waking state and cannot be measured by an external standard. To say that dream-contents are illusory because they do not conform to the measure of waking state is to prove nothing. From such a proof no further argument is possible.

Second, Gauḍapāda extends this proof to waking and says that like the dream-contents, the contents of waking state are illusory. We have already said that no extension is possible from dream, for dream has not been proved illusory. For the sake of argument we may grant that the illusoriness of dream has been proved. Now the illusoriness can be extended to waking only when waking has not yet been subjected to any proof. But the point is that waking was already proved true when it was accepted as the measure for judging the nature of dream-contents. Again for the sake of argument we may grant that waking has not been proved true. If this is so, then waking will not be a measure for judging dream-contents. In the absence of a measure dream cannot be proved illusory. If it is not proved so, it cannot serve as an analogy for showing the illusoriness of the world of waking. Thus Gauḍapāda's whole argument has failed to prove that the world is illusory.

Scripturally or logically, Gauḍapāda has not succeeded in arguing that the world is false. In like manner, he has not succeeded in proving that the Upaniṣad teaches Ātman through superimposition (*adhyāropa*) and subsequent denial (*apavāda*).

We may state the central teaching of the Upaniṣad in these words. Ātman is integral. For he is both cosmic and acosmic. He is cosmic, because he resides in the world as Prājña, Taijasa, and Viśva; He is acosmic, because he exceeds Prājña, Taijasa, and Viśva. Though he exceeds the world, he is the source of it, because in him it is stilled (*prapañcopaśamam*) into a supreme state of non-extension. From this two things are known — (i) the world was originally extended in names and forms; and (ii) its names and forms were subsequently destroyed. This compels us to conclude that the world is real, because it exists at all points of time — before creation, after destruction, and between creation and destruction. Lastly, He is to be realised (*sa vijñeyaḥ*)[25] as the four-footed (*catuṣpāt*)[26] and not otherwise.

NOTES

1. Chāndogya Upaniṣad, 3-14-4.
2. Bṛhadāraṇyaka Upaniṣad (hereafter Bṛ Up.), 3-8-8.
3. Ibid., 4-4-19.
4. Ibid., 2-4-6.
5. Ibid., 2-3-6.
6. Māṇḍūkya Upaniṣad (hereafter Mā. Up.), Mantra 7.
7. Ibid.
8. Ibid.
9. Bṛ Up., 2-3-6.

10. Gauḍapāda Kārikā (hereafter GK), 2-3.
11. Mā. Up., Mantra 5.
12. Ibid., Mantra 4.
13. Ibid., Mantra 3.
14. GK, 2-1.
15. Ibid., 2-5
16. Ibid., 3-13.
17. Ibid.
18. Mā. Up., Mantra 2.
19. Kaṭha Upaniṣad, 2-1-10.
20. GK, 3-14.
21. Mā. Up., Mantra 2.
22. Ibid., Mantra 6.
23. Ibid.
24. Muṇḍaka Upaniṣad, 1-1-7.
25. Mā. Up., Mantra 7.
26. Ibid., Mantra 2.

16

Catuṣpādātma-Siddhi

THE STATUS OF THE UPANIṢAD

The Māṇḍūkya is certainly one of the twelve authoritative Upaniṣads. But some hold that this Upaniṣad has a doubtful status in view of the fact that none of the *viṣayavākyas* in the Brahmasūtras, according to the commentators, can be traced to it. However, we cannot say with any degree of certainty that the authoritative Upaniṣads have been selected on the above basis. Also, it is difficult to say exactly when the authoritative Upaniṣads were first identified, before or after the composition of the Brahmasūtras. If it is the case that they were identified even before the composition of the *sūtras,* then the *sūtras* cannot be the basis for the assertion that the Māṇḍūkya has a doubtful status.

Assuming for the sake of argument that the identification was made after the composition of the *sūtras*, we may easily prove that one of their *viṣayavākyas* is from the Māṇḍūkya. The *sūtra, buddhyarthaḥ pādavat*[1] speaks of Brahman having feet. Since the idea of foot is generally applied to Brahman in the Upaniṣads, it will be quite appropriate to take the above *sūtra* to refer to all the Upaniṣads where the idea is mentioned. And the Māṇḍūkya is one of them. It speaks of *so'yam ātmā catuṣpāt.*[2] If the commentators do not take the above *sūtra* to refer to the Māṇḍūkya, it does not prove that the *sūtrakāra* has excluded the Upaniṣad from the scope of the *sūtra*. The help given by a commentator of the *sūtra* is indeed useful but not always indispensable. In the present case the commentators have excluded the Māṇḍūkya from the purview of the *sūtra* 3-2-33. But this does not necessarily deter us from considering that one of the *viṣayavākyas* of this *sūtra* has come from the Māṇḍūkya.

One thing is certain. If we go by the criterion of the homogeneity of substance, the Māṇḍūkya's affinity to the other

Upaniṣads is quite unmistakable. As will be shown later, the main idea of the Māṇḍūkya is found in the Upaniṣads like the Bṛhadāraṇyaka and Īśa (vide section 6). From this vital evidence we may conclude with a fair degree of certainty that the Māṇḍūkya is one of the twelve authoritative Upaniṣads. And the doubt about its status as an authoritative Upaniṣad is due to extraneous considerations and therefore baseless.

THE TRUE IMPORT OF THE UPANIṢAD

Of the twelve Upaniṣads the shortest is the Māṇḍūkya consisting of just twelve mantras. One of the later Upaniṣads, the Muktikā Upaniṣad (1-27), eulogizes the former thus: "By itself the Māṇḍūkya is sufficient to lead one to liberation, *māṇḍūkyam ekam evālam mumukṣūṇāṃ vimuktaye*." The earliest known commentary on the Māṇḍūkya is by the celebrated Advaitin Gauḍapādācārya. His commentary known as the Māṇḍūkya Kārikā became so famous that the Upaniṣad was rarely reproduced as a separate text. It always appeared along with the Kārikā. As a result, the mantras and the Kārikās were mixed up in such a way that some of the Kārikās came to be added to the Upaniṣad as if they were parts of the original text. This is what one witnesses in a version of the Māṇḍūkya provided by Madhvācārya who belongs to the thirteenth century (C.E).

According to Gauḍapāda, the true import of the Māṇḍūkya is in its declaration that since the world is a superimposition on Ātman, Ātman alone is the object to be known by rejecting the world as an imaginary creation (*sa ātmā sa vijñeyaḥ*). His Kārikā was designed to bring out this import from the Māṇḍūkya . But if one reads the Upaniṣad independently and refuses to be influenced by the Kārikā and the support extended to it by scholars till today, one finds no evidence at all in the Māṇḍūkya Upaniṣad to say that Ātman is to be realised by rejecting the world to be imaginary.

THE STRUCTURE OF THE UPANIṢAD

The whole Upaniṣad falls naturally into three successive divisions. In the first the word OM is said to be extended in all that exists — in the threefold becoming in Time and in that which is beyond the bounds of Time. Having shown that all this is fourfold, it concludes that since all this is Brahman and the Brahman is this Ātman, the Ātman is fourfold (*catuṣpāt*).[3]

In the second is given a brief description of the four quarters of Ātman — Viśva, Taijasa, Prājña and Caturtha. While the first three represent the world in its gross, subtle and causal conditions, the last one not only exceeds the world but exits as the supreme source of the same world. This Ātman is declared to be the object of knowledge (*sa ātmā sa vijñeyaḥ*).[4]

In the third the four quarters of Ātman are identified with the four parts of the word OM — the three letters A U M and the letter less or silent OM into which they resolve and out of which they evolve. From this fourfold identification arise two suggestions, one about Ātman and another about the worshipper of Ātman, the reality and the individual.

The first suggestion is left undeveloped in the Upaniṣad, for it is quite obvious from the context. According to it, though the eternal Ātman is quite distinct from the triple form of Viśva, Taijasa and Prājña, It is not divorced from the triple form but integrated with it, even as the letterless OM is perfectly integrated with the letters AUM. The second suggestion is fully developed in the concluding mantras, from 9 to 12. According to it, the worshipper of Ātman gets four results, depending on how Ātman is worshipped. He gets the highest result when Ātman is worshipped as the letterless OM. The resulting knowledge is total, for it is of the eternal Ātman as well as the Ātman manifest in triple form — Viśva, Taijasa and Prājña (*saṃviśatyātmanā ātmānaṃ*).[5] In short, it is of the fourfold Ātman.

GAUḌAPĀDA'S KĀRIKĀ

Gauḍapāda is the teacher of Śaṅkara's teacher Govindapāda. His Kārikā is acclaimed as an authentic exposition on the Māṇḍūkya Upaniṣad. Its aim is to bring out the definite conclusion of Vedānta as embodied in the original text (*vedāntaniścayaḥ*).[6]

The Māṇḍūkya speaks of the fourfold Ātman — Viśva, Taijasa, Prājña and the divine Ātman. If we follow the order of ideas in the Upaniṣad, it suggests two things: (i) it regards the first three as the triple term through which the world comes into existence from Ātman — while Prājña is the source of the world (*yoniḥ sarvasya*)[7] or the world in its unmanifest condition, Taijasa and Viśva represent respectively the two conditions of the manifest world, subtle and gross; (ii) through a total negation of the world (*prapañcopaśamaṃ*)[8] it arrives at its goal of realisation, namely, Ātman (*sa ātmā*).[9] From these two suggestions Gauḍapāda develops his arguments to demonstrate how the world is superimposed on Ātman as well as how the realisation of Ātman is possible when the superimposition is rejected.

(i) We say that there is no object in the world which does not exist in the middle even though it is without existence in the beginning and the end. Gauḍapāda's contention is that an object having no existence in the beginning and the end cannot have existence even in the middle (*nāstivartamāne api*).[10] For a nonexisting object cannot assume existence under any circumstance (*asatojanma . . . naiva yujyate*).[11] If it does, its assumption can only be through imagination (*kalpanā*)[12] and not otherwise. And the two instruments through which objects are imagined are inner Mind and outer Mind represented respectively by Taijasa and Viśva.

If the objects are imagined through Mind, then who uses the Mind and imagines them (*ko vai teṣāṃ vikalpakaḥ*)?[13] It is none else than the divine Ātman (*ātmā devaḥ*).[14] Though he is not subjected to any action (*avyavahāryam*),[15] he gets into self-delusion (*saṃmohitaḥ svayam*)[16] and regards himself as the all-source and the lord who creates all (*sarveśvaraḥ... yoniḥ sarvasya*).[17] The objects He creates are from himself [18] and the instruments he uses are from his Māyā (*svamāyā*).[19] The divine Ātman who creates the world through Māyā is known as Prājña.

In Gauḍapāda's view Prājña, Taijasa and Viśva are three forms of Māyā through which the imaginary world is brought into existence. While Māyā in the form of Prājña operates as the power of non-perception of the fact (*tattvam ajānataḥ*),[20] namely, the fact that Prājña in his true nature is none other than the divine Ātman, in the form of Taijasa as well as Viśva it operates as the power of false perception of the same fact (*anyathāgṛhṇataḥ*),[21] the power which wrongly sees the divine Ātman to be the manifold world. It may be seen that Gauḍapāda's view is the result of two factors, *nyāya* (logic) and *śruti* (scripture). Logically, objects are imaginary and these objects point to the existence of the relevant instruments and the cogniser behind the instruments; scripturally, the words *suṣupti* and *svapna* suggest that the world is the result of the joint-operation of two errors, non-perception and false perception.[22]

(ii) There are two essential attributes by which the divine Ātman is distinguished from the world, birthlessness (*ajaḥ*) and immortality (*amṛtaḥ*). He is inconceivable without them. Hence His nature (*prakṛtiḥ*)[23] consists in being birthless and immortal. Neither birth nor mortality can be affirmed of Him under any circumstance, because His nature is not subject to transmutation (*na anyathābhāvaḥ*).[24] Given His nature which is immutable, it is absolutely impossible for the world to appear from Him, for all beings in the world are characterised by birth and mortality. Even through Māyā the world cannot appear, for Māyā does not exist in Him (*sa ca māyā na vidyate*).[25] The divine Ātman is thus seen in the fourth quarter (*caturtha*) by sages versed in the Vedas (*munibhirvedapāragaiḥ*).[26]

Owing to lack of discrimination the unreal is seen as though real (*viparyāsāt*).[27] The world manifested through Prājña, Taijasa and Viśva is merely a creation of Māyā (*māyāmātramidaṃ*)[28] but it is viewed as though real (*sṛṣṭiriti*).[29] On account of this there arise in the world association with objects (*saṃkrāntam*), attachment (*saṅgam*), fear (*bhayam*) and misery (*duḥkham*). When the discrimination develops, the world is seen to be nothing but the divine Ātman imagined variously by Māyā (*ātmā vikalpitaḥ*).[30] As a result, the world imagined by Māyā ceases (*prapañcopaśamaṃ*),[31] and with the cessation of the world all association with objects, all attachment, all fear and misery cease (*nāsti*).[32] To know the divine Ātman to be unassociated with Māyā and the world (*aspṛṣṭaḥ*) and become united with the Ātman thus known is *asparśayogaḥ*.[33] This, according to Gauḍapāda, is the teaching of the Māṇḍūkya.

Here too, as in section (i), Gauḍapāda's conclusion is due to two factors, *nyāya* (logic) and *śruti* (scripture). Logically, the world cannot arise from the divine Ātman who is by nature birthless and immortal; hence it must be a superimposition. Scripturally, the word *prapañcopaśamam* affirms that in Him there is an absolute cessation of this world, of all things associated with Prājña, Taijasa and Viśva.

AN ANALYSIS OF GAUḌAPĀDA'S VIEW

(i) The first foundation of Gauḍapāda's Kārikā is logic, a logical analysis of the world. According to him, the analysis shows that the world is imaginary and does not have real existence.

All objects have a beginning and an end. In both they have no existence. But between the two stages they have existence. Here Gauḍapāda's point is that since they do not exist in the two stages, they cannot exist even in the middle. Hence he concludes that their existence in the middle must be imaginary and not real.

A careful scrutiny of Gauḍapāda's argument shows that his conclusion is not inevitable. His argument assumes that an object must be identical in all the three stages — beginning, middle and end. On this assumption he contends that an object which does not exist in the beginning and the end must be nonexistent even in the middle. It is quite possible to draw an opposite conclusion on the basis of the same assumption. If an object exists in the middle, it must necessarily exist in the beginning as well as the end. For an object possessing existence cannot be nonexistent under any circumstance. Its nonexistence in other conditions is a mere imagination. The nonexistence can only be an unmanifest existence of the object.

If the world is real and not imaginary, then Gauḍapāda's theory of imaginary creation becomes unjustifiable. Instead a theory of creation as a process of self-manifestation of the divine Ātman will be in order. The world implies the existence of Prājña, Taijasa and Viśva as the necessary terms of manifestation of Ātman. There is certainly Māyā, but it is a power of manifestation, not a power of imagination or illusory creation. It is a means by which the truths of Ātman are developed and manifested in space and time. Māyā is as real and divine as Ātman but absolutely under the latter's control. Such a view of creation is consistent with the fact that the world is a real phenomenon.

Ātman is said to be of four parts (*catuṣpāt*). According to Gauḍapāda, the first three are the three forms of the Lord subject to the influence of the delusive Māyā and the last and fourth is the Lord himself who is absolutely free from Māyā and bears no relationship to the forms of Māyā. For in the fourth, Māyā does not exist at all. In other words, Gauḍapāda views the first three to be false and the fourth to be true. But if we take his definition of Māyā, it is difficult to maintain that the first three are the false creations of Māyā. His definition is very clear. He defines Māyā to be the Lord's own instrument and power of creation (*svamāyā*).[34] If the Lord is real, then his Māyā must be as real as himself.* His Māyā must bring out what really exists in his eternal self and cannot be a source of imaginary objects. The Lord cannot see delusions if Māyā is his own. What He sees must be as real as himself. As a result, the dichotomous division of the four parts of Ātman cannot be consistently maintained by Gauḍapāda. Nor is it possible for him to conclude that *asparśayoga* is the teaching of the Māṇḍūkya Upaniṣad.

Gauḍapāda is conscious of these difficulties and therefore points out that Māyā and its existence in the Lord are affirmed merely for the sake of teaching (*upadeśāt*).[35] Since the Lord is incomprehensible (*agrāhyabhāvam*)[36] to the ignorant who see modification and diversity here, the Lord is first imagined to be the cause of the world and have created all through his apparent modifications. Then the Lord's real existence is easily brought home through a denial of all imagined for the sake of instruction (*upadeśādayaṃ vādaḥ*).[37] Māyā is therefore a power of imagination which creates the world through imagination. It is not real like the Lord and to treat it as a reality is a serious mistake. In a word, the Lord alone exists and not Māyā (*māyā na vidyate*).[38]

However, Gauḍapāda's view of Māyā is not borne out by the Upaniṣads. In the Śvetāśvatara, for example, there is a clear reference to Māyā, and the Lord is called the Lord of Māyā (*māyī*).[39] Here the word Māyā is not used in the sense of a power of imagination. The Upaniṣad says that this world is loosed forth by the Lord of Māyā (*māyī sṛjate viśvam etad)*.[40] It is significant that it does not say that this world is imagined by Māyī. To loose forth is to release into manifestation all that preexists in the Lord. Creation is therefore considered to be an act of manifestation (*sṛṣṭi*) and not imagination (*kalpanā*). It follows from this that according to the Upaniṣad, Māyā is real. Apart from this, on

Gauḍapāda's own admission, there are texts in *śruti* which speak about creation as a real process (*bhūtato ... sṛjyamāne ... śrutiḥ*).[41] So, when God is said to be the Lord of Māyā, Māyā is intended to be a real power of God.

According to Gauḍapāda, the word *prapañcopaśamaṃ*[42] in the Māṇḍūkya contains a clear suggestion that Prājña, Taijasa and Viśva represent the world in its causal, subtle and gross forms and that Ātman in the fourth quarter is to be realised by rejecting the world in all its three forms (*upaśamam*). And that the world is fit to be rejected is further strengthened by the words *suṣupti* and *svapna* which represent the two erroneous perceptions by which Prājña and the rest create the imaginary world. If we accept the interpretation of these terms — *upaśamam*, *suṣupti* and *svapna*, then we shall be compelled to agree with Gauḍapāda that the goal of realisation is the exclusive Ātman of the fourth quarter (*sa ātmā sa vijñeyaḥ*).[43] But the Upaniṣad places before us a larger ideal than this — the goal of the fourfold Ātman (*catuṣpāt-ātman*). If this is the goal, then we cannot accept Gauḍapāda's interpretation of the above three terms.

(ii) Gauḍapāda's position is that mortals can arise only through Māyā because they cannot arise directly from the Lord who is by nature immortal (*svabhāvena amṛtaḥ*)[44] and whose nature is always unalterable (*na prakṛter anyathābhāvaḥ*).[45] It is perfectly in order that the Lord's own nature consists in being immortal but Gauḍapāda's understanding of his nature is certainly not in agreement with the teaching of the Upaniṣads.

The Māṇḍūkya has defined Ātman as four-footed (*catuṣpāt*).[46] The four parts, as we all know, fall into two major categories: (i) the manifold world brought about by the triple Ātman — Prājña, Taijasa and Viśva; (ii) the divine Ātman who is beyond the world. These two correspond to the twofold division mentioned differently in different contexts in the Upaniṣads — the one and the many, the unborn and the born, the imperishable and the perishable, the formless and the formed, the eternal and the transitory, the immortal and the mortal, etc. Thus viewed, the above definition (*catuṣpāt*) very clearly says that not only is Ātman one, unborn, imperishable, formless, eternal and immortal but the same Ātman is everything stated on the opposite side. This gives us a sufficient insight into the Upaniṣad's view of Ātman's *svabhāva* (own nature). Ātman's *svabhāva* is a harmony of opposites and the harmony depends on how they are viewed. For instance, we shall take the opposites immortality and mortality and see how they are harmonised. Ātman is immortal, but the negation implied in its *svabhāva* is not an absolute negation. As a result, what is denied is not mortality but Ātman's limitation by mortality. From this it becomes clear that immortality and mortality are viewed not as opposites but as contraries. The teaching of the Māṇḍūkya is therefore that Ātman does not deny the world but the erroneous view that It is bound by the world. This is the true significance of the definition that Ātman is *catuṣpāt*.

Gauḍapāda's mistake lies in taking Ātman's nature to be absolutely negative. Hence he concludes that the mortals can never originate from the Immortal. But in real fact this is not what the Upaniṣads say. The immortal Ātman exceeds all. So It is not only not bound by the mortals here but also, by this very freedom, capable of assuming birth as the mortals. Given the flexibility proper to Ātman's *svabhāva*, we understand the secret significance of *catuṣpāt-ātman*. The Māṇḍūkya's aim is to precisely teach that to understand Ātman's *svabhāva* as implying an absolute negation of all we find here is to miss the true sense of Vedānta.

INTERPRETATION OF THE TEXT

The Māṇḍūkya defines Ātman in two ways — as *caturtha* and as *catuṣpāt*. As *caturtha*, Ātman implies the existence of the Three that precede — Viśva, Taijasa and Prājña; as *catuṣpāt*, Ātman exists not only as the Fourth but also as the preceding Three. In either way the Upaniṣad reinforces the idea that Ātman should be viewed in an integral sense and not otherwise. By the first (*caturtha*) it is implied that Ātman is to be taken not in isolation but always in relation to the three that precede; likewise, by the second (*catuṣpāt*) it is suggested that all the four are to be regarded collectively. This is the dominant note of the Upaniṣad. A right interpretation of the Upaniṣad is not possible if we do not give full credit to this note and abide by it.

We shall begin with the fourth quarter of Ātman (mantra 7). The seventh mantra has two lines and both of them speak in similar terms. The first line contains a series of denials — not this, not that (*neti neti*). It denies all that are affirmed in the previous mantras — not inward knowledge (mantra 4), not outward knowledge (mantra 3), not knowledge which is both inward and outward (mantras 4 and 3), not knowledge of the mass of conceptive forms (mantra 5). And the first line concludes with a denial of denials (*na prajñam na aprajñam*). Though all knowledge is thus denied (*na prajñam),* the subject of these denials is not a nothingness without knowledge (*na aprajñam*).

From the expression *na aprajñam* arise three important suggestions. First, denials do not negate the world in any of the three conditions — Viśva or Taijasa or Prājña, except limitation by the world. Second, they imply not a nothingness but an all-exceeding Ātman beyond the three divisions of time (*trikāla-atītam*). Third, since they permit the world, the world must preexist in Ātman and appear out of it as its real manifestation. The next line of the seventh mantra bears testimony to the validity of the suggestions (*na aprajñam*).

We now see that the suggestions of *na aprajñam* are taken up and fully worked out in the second line of the seventh mantra. It begins with another series of denials — *adṛṣṭam* (not that which is seen by the eyes), *avyavahāryam* (not that which is subjected to action), *agrāhyam* (not that which is grasped by the organs of action), *alakṣanam* (not that which is possessed of a mark), *acintyam* (not that which is an object of the thinking mind), *avyapadeśyam* (not that which bears a name). If we put a qualified sense into all these denials in keeping with the suggestion of *na aprajñam*, they speak differently. They do not deny *dṛṣṭam* and others as real manifestations of the fourth Ātman but limitation by them. As a result, the ultimate origin of the world is the one Ātman of knowledge which contains all in their essence (*ekātma-pratyaya-sāraṃ*).[47] Or it is Ātman in which the world is stilled into non-manifestation *(prapañcopaśamaṃ).*[48] By holding the world in its essence or in its stilled form of non-manifestation Ātman does not fall from its natural state of tranquillity and blissfulness, or from its oneness. For whatever exists in Ātman is nothing but Ātman. Therefore it is eternally tranquil, blissful and non-dual (*śāntaṃ śivam advaitam*).

According to the ancient sages, Ātman is *bhūman*, because Ātman expresses itself infinitely in names, forms, and works and at the same time exceeds all its expressions as the immeasurable and indefinable infinite. It is to express this all-exceeding sense that Ātman is described in negative terms. Ātman is therefore not nothingness but a supremely positive state. That is the integral Ātman the ancients had known; that very Ātman should be known by us also (*sa ātmā sa vijñeyaḥ*).[49] Apart from this, there is another reason why the integral Ātman should be our object. Given the ideal of *catuṣpāt-ātman*[50] its realisation is possible only through the knowledge of the integral Ātman.

In the mantras 3, 4, 5 and 6 Viśva, Taijasa and Prājña are described. Evidently they are the three forms of the fourth Ātman through which the world has come into existence. The world has three levels of existence — external, internal and causal. Correspondingly, its objects appear in three ways. At the first the objects are gross and projected by the all-pervasive Mind of Viśva; at the second they are subtle and projected by the illumined Mind of Taijasa; at the third they are in their original conceptive forms and projected by the all-wise Intelligence of Prājña. Thus the world has appeared through the three forms and the three powers of the fourth Ātman.

Apart from the forms and powers of Ātman, the Māṇḍūkya also speaks of three conditions of waking, dream and sleep (mantras 3, 4 and 5) as those of its dwelling in each soul. Generally waking, dream and sleep are taken to be the states of erroneous perceptions: while Viśva and Taijasa are endued with false perceptions, Prājña is endued with non-perception. False perception consists in seeing the fact wrongly (*anyathāgṛhṇataḥ*),[51] whereas non-perception consists in not seeing the fact *(tattvam ajānataḥ)*.[52] Therefore all objects brought into being by Taijasa and Viśva are said to be imagined by them (*kalpitā*).[53] In other words, the world thus imagined is the result of two factors: not-knowing the original fact as it is and knowing the fact wrongly.

If we take a glance at the words *bāhya-prajñaḥ*, *antaḥ-prajñaḥ* and *prajñāna-ghanaḥ*,[54] they reveal that none of the three forms of Ātman is conditioned by erroneous perception. The words *prajña* and *prajñāna* always give the sense of true knowledge or wisdom. The third compound word means a wise-knower of the mass (*ghanaprajñānaḥ*). Since this is a mass of causal or conceptive forms, it is appropriate to take *prajñāna-ghanaḥ* to mean a wise-knower of the world of conceptive forms. Invariably the compound words affirm that the world is an object of a wise-knower, a knower whose perception is perfectly free from error. From this it follows that the world thus known by the triple Ātman characterised by wisdom cannot be imaginary. Rather it must be a product of real creation.

In keeping with this view of Viśva, Taijasa and Prājña we have to interpret the three compounds *jāgaritasthānaḥ*, *svapnasthānaḥ* and *suṣuptasthānaḥ*.[55] Literally, they mean: "one who dwells in the waking state", "one who dwells in the dream state" and "one who dwells in the sleep state". Gauḍapāda takes each compound in an extended sense: "one who is identified with the waking state and bound by the error of false perception proper to that state", "one who is identified with the dream state and bound by the error of false perception proper to that state" and "one who is identified with the sleep state and bound by the error of non-perception proper to that state". But the extension given by Gauḍapāda is wholly unjustifiable for two reasons: (i) to dwell in a given state is not necessarily to be identified with that state and conditioned by its inherent error; (ii) in their extended senses the compounds do not agree with the other compounds *bāhyaprajñaḥ*, *antaḥprajñaḥ* and *prajñānaghanaḥ* where the bearer of these epithets is said to be a wise-knower, one who knows without any error. Hence there is absolutely no reason to go beyond the literal sense of the compounds *jāgaritasthānaḥ*, etc. and extend their original significance.

However, we should not fail to note that these compounds affirm an important fact: the Ātman who manifests himself in the world is a dweller in all the three states of waking, dream and sleep of the soul. In the waking state He dwells as Viśva, in the dream state He dwells as Taijasa and in the sleep state He dwells as Prājña. In them the indwelling Ātman (*antaryāmī*)[56] represents the highest ideal to be realised and possessed by the living soul. Even if the soul is ignorant and bound, it removes its veil now and then in the brief moments of its upward growth and comes into contact with the Indweller in any of the states of waking, dream and sleep and this makes its eventual entry into Him possible.

Now we shall take a look at the world created by the triple form of Ātman — Prājña, Taijasa and Viśva. Ātman is none of these forms, for It exceeds all forms. None of the forms can measure Ātman, for Ātman surpasses all measures. At the same time Ātman is not bound by its freedom from limitation; It freely manifests itself in all names, forms and works. If Ātman negates all, the very same Ātman affirms itself as the supreme source from which all arise. The world arises from Ātman in three distinct stages: first, as a mass of conceptive forms; second, as subtle forms; and third, as gross forms. In relation to the conceptive forms Ātman is spoken of as Prājña; in relation to the subtle and gross forms the same Ātman is known as Taijsasa and Viśva. At any stage in the process of manifestation the formed Ātman is not deprived of the knowledge of the Ātman beyond manifestation. Hence the epithets such as *prajñānaghanaḥ*. There is no veil of ignorance between Ātman and the triple form it assumes. As a result, the formed Ātman is always a faultless enjoyer who incurs no bondage. As Prājña, the Ātman enjoys delight (*ānandabhuk*),[57] the delight of manifesting the mass of conceptive forms; as Taijasa, the Ātman enjoys the delight of manifesting subtle objects (*praviviktabhuk*);[58] as Viśva, the Ātman enjoys the delight of manifesting gross objects (*sthūlabhuk*).[59] Thus in all these three stages there is a progressive development of the original content of Ātman but not a development away from the knowledge of Ātman.

Of the three forms of Ātman, Prājña is most important. From the point of view of the world, Taijasa and Viśva have no existence apart from Prājña; from the point of view of Ātman, without Prājña the world will be without a cause which makes Its temporal manifestation possible. There are several epithets by which the Māṇḍūkya brings out Prājña's central importance. He is *ekībhūtaḥ*,[60] because he is born from the self-nature of the eternal One* i.e. he is born from Ātman. He is *ānandamayaḥ*,[61] because he is full of delight as Ātman is. He is *prajñānaghanaḥ*,[62] because he is a wise-knower of the mass of forms from which arise subtle and gross objects. He is *cetomukhaḥ*,[63] because by turning his face towards conscious Mind, which perceives subtle and gross objects, he brings both Taijasa and Viśva into existence.

From the point of view of the world, Prājña is the source of all (*yoniḥ sarvasya*).[64] From him all manifesting themselves in subtle and gross forms appear and into him all deprived of these two forms enter (*prabhavāpyayau hi bhūtānām*).[65] In other words, Prājña is the source of both Taijasa and Viśva. In the order of manifestation the two appear successively. But in the manifest world the three are inseparable parts of a harmonious whole. So the Māṇḍūkya uses three significant epithets to show that Prājña embraces both the subtle and gross worlds. He is *sarvajñaḥ*,[66] because he knows the subtle and gross worlds in all their aspects — their origin, development and manifestation. He is *sarveśvaraḥ*,[67] because he is independent of the worlds. By virtue of this independence, he is extended in these worlds. He is *antaryāmī*,[68] because he is seated in the worlds and controls them through his omnipotence. As a result, Prājña, Taijasa and Viśva become a triply manifest Ātman, or a single Ātman indivisibly triple in name, in form and in work. If the eternal Ātman and Prājña are indivisible by virtue of the latter being the becoming of the former, so too Prājña and Taijasa and Viśva are indivisible by the strength of the latter two being the becomings of the former.

If Prājña as the causal world was originally the eternal One, Taijasa and Viśva as the subtle and gross worlds were enveloped in Prājña. In other words, the world is basically a becoming (*bhūta*) of what it was originally in the eternal being of the One and therefore a real manifestation (*sṛṣṭi*). This is the significance of the epithet *ekībhūtaḥ*[69] (he is born from the self-nature of the eternal One). In the face of this description Gauḍapāda's interpretation that the world is unborn (*na jāyate*)[70] and therefore imagined (*vikalpitā*),[71] is wholly unjustifiable and contrary to the explicit view of the scripture.

Having described the nature of the fourfold Ātman the Māṇḍūkya proceeds to show Ātman's identity with OM. OM too has four parts — the letterless OM (*amātra*) and the three letters A U M (*mātra*).[72] The purpose is to reinforce the idea that the fourfold Ātman is harmonious and without any opposition, even though the Caturtha Ātman is described in negative terms as if It is opposed to the first three quarters. Already we have found that the apparent opposition is removed through the key expression *na aprajñam*. In view of the importance given to the principle of fourfold Ātman the Upaniṣad seeks to resolve the opposition once again in terms of the harmony between the *amātra* and the *mātra* aspects of OM. The letterless silence and the letters expressive of sound and movement appear to be exclusive and mutually destructive. But in practice the two aspects complement and permit each other. When OM is uttered, the letters leap out from the letterless OM and in the same breath they get back into the original undifferentiated source.

In the next four mantras — 9, 10, 11 and 12 — the Māṇḍūkya is concerned with the results obtained through four forms of worship. As the word OM is essentially meant for meditation, the above four mantras are dealt with from the point of view of knowing Ātman through appropriate forms of meditation on the word.

First we shall take the three forms of Ātman — Viśva, Taijasa and Prājña. Each is made an exclusive object of worship through meditation. Thus a constant and disciplined meditation on the letter A leads one to gain control over the gross things of the world. A similar practice in respect of the letters U and M helps one attain mastery over things belonging to the subtle and causal worlds.

When the seeker is identified with Viśva who is the dweller in waking and the master of the gross world, all his desires are fulfilled and he becomes foremost among men.[73] When he is identified with Taijasa who is the dweller in dream and the master of the subtle world, his faculties of perception expand beyond their normal boundaries, and he rises to a position of equal regard from all and begets children who become the knowers of the Vedas (*brahmavits*).[74] When he is identified with Prājña who is the dweller in sleep and the master of the causal world, he can measure events by his original deeds and absorb the events as the results of these deeds.[75] Thus from the worship of the three forms of Ātman as A U M result three distinct realisations and three forms of mastery over the world.

The next and last in the series is the worship of the eternal Ātman through the letterless OM (*amātra*). Now we have to digress a little and note what the Īśa and Bṛhadāraṇyaka Upaniṣads have to say on the subject of worshipping Ātman.

According to the Īśa Upaniṣad, there are three forms of worship: (i) to worship Ātman as having taken birth in the forms of the world (*sambhūti*);[76] (ii) to worship Ātman as unborn, as not having taken birth at all (*asambhūti*);[77] (iii) to worship Ātman as both (*ubhayaṃ saha*).[78] Of the three the last one alone gives the truest and largest result: freedom from death and attainment of immortality (*mṛtyuṃ tīrtvā . . . amṛtam aśnute*).[79]

The Bṛhadāraṇyaka speaks of two conditions of Ātman: one where Ātman is manifest in forms of work (*karmanāmānyeva*)[80] and another where all forms of work have become one with Ātman (*sarva ekaṃ bhavanti*).[81] The right worship results in knowing the former through the latter (*anena hy etat sarvaṃ veda*).[82] In the former condition Ātman is only fragmentarily revealed (*akṛtsnaḥ*).[83] Therefore a complete knowledge of Ātman is possible only when the latter Ātman is worshipped as the means for the former Ātman manifest as all.

If we read the mantras 9, 10, 11 and 12 of the Māṇḍūkya in the light of the above teachings of the Īśa and Bṛhadāraṇyaka Upaniṣads, two things emerge. First, Viśva and the rest cannot give the full knowledge of Ātman; second, the full knowledge can arise only when the three forms of Ātman are known through the eternal Ātman. And this alone bestows upon us the highest results — freedom from death (*mṛtyu*) and attainment of immortality (*amṛta*).

Viśva, Taijasa and Prājña are the becomings in time of the potentialities of the eternal Ātman beyond time (*trikālātīta*).[84] As the figures of Ātman, they express the powers of Ātman and not Ātman behind the powers. As a result, the Ātman revealed in the figures of Viśva and the rest is necessarily fragmentary (*akṛtsnaḥ).*[85] As long as the seeker is bound by death, trapped in the smallness of being (*alpam*), he is incapable of exceeding the world and knowing the eternal Ātman. But when he meditates on the letterless OM as Ātman (*omkāra ātmaiva*),[86] he gets the highest result. For he is released from death and knows himself to be verily that Ātman in which are founded all the powers that have expressed themselves in the world.

Now the full significance of this realisation is unfolded to the seeker. The eternal Ātman is absolutely not limited by the works of Viśva, Taijasa and Prājña (*avyavahārya*).[87] This, however, does not mean that Ātman is a pure negation, a void without contents. On the contrary, It is the supreme source of the powers which Viśva and the rest represent through their forms and works. This source is the ultimate origin of the world. In fact, the world exists there in the form of absolute stillness, even as the letters A U M exist in the letterless OM. Hence Ātman is described as He in whom the world is stilled (*prapañcopaśamaḥ*).[88] Though the world thus exists in the eternal Ātman, Ātman does not fall from its blissfulness or from its oneness. Whatever exists in Ātman is nothing but Ātman. There is nothing other than Ātman. Hence It is eternally blissful (*śiva*)[89] and non-dual (*advaita*).[90]

When the seeker becomes the eternal Ātman beyond the triple Ātman manifesting the world, he is qualified to know Ātman in its completeness (*catuṣpāt-ātman*).[91] With the eternal Ātman he now penetrates the triple Ātman (*ātmanā ātmānaṃ*)[92] and the penetration is so perfect (*saṃviśati*)[93] that he sees his soul extended in all the four quarters of Ātman harmoniously and integrally, even as Ātman is eternally extended in Brahman *(ayam ātmā brahma)*. This is the supreme result of worshipping the eternal Ātman as the letterless OM (*amātra*) from which arise the letters A U M.

NEGATION OF NEGATION: A BASIC FORMULA OF THE UPANIṢAD

The Upaniṣads abound in passages which speak about Brahman both affirmatively and negatively. Sometimes they describe Brahman in affirmative terms without resorting to negations. For instance, the Chāndogya says: "The earth is one part, the sky is one part, heaven is one part, and the ocean is one part. This indeed, dear son, is the four-footed Brahman".[94] Sometimes they use negations and not affirmations in describing Brahman. For example, the Bṛhadāraṇyaka speaks thus: "It is neither gross nor fine, neither short nor long, neither red colour nor oiliness, neither shadow nor darkness, neither air nor space. It is unattached. It is neither taste nor smell, neither eyes nor ears. It eats nothing and no one eats it."[95] From them we understand that there are two important facts about the Upaniṣads: (i) When they use affirmations or negations in an exclusive manner, they do so only for the sake of emphasis and not for the sake of limiting Brahman to a single definition; (ii) they do not see any contradiction between negations and affirmations because they see Brahman through both of them.

How do the Upaniṣads see Brahman through both negations and affirmations? Generally, negation is taken in its absolute sense. Thus, when Brahman is said to be formless and immortal, Brahman is understood to be devoid of the characteristics of form and mortal existence. As a result, Brahman cannot be described as having a form or as being a mortal. If we so describe Brahman, we fall into the error of self-contradiction. However, it is a fact that the Upaniṣads do not face such a difficulty. We shall find out how this is possible. If we carefully read the negative terms used in describing Brahman, we find that none of them is used in its absolute sense. We must realise that the purpose is not to deny anything affirmed of Brahman but something incidental to the affirmation. Speaking in affirmative terms we may say that Brahman is a Kṣatriya. Now it is incidental to think that Brahman is nothing more than a Kṣatriya. To correct this error we have to add that Brahman is not limited by this affirmation. And this is done through a negation that Brahman is a Kṣatriya. This is the significance of all negative descriptions of Brahman. Therefore they do not conflict with the affirmative descriptions given of the same Brahman. As affirmations and negations are used as complementary aspects, there is no difficulty for the Upaniṣads to see Brahman through both of them.

But there is another equally serious error incidental to the negative descriptions of Brahman. We may rightly understand that they deny Brahman's limitation by name, form and work. In doing so we are likely to fall into an opposite error of thinking that since Brahman denies limitation by all, Brahman is a void, a nothingness where names, forms and works somehow have their foundations. If the world exists there without setting a limit to the

Brahman, then we do not know how it originally came to exist in Brahman which is a pure void. It is a riddle which we find extremely difficult to solve. In an attempt to solve the riddle the theory of Māyā (*māyā vāda*) is introduced, but the theory itself is proved to be a riddle.

Rightly understood, just as the purpose of a negative description is not to deny affirmation but limitation by affirmation, so also its another equally important purpose is to deny that transcendence is a nothingness. It affirms by implication that transcendence is a higher state supremely rich and full of contents. Hence Sri Aurobindo rightly points out that a negation is really a "negating positive".[96] If transcendence is a supreme positive, then it becomes the ultimate source from which all revealed by affirmations come into existence. As a result, we do not see any difficulty, much less a riddle, in understanding how the world originally came to exist in Brahman which exceeds all. In other words, the real significance of a negation is that it must be viewed as a negation of negation. For example, when Brahman is defined as *arūpam*, *aśabdam* and *asthūlam*, they have to be expanded as *arūpam na arūpam, aśabdam na aśabdam*, and *asthūlam na asthūlam*. The negative definitions, when thus expanded, tell us that though Brahman is not limited by form, sound and grossness, Brahman is not a negative state. In other words, Brahman admits form, sound and grossness but exceeds them all as an absolute positive. Though the formula of negation of negation is implicit in the teachings of all Upaniṣads, nowhere except in the Māṇḍūkya is it explicitly stated.

After denying all forms of knowledge affirmed in respect of Viśva, Taijasa and Prājña *(aprajñam)* the Māṇḍūkya goes on to deny that the transcendent Ātman is a pure negation *(na aprajñam)*. Through the negation of negation it affirms that this Ātman is a supreme positive full of contents. Hence the two significant expressions *ekātmapratyayasāraṃ*[97] (Ātman of the same nature contains all as essence in its consciousness) and *prapañca-upaśamaṃ*[98] (the world stilled in Ātman). A true knowledge of Ātman is possible only when all negations are rightly negated. The chief merit of the Māṇḍūkya lies in the fact that it has retrieved the formula of negation of negation from obscurity and offered it to us so that we may apprehend Ātman even as the ancient seers apprehended It.

NOTES

1. Brahmasūtra, 3-2-33.
2. Māṇḍūkya Upaniṣad (hereafter Mā. Up.), Mantra 2.
3. Ibid.,
4. Ibid., Mantra 7.
5. Ibid., Mantra 12.
6. Gauḍapāda Kārikā (hereafter GK), 2-12.
7. Mā. Up., Mantra 6.
8. Ibid., Mantra 7.
9. Ibid.
10. GK, 2-6.
11. Ibid., 3-28.
12. Ibid., 2-10.
13. Ibid., 2-11.
14. Ibid., 2-12.
15. Mā. Up., Mantra 7.
16. GK, 2-19.
17. Mā. Up., Mantra 6.
18. GK, 2-12.
19. Ibid.
20. Ibid., 1-15.
21. Ibid.
22. Ibid.
23. Ibid., 4-29.
24. Ibid.
25. Ibid., 4-58.
26. Ibid., 2-35.
27. Ibid., 4-41.
28. Ibid., 1-17.
29. Ibid., 2-28.
30. Ibid., 2-17.
31. Mā. Up., Mantra 7.
32. GK, 4-73.
33. Ibid., 4-2.
34. Ibid., 2-12.
    * Cf. S. Radhakrishnan, *Indian Philosophy* (1958), Vol. II, p.460.
35. GK, 1-18.
36. Ibid., 3-26.

37. Ibid., 1-18.
38. Ibid., 4-58.
39. Śvetāśvatāra Upaniṣad, 4-9.
40. Ibid.
41. GK, 3-23.
42. Mā. Up., Mantra 7.
43. Ibid.
44. GK, 3-22.
45. Ibid., 3-21.
46. Mā. Up., Mantra 2.
47. Ibid., Mantra 7.
48. Ibid.
49. Ibid.
50. Ibid., Mantra 2.
51. GK, 1-15.
52. Ibid.
53. Ibid., 2-15.
54. Mā. Up., Mantra 3,4,5.
55. Ibid.,
56. Ibid., Mantra 6.
57. Ibid., Mantra 5.
58. Ibid., Mantra 4.
59. Ibid., Mantra 3.
60. Ibid., Mantra 5. (* *ekaḥ nityaḥ svabhāvāt sambhūtaḥ*)
61. Ibid.
62. Ibid.
63. Ibid.
64. Ibid., Mantra 6.
65. Ibid.
66. Ibid.
67. Ibid.
68. Ibid.
69. Ibid., Mantra 5.
70. GK, 4-71.
71. Ibid., 2-17.
72. Mā. Up., Mantra 11,12.
73. Ibid., Mantra 9.
74. Ibid., Mantra 10.
75. Ibid., Mantra 11.
76. Īśa Upaniṣad, Mantra 13.
77. Ibid.
78. Ibid., Mantra 14.
79. Ibid.
80. Bṛhadāraṇyaka Upaniṣad (hereafter Bṛ. Up.), 1-4-7.

81. Ibid.
82. Ibid.
83. Ibid.
84. Mā. Up., Mantra 1.
85. Bṛ. Up., 1-4-7.
86. Mā. Up., Mantra 12.
87. Ibid.
88. Ibid.
89. Ibid.
90. Ibid.
91. Ibid.
92. Ibid.
93. Ibid., Mantra 2.
94. Chāndogya Upaniṣad, 4-6-3.
95. Bṛ. Up., 3-8-8.
96. Sri Aurobindo, *The Life Divine* (1973), p. 316.
97. Mā. Up., Mantra 7.
98. Ibid.

17

The Example of Clay

VIDYĀRAṆYA'S COMMENTARY

Among the post-Śaṅkara teachers Vidyāraṇya is the foremost. He is the author of many important works in the field of Vedānta. His work the Pañcadaśī is a classic known for its depth and comprehensiveness. It is a manual on Advaita. It is not only a systematic exposition of the tenets of Advaita but also a cogent presentation of the teachings of the Upaniṣads in the light of those tenets. In one of its chapters Vidyāraṇya tries to establish through the example of clay that Brahman is real and the world projected from It is illusory. This teaching is a fundamental tenet of Advaita. The example is originally given in the Chāndogya Upaniṣad by Uddālaka to his son Śvetaketu.

Śvetaketu returns home after twelve years of study under a competent teacher of the Vedas. He has mastered all the Vedas and is very proud of his achievement. Finding that his achievement is not complete, Uddālaka asks Śvetaketu: "Did you not ask for that instruction by which the unheard becomes heard, the unperceived becomes perceived, and the unknown becomes known?"[1] He replies that this was not taught to him by his teacher with whom he lived.

What is this instruction? Uddālaka explains it through examples. One of them is clay. This is as follows: By one clod of clay (*ekena mṛtpiṇḍena*) all made of clay (*sarvammṛnmayam*) becomes known. To it a statement about the modification (*vikāra*) and another about the clay (*mṛttikā*) are added — *vācārambhaṇaṃ vikāro nāmadheyaṃ*; *mṛttiketyeva satyam.*[2] The meaning of the example will be clear only when the two statements are rightly grasped. The first speaks about clay and modifications of clay; the second and third point out that while the modifications are unreal (*vācārambhaṇaṃ vikāro nāmadheyaṃ*), the clay is real (*satyam*). This leads to the question why they are so regarded. Vidyāraṇya explains that the modifications are unreal because they are of the nature of *māyā* and the clay is real because it is the locus of the modifications.[3] If the clay is real, how is it possible to say that its modifications are of the nature of *māyā*? They must be as real as the clay. This objection cannot be raised. For, according to Vidyāraṇya, prior to its production the effect does not exist in the cause; however, when the effect arises, it is produced from *māyā*. A nonexistent effect cannot come into existence in any other way except through *māyā*. The appearance of the effect in this way is comparable to the elephant and others seen in a dream (*yad-asadbhāsamānaṃ tanmithyā svapnagajādhivat*).[4] Actually, the elephant does not exist in the mind of the dreamer. It exists elsewhere. However, it is witnessed in the dream i.e. in the mind of the dreamer. From this the elephant is inferred to be a mere illusory experience (*mithyā*). This is the appropriateness of the metaphor. Now we pass on to the next question about the clay. It is said to be real because it is the locus of the modifications. How can the locus be real while the modifications are illusory? Vidyāraṇya says that it is real because its nature is always the same — before the creation of the effect, while the created effect is in existence, and after the disappearance of the effect from its manifest existence (*vyaktakāle tataḥ pūrvamūrdhvam-apyekarūpabhāk*).[5] This is how he has justified the reality of the clay and the illusoriness of its modifications.

In this connection Vidyāraṇya mentions another point about the modifications of clay. Though scripture views them to be illusory (*vikāro nāmadheyaṃ*), they are not viewed to be so by common people (*janāḥ*). They cognise them to be real. This is a contradiction. Vidyāraṇya removes the contradiction in favour of the scripture by pointing out that as the common people lack in discrimination (*vicāravikalā janāḥ*),[6] their cognition must be set aside as erroneous.

What is the outcome of this discussion? What is meant by the words "all made of clay become known? " There is clay and there are modifications of clay resting on the clay. By knowing the clay, it is cognised to be changeless and its modifications to be projections of *māyā*. The point is that the purport of the scripture is not conveyed by the knowledge of the modifications (*śrutau naiva nānātvasya vivakṣayā*)[7] as by that of the clay.

By giving the example of clay the ultimate aim of Uddālaka is to speak about Brahman and the modifications of Brahman viz. the world.[8] In Brahman the world does not exist before its creation or after its destruction. However, it exists only after its creation. This means that the world is an illusory appearance in Brahman. That it is illusory is conveyed by an apparently simple formula — by knowing Brahman all modification of Brahman is known. The goal of human life consists in realising Brahman which becomes never otherwise (*kūṭastham brahma nānyathā*)[9] and abandoning the world which is an illusory modification.

AN ANALYSIS OF THE COMMENTARY

Māyā is said to be of the nature of existence (*bhāvarūpa*). For it is inferred from the existence of the world in Brahman. There are two premises from which the existence of Māyā is inferred. (i) Before creation the world does not exist in Brahman. It comes into existence only after its creation. (ii) The world which now exists in Brahman is an illusory creation, because it is not derived from Brahman. The illusory world must be from a cause other than Brahman. And this cause is Māyā, the power from which illusory creations appear. Māyā has another description which says that it is of the nature of nonexistence (*abhāvātmaka*). It means that it has no essence of its own (*niḥsāra*) which contains all in a latent state. Therefore its creations proceed not from latent existence but from imagination (*kalpanāśakti*). A magician creates birds without eggs, plants without seeds, or flowers without creepers. No material cause is required for his creations. He creates all through mere imagination. This is why Māyā is often compared to him and thought to be, like him, capable of achieving what is not possible of achievement (*aghaṭana ghaṭanā paṭiyasi*). In this respect Māyā is unlike Prakṛti which produces all from the material hidden in its essential being (*svabhāva*). Generally, the supporters of the theory of Māyā state it to be the material cause of the world. But this is just a figurative statement. Strictly speaking, Prakṛti alone is fit to be the material cause of the world, not Māyā. For Prakṛti alone is possessed of the essential being, not Māyā.

If we examine the words of the Upaniṣads, we find that they speak of the creation of the world from Brahman. But there is no evidence in any of the texts to say that the world thus created is an illusory appearance. This is patent. Some try to produce counter evidences to deny the above observation. Let us consider two of them. (i) A text from the Śvetāśvatara Upaniṣad[10] says that the Lord of the world is to be known as Māyin (a conjuror). From this it follows that the world created by Him is of the nature of Māyā (illusion). Thus the world is indirectly mentioned by the Upaniṣad to be illusory. The conventional sense of the word Māyin definitely refers to a conjuror. However, if we carefully study the evidence, we note that the word is made to give up its conventional sense. In the word Māyin the stem is *māyā*. And from the stem, *māyin* gives the sense of a possessor or holder of *māyā*, without prejudice to its conventional sense. Since the stem is used in several senses, one is free to give up the sense of illusion and adopt any suitable sense from them. This is what the seer of the Upaniṣad attempts to do. He says, "Know Māyā to be Prakṛti". By Prakṛti is meant the material cause, the cause which produces the effects from the state of unmanifest existence. Hence Māyā is to be known not as devoid of essence (*niḥsāra*) but as having latent existence in which the effects lie hidden and wait for their manifestation. Having thus redefined the word Māyā, the seer proceeds to the next command which goes thus: "Know the holder of Māyā to be the great Lord (whose Māyā produces not illusions but real forms from hidden effects)." The great Lord is thus the creator of the real world. From this it is clear that the first evidence has turned out to be fruitless. (ii) We shall come to the second evidence. It is from the Kaṭha Upaniṣad.[11] It says that Ātman (there) and the world (here) are one and inseparable, because while Ātman is manifest as the world, the world remains unmanifest as Ātman. Therefore there is absolutely no existence for the Many apart from Ātman (*neha nānāsti kiñcana*). In this context the following line occurs: he who sees as if there are the Many here (*ya iha nāneva paśyati*) goes from death to death i.e. transmigrates. The words "as if there are the Many here" are quoted to prove the contention that the world is an illusory appearance. What the line intends to say is this: the world of plurality stands unseparated from Ātman;

however, the mortal sees the world otherwise; he sees as if the world exists independent of Ātman. This perception of the mortal is false, not the world of plurality. Like the previous one, the present evidence also fails to produce the desired result. Therefore our original observation about the world in the Upaniṣads stands vindicated.

Now we are prepared to come to the main point in our discussion. Vidyāraṇya maintains two views about the world. First, the world does not preexist in Brahman; second, after creation it exists in Brahman as an illusory appearance, because it is not possible for the nonexistent to assume existence except through illusion. From these two views he interprets the texts on Brahman and those on the world created from Brahman. To him the world presented in them is illusory. In the previous discussion we have examined two evidences, one from the Śvetāśvatara and another from the Kaṭha, and proved that they do not speak about *illusory* world. Now we shall produce two other evidences and prove that the world spoken by them is *real*. (i) In the Chāndogya Upaniṣad[12] it is said that in the beginning the world was (*idam agra āsīt*) really one with Brahman (*sadeva*) i.e. it was in a state of absolute oneness with Brahman (*ekamevādvitīyam*). (ii) Likewise, the Muṇḍaka Upaniṣad[13] asserts that the world is born from the Imperishable (*akṣarāt saṃbhavatīha viśvam*). From the two evidences it is clear that the world is real, because it has preexisted in Brahman and also because it is born from the state of preexistence in that imperishable Brahman. However, there is a reason why Vidyāraṇya thinks that the world appears in Brahman through illusion. Everywhere the Upaniṣads proclaim Brahman to be imperishable (*avyaya*) and immutable (*akṣara*). Unless Brahman undergoes transformation and loses thereby his original nature, it is not possible for the world to appear from Him. From this Vidyāraṇya concludes that the Upaniṣads overcome the difficulty through the assumption of Māyā. With the power of illusion, Māyā produces the world without causing damage to the imperishable nature of Brahman. However, he cannot uphold his conclusion without abandoning the other texts where the preexistence of the world in Brahman is affirmed in clear terms. They imply that the world is created from Brahman through transformation. As a result, Vidyāraṇya's method of interpretation must be given up as opposed to the Upaniṣads.

We have abandoned Vidyāraṇya's theory of Māyā. But the original problem remains unsolved. If the texts on creation are obscure, their obscurity must be removed only through the light of other texts. In this task logic is absolutely necessary, but its role is secondary. For the authority of scripture is greater than that of logic. In this connection the Muṇḍaka text[14] comes in handy. It helps us to remove the obscurity of the creation-texts.

The Muṇḍaka[15] speaks of a higher reality than the Imperishable. It is called That (*tat*) which is exceedingly subtle (*susūkṣmaṃ*). In view of the gross beings (*bhūtas*), the Imperishable (*avyaya*) is subtle. In view of the Imperishable, That is exceedingly subtle. If the Imperishable is free of the limitations of the gross beings, That exceeds even this freedom possessed by the Imperishable. However, by the absolute freedom That does not stand separated from the Imperishable and the world of gross beings. On the contrary, That is present in both of them (*sarvagataṃ*). That is indeed imperishable, but by the imperishability That is not prevented from producing the world from itself. Thus That is simultaneously *avyaya* and *bhūtayoni*. This is how the wise see That (*paripaśyanti dhīrāḥ*).

That is called elsewhere the supreme Imperishable (*parātparaṃ*).[16] It produces the world through transformation without ceasing to be imperishable. Imperishability and transformation are simultaneously possible for That. For they are not opposites. In the state of absolute freedom one permits the other. This is the real theory of transformation enunciated in the Upaniṣads — the theory of transformation of the highest Imperishable (*parāvyayapariṇāmavāda*). Vidyāraṇya knows the existence of the imperishable Brahman, but not of the supreme Imperishable. This is why he clings to the theory of Māyā which has caused extensive damage to the Upaniṣads. A correct understanding of them is possible only when this theory is banished from the mind of the scholar.

ĀTMAN AND THE WORLD

In metaphysical discussions the role played by examples is very important. What is subtle and, therefore, difficult to comprehend is made comprehensible through concrete instances. They are taken from things known to people whose intelligence is meagre and ordinary. But unfortunately the example itself is made unintelligible by commentators whose motive is to justify their own pre-conceived views. Uddālaka's clay example, as explained by the commentators, is one such instance.

Vidyāraṇya makes out that through the clay example Uddālaka teaches two things. (i) Clay alone deserves attention and (ii) not things made of clay. This is why clay is said to be real (*satyam*), while clay-things are dismissed as unreal (*vikāro nāmadheyaṃ vācārambhaṇaṃ*). This makes the common man react in these words: "If clay is real, then clay-things too must be real, they cannot be otherwise."

By one lump of clay, says Uddālaka, all that is made of clay becomes known. By itself this proposition is clear. Since clay is present in the lump and the things that come from the lump, it is possible to pass from one to other, from the source to the products. However, the correct import of the above proposition is to be determined in relation to the two other propositions — (ii) *vācārambhaṇaṃ vikāro nāmadheyaṃ*; (iii) *mṛttiketyeva satyam*. The link between the first and the next two is provided by the words *vikāra* (modification) and *mṛttikā* (clay).

According to Vidyāraṇya, clay in proposition (iii) means the locus (*ādhāramṛdvastu*)[17] which undergoes no transformation and produces no clay-things (*ekarūpabhāk*).[18] In proposition (ii), by modification of clay is meant the appearance of clay-things such as pot in the locus through the action of Māyā.[19] In the light of these elucidations Vidyāraṇya determines the correct import of the first proposition. Its import is this: By knowing a clod of clay which is changeless all that is made of clay is known to be an illusory creation of Māyā.

In this connection two points mentioned by Vidyāraṇya deserve attention. (a) Vidyāraṇya has resolved the contradiction between the cognition of the common people and the teaching of the scripture by attaching a greater authority to the latter. As a result, the former is rejected as erroneous.

The clay and its modifications belong to the domain of physical things and come under the authority of perception (*pratyakṣa*). Apart from this, there is another domain, the domain of supraphysical things which comes under the authority of scripture (*śruti*). In principle no conflict between the two authorities is possible, for their domains are exclusive of each other. If a conflict arises between the two, then it must be resolved without prejudice to their mutual autonomy. When the scripture happens to speak about a subject that actually comes under the domain of physical things, it would speak about it without causing injury to the authority of perception. It would restate the revelations of the senses and not contradict them.

From this discussion it becomes clear that Vidyāraṇya has removed the contradiction between the cognition of the common people and the teaching of the scripture not only by pushing the scripture beyond its legitimate limit of authority but also by causing deliberate damage to the authority of perception. This is certainly indefensible. But then how to get rid of the error of contradiction without overlooking the testimonies of perception and scripture? There is only one way of doing it and it is by attributing the error to our understanding of the scripture and putting the correct and proper meanings into its words — *vācārambhaṇaṃ vikāro nāmadheyaṃ* and *satyam*.

(b) Vidyāraṇya points out that in giving the formula of knowing the many from the one, Uddālaka's intention is to teach not of the many (*naiva nānātvasya vivakṣayā*)[20] but of the one which alone is the aim of human life (*pumarthaṃ syāt*).[21] His view of Uddālaka's intention about the modifications of clay is a direct result of his other view that scripture denies the testimony of perception and looks upon the modifications as illusory. It is a case of one mistake culminating in another mistake. It means that the first is surely a mistaken view. From this we are compelled to conclude that his interpretation of Uddālaka's formula itself is responsible for these mistakes.

A comparison between the original text and the meanings assigned to its words by Vidyāraṇya brings to light serious discrepancies. (i) He has driven a wedge between the clay and the effects that lie in it in an unmanifest state. He has taken away the effects and named the clay as the immutable locus (*ādhāra-mṛdvastu*)[22] where they are nonexistent (*asat*).[23] This is not only a gross distortion of the original word but in contradiction to the Brihadaranyaka[24] and Chāndogya[25] texts. They speak in unmistakable terms that the effect preexists in the cause. After distorting the original sense of the cause, Vidyāraṇya has converted the unmanifest state as the power of Māyā (*acintyaśaktirmāyaiṣā ...avyākṛtābhidhā*)[26] from which the effects arise not as real creations but as illusory appearances. This contradicts the texts like the Muṇḍaka where the birth of the effect (*viśvam sambhavati*)[27] from the cause (*akṣarāt*) is proclaimed. The word *sambhavati* is significant. It signifies birth of something which preexists. Hence the effect is a real manifestation. In the birth of the effect the action of Māyā is absolutely irrelevant.

(ii) We have found how Vidyāraṇya has mutilated the original words of the Upaniṣad. As a result, the first proposition has become disjointed. In the view of the Upaniṣads the cause and the effect are indivisible. But Vidyāraṇya has divided the two as if they are opposites. The reason for doing so is to be found in his understanding of the second and third propositions. For his reading of them is not in harmony with the spirit of the Upaniṣads in general. The words *nāmadheyam* and *satyam* are wrongly understood by him. He takes *nāmadheyam* [28] to be standing for illusory appearance and *satyam* [29] to be a substratum which undergoes no transformation. If we insist on unfolding from them meanings not inharmonious with the teachings of other Upaniṣads, particularly the Bṛhadāraṇyaka and the Muṇḍaka, it is definitely possible to grasp the intended teaching of the first proposition. For nowhere do they teach that the effect is nonexistent in the cause or that it is an illusory appearance from the cause. This is clearly known from them.

(iii) A cursory glance at the first proposition clearly shows that Uddālaka has two kinds of knowledge in view — knowledge of the one and knowledge of the many. But Vidyāraṇya says that Uddālaka is interested only in the first, for this alone constitutes the goal of human life (*pumarthaṃ*) and not the second. The reason for his assertion is his preconceived view of causation according to which the cause is real while the effect is a mere illusion. There are definitely two forms of knowledge and both are to be attained. The distinction between the two is so clearly pronounced that no one can lose sight of it. While the first is the means (*ekenamṛtpiṇḍena*), the second is the end achieved by the means (*sarvammṛnmayam vijñātaṃ syāt*). The first is essential knowledge and the second is comprehensive knowledge elsewhere referred to as the highest attainment (*param*).[30]

Now we have arrived to the crucial part in our discussion — what do the second and third propositions actually say? Let us reproduce the text under discussion: *vācārambhaṇaṃ vikāro nāmadheyaṃ; mṛttiketyeva satyam.* Before we proceed we shall make two preliminary observations. First, the word *vikāra* means a modification of clay. It is a modification of something which preexists in the clay. This means that it is a real modification from the clay. Hence it cannot be called an illusory product (*vācārambhaṇaṃ nāmadheyaṃ*). Second, the word *satyam* cannot imply that the clay undergoes no transformation. From this it is evident that the words *vācārambhaṇaṃ vikāro nāmadheyaṃ* and *satyam* are not correctly understood by Vidyāraṇya. Though we have already established this point through a detailed analysis, we now present the same point through a prima facie view of the above words. Now we shall go back to our main discussion.

The word *vikāraḥ* refers to the modification of clay. The words *nāmadheyaṃ vācārambhaṇaṃ* emphasise the relation of the name to the language consisting of words. Hence *vikāro nāmadheyaṃ vācārambhaṇaṃ* assert that the modification is of the nature of the name produced from the words of the language. By this assertion a comparison is intended. The name is a word and the word is derived from the language. Hence the name is a derivation from the language. When the language is known, the name is known to be its own word. For it was implicit in the language. To the language and the name are respectively compared the clay and the modification of clay. Just as the name is derived from the words of the language where all name exists in an unmanifested state, so also the modification is produced from the clay where all product is in a state of unmanifestation. As the language is the means of knowing the name, so the clay (*mṛttikā*) is the right means (*satyam*) of knowing the modification. From this comparison two points emerge. (i) The clay-things, before their creation, preexist in the clay; therefore they are created from their preexistent state in the clay. (ii) By knowing the clay, the clay-things are known to be modifications of the clay itself, for they had their preexistence in the clay.

By taking *nāmadheyaṃ* to be a comparison given in respect of *vikāraḥ* Uddālaka's example is found to be quite intelligible and instructive. Like the language and the name, the clay and the modification of clay belong to the same order of existence. They do not present themselves as two opposites, one as real clay and the other as unreal modification of clay, as in the system of interpretation of Vidyāraṇya. The name (*nāmadheyaṃ*) derived from the language (*vācārambhaṇaṃ*) is never thought to be an illusory appearance by the knower of the language. For it is an expression of what was already there in the words of the language. In the same way the relation of the modification of clay to the clay is to be understood. This is the pure and original teaching of Uddālaka.

How does the clay undergo modification and yet remain unmodified in its original nature? For Uddālaka this question is irrelevant. There is a lump of clay and there are many clay-things that have come out from the lump. Though the clay-things are numerous, they are known by merely knowing a single lump of clay. This is the main point of Uddālaka's teaching. All other points connected with his teaching do not engage his attention. However, the above question is not unanswerable. For the clay both change and changelessness are simultaneously possible without any contradiction. The pot rises from the clay. The presence of clay in it is an evidence that the pot is a modification from the clay and not from any other cause. Likewise, the clay in the pot has not deviated from its original clay-nature. This is a parallel evidence that the pot rises from the clay without causing damage to the clay-nature. If there is a question whether the pot is real like the clay, the answer is in the affirmative. For it preexisted in the clay and has not abandoned its oneness with the clay in the process of transformation of its preexistence. It has now become the continent of the clay. In other words, the pot is real for two reasons: first, it was a content of the real clay; second, now it has the real clay as its content.

In giving the example of clay Uddālaka's ultimate aim is to teach of Ātman and the world. Before creation the world existed in Ātman. It was in an unmanifest state. It was so completely united with Ātman that it was as if nonexistent (*asat*).[31] The word *asat* is used here as a figure for absolute union. When the world is released from the unmanifest existence, it is cognised to be a real manifestation of the essence of Ātman. For it had preexisted in Ātman. As the world has no other cause than Ātman, the question of its being an illusory creation cannot arise. The clay-things are known from knowing the clay. Likewise, all in the world become known by knowing Ātman.

There is no dichotomy between Ātman and the world. For the world too is Ātman, Ātman self-extended in names and forms. Knowledge of Ātman is not an end in itself; it is a means to another knowledge — knowledge of the world. If Ātman is sought for its own sake, then the world is neglected — it becomes *aśrutam*, *amatam* and *avijñātam*.[32] This is incomplete knowledge. If it should become *śrutam, matam,* and *vijñātam,* it is possible only through complete knowledge. As the Upaniṣads are not unanimous about the ideas of means and end, we shall leave them aside and give attention to what the sages have said about complete knowledge. They now and then stress that complete knowledge alone is worthy of pursuit. The Kaṭha Upaniṣad is a case in point. It says that Ātman (there) and the world of plurality (here) are one and inseparable.[33] However, the mortal separates the world and sees as if it exists without Ātman (*nāneva paśyati*). In reality the world of plurality has no existence independent of Ātman (*neha nānāsti kiñcana*).[34] As the mortal's cognition of the world is contrary to the fact, he goes from death to death.[35] From these words it is clear that the correct view consists in seeing both Ātman and the world as one (*ekadhaivānudraṣṭavyam*).[36]

In the Īśa Upaniṣad the same point is stated differently. It speaks about *vidyā* (knowledge of the one) and *a-vidyā* (knowledge of what is other than the one viz. knowledge of the many or the world).[37] He who pursues Avidyā to the neglect of Vidyā goes to darkness (*tamaḥ*), whereas he who pursues Vidyā to the neglect of Avidyā goes to greater darkness (*bhūya tamaḥ*).The point is that both Vidyā and Avidyā must be attained. He who attains both (*ubhayaṃ saha*) overcomes his ego (*mṛtyu*) through embracing the many and enjoys immortality (*amṛtam*) through living in the One.[38] It is worthy of note that the Īśa does not stop with its instruction but goes further and adds how exclusive pursuits produce undesirable results. In this respect the teaching of the Īśa is more comprehensive and insistent. The law by which Ātman and the world are held together is referred to by Yājñavalkya as the law of the Imperishable (*anucchitti-dharmā*).[39]

Uddālaka's example is very simple and most appropriate. Vidyāraṇya's interest is to make Uddālaka a spokesman of the theory of Māyā. In this connection he has used all his resources — his skill, scholarship, and personal experience. Yet the words of Uddālaka speak only what is intended by him, not otherwise.

NOTES

1. Chāndogya Upaniṣad, (hereafter Ch. Up.), 6-1-13.
2. Ibid., 6-1-4.
3. Swāmī Vidyāraṇya, *Pañcadaśī* (hereafter PD), 13-38.
4. Ibid., 2-70.
5. Ibid., 13-44.
6. Ibid.13-33.
7. Ibid., 13-60.
8. Ibid., 13-61.
9. Ibid., 13-100.
10. Śvetāśvatara Upaniṣad, 4-10.
11. Kaṭha Upaniṣad (hereafter K. Up.), 2-1-10, 11.
12. Ch. Up., 6-2.
13. Muṇḍaka Upaniṣad (hereafter M. Up.), 1-1-7.
14. Ibid., 1-1-6.
15. Ibid.
16. Ibid., 3-2-8.
17. PD, 13-38.
18. Ibid., 13-44.
19. Ibid., 13-38.
20. Ibid., 13-60.
21. Ibid., 13-56.
22. Ibid., 13-38.
23. Ibid., 2-70.
24. Bṛhadāraṇyaka Upaniṣad (hereafter Bṛ. Up.), 1-4-10, 11,17.
25. Ch. Up., 6-2-2.
26. PD, 13-65.
27. M. Up., 1-7-7.
28. PD, 13-43.
29. Ibid., 13-44.
30. Taittirīya Upaniṣad, 2-1-1.
31. Ibid., 2-7-1.
32. Ch. Up., 6-1-3.
33. K. Up., 2-1-10.
34. Ibid., 2-1-11.

35. Ibid.
36. Bṛ. Up., 4-4-20.
37. Īśa Upaniṣad, Mantra 9.
38. Ibid., Mantra 11.
39. Bṛ. Up., 4-5-14.

18

Scripture, Knowledge, and Delusion

THE TWOFOLD KNOWLEDGE

In India the ancient system of education aimed at complete mastery — mastery of this world and mastery of the world beyond (*ayaṃ ca lokaḥ paraśca lokaḥ prajñāyante*).[1] From the study of this world arose a number of *vidyās*; likewise, from the study of the higher world *brahmavidyā* arose. All these were meticulously taught and men of knowledge and wisdom were moulded by this type of education. There were two methods of learning the *vidyās*. One method was to learn them one by one. This was very tedious. Another method was to learn the most important *vidyā* first and, afterwards, the others through this *vidyā*. The sages of the Upaniṣads favoured the second method. They were of the view that by mastering the Brahmavidyā all the others could be easily mastered. Hence they declared that all *vidyās* have the Brahmavidyā as their foundation (*brahmavidyāṃ sarvavidyā pratiṣṭhām*).[2] The seekers of wisdom generally approach their masters with this question: What is that by knowing which all else becomes known (*kasminnu bhagavo vijñāte sarvamidaṃ vijñātam bhavati*)?[3] As we have said, their intention is first to acquire the science of Brahman and then all other sciences from that higher science.

As the science of Brahman is enshrined in the Vedas and Upaniṣads, it is necessary for the seekers of wisdom to learn their teachings in the proper manner under the guidance of those who have mastered the texts and established themselves in Brahman (*śrotriyam brahmaniṣṭham*).[4] In this connection it is important to note a famous distinction made by the Muṇḍaka Upaniṣad between two *vidyās*, lower (*aparā*) and higher (*parā*).The relevant text runs as follows:

> *tatrāparā ṛgvedo yajurvedaḥ sāmavedo atharvavedaḥ śikṣā kalpo vyākarṇaṃ niruktaṃ chando jotiṣamiti; atha parā yayā tadakṣaram adhigamyate.*[5]

The above text says two things. (i) Lower knowledge is from the Vedas (Rig Veda etc.) and the six works (Śikṣā etc.). (ii) Higher knowledge is that by which (*yayā*) Tadakṣaram is attained. The wording of the text makes it very difficult to comprehend. There are two reasons for this difficulty. First, though it speaks about the Vedas etc. as the means of lower knowledge, it does not say what is the object to be achieved by this means. Second, though it speaks about the means of achieving Tadakṣaram, it says nothing about the means *yayā* except that it is higher knowledge. Therefore there are two questions to be answered: (i) What is the object of lower knowledge? (ii) What is the higher means of attaining Tadakṣaram?

A careful study of the text helps us to discover the two missing ideas. In the second line the word *tad-akṣaram* occurs. The prefix *tad* in it indicates that some *akṣaram* is already known. From where is this known? Evidently, this is known from the first line where the Vedas are mentioned. This means that this *akṣaram* is known from the study of the Vedas. From this we get the answer to the first question what is the object of lower knowledge. The answer is: Akṣaram. It is this Akṣaram that is referred to as Tadakṣaram in the second line of the text. But then why is this knowledge called lower? We know that the six works *śikṣā* etc. are the aids with which the Vedas are studied. Obviously, this is the traditional method for studying the Vedas. By studying in this way we arrive at the knowledge of the Imperishable (*akṣaram*) from them. The Imperishable known through the above method is nothing but a word. As the word Imperishable is not the real Imperishable, the knowledge obtained from the Vedas is definitely of a lower category.

Now we come to the second question, what is the higher means of attaining Tadakṣaram? We know that there are only two means for attaining the Imperishable. One is the study of the Vedas. The other is the Imperishable itself. Since we are concerned with higher knowledge here, the first is ruled out. How is the Imperishable attained by the Imperishable? It is attained by merging oneself into the Imperishable. This way is proclaimed everywhere in the Upaniṣads. In the Muṇḍaka itself there are many references to this way. For example, it says in 3-2-9 that a knower of Brahman becomes Brahman Himself (*brahmaveda brahmaiva bhavati*). As this means is well-known among the Upaniṣads, text 1-1-5 equates *yayā* with it under the notion that it is not necessary to name it. This knowledge by merger is called higher because this is obtained directly from the Imperish-able and it is certainly superior to the one gained through the study of the Vedas. Now the text 1-1-5 shines forth without any obscurities that made it unintelligible.

The Upaniṣad emphatically says that both the *vidyās*, *parā* and *aparā*, are to be acquired (*dve vidye veditavye*).[6] By the lower, one mentally understands what is the Imperishable and what are the practical conditions necessary for its attainment. By the higher, one enters and attains the Imperishable previously understood by the mind from the study of the Vedas.

Just as the two *vidyās* are to be acquired, so also both have to be discriminated from each other. Otherwise confusion of *vidyās* is inevitable. From this confusion arises delusion. As the deluded makes false claims to higher knowledge, the Muṇḍaka Upaniṣad admonishes against the delusion — the Imperishable Ātman is attained not through delusion created by the word (*na ayam ātmā labyaḥ pramādāt*).[7] The admonition is repeated in different words in different contexts in the Upaniṣads.

UDDĀLAKA AND ŚVETAKETU

Śvetaketu, son of Uddālaka, is a Brāhmaṇa by birth. His father sends him to a teacher for learning the Vedas. He lives with his teacher for twelve years and completes his study. We shall note how his psychological condition is described when he returns home after a long period of study with his teacher.

There are three words in the text which give us sufficient insight into his inner condition. He has studied all the Vedas (*sarvān vedān*)[8] and mastered them systematically. On account of this achievement he becomes proud (*anūcānamānī*).[9] Beyond a particular point pride becomes a source of intellectual blindness and brings about the fall of the proud. In this way one may find him stuck with the words of the Vedas (*stabdhaḥ*).[10] From this two consequences are possible — arrogance and delusion. And Śvetaketu seems to have been overtaken by both. The third word *mahāmanāḥ*[11] in the text is used to convey both the senses of arrogance and delusion. He is arrogant, because he has an exaggerated *opinion* about his achievement as a scholar (*vedavid*); he is deluded, because he *imagines* himself to be a great knower of reality (*tattvavid*). It is wrong to take the word *mahāmanāḥ* to convey the sense of mere arrogance, as is taken generally by commentators. To view Śvetaketu merely as an arrogant person is to lose sight of the deeper condition of his personality. As a matter of fact, his father Uddālaka himself seems to consider him to be both arrogant and deluded. This is clearly borne out by the teachings given subsequently by him to his son.

Uddālaka teaches Śvetaketu two important things. One is about reality (*satyam*)[12] and another is about delusion caused by word (*vācārambhaṇaṃ vikāraḥ*).[13] As for the first, the reality of the world is to be known by the reality of the One. Generally, men (including those who have studied the Vedas and obtained good proficiency in them) try to know the reality of the world as if there is only this world and no other reality (*ayam loko nāsti para iti mānī*).[13] Since the One is veiled from them, their attempts at knowing the world are fruitless. Therefore they see the world to be unrevealed (*aśrutaṃ*),[14] ungrasped (*amataṃ*), and uncomprehended (*avijñātaṃ*).[15] In this connection Uddālaka points out that from the knowledge of the One, the world becomes known (*śrutaṃ, matam,* and *vijñātam*). This is the significance of the question put to Śvetaketu by him: Did you ask your teacher for the instruction by which the unrevealed becomes revealed, the ungrasped grasped, and the uncomprehended comprehended?[16] Through the examples of clay, gold and iron Śvetaketu's attention is repeatedly drawn to the need for knowing the world by knowing the One.

As regards the second teaching, it is always necessary to maintain the fundamental difference between word (*vāk*) and reality (*satyam*)[17]. Otherwise one is assailed by confusions and delusions. A knower of word (*vedavid*) mistakes himself to be a knower of reality (*tattvavid*). Word is illusorily modified into reality, and the word ceases to be a representation of the reality. The way to escape from the delusion is to recover the sense of discrimination and see clearly that word and reality belong to two mutually different orders of existence. This is the reason why Uddālaka repeatedly talks about the distinction between *vāk* and *satyam*.

If we examine the teachings of Uddālaka from his personal point of view, certain things about his son are known from his words. Śvetaketu is wrong in thinking that he has learnt everything from his prolonged study of the Vedas. He has to see his deficiency as a knower of the Vedas. He must know the reality of the Many by the reality of the One and learn that in the absence of discrimination word is illusorily modified into reality and the knower is made into a victim of delusion. He must be able to discriminate and overcome the illusory modification of word. Unless we grant these things it is very difficult to justify the words Uddālaka has spoken to his son.

We may speak of two versions of Uddālaka's teachings, first and second. In the first his instructions are very brief and given mainly through examples such as clay, gold, and iron. In the second the implications of the original instructions are taken up and elaborated as clearly as possible. This becomes a complete statement on the metaphysics of Being (*sat*). This has come to be described as the science of Being (*sadvidyā*).[18] If we view the two versions together, we are sure to be convinced that the final version is the logical culmination of the earlier version. Thus in them analogies and metaphysics go hand in hand and complement each other through mutual help.

EXAMINATION OF THE ORIGINAL TEXTS

(i) There are three texts and all three deal with examples. We shall explain the first where clay is given as an example, and omit the rest. For in them the same teaching is given using gold and iron as two other examples. The text goes like this:

ekena mṛtpiṇḍena sarvaṃ mṛnmayaṃ vijñātaṃ syāt;
vācārambhaṇaṃ vikāro nāmadheyaṃ mṛttikā iti eva satyam.[19]

The text begins by speaking about a clod of clay (*mṛtpiṇḍa*). What is called clay here is alone real (*mṛttikā iti eva satyam*). For it rises from earth (*mṛdārambhaṇam*). The word clay is not real, for it rises from speech (*vācārambhaṇaṃ*) and belongs to the order of names.

From the clay all things made of clay (*mṛnmayaṃ*) become known. But from the word clay they do not become known. For the clay and not the word is the material cause of clay-things.

Though the word clay and the clay belong to two different orders, it is possible for the mind to come under delusion begun by the word (*vācārambhaṇaṃ vikāraḥ*) and consider the word as if it is the clay. But actually this illusory product is but the name clay (*nāmadheyaṃ*) and not the clay.

When does the delusion take place? We know that scholars are preoccupied with the words they have heard from their masters. By means of constant reflection and enquiry they try to learn them as perfectly as possible. When they are overcome by passions such as attachment and pride, as in the case of Śvetaketu, they lose their sense of discrimination and get stuck with the words. It is a condition where the words produce delusions and make the scholars their poor victims.

The main aim of the text under discussion is to teach that by knowing a clod of clay all things made of clay become known. In this connection the text says that in the absence of discrimination between the word clay and the clay, the above formula of knowledge does not work and we are overcome by a delusion begun by the word. Then how do we come out of the delusion and get the discrimination necessary for the formula to produce the desired result? By remembering that the clay alone is real (*mṛttiketyeva satyam*) and not the word clay (*vāk*) which belongs to the order of names (*nāmadheyaṃ*).

(ii) Now we pass on to the texts on the science of Being (*sadvidyā*). Let us take the text which speaks about the sun (*āditya*).[20] Other texts are omitted. Because they present the same idea by speaking about objects such as the moon. The text about the sun is as follows:

1.*yad ādityasya rohitaṃ rūpaṃ tejasas tad rūpaṃ; yacchuklaṃ tad apām; yat kṛṣṇaṃ tad annasya.*
2.*apāgād ādityād ādityatvaṃ.*
3.*vācārambhaṇaṃ vikāro nāmadheyaṃ.*
4.*trīṇi rūpāṇīty eva satyam.*[21]

Before we discuss the above text we shall bear in mind what the Upaniṣad says about the world. From the supreme God (*parā devatā*)[22] three original material elements have appeared — Fire (*tejaḥ*), Water (*āpaḥ*), and Earth (*annam*).[23] All in the world have arisen from the three Elements. In other words, the supreme Being (*sataḥ*) is the material cause of the world. Of this world two things are asserted by the Upaniṣad. First of all, it is verily this Being and not other than that (*ātmaiva idaṃ sarvam*).[24] Secondly, it exists only in this Being and not elsewhere (*satpratiṣṭhaḥ*).[25] Hence from the knowledge of the Being, the whole world becomes known (*vijñātaṃ bhavati*).[26] Wise men do not see the world as seen by men without discrimination or the knowledge of the Being.

Apart from this view of the world, it is important to note the Upaniṣad's observation about the custodians of the science of Being. This science was in the custody of the knowers of the Vedas who had flourished in olden times. They were not mere knowers of the Vedas, but they had also known their underlying reality (*satyam*) through *upāsanās*. By *upāsanā* is meant the discipline by which they kept their mind seated (*āsana*) closely (*upa*) to the reality behind the words of the Vedas and attained higher knowledge thereof (*parā vidyā*). As they had this higher knowledge, they were regarded as wise men (*tadvidvāṃsaḥ*)[27] and great knowers of the Vedas (*mahāśrotriyāḥ*).[28] From this we understand that Uddālaka's theory of Being owes its origin to the great knowers of the Vedas who were much anterior to him.

Now we shall come to the text 6-4-2. For the sake of convenience we may divide the text into four parts. Part one speaks about knowing the sun from the three Elements. Part two refers to the disappearance of *ādityatvam* from Āditya. Part three makes mention of the delusive modification begun by the word, and the name being the product of the modification. Finally, part four insists on the discrimination between word and reality.

Part one says that from the three Elements the sun (*āditya*) is known. It is known as an object produced from and supported by the Elements. This is the significance of the equation worked out between the sun, on the one hand, and the Elements, on the other, by the text. The sun's essential nature (*ādityatvaṃ*) consists in being a product of the Elements. The knowers of the Being (*sat*) know the sun by knowing its essential nature.

However, in part two an important point is made. The text says that the sun's *ādityatvaṃ* disappears from the sun (*apāgād ādityād*).

The presence or absence of *ādityatvaṃ* in the sun depends on the sun's relationship to the Elements. If it is related to the three Elements, its *ādityatvaṃ* is present, otherwise it is not. In other words, its *ādityatvaṃ* disappears when the sun is not related to the Elements from which it has come into existence.

Part three explains why the sun is not related to the three Elements. In order to relate it to them there must be the discrimination between the words (*vāk*) and the Elements denoted by them. In its absence the Elements are begun by the words. As the Elements thus begun are illusory (*vācārambhaṇaṃ vikāraḥ*), there are actually the names (*nāmadheyaṃ*) and not the Elements. When the Elements are not there, the sun cannot be related to them.

Part four completes the argument of the text. In order for the sun to be known by its essential nature the knower should be endowed with discrimination, the discrimination between the word and the reality, the names and the three Elements. The text *trīṇirūpāṇītyeva satyam* is intended to teach the sense of discrimination. It clearly says that what are called (*iti*) the three Elements alone (*eva*) are real (*satyam*). If they alone are real, then what do they exclude from themselves to be *not real*? They are certainly the names by which they are called. For all name is a word and not a reality. Therefore from the three Elements the sun is known to be their product.

Though the text talks about Āditya, its teaching is to be extended to the whole world. On the analogy of Āditya the world is to be known as a product of the three Elements of the Being (*sat*). This is how the world is known by the knowers of the Being.

THE REALITY OF THE WORLD

We started with the view that Śvetaketu, an accomplished scholar in the study of the Vedas, was assailed by the evils of arrogance and delusion. We made an attempt to show that Uddālaka's desire was to correct Śvetaketu and extricate him from the two evils. This brings us to the end of our discussion. But still it is not out of place to note how the reality of the world is presented in the sixth chapter of the Chāndogya Upaniṣad.

The above Upaniṣad has earned the reputation of teaching the unreality (*anṛtatvam*)[29] of the world in decisive terms. In this light, relevant passages from the Upaniṣad were interpreted time and again by great scholars as if to show that they were not to be understood otherwise. But this is resented by many good scholars, both eastern and western. As the former were highly skilled and well equipped, they were hardly challenged. In history two attempts have been made to oppose their interpretations. Both the attempts are unsatisfactory.

Here an attempt has been made to put forward alternative interpretations of the texts 6-1-4 and 6-4-2. But this is not enough. It must be proved that the theory of illusory creation of the world (*māyāvāda*) is contrary to the tenets of Vedānta.

Toṭaka is a direct disciple of Śaṅkara. He is the author of a concise work entitled *Śrutisārasamuddharaṇam.*[30] It is a less known but a very important treatise on the Upaniṣads. It argues that through hundreds of illustrations the Upaniṣads teach the unreality of the world (*janimajjagadetadabhūtamiti śrutayaḥ pravadantyupamānaśataiḥ*).[31] It speaks as if this theory is a settled matter beyond dispute.

Toṭaka takes the example of gold. He points out that the necklace etc. do not exist in the gold either before their production or after their destruction, but however they appear from it and exist in the present. According to his view, whatever does not exist in the gold before and after, is produced from it only through illusory modification. From this he concludes that they exist in the present merely through illusion. To quote his words: *kanake rucakādi na pūrvamabhūccaramaṃ ca na vidyata ityanṛtam adhunāpi.* [32] (The necklace etc. did not exist in the gold before and they do not exist in the gold later. So they are unreal even in the present.) Applying this theory to the Muṇḍaka text 2-1-3, the author comes to the conclusion that the entire world that has originated, from space onwards, is taught to be unreal (*tathaiva samastamidaṃ janimadvyadādi bhavedanṛtam*).[33] This is one of the arguments by which he establishes that all Upaniṣads where creation of the world is mentioned, teach the unreality of the world of names and forms.

But in the Upaniṣads the theory of creation is presented differently. In the Īśa, for example, there is a concise but a vivid statement of the theory.[34] It says that the world is created through a triple process of seeing, conceiving and realising by God. As the

Kavi, He sees the hidden potentialities in the eternal being; as the Manīṣī, He thinks out and conceives the world from the potentialities; as the Paribhū, he realises the world thus conceived. As there is a perfect accord between what the objects are and what they should be according to their eternal natures (*yāthātathyataḥ arthān vyadadhāt śāśvatībhyaḥ samābhyaḥ*),[35] they do not appear without any law of development. On the other hand, they appear in obedience to the law of triple development as mentioned above. Thus, according to the Īśa, the creation of the world is a real manifestation and not an illusory modification. This view is shared by all Upaniṣads. No further proof is required to understand their position in this regard. From this we are compelled to conclude that the created world cannot be considered unreal (*anṛta*), as argued by Toṭaka. The theory put forward by him is his own and not the one discussed in the Upaniṣads.

Now we shall turn to the Chāndogya texts where the world is said to have been declared unreal (*asat*). Referring to the texts 6-4-1, 6-4-2 and 6-4-3, Toṭaka advances this argument. The above texts speak about three things — fire, the sun, and the moon. By speaking about them they intend to speak about this world (*idaṃjagad*).[36] The three Elements Fire, Water, and Earth, according to them, are the material cause of the world; fire, the sun, and the moon are the three modifications of this material cause. The texts go further and declare that while the modification is unreal (*vācārambhaṇaṃ nāmadheyaṃ*), the material cause is real (*satyam*). In the words of Toṭaka: *vitathā vikṛtiḥ satataṃ sakalā na tathā prakṛtiḥ.*[37] From this he concludes that the world is proved to be unreal by the Upaniṣad (*jagadetadabhūtamiti*).[38]

In essence there is no difference between this argument and the earlier one. As this argument is text-based, unlike the earlier one, we have to oppose it by two means. First, we repeat that this argument, like the previous one, runs counter to the view of creation set forth in the Īśa Upaniṣad. There it is stated very clearly that in creation the objects (*arthān*) are moulded in accordance with the eternal natures which predetermine what they should be when released into manifestation (*yāthātathyataḥ vyadadhāt*).[39] From this it may be seen that the created world is certainly real and not unreal by any reason. Second, if what we have stated is correct, it must be proved correct by removing the contradiction between the two Upaniṣads in this regard.

Let us now go back to the previous section 3. There the Chāndogya text about the sun is fully elaborated. For our purpose parts 3 and 4 of the above text are important. Part 3 does not speak about causal modification and its unreality. It speaks about another type of modification and its product — the delusive modification begun by the word (*vācārambhaṇaṃ vikāraḥ*), and the product of the modification being the name (*nāmadheyaṃ*). From this it must be borne in mind that part 3 does not condemn causal modification as unreal creation. In part 4 the reality of the three Elements is asserted. They are real (*satyam*) as discriminated (*iti*) from the names (*nāmadheyaṃ*) by which they are called. In other words, the three Elements alone are real and not the names that denote these Elements.

Now that the contradiction between the Īśa and the Chāndogya is eliminated the former's view of the world as a real creation from God stands vindicated. As a result, Toṭaka's interpretation is to be dismissed as *aśrutakalpanā*. To associate the Chāndogya or any other Upaniṣad with the theory of false creation (*māyāvāda*) is undoubtedly an attempt at misreading the Vedic teaching of Vedānta.

NOTES

1. Bṛhadāraṇyaka Upaniṣad, 4-1-2.
2. Muṇḍaka Upaniṣad, 1-1-1.
3. Ibid., 1-1-3.
4. Ibid., 1-2-12.
5. Ibid., 1-1-5.
6. Ibid., 1-1-4.
7. Ibid., 3-2-4.
8. Chāndogya Upaniṣad (hereafter Ch. Up.), 6-2-1,2.
9. Ibid., 6-1-2.
10. Ibid.
11. Ibid.
12. Ibid., 6-1-4.
13. Ibid., 6-1-4; Kaṭha Upaniṣad, 1-2-6.
14. Ibid, 6-1-3.
15. Ibid.
16. Ibid.
17. Ibid., 6-1-4.
18. Ibid., 6-2-1.
19. Ibid., 6-1-4.

20. Ibid., 6-4-2.
21. Ibid.
22. Ibid., 6-3-2.
23. Ibid., 6-2-3,4.
24. Ibid., 7-25-2.
25. Ibid., 6-8-4.
26. Ibid., 6-1-3.
27. Ibid., 6-4-3.
28. Ibid.
29. Śaṅkara, *Muṇḍaka Upaniṣad Bhāṣya*, 2-1-3.
30. Michael Comans, *Extracting the Essence of the Śruti* (hereafter EES), Motilal Banarsidass, Delhi, 1996.
31. Ibid., verse 116.
32. Ibid., verse 134.
33. Ibid.,
34. Īśa Upaniṣad (hereafter Īś. Up.), Mantra 8.
35. Ibid.
36. EES, verse 117.
37. Ibid., verse 124.
38. Ibid., verse 127.
39. Īś. Up., Mantra 8.

19

Therefore That Became the World

THE THREE REALITIES

That (*tad*) is the highest reality, but it has become the world (*tat sarvam abhavat*). This statement occurs in the text 1-4-10 of the Bṛhadāraṇyaka Upaniṣad. In this important text three different realities are mentioned and they are harmoniously arranged. They are: (i) the reality of That which surpasses all (*sarvātīta*); (ii) the reality of Brahman which contains all (*sarvabhūtayoni*); (iii) the reality of all existences which arises out of That (*sarvāṇi bhūtāni*). The text shows that a complete knowledge consists in knowing all the three realities successively and simultaneously. Knowledge begins by knowing That which exceeds all; it becomes complete by knowing all as the modifications of That. The intervening step is provided by the knowledge of That as Brahman in which all are deeply hidden. This is the central teaching of the text 1-4-10 of the Bṛhadāraṇyaka.

TEXT AND TRANSLATION

Let us look at the text under discussion. We may speak of five divisions in it. They are as given below:

(i) *brahma vā idam agra āsīt. tad ātmānam evāvet ahaṃ brahmāsmīti. tasmāt tat sarvam abhavat.*

(ii) *tad yo yo devānāṃ pratyabudhyata sa eva tad abhavat; tathā ṛṣīṇāṃ; tathā manuṣyāṇāṃ; taddhaitat paśyan ṛṣir vāmadevaḥ pratipede ahaṃ manur abhavaṃ sūryaśceti.*

(iii) *tad idaṃ api etarhi ya evaṃ vedāhaṃ brahmāsmīti sa idaṃ sarvaṃ bhavati; tasya ha na devas ca nābhūtyā īśate. ātmā hy eṣāṃ sa bhavati;*

(iv) *atha yo anyāṃ devatām upāste anyo asau anyo ahamasmīti na sa veda; yathā paśur evaṃ sa devānām. yathā ha vai bahavaḥ paśavo manuṣyaṃ bhuñjyuḥ; evam ekaikaḥ puruṣo devān bhunakti; ekasminn eva paśāv ādiyamāne apriyaṃ bhavati, kim u bahuṣu;*

(v) *tasmād eṣāṃ tan na priyaṃ yad etan manuṣyā vidyuḥ.*

Now follows a translation of the original text:

(i) This was indeed Brahman in the beginning. That itself knew as "I am Brahman." Therefore That became the world.

(ii) Whoever among the gods knew That, he, indeed, became That. It is the same in the case of seers and in the case of men. Realising That to be this Brahman, the seer Vāmadeva knew "I was Manu and the Sun too".

(iii) That is this Brahman even now. Whoever in this manner knows That as "I am Brahman" becomes this world. Even the gods cannot prevent him from becoming thus, for he becomes their Self.

(iv) On the other hand, he does not know That, he who worships the god who is other than That. He thinks thus "He is one and I am one". He is like an animal to the gods. As many animals serve a man, so does each man serve the gods. Even if one animal is taken away, it causes displeasure to them, what should one say of many animals kept by them?

(v) Therefore it is not pleasing to the gods that men should know this formula of knowledge and become this world.

Having given the text and its translation, we shall now make an attempt to show how its central teaching is presented and developed. Before we do so, it is necessary to state and examine the existing commentary on the text by Śaṅkara. He explains the text as if it deals with the reality of Brahman alone and not with the other realities of That and the world. Thus his interpretation raises an important question about the text, and it has to be examined how far the text lends support to this interpretation.

THE METHOD OF SUPERIMPOSITION
(ADHYĀROPA PRAKRIYĀ)

Śaṅkara's interpretation of the text is well known. This Brahman in the body, he says, is certainly Brahman even before it is realised to be so (*brahma vā idam agra āsīt*). But owing to superimposition of ignorance Brahman thinks that it is not Brahman and, therefore, not all (*abrahmāsmyasarvaṃ ca ityātmanyadhyāropāt*).[1] By whom are ignorance and error caused? By Brahman, for there was none else before the two were superimposed. On whom are the two superimposed? On Brahman itself. Therefore by Brahman the two evils have come to exist in Brahman. It means that freedom from the two evils is to be won only by Brahman. This is why the text says thus — That knew Itself as "I am Brahman" (*tat ātmānam eva avet ahaṃ brahma asmīti*). By knowing in this manner Brahman became all (*tasmāt tat sarvam abhavat*). Śaṅkara points out that by the cessation of the superimposed notion of not being Brahman its effect viz. the notion of not being all ceased and from this, that Brahman became all (*abrahma-adhyāropaṇa-apagamāt-tatkāryasyāsarvatvasya-nivṛttyā sarvamabhavat*).[2] This means that the sentence "That knew Itself" should be understood as referring to the cessation of superimposition of ignorance (*ajñānādhyāropaṇa nivṛttireva*).[3]

Having dealt with the nature of the knowledge of Brahman, the text proceeds to unfold its significance for the gods, the seers, and men. From another text of this Upaniṣad[4] we know that Brahman has entered everywhere and dwells in all bodies. On account of this, whoever among the gods is awakened to Brahman becomes all. In like manner whoever among the seers and the men is awakened to Brahman attains the same result, the result of becoming all. That the knowledge of Brahman leads to this result (*brahmavidyāyāḥ sarvabhāvāpattiḥ*)[5] is supported by a quotation from the Ṛg Veda[6] where a seer called Vāmadeva says that by his knowledge of Brahman he was Manu and the Sun also. Here he is certainly speaking about the result of knowing Brahman, namely, the attainment of all by him (*sarvabhāvāpattiṃ brahmavidyāphalaṃ*).[7] It proves that the result viz. liberation (*mokṣa*)[8] is attainable through the knowledge of Brahman.

One may think, despite the assurance given about men, that this result is possible of attainment only in the case of the gods and the seers. In order to remove this wrong opinion the text adds that even the gods cannot prevent the man from getting the result. This implies two things. (i) The result is surely possible in the case of man; (ii) though the gods can prevent the result through their powers (*devāḥ prabhāvavantaḥ*),[9] they do not do so. Why do they not prevent it from him? For by knowing Brahman he becomes their self. As they cannot go against their own self, they have no option but to restrain themselves (*nātmanaḥ pratikūlatve devānāṃ prayatnaḥ sambhavati*).[10]

This leads to the question what is the position of the ignorant man in relation to the gods. To them he is bound by his indebtedness (*ṛṇivat*).[11] Hence he worships his god thinking "He is one and I am another" (*anyo asau anyo ahaṃ*) and does not know the truth (*na vijānāti tattvam*).[12] As an animal gives all kinds of services to its master, so he serves Him. If he sets aside the idea that he is a creature to the gods, it is not liked by them. For by this should he know his identity with Brahman, he would cease to be their object of enjoyment (*upabhogyam*).[13]

The aim of the text, according to Śaṅkara, is to show the difference between the two spheres — knowledge, on one side, and Ignorance, on the other (*vidyā-avidyā-vibhāga-pradarśnenaiva-upakṣīṇā*).[14] Knowledge raises him to Brahman beyond the gods; whereas Ignorance compels from him submissiveness and service to the gods.

THE METHOD OF VEDĀNTA (*VEDĀNTA PRAKRIYĀ*)

The present interpretation is based on the authority of the text itself — its original words, its natural meanings, and its subtle suggestions. In this respect it is unlike the interpretation based on the method of superimposition.

The highest Brahman is that which exceeds all limitations. Hence it is denoted by the word That (*tad*). However, there is another reality where all this is one with Brahman (*brahma vā idam agra āsīt*). When That and none else knows itself as this all-containing Brahman (*aham brahmāsmi iti*), That becomes the ultimate source of the world. As the source of the world, it is but natural for That to become all existences of the world. Therefore That becomes the whole world (*tasmāt tat sarvam abhavat*).

Now the Highest (*tad*) has become the entire world. However, all existences, especially the higher ones, are aware of themselves and not of the Highest from which they have arisen. Among the existences the text speaks of three categories — the gods (*devas*), the seers (*ṛṣis*), and men (*manuṣyas*). The gods are superior to the other two, for they are endowed with extra-ordinary powers by which they can alter the destinies of the two. The seers come from the family of enlightened men, whereas men come from ordinary families. However, the seer and the ordinary man are not different from each other, for both are mortals by birth. The text puts the gods, the seers, and men in a common category because all of them are ignorant of the Highest. If the ignorance is removed by being awakened to the reality of the Highest, the awakened one becomes That and is united with all existences in the world (*sa eva tad abhavat*). This is true of all the three — the gods, the seers, and men. In support of this observation the text quotes from the Ṛg Veda,[15] the earliest authority in these matters, where the seer Vāmadeva says that he was Manu and the Sun also (*aham manur abhavam sūryaśceti*). This was the result of his realisation of That as Brahman (*taddhaitat paśyan*). Note that Manu and the Sun are cases of modification into the world of names and forms.

This formula of knowledge is effective even now, says the text. Whoever knows the Highest as the all-containing Brahman (*ahaṃ brahmāsmīti*) becomes all existences in the world (*sa idaṃ sarvaṃ bhavati*). Even the gods cannot prevent him from being united with all in the world. Actually this is a result determined by That (*tad*). The gods are indeed superior to men, but they are not superior to That. For they have come from That and have That as their Self (*ātmā*). Strictly speaking, man becomes the world by becoming That (*sa eva tad abhavat*). In the circumstance no god can obstruct the result, the result of becoming the world by him.

In the condition of ignorance man is separated from the Highest. And the god is no exception to this consequence (*anyāṃ devatām*). He views himself as one (*anyo aham*) and the god as one (*anyo asau*). For him the highest in the world is the god. Hence he offers worship to Him. As his worship proceeds from ignorance, he does not know the true Self that stands behind him and the god (*sa na veda*). What is the result of this worship? Like an animal (*paśuḥ*) he serves the god. And the god does not want him to be taken away from Him. For He is attached to him as an object of enjoyment. From the side of man he is attached to the god. For He fulfils all his desires and brings happiness to his life. Thus his dependence is secured on both sides — on one side by his own attachment and on the other by the attachment of the god. To the above question what is the result of giving worship by an ignorant man to an ignorant god the answer is that he becomes dependent on the god and his dependence hardens into an eternal bondage.

What happens when there is an opportunity for man to escape this bondage through the knowledge of That and become absolutely free like That? As the text has already indicated, it causes displeasure to the gods (*eṣām tan na priyaṃ*). For they do not want that he should know this formula of knowledge (*etat*) and attain freedom from bondage. However, their displeasure and unwillingness become ineffective when he seizes the opportunity and sees that he is really independent of them.

Knowledge brings completeness of being and freedom from bondage. On the contrary, ignorance imposes smallness, submissiveness, and irrevocable bondage. Hence knowledge is desirable. The object of knowledge is to know the Example set by That (*evaṃ veda*) and become the world (*sa idaṃ sarvaṃ bhavati*) like That. This is the teaching of the text 1-4-10.

THE IMPORTANCE OF THE TEXT

In part 1 of the text 1-4-10 the word *idam* occurs. It conveys the same sense as conveyed by it in the preceding and the succeeding mantras of the Upaniṣad, namely, the mantras 1-4-7 and 1-4-11. As in 1-4-10 so in 1-4-7 and 1-4-11 the word is used in their opening sentences. In all of them it conveys the sense of the world. In the text under discussion (1-4-10) the sense of *idam* is clearly expanded and stated as *idam sarvam* (part 3). In another text[16] of the Bṛhadāraṇyaka Upaniṣad the expanded version of *idam sarvam* occurs repeatedly. Besides this the word, unless and otherwise specified, is used everywhere in the Upaniṣads to convey the same sense, namely, the sense of the world. Hence *sarvam* (the world) is the natural sense of the word *idam* (this). As a result, the words *idam agra āsīt* describe the condition of the world before it came into existence. From this it is clear that the word *agra* refers to a condition before the actual creation of the world (*sṛṣṭi*). What was its condition before creation? It existed in a supreme state of oneness with its cause, namely, Brahman (*brahma vā idam agra āsīt*). It agrees with the creation-texts of all Upaniṣads where Brahman is presented as the ultimate cause of the world. Here in part 1 Brahman is presented as the highest source in which the whole world exists unextended and unevolved. In other words, part 1 begins by speaking about the all-containing reality of Brahman.

An advocate of the theory of superimposition (*adhyāropa*), Śaṅkara does not want to take the first sentence in part 1 as it stands. Therefore he explains the words *idam*, *agra,* and *āsīt* differently — *idam* as the Brahman (Ātman) perceived in the body of the individual; *agra* as the condition preceding his enlightenment or liberation; *āsīt* as the ever-accomplished state of Brahman. If we look at 1-4-10 in relation to its previous and subsequent texts, 1-4-7 and 1-4-11, we are sure to be convinced that Śaṅkara's interpretation of the above three words is totally out of context. The meanings he has assigned to them are not supported by the scripture. He has rejected their intended senses because they speak something not acceptable to his theory of Brahman. According to his theory, Brahman alone is real (*sat*) and the world is a non-real superimposition (*a-sat*). Between the two there can never be a relation of oneness. Hence he is compelled to deviate from the natural meanings of the above words and give them his own independent meanings. Even if his theory is correct, it does not qualify him, under any circumstance, to reject the natural meanings of the words of the Upaniṣad. It is impermissible.

We have to note how the first and the second sentences in part 1 are connected with each other. The second goes like this: That and none else knew itself as "I am Brahman." In the Upaniṣads the word *tad* (That) has a special significance. Though Brahman is said to be the highest reality, another reality higher than the Brahman is also recognised. This is referred to as the supreme Brahman (*paramambrahma*)[17] or as That Brahman (*tadbrahma*).[18] This is designated as simply That (*tad*). That is beyond all classifications, all predications, and all words. For it is limitless and absolutely free. On account of this very fact, That assumes limitations. And this assumption by That causes no bondage whatever. For even after the assumption That remains completely free. This is the true significance of the word *eva* in the second sentence in part 1. That Brahman assumes the status of the ultimate cause of the world by knowing itself to be the all-containing Brahman. By assuming thus That does not cease to be what it was originally. For the assumption by That is an act of absolute freedom. In short, That becomes Brahman, but by becoming thus That has not lost its original freedom. It remains the same as ever. This is the connotation of the word That (*tad*). In the expression "I am Brahman" the subject stands for the reality of That; the predicate for the reality of Brahman as defined in the opening sentence; and lastly, the verb for the act of assumption of the form of Brahman by That. This explains how the connection between the two sentences is effected by the text.

In Śaṅkara's view the connection between the two sentences is worked out differently. The first sentence, according to him, means that Brahman is an eternally accomplished fact. But the second sentence speaks as if this accomplishment is possible only after knowing Brahman. This is a contradiction. Therefore he thinks that a proper connection between the two sentences is not possible if the second sentence is to be taken as it is. He tries to overcome this difficulty by bringing in the theory of superimposition. Though Brahman is eternally accomplished, it does not cognise the fact. For it has superimposed on itself the notion of ignorance (*adhyāropayati*)[19] and thinks that it is not Brahman and not all (*abrahmāsmyasarvaṃ ca*).[20] The superimposition is removed when it knows itself (*ātmānam*) as "I am Brahman" (*aham brahmāsmīti*). This eliminates, says Śaṅkara, the seeming contradiction between the first two sentences in part 1. He goes further and points out that the words "That knew only Itself" are to be understood not as a process of knowledge but as a process of removal of superimposition of ignorance. But if we examine the original text, we are convinced that Śaṅkara's interpretation is totally unwarranted. There is absolutely nothing in the text to suggest that the connection between the above two sentences is made through the idea of superimposition of ignorance on Brahman and its subsequent removal from Brahman.

The second sentence says that the supreme Brahman (That) assumes the form of Brahman. But what exactly is the nature of the form thus assumed by That? This is clarified by the first which defines the Brahman as the ultimate cause of the world. While the second is the primary statement, the first precedes it merely as a statement of clarification which throws light on the significance of the word Brahman. Thus there is really no contradiction between the two sentences and, therefore, no need to resolve it. Actually, the second sentence embodies a transition from knowledge to knowledge, from the all-excluding consciousness to the all-including consciousness, from That (*aham*) to That-is-Brahman (*brahmāsmi*). In this process there is no place at all for the play of ignorance and its removal.

The third sentence in part 1 is the logical culmination of what is affirmed by the second sentence. Brahman holds within itself all the contents of the world. When That knows itself to be Brahman, That becomes the source of the world (*sarvabhūtayoni*). This is the affirmation of the second sentence. The law of development requires that whatever is implicit becomes explicit, whatever is unmanifest becomes manifest. In fulfilment of the law That becomes all, i.e., all existences of the world (*sarvāṇi bhūtāni*). This is what the third sentence says — *tasmāt tat sarvam abhavat*. The word *tasmāt* in it is very important. It signifies that the world comes into existence not fortuitously but in fulfilment of an eternal necessity inherent in the very nature of That. Likewise, the word *abhavat* in it indicates that the world is not a falsehood but a creation of a truth of That. The above word comes from the root *bhū* which always means a real process, a real modification.

Śaṅkara is not inclined to accept the deep meanings attached to the words *tasmāt* and *abhavat*. He takes them in their most ordinary senses — *tasmāt* in the sense of result (*phala*) and *abhavat* in the sense of attainment (*prāpti*). As for the word *sarvam*, he gives up its natural sense. It occurs very frequently in the Upaniṣads in the nominative and accusative cases and in all of them it stands for all creatures of the world, or simply the world (*prapañca*). In the present text (1-4-10) the words *aham manur abhavaṃ sūryaśceti* clearly suggest that by *sarvam* is meant the world. This is confirmed by the words that come subsequently — *sa idaṃ sarvaṃ bhavati*. However, he wants to make it speak something else not inconsistent with his theory of superimposition. Hence he reads *sarvam* as an attribute — *sarvātmabhāva*[21] (all-selfness) or *sarvabhāva*[22] (all-ness). All-selfness, according to him, is an attribute of Brahman (*sarvātmatvam*).[23] The third sentence in part 1 of the text *tasmāt tat sarvam abhavat* is forced to say this: "Therefore Brahman attained the *nature* of Brahman." This, he says, is the result of *knowing* Brahman. In this way the word *sarvam* is made to forgo its original reference to the world. Nowhere in the Upaniṣads it conveys the sense of the nature (*sarvātmatva*) of Brahman. If we compare the second sentence with the third one, we may find that the third is reduced to a mere tautology. For it says nothing beyond what the second has already said. Thus the third sentence is skilfully nullified.

In this connection another point is to be made. The original text refers to a mantra from the Ṛg Veda where Vāmadeva speaks about his knowledge "I was Manu and the Sun too." The mantra is mentioned with a view to show how by the knowledge of That he became the world.This is very clear. But Śaṅkara's interpretation of the mantra is different. Having taken *tat sarvam abhavat* as saying that Brahman attained Brahman's *sarvātmabhāvam* or *sarvātmatvam*, he points out that the words "I was Manu and the Sun too" refer to the attainment of *sarvātmatvam* of Brahman through the knowledge of Brahman (*brahmavidyā*). Definitely this interpretation is not borne out by the words "I was Manu and the Sun too". For the words simply mean that Vāmadeva became this world. This proves that *sarvam* in *tat sarvam abhavat* cannot be given the sense of *sarvātmatvam* or *sarvātmabhāvam* of Brahman. It (*sarvam*) is used in the text, as we have already said, only in the sense of the world (*prapañca*) extended in names and forms.

Man is born as an ignorant individual, as one who does not know That (*na sa veda*). Hence he is attached to the gods, like an animal attached to its master. He is helpless and incapable of going beyond their influence and control. However, when he knows That, he must know even as That knows itself and becomes the world. Otherwise he may know That but not know *like* That. His knowledge will be incomplete and limited to one aspect of That. Complete knowledge is possible only when he is united with the whole world and attains likeness to That (*sā-dharmya*). Having become like That, he is absolutely un- attached and free. There are two things to be noted. At one level he is united with the gods. That is not only his Self but also the Self of the gods. At another level he is similar to them. He and the gods are but two types of modification of That. As a result, the original relations between the two disappear — there is neither the dependence of man nor the domination of the gods. If men give their attention to the knowledge of That and neglect the other equally important knowledge, namely, That-is-Brahman, they become escapists and enter That as if into a great darkness (*bhūya iva te tamaḥ praviśanti*)[24] or into a state of non-existence.

If man can go beyond the power of the gods and become absolutely free like That, how is he prevented by them from knowing the reality of That? He is prevented by his own worship (*upāsanā*), by the worship he offers to them. Always he has the option to abandon his worship and escape enslavement by the gods. As long as he does not make up his mind and exercise the option open to him, he cannot cross the boundaries set and watched by them. If, on the other hand, he changes his mind and drops all his worship, then the gods cannot prevent him from knowing That. For the cause behind his blind subservience to them is now completely removed.

The text speaks about three distinct orders of reality — That (*tad*), Brahman (*brahma*), and the world (*sarvam*). All the three are to be known in order to know in the same manner (*evam veda*) as That knows itself. However, Śaṅkara interprets the text as if it deals only with the reality of Brahman. This raises two questions: (i) what is the reason for his own reading of the text (ii) and how does he accomplish his task? (i) According to his theory, there is no other reality than that of Brahman — neither That, which is higher than Brahman, nor the world, which is dependent on Brahman. This answers the first question. (ii) By explaining away the two important words *tad* and *sarvam* he establishes that Brahman is the only reality besides which no other reality exists. He takes *tad* as another word for Brahman, while *sarvam* is twisted by him to mean the nature of Brahman. This answers the second question. Now it is clear how the original text is completely distorted and compelled to say that Brahman is the only reality to be known.

An important distinction is to be made between two forms of knowledge — knowledge of That and knowledge of Brahman. The eligible persons for the two are different from each other. While the first is meant for the ignorant (*avidvān*), the second is prescribed for the knower of That (*vidvān*). However, Śaṅkara thinks that the text 1-4-10 is concerned with the knowledge of Brahman alone for which the eligible is the ignorant (*sukhī duḥkhī saṃsārī*).[25] He thinks so because he does not grasp the subtle difference between the two forms of knowledge presupposing two different eligible persons.

There is absolutely no opposition between the two realities — That and the world. There are two major powers. By the one, That conceives all. By the other, That creates all according to the original conception. Thus conception and creation are the two eternal powers by which That becomes the world. As the world is made from That the two are one and inseparable. This is the Advaita of the Bṛhadāraṇyaka Upaniṣad.

There are two methods for interpreting the text 1-4-10 — the method of Superimposition (*adhyāropaprakriyā*) and the method of Vedānta (*vedāntaprakriyā*). The results of the first are really shocking and amazing. For the original words of the scripture are deliberately twisted and even nullified. Therefore we must reject the first and favour the second. The method of Vedānta proceeds from the clues and the logical connections supplied by the original words themselves. As a result, all its interpretations are determined by the authority of the scripture. This is why they are always natural and trustworthy.

NOTES

1. *Ten Principal Upaniṣads* (with Śaṅkarabhāṣya) (hereafter TPU), Motilal Banarsidass, Delhi, 2000, p. 672.
2. Ibid., p.674.
3. Ibid.
4. Bṛhadāraṇyaka Upaniṣad (hereafter Bṛ Up.), 2-5-18
5. TPU, p.674.
6. Ṛg Veda (hereafter RV), 4-26-1.
7. TPU, p.674.
8. Ibid.
9. Ibid., p. 675.
10. Ibid., p. 676.
11. Ibid., p. 679.
12. Ibid.
13. Ibid., p. 680.
14. Ibid., p. 679.
15. RV, 4-26-1.
16. Bṛ Up., 2-5.
17. Ibid., 4-1-7.
18. Kaṭha Upaniṣad, 2-3-1.
19. TPU, p.672.
20. Ibid.
21. Ibid., p.674.
22. Ibid.
23. Śaṅkara, *Brahmasūtra Bhāṣya*, 1-3-9.
24. Bṛ Up., 4-4-10.
25. TPU, p.672.

20

Death and Immortality

THE WRONG METHOD

Interpretations of the Bṛhadāraṇyaka Upaniṣad by ascetics have their own merits. Their merits relate to the minor insights preserved by them. Fundamentally, they have mutilated the text and made it speak in a tone not in consonance with the vigorous voice of the Vedas. The mutilation is due to *adhyāropāpavāda prakriyā*, their method of interpretation. It is a method quite alien to the genius of the Upaniṣad. There is absolutely no justification for the method either through utility or through scriptural authority. As for utility, the measure of harmony it has brought out in the text is much less than the numerous instances of violence committed upon the original words, phrases and passages. As regards scriptural authority, there is not a single evidence in the original in support of the method. As a result, the Upaniṣad remains an ill-understood text, not having anything to do with its exposition of the inner sense of the Vedas (*vedānta*).

THE LAW OF THE TRUTH (*SATYADHARMA*)

In its self-form (*svarūpa*) Being is Ātman and the same Being in its self-becoming (*svabhāva*) is Jagat. Thus both Ātman and Jagat are one Being (*sat*). Ātman is immutable, unmanifest and one, whereas Jagat is mutable, manifest and manifold.

Jagat has two aspects, higher and lower. In the higher aspect it is Prāṇa, Life-Force. It is absolutely free and without mortal characteristics (*tad etad amṛtaṃ*)[1]. In the lower aspect it is Prāṇa veiled by nāma and rūpa (*tābhyām ayaṃ prāṇaś channaḥ*)[2] because they are overcome by death (*mṛtyunābhipannam*)[3]. Basically nāma and rūpa are *sat* (*nāmarūpe satyam*),[4] as is Prāṇa, and, therefore, cannot veil the latter. But still they veil it because they are now in the grip of death. In other words, Jagat will be absolutely free of death when *nāma* and *rūpa* are recognised to be the becomings (*bhūtas*) of the immortal Prāṇa and, therefore, one in essence with it which is no other than Ātman in Movement.

Take any being here. It has two aspects, individual and universal. In both these aspects Prāṇa is the self (*ayam eva sa yo'yam ātmā*).[5] When one knows Prāṇa to be the Life-Force of Ātman and the individual and universal to be two manifestations of the Prāṇa, all relations between the two give up their mortal characteristics and express sweetness and delight (*madhu*). This is the essential teaching of Madhu Brāhmaṇa (2-5).

Jagat is a harmonious arrangement of three fundamental truths — the truth of name and form (*nāmarūpa*), the truth of Life-Force which is the image of Ātman (*pratirūpa*) and the truth of the immortal Ātman (*svarūpa*). All three complement and support one another. This is the Law of the Truth (*satyadharma*).[6] He who knows and transacts here according to the Law is an all-knower (*sarvavit*)[7] and a winner of the world (*lokajit*).[8]

THREE PARABLES OF PRĀṆA

Bṛhadāraṇyaka extols the excellence of Prāṇa through significant parables. According to one (1-5-21), the Lord of beings created the organs. After this they quarrelled with one another. The organ of speech resolved, "I will go on speaking", the eye, "I will go on seeing", the ear, "I will go on hearing". So did the other organs according to their functions. Death seized them all in the form of weariness. Having overtaken them, it restrained them. As a result, the organs, one by one, became tired. However, death could not overtake Prāṇa in the body. The other organs, therefore, resolved to know it and said, "This is verily the greatest among us (*naḥ śreṣṭhaḥ*). Whether moving or not moving, it neither suffers nor is injured. Well, let us assume its form alone". Having known the fact about Prāṇa, they assumed its form alone.

According to another parable (1-5-22), which is a variation of 1-5-21, the gods quarrelled with one another. Fire resolved "I will go on burning". The sun said, "I will go on giving heat". The moon said, "I will go on shining". And so did the other gods according to their functions. As Prāṇa among the organs holds the central position, so does Vāyu among the gods. On account of this uniqueness, Vāyu continued to function without obstruction, but the other gods could not. Vāyu is the one god for whom there is no decline.

A third parable (1-3-1 to 7) tells us that there was a rivalry between Devas and Asuras. Devas were few and Asuras many. They struggled with one another for mastery of the worlds. Devas tried to overcome Asuras through Udgītha at the sacrifice. So they asked the organ of speech to chant Udgītha for them. As Asuras knew that through this chanter Devas would overcome them, they charged the organ and pierced it with evil. As a result, it could not help Devas. So Devas tried to get the support of the other organs such as the organs of smelling, seeing and hearing. Overtaken by Asuras, they also failed to support them. Then Devas turned to mind only to be outwitted again by their adversaries. At last Devas approached Āsanya Prāṇa (Prāṇa in the mouth) and asked it to chant Udgītha for them. In order to prevent the Prāṇa from helping Devas, Asuras charged it, hoping to pierce it with evil. But like a clod of clay, they were crushed and destroyed and scattered in all directions.

The parables establish that Prāṇa manifests itself both in the individual (physical body) and universal (god-form). But in neither of them is it overcome by death, for it is verily immortal (*prāṇo vā amṛtam*).[9] When it is known to be such, one conquers death which keeps spoiling all our interactions with the world and makes life a life of recurrent fear and misery (*punar mṛtyuṃ jayati*).[10] As a result, life in the world becomes a harmonious play of relations invested with sweetness and delight (*madhu*). This is the real significance of Mind and Senses assuming the nature of Prāṇa (*ta etasyaiva sarve rūpamabhavan*)[11] and of the gods achieving world-mastery through the chanter of Udgītha (*ta eṣu lokeṣvaspardhanta*).[12] Moreover, this explains why Prāṇa is extolled as the greatest and the most excellent power in the world (*jyeṣṭhaṃ ca śreṣṭhaṃ ca*).[13]

DEATH AND ITS MEANING

Generally, death is regarded as the opposite of life. Thus cessation of physical life is called death. In ancient days physical life lasting for a hundred years was considered to be the full term of embodied existence for a human being. It was referred to as *dīrghāyu*. In the Veda the sages insist on living a hundred years in the world (*śataṃ himāḥ*) (hundred winters). The same insistence is found in the Upaniṣads also, but less frequently. The Īśa says that one should desire to live a hundred years performing works here (*jijīviṣet śataṃ samāḥ*).[14] The concern of the sages is that death should not occur before they completed their full term of existence. But they do recognise the fact that death is inevitable and that no one can live without facing it at all. Hence the Īśa speaks of the body being consumed by the fire at the end (*bhasmāntaṃ śarīram*).[15]

There is another sense according to which death is understood. In this sense death and immortality are regarded as opposites. The Īśa Upaniṣad says that one attains immortality by passing out of death (*mṛtyuṃ tīrtvā ... amṛtam aśnute*).[16] Here escape from death does not mean freedom from physical death. Nor does attainment of immortality mean that by immunizing against the causes of death the body is made immortal. For in another verse, as we have already mentioned, the same Upaniṣad says that ashes are the end of physical life (*bhasmāntam*).[17] If one can escape death and at the same time the body is not freed from the necessity of death, then death in the first instance signifies something other than physical dissolution of the body.

If we know what immortality stands for, then we may easily understand the sense given to death. In the Upaniṣads immortality is an essential attribute of Brahman. Hence they affirm that by knowing Brahman one becomes immortal or that by becoming immortal one knows Brahman. Thus Brahman and immortality are used as mutually convertible terms. As Brahman is absolutely free of imperfections, limitations, deficiencies, untruths, bonds, injuries, sufferings and the like, the negative expression *immortality* signifies absence of these faults in Brahman. From this we may easily infer that death, which is the opposite of immortality, stands for all the faults listed above. In the Bṛhadāraṇyaka death is used in the following senses: hunger,[18] evil,[19] darkness and falsehood,[20] weariness, obstruction, suffering and injury [21] and ignorance of right relations.[22] This bears ample testimony to the fact that death is equated with all types of faults.

If we go one step further and examine the faults, we may get a deeper view of them, i.e., they all have smallness as their essence. For when we live and act within the boundaries of smallness, faults are the inevitable results. Hence death may be defined as smallness. For this profound insight we are indebted to the Chāndogya, another ancient Upaniṣad like the Bṛhadāraṇyaka. It says that while immortality consists in being immense (*yo vai bhūma tad amṛtam*),[23] death as its opposite consists in being small (*yad alpaṃ tan martyam*).[24]

If death is smallness, we must know what this smallness is. We must remember that the world is a harmonious arrangement of three truths — truths of Ātman, original Life-Force and Nāmarūpa. This is the Law of the Truth. If we know our self to be all three in themselves and in their mutual relations, there is no veil between us and the gods and the Life-Force is a means of mutual nourishment and enjoyment. This is to know and live according to the law, this is to dwell in immensity. On the contrary, if we disregard the Law and exclusively attach ourselves to the individual name and form consisting of mind and senses, we create a veil between us and the gods and convert the Life-Force into a means of mutual isolation and dissatisfaction. Hence smallness consists in being identified with one's mind and senses, a portion of one's original existence.

From this it is clear that smallness arises from immensity when the Law of the Truth is disregarded. Conversely, it disappears into the immensity when the truth of Nāmarūpa is united with those of Life-Force and Ātman and with this the Law of the Truth is upheld. Therefore, the way to conquer death is to enlarge its boundaries till they are completely dissolved in the immortal Ātman. This is referred to as death becoming one's Ātman (*mṛtyur asya ātmā bhavati*).[25]

Thus death is understood in two distinct senses: (i) as a departure from life; (ii) as a deviation from immensity into smallness. Etymologically, both senses are valid. From *mṛta*, death is a condition of being dead; likewise, it is also a condition of being reduced and made into tiny particles. A right understanding of death as dealt with in the Upaniṣads is possible only when the two senses of the word are clearly comprehended.

ATTAINMENT OF IMMORTALITY

Yājñavalkya, being himself a seer of non-duality (*draṣṭādvaitaḥ*),[26] expounds the nature of immortality to his wife Maitreyī who is acquainted with the metaphysics of Brahman (*brahmavādinī*).[27] He tells her that immortality is won not by wealth but by the knowledge of Ātman.

Yājñavalkya's account of immortality has two parts, one dealing with the non-dualistic view and another with the dualistic view. The non-dualistic view consists in seeing the world as a manifestation of Ātman and, therefore, all names and forms to be invested with the light of Ātman and to be in harmonious relation with the Ātman and with one another, whereas the dualistic view consists in excluding Ātman from the world and seeing the world as an aggregate of separate names and forms each measuring all in terms of its self-sufficiency. As a result, all relations between beings are exclusive and without harmony. He who lives in the dualistic view is a mortal, but he who gives up the dualistic view and embraces the non-dualistic one ceases to be a mortal and attains immortality (*amṛtam aśnute*).

(i) According to Yājñavalkya, the worlds, the gods, the beings and all else possessing names and forms are Ātman. For all of them are breathed forth by Ātman (*asyaiva etāni sarvāṇi niḥśvasitāni*).[28] The image of breath is intended to affirm that the world is brought into existence by means of Prāṇa which is no other than Ātman's Life-Force. Thus Ātman is not only the ultimate source of the world but also the world itself — the original Life-Force and the names and forms that are its becomings (*imāni bhūtāni*). In fact, there are three truths: in the beginning, the truth of Ātman; in the middle, the truth of Life-Force; and in the end, the truth of Nāmarūpa. Though three, they are indivisible; they are one Ātman in three modes. The highest and the lowest are held together in perfect harmony by Prāṇa which exists in both: in Ātman it exists as its very form and in Nāmarūpa it exists as its inner controller (*antaryāmī*).[29] Hence it is aptly called the Thread (*tad sūtram*).[30] That the three stand together in perfect harmony and union is brought out by a revealing image in the Bṛhadāraṇyaka — the image of a chariot wheel (*ratha-cakra*).[31] There are three parts in the wheel and they correspond to the three truths mentioned above — the hub (*ratha-nābhiḥ*) to Ātman; the felly (*ratha-nemiḥ*) to Prāṇa; and the spokes (*arāḥ*) to Nāmāni Rūpāni. Just as the spokes are held together by the felly and hub, so all names and forms are held together by both Prāṇa and Ātman. To know Ātman thus is to possess a complete knowledge of it (*saṃjñā*).[32] The harmonious arrangement of the three truths is referred to as the Law of the indestructible Ātman (*anucchittidharmā*)[33] by Yājñavalkya.

To bring home the importance of complete knowledge Yājñavalkya gives several examples. The examples fall into two classes. In the first are included the examples of drum, conch and *vīṇa*; in the second are put those of the ocean, the skin, the nostrils, etc. Harmonious sounds arise when a drum is beaten, a conch blown and a *vīṇa* played. In each case what strikes us first is the particular notes. With them the underlying harmony cannot be grasped. But when the general note is taken into account, the harmony behind the particular notes is grasped. There are many waters such as rivers, lakes, etc.; there are many kinds of touch; there are many kinds of smell. But all waters, all kinds of touch and all smells do not exist in themselves. The waters meet at the ocean, the various kinds of touch at the skin, and all smells at the nostrils. In other words, the examples teach that all diversities are incomplete in themselves and become complete only when they reach the highest point at which they are united.

He who knows and acts according to the Law of the imperishable Ātman is immortal and has rid himself of all mortal characteristics by possessing which he lived in his separate self and hurt others around him through his egoistic attitude. As a result, he is now full of love for Ātman and all that have come from and belong to Ātman. He loves all for the sake of Ātman (*ātmanaḥ ... kāmāya*).[34] And all his relations with the world are based on this love. What he gives to the world, the world returns to him. For this is the rule: He receives happiness from all beings in return for giving happiness to the world of which he is a citizen.[35]

(ii) He who is ignorant of Ātman abides in a place other than Ātman (*anyatrātmanaḥ*).[36] Evidently he abides in smallness which is the same as death. Thus abiding, he looks upon himself as *anyaḥ* (another) and the person who is before him also as *anyaḥ* (another) (*anyo'sau anyo'ham asmi*).[37] This outlook is inevitable for a person who lives in death and bound by death. For, as the Chāndogya puts it, when one sees something else (*anyat*), that is smallness.[38] We know that smallness is another word for death. Therefore a person bound by death can uphold only relations that estrange him from others in the world. We see how by estrangement from the gods he is brought to the level of a brute, an object of contempt (*yathā paśur evam sa devānām*).[39] He hurts the gods by estranging himself from them and so they hurt him back by treating him as a beast. This is true of all relations he establishes with the world. As they are conditioned by death, they bring him only evil and misery. By failing to know and live according to the Law of the imperishable Ātman he has fallen into death and assumed mortal attributes. However, death is falsehood (*asat*) and falsehood disappears when he passes from the dualistic to the non-dualistic view of the world.

Attention must be drawn to the two passages 2-4-12 and 2-4-14. They are most misunderstood from the time of Śaṅkara, the first known commentator of the Upaniṣads. In them Yājñavalkya sums up his view of immortality.

(i) If we carefully analyse 2-4-12, we may find that it has three parts. In the first, the sage speaks of water into which a lump of salt is thrown and dissolved. And the water is salty wherever one tastes it. In the second, the salty water is compared to the great Being (*mahat bhūta*) which is infinite and without boundaries. The Being is verily a mass pervaded by consciousness (*vijñāna-ghanaeva*). Like the water which is salty everywhere, the mass is conscious at all points. The Being is called a mass (*ghanaḥ*) because It is a multitude of forms. In other words, the great Being is Ātman which has become the world by assuming a multiplicity of names and forms, The expression *mahat bhūta* is significant. The word *bhūta* gives two senses, being and becoming. So the phrase means Being that has become great through infinite (*anantam*) forms and boundless (*apāram*) extension in space and time. In the third, he speaks about an individual soul possessing mind and senses and living and enjoying in the world. The soul, mind and senses are the different becomings of Ātman (*etāni bhūtāni*). As his soul, mind, etc., are overcome by death, he lives here as a mortal being. Abiding in death, he is attached to his mind and senses and lives in a place other than Ātman (*anyatrātmanaḥ*). He is ignorant of his individual self, the self of others and the original Ātman which lives everywhere having built its numerous habitations through Prāṇa, its Life-Force. Thus he lives in falsehood (*asat*) without knowing the fact. Only after he destroys the forms of death (*tāny eva anuvinaśyati*) does he come out of his attachment for the becomings consisting of mind and senses (*etebhyo bhūtebhyaḥ samutthāya*). But certainly he does not destroy his mind and senses by abandoning them. For what is actually destroyed is death which keeps him in bondage to his body. Thus he passes out of death but does not pass out of his body (*na pretya*).[40] The words *na pretya* are carefully chosen to tell us that *vinaśyati* refers to the destruction of something else and not the body. By staying here with mind and senses, he gets complete knowledge — knowledge of Nāmarūpa, Prāṇa and Ātman (*saṃjñā*).

After Yājñavalkya speaks thus, Maitreyī complains that he has bewildered her through the words *na pretya saṃjñāsti*. She is confused because she has understood *vinaśyati* to mean destruction of mind and senses causing thereby physical death. She thinks that immortality is attained after leaving the body.[41] Hence the closing words *na pretya* (not having departed from physical body) bewilder her. This is a mistake she can rectify herself by carefully going through his words once again. For she is a Brahmavādinī.[42] Reflection is necessary to avoid a mistake of this type. Therefore he replies that he has not said anything bewildering. Having said this, he tries to explain his statement in the next passage.

(ii) The other passage 2-4-14 is about transition from death to immortality, from the condition of duality to that of non-duality. There are two parts in the passage. In the first is given the condition of one bound by death. By living and acting in death he lives and acts in a place other than Ātman (*anyatrātmanaḥ*).[43] As a result, his relations in life have become relations between *itara* and *itara*, other and other: other smells other, other sees other, other hears other, other speaks to other, other thinks of other, other understands other. In fact, these dual relations are false, for they are the results of living in falsehood which is death. Hence the particle *iva* qualifies duality (*dvaitamiva*).

In the second part is stated the condition of one who has passed out of death and attained immortality. For him Ātman has become everything here, himself and all around him (*sarvam ātmaivābhūt*). He finds everything to be a becoming of Ātman. As a result, all his relations in the world undergo a drastic change. They cease to be dual and have become non-dual. Now Ātman smells Ātman; Ātman sees Ātman; Ātman hears Ātman; Ātman speaks to Ātman; Ātman thinks of Ātman; and Ātman understands Ātman. Thus there are two forms of Ātman: Ātman who knows and Ātman who is known. Since one is known by the other, does it mean that the knower-Ātman too is known by another Ātman? No, it is inconceivable. Because the knower-Ātman is the highest and He alone and none else has become all here (*sarvam ātmaivābhūt*). Hence the Upaniṣad elsewhere says: "There is no other knower besides the knowner-Ātman (*na anyat ataḥ asti vijñātṛ*)".[44] He who sees everything abiding in Ātman is a seer of non-duality (*draṣṭādvaitaḥ*).[45] He is an immortal being who maintains all relations in the world through Ātman and loves all for the sake of Ātman (*ātmanaḥ ... kāmāya bhūtāni priyāṇi bhavanti*).[46] He lives and interacts with the world without obstructions from death. In fact, this whole passage (2-4-14) is a detailed commentary on the key phrase which occurs in 2-4-12, namely, *na pretya saṃjñāsti*.

THE TWO ASPECTS OF IMMORTALITY

Immortality consists not only in knowing the immortal Ātman but also in expressing the immortal Prāṇa through soul, mind and senses and living as an image of Ātman in the world. Thus immortality is both Knowledge and Life. The best among the knowers of Brahman, says the Muṇḍaka Upaniṣad, is one who is a doer of works (*kriyāvān*), delights in Ātman and brings about the play of Ātman in his active life (*ātmakrīḍa ātmaratiḥ*).[47]

(i) According to the Law of the imperishable Ātman, the world is the great Ātman having assumed infinite names and forms and extended in boundless Space and Time. This huge Mass is verily conscious everywhere and nothing in it is devoid of consciousness (*vijñānaghana eva*). In this all are true (*sat*). There is no place for anything false (*asat*). Names and forms are true, Prāṇa through which Ātman has become huge (*mahat*) is true, and Ātman, the ultimate source of names and forms, is also true. In the words of the Upaniṣad Ātman is the truth of truths (*satyasya satyam*).[48] Of course, death (*asat*) is there in the world, but it is an accidental and not an essential aspect. When a person becomes immortal, his knowledge is not limited to Ātman but extended to Prāṇa and all names and forms. It excludes only limitation of knowledge. It is for this reason that Yājñavalkya speaks of a liberated person getting complete knowledge (*saṃjñā*).[49] If for any reason we think that the Upaniṣad is concerned with Ātman to the exclusion of the rest, we are mistaken. Its teaching is very clear and it insists on becoming an all-knower (*sarvavit*),[50] a knower of the whole scale of existence (*sat*).

(ii) As long as a person is mortal, he is a dualist who regards everything as abiding in a place other than Ātman, namely, death. To him all abiding in death are estranged from one another. In them the subject is other, the object is other and the relations between the two are other-based relations. As all other-based relations are conditioned by death, they only express death, namely, fear, hatred and grief. On the contrary, when the person passes from mortality to immortality, he becomes a non-dualist who regards everything as abiding in Ātman. To him all abiding in Ātman exist together and are not estranged from one another. In them the subject is Ātman, the object is Ātman and the relations between the two are Ātman-based relations. As all Ātman-based relations are free from death, they naturally express immortality, namely, love, friendship and joy. When death is abolished, duality is abolished but not names and forms nor their relations. All of them continue to exist but with the light and bliss of Ātman. Thus immortality is not only attainment of Knowledge but of Life expressive of sweet and delightful relations with all in the world. This is the justification for the commencement of Madhu Brāhmaṇa immediately after the teaching on the nature of life founded upon the knowledge of non-duality in 2-4-14. If for any reason we think that the Upaniṣad deals with knowledge and not with life, it is like entering into a great darkness (*bhūya tamaḥ*).[51] Its call is definitely for a life of total mastery, for becoming a master of the world (*lokajit*),[52] not conditioned by death.

If Prāṇa is Ātman and the same Prāṇa is the builder of habitations for Ātman, then Knowledge and Life are indivisible. But if we think that they are separate and opposed to each other, we miss the real teaching of the Upaniṣad.

NOTES

1. Bṛhadāraṇyaka Upaniṣad (hereafter Bṛ Up.), 1-6-3.
2. Ibid.
3. Ibid., 3-1-3.
4. Ibid., 1-6-3.
5. Ibid., 2-5-14.
6. Ibid., 5-15-1.
7. Ibid., 3-7-1.
8. Ibid., 1-3-28.
9. Ibid., 1-6-3.
10. Ibid., 3-3-2.
11. Ibid., 1-5-21.
12. Ibid., 1-3-1.
13. Ibid., 6-1-1.
14. Īśa Upaniṣad, verse 2.
15. Ibid., verse 17.
16. Ibid., verses 11, 14.
17. Ibid., verse 17.
18. Bṛ Up., 1-2-1.
19. Ibid., 1-3-11.
20. Ibid., 1-3-28.
21. Ibid., 1-5-21.
22. Ibid., 3-1-3.
23. Chāndogya Upaniṣad (hereafter Ch. Up.), 7-24-1.
24. Ibid.
25. Bṛ Up., 1-2-7.

26. Ibid., 4-3-32.
27. Ibid., 4-5-1.
28. Ibid., 2-4-10.
29. Ibid., 3-7-2.
30. Ibid.
31. Ibid., 2-5-15.
32. Ibid., 2-4-12.
33. Ibid., 4-5-14.
34. Ibid., 2-4-5.
35. Ibid., 1-4-16.
36. Ibid., 2-4-6.
37. Ibid., 1-4-10.
38. Ch. Up., 7-24-1.
39. Bṛ Up., 1-4-10.
40. Cf. Ibid., 4-4-7.
41. Vide Ibid., 6-2-15.
42. Ibid., 2-4-4.
43. Ibid., 2-4-6.
44. Ibid., 3-8-11.
45. Ibid., 4-3-32.
46. Ibid., 2-4-5.
47. Muṇḍaka Upaniṣad, 3-1-4.
48. Bṛ Up., 2-1-20.
49. Ibid., 2-4-12.
50. Ibid., 3-7-1.
51. Ibid., 4-4-10.
52. Ibid., 1-3-28.

21

Ātma Vidyā and Madhu Vidyā: Two Expositions

FULFILMENT THROUGH MUTUAL LOVE OF ĀTMAN

The Bṛhadāraṇyaka, like the Chāndogya, is an old Upaniṣad. There are six Brāhmaṇas in the second chapter of this Upaniṣad. Among the six, two are considered to be very important, 2-4 (Maitreyī Brāhmaṇa) and 2-5 (Madhu Brāhmaṇa). Not only do they appear together but even their subject-matter is essentially the same. Therefore a question arises as to why they are separate from each other as if they are two independent Brāhmaṇas without a common basis.

According to Śaṅkara, while 2-4 sets forth a proposition about the world and its absolute oneness with Ātman and elucidates it, 2-5 brings the elucidation to a close by restating its substance. Thus the latter is considered to be without a teaching of its own. But Kapāli Śāstry (1886-1953), a Vedic scholar, does not think so. He says that while 2-4 holds that Ātman is real and the world illusory, 2-5 runs counter to it and corrects its view by affirming that the world is a real manifestation of Ātman. Hence, in his opinion, 2-5 is a corrective to 2-4. Apart from the two, a third view is possible. It maintains that while 2-4 is inconclusive, 2-5 develops its thought and takes it to its natural conclusion. Thus 2-5 is regarded as the culmination of 2-4. In the following pages a study of the two Brāhmaṇas is made in this light to see how far it will be fruitful to do so.

First we shall state the views of Śaṅkara and Kapāli Śāstry, then examine them in the light of the original text, and finally conclude with the proposed study. In doing so we shall demonstrate that the Bṛhadāraṇyaka is a gospel of fulfilment through mutual love of Ātman, a fact long ignored by the commentators and scholars.

THE TRADITIONALIST ACCOUNT

The Maitreyī Brāhmaṇa is in the form of a dialogue between Maitreyī and her husband Yājñavalkya. The dialogue is about immortality, its means, realisation and result. Its means is renunciation; its realisation is the attainment of Ātman; and its result is the destruction of interaction with the world.

(i) Man is generally attached to his family, possessions, society, the worlds, the gods, and the creatures of this world. He renounces them all by recognising that he is bound by them. By doing so he becomes fit for becoming immortal. (ii) Through ignorance he has superimposed on Ātman the notions of caste, order of life, actions and their factors and results, and mistaken It for these notions. The ignorance is removed through *śravaṇa* (hearing), *mata* (reflection) and *vijñāna* (understanding). Through hearing he learns that Ātman is pure and devoid of superimpositions; through reflection he destroys the superimpositions; through understanding he realises that all this is Ātman (*idaṃ sarvaṃ viditam*).[1] By knowing all to be Ātman, he becomes a knower of Ātman; by being a knower of Ātman, he becomes immortal and breaks the bonds of mortality.

An immortal knows all to be not otherwise than Ātman (*nānyatrātmanaḥ*). On the contrary, he who knows all to be otherwise than as of the essence of Ātman (*anyatrātmanaḥ*)[2] is a mortal whom all reject (*parāduḥ*).[3] Why is the mortal so rejected? By speaking about the rejection Yājñavalkya intends to affirm that one should give up mortality and become immortal.

According to the Upaniṣad, there are three conditions under which the world exists. First, when it stays in manifest existence; second, before it comes into existence; third, when the world is dissolved into its original source. Several examples are given with a view to bring out how in each of these conditions the world is known to be non-different from Ātman.

First come the three examples of drum, conch and *vina*.[4] They are instruments of music. When they are used according to the science of music, two notes are produced from each, general and particular. Those who are trained in the science say that while the particular notes cannot be grasped by themselves, they can be grasped by including them in the general note. In the same way no object by itself is rightly known. But it is rightly known when it is included in Ātman.

The next two examples are about the great Being (*mahad bhūta*) and the fire.[5] When the Being breaths out, many kinds of compositions come into existence — Ṛg Veda, Yajur Veda, Sāma Veda, Atharvāṅgirasa, history, mythology, arts, Upaniṣads, pithy verses, aphorisms, elucidations and explanations. Śaṅkara points out that all these fall into two major categories, Mantras and Brāhmaṇas. In other words, the Vedas with these two categories appear out of the Being *like* the breath. What are they before they come forth from the great Being? They are nothing but the great Being in the same way as different kinds of smoke, which appear out of a fire kindled with wet faggot, are nothing but the fire before their appearance (*agnireva*).[6] Like the Vedas and the smoke-forms, the world of names and forms, before its manifestation, is nothing but Ātman.

The fifth and sixth examples concern the instruments of knowledge and action and the sea.[7] First come the instruments of knowledge — skin, nose, toung, eye, ear, mind and intellect. Each instrument has its own movement, like the skin which has the movement of touch. And each movement has its own goal, like the touch which has its goal in the skin. Now come the instruments of action which are five in number, from the hands to the organ of speech. Each has its own movement, like the organ of speech which is engaged in the recitation of the Vedas. And each movement has its own goal, like the recitation of the Vedas the goal of which is in the organ of speech. Śaṅkara says that all these examples, whether they are the instruments of knowledge or of action, are illustrative of dissolution, dissolution of movements in their respective instruments. How are they dissolved? Like the different kinds of water in the ocean.[8] Through successive dissolutions, all instruments are subjectively merged in pure consciousness and have no existence apart from the consciousness. In a like manner the universe, when objectively dissolved in successive stages, has no existence apart from Ātman.

The universe is Ātman, because in its dissolved condition it is nothing but Ātman. Ātman is compared to water into which a lump of salt is dropped and dissolved and which tastes saline whichever part one takes. Śaṅkara takes the water to stand for the water of the sea, and the sea to stand for the great Being or Ātman which is endless, infinite and pure consciousness (*mahadbhūtam anantam apāram vijñānaghanaeva*).[9] The lump of salt is regarded as the sea water in its solidified condition. It represents the individual who is a modification of Ātman, the individual who comes out as a separate entity on account of the elements i.e. the body and senses formed out of the elements. But when he destroys them (*tāny anuvinaśyati*)[10], two things happen. First, his individual consciousness is destroyed (*na saṃjñāsti*),[11] the consciousness conditioned by the elements. Second, like the lump of salt thrown into the sea (*udake prāsta*),[12] he is merged in Ātman and attains his original nature. Just as the individual is Ātman through subjective dissolution of his separate existence, so also the universe, when objectively dissolved of its separate existence, is Ātman (*vijñānaghanaeva*).[13]

Now we come to the third aspect viz. the result arising from the realisation of immortality (vide above). As a mortal, an individual was conditioned by the dualities of the world. In smelling or seeing or hearing, something was smelled or seen or heard by him. In this there were two sets of dualities that conditioned him, (i) an action and a doer of action and (ii) an action and a result of action i.e. an object grasped by the action. Now he is an immortal by being a knower of Ātman. Ātman is the cogniser for whom there is *nothing else* to be smelled or seen or heard and there is *no one else* who smells or sees or hears. As a result, there is neither the world nor the individual who interacts with the world. As Ātman is known through an extreme dissolution of the world, or as the world has become Ātman (*sarvam ātmaivābhūt)*, all interaction and all duality cease for a knower of Ātman. This is the unique result of knowing Ātman.

Thus the Maitreyī Brāhmaṇa teaches three things: first, a seeker of immortality begins by renouncing the world; second, he becomes a knower of Ātman by merging the world in Ātman through *śravaṇa, mata* and *vijñāna*; third, he enjoys complete freedom and has escaped the necessity of interacting with the world. They are the instructions given to Maitreyī by Yājñavalkya.

(ii) Now comes the Madhu Brāhmaṇa. It comes close on the heels of the Maitreyī Brāhmaṇa. In it Ṛṣi Dadhyaṅ teaches the science of Madhu to gods Aśvins. According to Śaṅkara, the word Madhu is used in two distinct senses, dependence and effect. It means dependence, because bees eat it and depend on it for their existence. It also means effect, because it is produced by the work of the bees. The world has two major forms, individual (*adhyātmā*) and universal (*adhidaiva*). Just as they exist through mutual dependence, so also they act on each other and produce effects through their interaction. As Dadhyaṅ's teaching is about their mutual dependence and mutual influence, it is referred to as the Madhu Vidyā.

The Madhu Brāhmaṇa deals with a number of instances of mutual dependence between the two cosmic forms, individual and universal. Earth is mentioned as the first of these instances. Let us see what Dadhyaṅ says about earth. First, this earth (individual) is honey for all beings (universal) and all beings are honey for this earth. Second, there is a bright and immortal person in each — in the earth and in the body of the beings. Third, the two inner persons are only Ātman which is greater than the cosmic forms. In other instances, if we leave aside the names given to the individual forms, the same ideas and the same words are repeated. The purpose of this refrain is to emphasise that Ātman "alone [is] real" and "everything else ... an effect, a modification, a mere name, an effort of speech only."[14] This means that the first fourteen mantras of 2-5 teach the same thing — Ātman is the only reality and all else an effect.

In the mantra 2-5-15 is found the culmination of the previous mantras of 2-5. It speaks of the knower of Ātman as the ruler and king of all beings. For he is "the object of universal homage." The above mantra further says that the whole universe is fixed in the knower of Ātman.[15] How is it fixed in him? "[L]ike a reflection of the moon in water" is fixed in the original moon.[16]

Śaṅkara holds that in the first fifteen mantras of 2-5 the teaching given to Maitreyī about Ātman in 2-4 is reaffirmed through a new type of reasoning. The rest of the mantras (16 to 19) support it with scriptural evidences.[17] It may be seen that mantras 16 and 17 have been taken from the Ṛg Veda. They speak about two things. (i) Dadhyaṅ teaches the Madhu Vidyā to the Aśvins through a horse's head; (ii) the horse's head is fixed on Dadhyaṅ by the Aśvins. In this connection Śaṅkara draws our attention to a story found in the Śatapatha Brāhmaṇa.[18]

According to the story, the Aśvins wanted to learn the doctrine of Madhu from Dadhyaṅ. But he was unwilling to teach them, because he was afraid that if the doctrine was revealed to anyone else, Indra would cut off his head. For it was the condition Indra put when he taught the doctrine to Dadhyaṅ. The Aśvins said that if he accepted them as his disciples, they would remove his head and fix a horse's head there, so that he could teach them through this head. They assured that when Indra cut off his head, they would restore him his original head. Dadhyaṅ agreed to teach them. When he taught the Aśvins, Indra instantly knew about it and removed his head. Upon this the Aśvins refixed Dadhyaṅ's original head.

By connecting the above two mantras with the story Śaṅkara concludes that the latter is an elucidation of the contents of the former. Further he concludes that the story is meant as a eulogy and not a description of the circumstances under which Dadhyaṅ taught the twin gods Aśvins. The aim of the story is to teach that the Madhu Vidyā is so great that even the gods have to face extreme difficulty in learning it. In other words, the mantras 2-5-16 and 2-5-17 are to be considered as eulogistic compositions about the Madhu Vidyā.

The last two mantras 2-5-18 and 2-5-19 say two things: (i) there is nothing that is not covered, nothing that is not pervaded by Him; (ii) this Ātman is Brahman and All-perceiver. Of the two mantras, the second is taken from the Ṛg Veda.[19] They both teach that Ātman is the absolute reality in which all particular consciousness ceases (2-4) and all interdependence is a matter of effect, an effort of speech only (2-5).

Thus in both the Brāhmaṇas, Maitreyī and Madhu, the same doctrine of Ātman is taught. While the first sets forth that all this is Ātman (2-4-6) and explains it through analogies, the second supports the proposition through a different type of reasoning[20] and through evidences taken from the Ṛg Veda.[21] In short, 2-5 restates and reinforces the original doctrine of 2-4.

KAPĀLI ŚĀSTRY'S ACCOUNT

Kapāli Śāstry's approach is different from that of Śaṅkara. His main interest is in the Madhu Brāhmaṇa and all his comments about the Maitreyī Brāhmaṇa occur only in connection with his study of the former Brāhmaṇa. His conviction is that the Vedānta develops out of the Mantras and reveals "the soul of the Veda."[22] Influenced by Sri Aurobindo, he does not share the view of the traditionalists who say that the Vedānta has no organic connection with the Mantras because their subject-matter is *karma*. He notices that the Madhu Brāhmaṇa, which commences immediately after the Maitreyī Brāhmaṇa, has a close connection with the latter. He thinks that even if a scholar is engaged in an exclusive study of the Madhu Brāhmaṇa, he cannot conclude his study without taking into consideration the connection it has with the other Brāhmaṇa. Accordingly, he brings his study to a close by adding a note on the connection between the two Brāhmaṇas.

In his view the Madhu Vidyā is concerned with three things. (i) In the creation the whole and the part are honey to each other, because the Honey, otherwise known as "the secret Delight" or "the Self", abides in them and makes the world "intact" and "enjoyable".[23] (ii) This Self, "the basic principle of Madhu", is "the Master and King of all things and beings and holds together — as the hub and felly hold the spokes — all beings, all gods, all worlds, all lives, all selves." [24] (iii) A "necessary step towards a knowledge of the secret Delight" is the realisation of "the interdependence of things and beings, human and others".[25]

How is one led from interdependence to the secret Delight? The passage is effected through a realisation that there is no self-sufficiency in a world where all are interdependent. The relation that holds all together is "that of a balance and harmony but neither of them can be explained by itself without the term of the other and therefore their mutual dependence and balance and harmony can be explained by that one secret, the Madhu, the Delight of being in all existence which effects, supports and holds them in close affinity".[26] Not only is the secret Delight the explanation of interdependence but it is the very source of all that are interdependent. As Śāstry says, "It is this Delight that makes possible ... the necessity of diverse forms in the manifested existence and gives them their value".[27]

In this connection we may note that the important word Madhu is understood more or less in the same sense in which Śaṅkara has understood it. Śāstry differs from him only in one respect — in not twisting the word and getting out of it the sense of a false modification.

The honey doctrine revealed to the Aśvins is supported and evidenced by two Ṛks.[28] They say that the Aśvins put a horse's head on Dadhyaṅ and that Dadhyaṅ revealed the honey doctrine to them through the horse's head. According to Śāstry, this raises three important questions.[29] (i) Who is this Dadhyaṅ? (ii) What is the Madhu that he knows and gives out to the Aśvins? (iii) Why are the Aśvins attracted to him? And the full significance of the honey doctrine can be unfolded only by answering these questions.

Before answering these questions, Kapāli Śāstry refers to the story mentioned in the Śatapatha Brāhmaṇa only to remind us that "legends are often a morbid growth" and prove "a false light, a light that rather obscures than illuminates".[30] Unlike his counterpart, Śaṅkara, he takes the two Ṛks, concerning Dadhyaṅ, very seriously and tries to understand the Madhu Vidyā in a deeper perspective with the help of the Ṛks.

(i) He seeks to understand Dadhyaṅ from two sides, from an analysis of the words *dadhyan atharva* and from a study of *pravargya karma* of which the Madhu Vidyā is said to be a limb. First of all, the word *atharva* means "not moving out" or "fixation".[31] The idea of fixation is found in the word *dadhyan* also, especially the component *dadhi*. According to Śāstry, *dadhyan* from *dadhi* is Agni brought forth and fixed in human being. So Dadhyaṅ is not just Agni, but a son of Atharvan, "a specially developed power" of Agni in human mind.[32] From the other component *anc* we must note that *dadhyanc* is a power that *moves* "in the ladder of the progress of human mind". [33]

Second, the *pravargya karma* throws further light on the word *dadhyan*. The *karma* is connected with three things — *gharma*, *pravargya*, and *mahāvīra*.[34] The first is "an eatable cooked food for offering in the ritual"; the second is the preparation of the food "by pouring fresh milk in the heated clarified butter"; and the third is the vessel, "the earthenware in the shape of a mortar" used for making the food. According to the system of Vedic symbolism which Śāstry adopts from Sri Aurobindo, the three terms stand for three things connected with the inner development of the sacrificer — the heat of *tapas* (*gharma*), the rigours of *tapasya* which purify and discipline (*pravargya*) and the human vessel (*mahāvīra*) in which the heat is produced and by which sacrifice is effected.

When the human soul offers itself to the gods, their gifts begin to flow into the soul in response to the offering. The gifts are the higher powers that descend and lodge themselves in the sacrificer. In order to hold them the vessel of the sacrificer viz. his body must be sufficiently strong and possessed of "heroic mettle". Even for getting this body he depends on the gods who alone have the power to give a suitable body for receiving the gifts and using them in the right way.

Now we know who Dadhyaṅ is. He is "a flaming power" progressing towards higher levels beyond mind, but a power operating at the mental level. But his higher progress is possible only when his body becomes fit through the help of the gods who infuse abundant strength and holding-power into the body. In short, Dadhyaṅ is a sacrificer who seeks a fit body for higher progress through the grace of the Aśvins.

(ii) The next thing to be understood about Dadhyaṅ is the object he offers as a sacrifice. He has a very valuable possession with him and this is his Madhu Vidyā. He has discovered that everything depends on everything else and that their secret Honey, the eternal Self, the Master and King, holds all together and maintains them in harmony. As the gods come to man for giving him help and their help is made possible through a suitable sacrifice, Dadhyaṅ gives his Madhu Vidyā as a sacrifice to them. This answers the second question what the Madhu Dadhyaṅ knows and gives out to the gods.

Dadhyaṅ's aim is to progress beyond mind, and Indra, the lord of the gods, is yet to come and assist him in the progress. But before that he must win help from other gods who can work on his body and make it a perfect vessel which does not break or sink under the weight of the higher substance descending into his physical-vital system. Hence the gods Aśvins are invoked. They are "the riders on the path, symbolic of force, especially of life-energy and nervous force; they are seekers of honey, Madhu, gods of enjoyment, physicians, bring back youth to the old, health to the sick, wholeness to the maimed".[35] To them is given the Madhu Vidyā as a sacrifice.

In this connection Kapāli Śāstry explains why Dadhyaṅ teaches through a horse's head. The Madhu Vidyā is a secret held by him. It is to be communicated through "a password" and not through "the language of the intellectual mind".[36] Dadhyaṅ is provided with a horse's head because it serves as a password between him and the Aśvins. This, says Kapāli Śāstry, is the meaning of the horse-head through which Dadhyaṅ teaches.

(iii) The Aśvins, according to Śāstry, are an archetype of interdependence and harmony. The Veda "likens them to a splendid married pair, to the two lips that speak sweet words, to the two nostrils, two hands and to many other pairs all of which have their common objects".[37] They are attracted to Dadhyaṅ because he is in possession of the very secret honey of the Self by knowing which they, as a symbol of interdependence, may find their mutual fulfilment. This is the answer to the question why the Aśvins are attracted to Dadhyaṅ. Though Kapāli Śāstry thinks that the Aśvins are attracted to Dadhyaṅ just by being an archetype of interdependence and does not develop the point further, the full significance of their attraction comes out only when it is related to their own fulfilment.

Let us now see what Kapāli Śāstry's note says about the connection between the two Brāhmaṇas, 2-4 and 2-5. He says: "It is significant that it [the Madhu Brāhmaṇa] comes close upon the Maitreyī Brāhmaṇa which concludes with famous passages often quoted in support of the lofty idealism represented in Śaṅkara's exposition of Advaita doctrine of later times".[38] Here the passages he has in mind refer to 2-4-12 and 2-4-14. We must note that the passages are not only "often quoted" in support of Śaṅkara's Advaita but also interpreted by him as teaching that when knowledge of Ātman arises, the appearance of the world is dissolved and all world-transactions come to an end.[39] What is Kapāli Śāstry's own view about the passages? Do they teach that the world is illusory, *mithyā*? He thinks that they "tend" to do so.[40] He holds that they set forth the view of "Absolute Idealism" otherwise called "Absolute Monism" or "Lofty Illusionism".[41] How then does 2-5 stand to 2-4? He says that the former is related to the latter in two ways. First of all, it is "a corrective to the metaphysical excesses"[42] of the latter. Second, it "reconciles the Absolute Idealism to which the [latter] Brāhmaṇa tends with the relative Realism of World-existence in which an all-embracing dualism is the dominant note" .[43]

So the two Brāhmaṇas are to be seen thus — one as dismissing all dualism as illusory[44] and the other as correcting it by preserving the reality of dualism;[45] one as maintaining an absolute idealism and the other as reconciling the idealism with its realism. This is Śāstry's note on them.

A CRITICAL STUDY OF THE TWO ACCOUNTS

(i) In the Maitreyī Brāhmaṇa Yājñavalkya teaches how the world is to be loved by us. It may be loved in two ways, in the mortal way or in the immortal way. To love the world for its own sake, for the satisfaction it gives to the ego is the mortal way; to recognise that Ātman is the sole possessor and inhabitant of the world and the sole enjoyer of habitation in the world and to love the world for Ātman's sake is the immortal way. Therefore immortality consists in rejecting the mortal love and loving all for the sake of the immortal Ātman.

If we think that immortality is just attainment of Ātman and love of Ātman, we are mistaken. It must culminate in the love of the world for the sake of Ātman. This is the most important aspect of immortality. There are three steps for one who desires to become immortal. First, knowledge of Ātman (*ātmā draṣṭavyaḥ*).[46] It is attained through *śravaṇa*, *manana* and *nididhyāsana* about Ātman. Second, knowledge about the contents of Ātman. It is attained (through *śravaṇa*, *mata* and *vijñāna*) from Ātman (*ātmanaḥ*).[47] Third, from the contents the world is known to be an extension of Ātman (*idaṃ sarvaṃ viditam*)[48] and, therefore, an object to be loved for the sake of Ātman.

If we do not know Ātman and Ātman's cosmic extension, we see the world to be elsewhere than in Ātman (*anyatrātmanaḥ*).[49]

That is to say, we see the world to be existing for our ego. We love the world for its own sake, for the joy it gives to our ego. Likewise, the world loves us for our own sake, for the joy we give to the collective-ego. As a result, it abandons us to the forces of death (*parādād*).[50] In other words, we are destroyed and used as food for the world. Conversely, if we see the world to be existing for Ātman, we love it for Ātman's sake and make it an ideal habitation for Ātman's enjoyment; in return for our love the world loves us and gives us all it has and makes us all perfect habitations for Ātman in us. As a result, we are saved from the law of necessity and delivered into a life of freedom and bliss. Thus an individual lives for the good of the world and the world, in return, lives for his good.

Śaṅkara's reading of 2-4-5 is different. He says that we are mortal because we have mistaken Ātman for the world superimposed on Ātman through ignorance. Hence mortality is put aside when we renounce the world, remove the superimpositions through *śravaṇa*, *mata* and *vijñāna* and know Ātman by knowing that all this is Ātman. In other words, we become immortal when we no longer mistake Ātman for the world and when we rightly know that the world is of the same nature as Ātman.

If we analyse the original text, we find that Śaṅkara's reading is not faithful to the text. First, it does not teach renunciation of the world. Rather it teaches that the habit of loving the world for its own sake is to be renounced. Second, it does not say that Ātman alone is to be loved and the world to be abandoned. Rather it says that all are to be loved for the sake of Ātman. This implies that as Ātman is the object of love, all in whom Ātman resides are to be loved for the sake of Ātman. Third, it does not state that knowledge of Ātman is the same as the knowledge that all this is identical with Ātman. Rather it states that knowledge of Ātman is first an independent attainment (*ātmā draṣṭavyaḥ*)[51] and then a means to another knowledge, knowledge about the world from Ātman (*ātmanaḥ idaṃ sarvaṃ viditam*).[52] With this knowledge the world is rightly known as the extension of Ātman. When the world is thus known, love of the world for the sake of Ātman is inevitable. On the contrary, if the world is known that it is of the same nature as Ātman, then love of Ātman may be possible but not love of the world for the sake of Ātman, for there is no world except Ātman. All these points go to show that Śaṅkara's reading of 2-4-5 is unacceptable.

In 2-4-5 Ātman is shown to be the cause, and the world the consequence of Ātman i.e. the self-extension of Ātman in names and forms. Accordingly, the proposition *idam sarvam yad ayam ātmā*[53] is to be interpreted. Literally, it means: "What this Ātman brings into existence, that is this world". From this we get the true knowledge of the world, the knowledge that the world is the manifestation of the very essence of Ātman. All subsequent examples given in the text 2-4-7 to 12 support this point in one way or the other.

Śaṅkara takes *ātmanaḥ idaṃ sarvaṃ viditam*[54] to mean that the world in reality is Ātman itself. Hence he understands the proposition in 2-4-6 as setting forth a perfect identity between the world and Ātman. If they are identical, no duality is possible between the two. But the subsequent examples do not support their absolute oneness.

According to Śaṅkara's own interpretations, the examples illustrate the following relations between the world and Ātman. First, in its manifest condition the world has a dependent existence in Ātman;[55] second, in its original condition the world exists as a potential in Ātman;[56] third, in its dissolved condition the world exists like Ātman.[57] In all these the world is distinct from Ātman, and their relation is one of duality. As this goes against the absolute identity affirmed through the proposition "all this is Ātman",[58] Śaṅkara invokes the rule that "if a thing cannot be perceived apart from something else, the latter is the essence of that thing".[59] By doing so he has changed duality into identity. Here he has imported the above rule from outside under the pretext that it is one of the suggestions of the examples. The examples suggest that the world originates from, stays in existence in, and resolves again into, Ātman; and there the utility of the examples ceases. To argue that the suggestions themselves point to another suggestion is a case of stretching beyond the utility intended by the examples. As a matter of fact, Śaṅkara has taken refuge in abstract reasoning under the pretext of explaining the examples. This is unwarranted. For examples *suggest* and do not *argue*. His struggle with the examples proves that his interpretation of the proposition "all this is Ātman" is wrong.

His struggle is more in evidence when he explains the mantra 2-4-12. The mantra speaks about a lump of salt dissolved in water and the particles of water becoming saline in taste. The text is very clear about what it says: the original water is not saline but becomes so only after the lump of salt is dissolved into it. But Śaṅkara takes the word water (*udakam*) to stand for sea-water and says that the lump of salt is a product of this water. By doing so he has reversed the original text.

Further, he equates the water with the supreme Being and the lump of salt with the individual being. He argues that the dissolution of the lump into the water speaks about the merger of the individual in the supreme Being and the attainment of the latter's nature. But the equation and argument are both wrong, because the original text says that by the dissolution of the lump the water gets the saline taste of the lump. If this is so, then by the merger of the individual the original nature of the supreme Being should undergo change. This is sheer absurdity. If we try to overcome the difficulty by reading "the water" as "the sea-water", we will face another difficulty, the difficulty of saying that when the lump of salt is dissolved the sea water becomes saline as if it was not so before. This is another absurdity. From this it is clear that the salt example, as understood by Śaṅkara, throws no light on the sense given by him to the proposition "all this is Ātman".

The last mantra 2-4-14 is about the conquest of immortality and the result the conquest gives. When a person knows Ātman by knowing the world to be but Ātman, he becomes immortal. As a result, he is freed from all dealings with the world which are of *kriyā-kāraka-phalātmaka* (the nature of action, doer of action, and result of action). This is the teaching of the above mantra. The important point here is that if this were the result, then Yājñavalkya would have found it impossible to give the teaching to Maitreyī. For he is a knower of Ātman. By teaching her he contradicts himself, for he has not given up action and its factors. He is a teacher (doer of action) from whom Maitreyī hears about Ātman (result of action) through his instructions (action). Thus the interpretation Śaṅkara has put on the text is nullified by the text itself. He is now caught in a dilemma, for he cannot defend either his interpretation or the original text.

If he defends his interpretation, he will have to deny Yājñavalkya's conversation with Maitreyī; if he accepts his involvement in the conversation, then Śaṅkara's interpretation that an immortal is freed from action and its factors will be automatically denied. This is the worst among the difficulties Śaṅkara faced in interpreting the Maitreyī Brāhmaṇa.

Now we go to the Madhu Brāhmaṇa. According to Śaṅkara, mantras 1 to 14, which deal with things mutually dependent, teach that Ātman alone is real and all else — all that is interdependent — is an effect (*madhu*). By being so all is "a modification, a mere name, an effort of speech merely". Here the extension given to the word *madhu* is unwarranted. As a figure, the word may mean "an effect", but cannot mean a modification of *avidyā*, a mere name, a false appearance. It can never be a figure for false appearance (*mithyā*). All the above mantras (1 to 14) affirm that the two main forms of the world, individual and universal, are really the dual forms of Ātman. They do not reduce them to the status of mere appearances of Ātman but are viewed as the manifestations of the very essence of Ātman. This agrees with the text in the previous section 2-4-14 which says that all is a becoming of the very essence of Ātman (*sarvam ātmaivābhūt*).[60]

Mantra 2-5-15 occupies an important position in the Madhu Brāhmaṇa. For it shows beyond a shadow of doubt how the world and Ātman are related to each other. It says that while Ātman is the ruler and king, all beings, all the gods, all the worlds and all organs are fixed in him i.e. dependent on him. But Śaṅkara interprets the mantra to mean that it is rather about the knower of Ātman than about Ātman. He is called the ruler and king because he has become "an object of universal homage" through his knowledge. Since Ātman is reflected in the bodies like the moon in water, they are said to be fixed in the knower of Ātman. Here we may note how the mantra is compelled to speak differently. There are three words — *ātmā*, *samarpitāḥ* and *sarvāṇi bhūtani*. Their meanings are very clear. The first does not mean a knower of Ātman; there is nothing in the second to suggest that the reflections are fixed in the original; the third does not give the sense of bodies which produce reflected images. Apart from these, the wheel example disproves in one stroke all Śaṅkara has said about Ātman and the world. Since the example does not lend itself to be twisted, he has to leave it as it is. It clearly shows that Ātman is the higher reality and the world abides in it as the lower and dependent reality.

Finally, Śaṅkara holds that the central teaching of the Maitreyī Brāhmaṇa is the equation between the world and Ātman[61] and then this teaching is reaffirmed in the Madhu Brāhmaṇa. If we examine the relevant text i.e. 2-5-15, we find that there is no such reaffirmation in it. For the text actually means that the world *abides* in Ātman because it is subject to Ātman who is its lord (*adhipati*). From this we are compelled to conclude that, according to the former text 2-4-6, the world is Ātman because it is created (*bhūta*) from Ātman who is the source and lord of creations (*bhūtādhipati*).

(ii) Now we shall examine the account given by Kapāli Śāstry. We know that the Madhu Brāhmaṇa closes with three mantras taken from the Ṛg Veda. Two of them contain the names of Dadhyaṅ and Aśvins. From this, Śāstry concludes that the Brāhmaṇa is a material fit for study according to the system of Vedic symbolism developed by Sri Aurobindo.

We must remember that the Madhu Brāhmaṇa is basically a work of Vedānta. The Vedānta is primarily philosophical and secondarily psychological. Accordingly, its exegesis is determined. The Vedāntic exegesis keeps itself close to the philosophical ideas and reads the other ideas in accordance with the former. Therefore all Vedic mantras appearing in the Upaniṣads must be considered as Vedāntic mantras. Kapāli Śāstry's mistake is that he regards the Ṛks in the Madhu Brāhmaṇa as Vedic and forgets that the Brāhmaṇa is a Vedāntic work.

He starts his study with a brief analysis of the Pravargya rite. The Śatapatha Brāhmaṇa speaks of it as a limb (*aṅga*) of the Madhu Vidyā. However, the Madhu Brāhmaṇa, as found in the Bṛhadāraṇyaka Upaniṣad, makes no mention of the rite. As a result, the text on hand must be considered self-sufficient and studied as such. Materials from other sources can be brought within the scope of the text only when the text cannot be understood otherwise. The Madhu Brāhmaṇa can stand by itself and make sense without being connected with the Pravargya rite mentioned in the Śatapatha Brāhmaṇa.

For the sake of argument let us admit that the above section is relevant for the study of the Madhu Brāhmaṇa and see how far it helps Kapāli Śāstry to unfold the latter's significance.

The Pravargya rite is concerned with three things — *gharma*, *pravargya*, and *mahāvīra*. By taking them as symbols of inner progress Śāstry points out that Dadhyaṅ is a sacrificer who needs help from the gods for making his body a strong vessel capable of receiving and holding the descending powers of the higher worlds. The twin gods, he says, are invoked for this purpose. Further, from an analysis of the words *dadhyan atharva* he concludes that *dadhyan* is a soul that has progressed far beyond the level of a knower of Madhu Vidyā and is seeking further development with the help of Indra, the lord of mind. Before Indra comes, the Aśvins must come and make Dadhyaṅ's body a fit vessel to receive the gifts of the gods.

If we turn to the original text of Madhu Brāhmaṇa, there is no indication whatever that Dadhyaṅ is seeking a goal higher than the Madhu Vidyā. If, on the contrary, he is a seeker of a higher goal, then the Madhu Vidyā will not be a central issue in the Madhu Brāhmaṇa, but something secondary or inferior. If the Vidyā is an inferior issue, then it is difficult to explain why the Madhu Brāhmaṇa has devoted so many mantras for expounding its teaching and so much space for emphasising its importance.

Strictly speaking, the Madhu Vidyā, on Śāstry's showing, is the means of personal fulfilment: to Dadhyaṅ it is the means for winning a fit body; to the Aśvins it is the means for finding their mutual oneness. If we look into the original text, there is hardly any suggestion that the Madhu Vidyā is the means for personal fulfilment. On the other hand, Dadhyaṅ is said to be acting according to truth (*ṛtāyan*),[62] the truth that demands love of all for the sake of Ātman in all. When he so acts, the Madhu Vidyā cannot be a means of personal fulfilment for him. Similarly, the Aśvins are called the doers of noble deeds for the sake of gain (*sanaye*),[63] the gain intended for the world's good. If what they gain is not for the larger good, then their deeds cannot be called noble. Therefore the Aśvins cannot be seekers of personal fulfilment. From these it is clear that the Madhu Vidyā is not intended to be a means of personal satisfaction either for Dadhyaṅ or for the Aśvins.

There is no mystery about Dadhyaṅ. He is the knower and teacher of the Madhu Vidyā. This is all we need to know about him and we know him to be both from the Madhu Brāhmaṇa. Hence the question "Who is this Dadhyaṅ?" is pointless.

Equally pointless is the next question, "What is the Madhu that he knows and gives out to the Aśvins?" The Madhu that he knows and gives out to them has been very clearly set forth in the first fifteen mantras in the Madhu Brāhmaṇa. Apart from this, no other Madhu is spoken in the Brāhmaṇa.

A teaching is a secret only for the purpose of right qualification. It is withheld from others because they do not have the right qualification to learn the teaching. On the other hand, if a teacher accepts someone as a disciple, then the latter is regarded as a qualified individual. To the qualified individual the teaching is revealed. Therefore Dadhyaṅ needs no password for teaching the gods, for the password does not reveal but hides the teaching.

Even if we assume that a password is needed for the teacher, it is his responsibility to find it and not the responsibility of the disciple who learns the secret from him. But the text clearly says that the password, namely, the horse's head, is given by the disciples to their teacher. Therefore, Kapāli Śāstry's explanation of the horse's head does not agree with the original text.

The third question, "Why are the Aśvins attracted to Dadhyaṅ?", is baseless. If it is true that they are attracted to him, then they will be under compulsion to seek him for some purpose or other. But there is no such compulsion to be found in the text.

The conceptions of Dadhyaṅ, Madhu Vidyā and Aśvins are very clearly stated in the original text. But they are misunderstood by Kapāli Śāstry. This is because he has overlooked the dividing line between the Madhu Brāhmaṇa and the section on the Pravargya ritual in the Śatapatha Brāhmaṇa, and strayed away from the main subject of Madhu Vidyā.

Both Śaṅkara and Śāstry have failed to unfold the true import of the Madhu Brāhmaṇa. The former has failed because he has a preconceived view that the Brāhmaṇa is speaking about the false appearance of Ātman. The latter has failed because he cannot distinguish between the Vedic and the Vedāntic exegesis. A right study of the Brāhmaṇa is possible only when we reject both the approaches as faulty.

Finally, we come to Śāstry's comments on the Maitreyī Brāhmaṇa and its connection with the Madhu Brāhmaṇa. He thinks that the first "tends" to teach a theory of "Absolute Idealism" or "Lofty Illusionism" and the second appears as "a corrective" to the first.

Here we note two things about the Maitreyī Brāhmaṇa. (i) The closing passages 2-4-12 and 14 are "often quoted" in support of Śaṅkara's Advaita, a system which teaches absolute idealism or lofty illusionism. (ii) The above passages tend towards Śaṅkara's system. Kapāli Śāstry cannot make up his mind whether Śaṅkara reads his Advaita into the passages or the passages themselves set forth a view akin to the view of Śaṅkara. Hence the doubtful word "tend" used by him. However, he is certain that the Madhu Vidyā is a corrective to the previous section 2-4. This lands him in difficulties from which he cannot escape. For his conclusion about the Brāhmaṇa is unfounded.

If one Brāhmaṇa teaches illusionism and another comes in to correct it, we should know why the Upaniṣad is blowing hot and cold about illusionism. If the Upaniṣad is bent upon setting aside the view of illusionism through the Madhu Brāhmaṇa, why should it at all express such a view through the Maitreyī Brāhmaṇa? With Sri Aurobindo, Śāstry thinks that the Upaniṣads represent "the soul of the Veda." If he so thinks, does he believe that the illusionism as reflected in the Maitreyī Brāhmaṇa is traceable to the hymns of the Veda? We know that Sri Aurobindo does not find any basis for illusionism either in the hymns (*sūktas*) or in what he calls the early Upaniṣads which include the Bṛhadāraṇyaka.[64] If Śāstry is guided by the luminous hints provided by Sri Aurobindo, why has he not viewed the Maitreyī Brāhmaṇa in the light of those hints? If 2-5 does not favour illusonism, in keeping with the spirit of this Brāhmaṇa 2-4 also cannot favour this view. If this is so, why has he not studied 2-4 in this light?

These are some of the questions Śāstry's comments on 2-4 and 2-5 raise and keep us wondering as to how he has not realised the consequences of his own words. But one thing is very clear. He has not understood either the Madhu Brāhmaṇa or the Maitreyī Brāhmaṇa. As a matter of fact, there are valid reasons to say that 2-5 develops directly out of 2-4 and takes the latter to its logical conclusion.

THE DOCTRINE OF MUTUAL LOVE AND FULFILMENT

(i) Life is an interplay of forces and progresses through the interplay. As long as life is there, its progress through the play of forces will be the law. In the condition of ignorance the progress takes place through conflict and confusion, struggle and opposition. Each seeks its own development and uses all for its own separate good. In this process each is compelled to serve as a means for all, as something to be destroyed and used for the good of all. In the Upaniṣad the development through self-aggrandizement is referred to as hunger (*aśanā*).[65] As death is the result of an insatiable hunger for self-aggrandizement, hunger is identified with death (*aśanāya hi mṛtyuḥ*).[66] In other words, the progress of life is conditioned by the law of hunger and death (*mṛtyunaivedam āvṛtam āsīt aśanāyayā*). This law is beautifully rendered by Sri Aurobindo as "the eater eating is himself eaten".[67] But in the condition of knowledge the law disappears and gives place to another law by which life begins to progress, the law of love and fulfilment. This is the law by which an immortal lives here. He gives himself freely to the world, and the world gives itself freely to him. He loves all and fulfils their good and, in return, all love him and fulfil his good. So the real law of progress is this: the lover loving is himself loved.

It is not without purpose that the Bṛhadāraṇyaka opens with a declaration that everything is enveloped by hunger and death. For hunger which is death is a problem to be faced and resolved through knowledge. If the first chapter begins with the problem of mortality, the second closes with the conquest of mortality. In the first occurs the prayer for passage from death to immortality (*mṛtyor māmṛtaṃ gamaya*);[68] in the second the prayer is fulfilled through the Madhu Vidyā (*ayam ātmā sarveṣām bhūtānām madhu; asyātmanaḥ sarvāṇi bhūtāni madhu*).[69]

Yājñavalkya teaches two things about love for the world: (i) in one sense it must be given up; (ii) in another sense it must be cultivated. We live in the midst of many things — wife, sons, wealth, Brāhmaṇas, Kṣatriyas, the worlds, the gods and the beings. If we love them for their own sake, we regard them as objects which give satisfaction for our ego and by which our ego enjoys aggrandizement. To live for the ego is to be conditioned by it; to seek satisfaction for it is to be bound by mortality. If we want to get rid of mortality, we must get rid of the habit of seeking satisfaction for the ego. We can break the habit only when we stop loving all for the sake of all. In this sense the love for the world is to be abandoned. Hence Yājñavalkya's instruction: all is to be loved not for the sake of all.[70]

If we cease to love all for the sake of all, then we conquer our ego. We become fit for immortality and for loving all in the right way. By hearing (*śravaṇa*), reflection (*manana*) and contemplation (*nididhyāsana*) we realise Ātman; by again hearing (*śravaṇa*), reflection (*mata*) and understanding (*vijñāna*) about Ātman's contents all is known (*idaṃ sarvaṃ viditam*) from Ātman (*ātmanaḥ*) and loved for the sake of Ātman. By knowing and loving thus we surrender all to Ātman who is the sole inhabitant and enjoyer of the world. Hence Yājñavalkya's other instruction: all is to be loved for the sake of Ātman.[71]

As the individual is to the world, so is the world to him. In the condition of ignorance he sees all to be elsewhere than in Ātman (*anyatrātmanaḥ*).[72] In other words, he sees all to be existing for his ego and loves all for their own sake, for the satisfaction they give him. In the same way all see him as existing for their collective-ego and love him for his own sake, for the satisfaction he gives them. Eventually, all abandon him to the forces of destruction (*parāduḥ*)[73] and use him as food for their collective-ego. In the condition of knowledge he sees all to be from Ātman (*ātmanaḥ*).[74] That is to say, he sees all as modifications of Ātman and loves all for the sake of Ātman in them. In the same way all see him as a modification of Ātman and love him for the sake of Ātman in him. Eventually, all offer themselves as food for his Ātman. Therefore, while a mortal is abandoned to death by all, an immortal abandones himself to Ātman in all.

Immortality is not a one-sided attainment. It changes the individual's attitude towards the world and the world's attitude towards the individual. Also, it destroys the false and restores the true relationship between the individual and the world. We discover these truths when we supply the connecting steps in thought between the two significant propositions *sarvam priyam bhavati*[75] and *sarvaṃ tam parādād*[76] and draw relevant conclusions.

If mortality is the result of seeing all otherwise than as having their real relations to Ātman (*anyatrātmanaḥ*),[77] immortality is the result of removing the wrong knowledge and seeing all in the right way. In other words, what is by right relations this Ātman, that is this world (*idaṃ sarvaṃ yad ayam ātmā*).[78] This is how the world should be seen. A series of examples is given with a view to draw our attention to the right relations that hold between the world and Ātman.

We shall first state the examples and then bring out their relevance. (i) The examples of drum, conch and *vīṇa*. As the same idea is repeated through three different examples, let us confine ourselves to one viz. drum and leave out the rest. Let us suppose that a person is far removed from the place where a drum is kept and beaten and that he has not seen the drum before. As the sounds reach his ears, he cannot grasp them, because their source is not known to him (*bāhyān śabdān*).[79] But they are grasped when their source is seen by him viz. the drum (*dundubheśtu grahaṇena śabdo gṛhītaḥ*).[80] (ii) The examples of fire and *mahad bhūta*. In a solid fire no smoke is seen. But when associated with wet faggot, different forms of smoke come out of the fire. As distinguished from the *bhūta* of fire, *ākāśa* is *mahad bhūta*. It is pure extension and does not produce words by itself. But through the force of *vāyu* many kinds of words are produced (breathed forth) from *ākāśa*.[81] (iii) There are thirteen examples, but they may be classed under three heads — the sea, the instruments of knowledge, and the instruments of action. The sea is the abode of all waters such as tank water, river water, etc. The cognitive movements such as touch, smell, etc. have their abodes in the instruments of knowledge. Lastly, the physical movements such as enjoyment, speech, etc. have their abodes in the instruments of action. [82]

All these examples — (i), (ii) and (iii), are intended to emphasise three important relations. First, that the world has its source in Ātman; second, that the world and Ātman are materially the same; third, that the abode of the world is Ātman.

Just as the drum-beat is grasped when its source viz. the drum is grasped, so also the world is truly understood when it is related to its source viz. Ātman. Just as the smoke-forms are not different from the fire, just as the words are not different from *ākāśa*, so also the world is not materially different from Ātman. Just as the waters of different kinds have their abodes in the sea, just as the cognitive movements their abodes in the instruments of knowledge, just as the physical movements their abodes in the instruments of action, so also the world has its abode in Ātman. Thus the world has three things in Ātman — its source, stuff of existence and abode.

There is another example, the example of a lump of salt (*saindhava khilya*).[83] When the lump is dissolved in water, it pervades the entire volume of water and enters all particles without exception (*yato yatastvādadīta lavaṇameva*).[84] Like the lump dissolved in water is Ātman (*mahad bhūtam*).[85] Ātman has assumed an infinite of forms (*anantam*)[86] and attained limitless extension by entering all these forms (*apāram*).[87] As a result, the entire world is a mass of conscious forms (*vijñānaghanaeva*)[88] forms that are conscious both inwardly and outwardly — inwardly as the self identified with the conscious Ātman, and outwardly as the dwelling pervaded by the consciousness of Ātman. From the description of Ātman based on the above example another relation of the world to Ātman is brought to our attention, a relation not mentioned previously: that there is not a single object in the world which is not a habitation of Ātman. Thus from the whole series of examples we understand that the world bears a fourfold relation to Ātman. Its source and substance, abode and abider are in the same Ātman.

In the second part of the mantra 2-4-12 another important matter about the appearance of the world from Ātman is discussed. From the boundless becomings of Ātman the world is born. In this process the individual, coming forth from these becomings (*etebhyo bhūtebhyaḥ samutthāya*),[89] as a being with other beings, destroys his original relations with Ātman (*tānyevānu vinaśyati*).[90] As a result, he is overtaken by death (*mṛtyunā-abhipannam*)[91] and finds himself and others elsewhere than in Ātman (*anyatrātmanaḥ*).[92] A dead person has no consciousness, self-consciousness or other-consciousness. In the same way the individual who has abandoned his original relations with Ātman is practically dead to Ātman. Having gone into the condition of death, there is no consciousness of Ātman (*pretya na saṃjñāsti*).[93] He does not see Ātman either in himself or in others.

There is nothing unintelligible about the individual not possessing the consciousness of Ātman. He may arise from Ātman, but if he separates himself from his original source, it is but natural that he does not have original consciousness and sees himself elsewhere than in Ātman. Just as he sees himself elsewhere, so also he sees all elsewhere — wife, sons, Brāhmaṇas, Kṣatriyas, the worlds, etc.[94] This is the law of the imperishable Ātman.[95] According to the law, one is conscious by union with Ātman, otherwise one is like a dead person for whom everything is elsewhere, self-consciousness and other-consciousness. Therefore whether or not a person is conscious of Ātman depends on whether or not he maintains his original relations with Ātman.

For a person who has abandoned his true relations with Ātman, the world is conditioned by false duality (*dvaitamiva bhavati*),[96] the duality of other and other. He considers himself as other and all else before him as other (*anyo asau anyo aham*).[97] His dealings with the world are governed by this sense of otherness: other (*itaraḥ*) smells other (*itaram*), other sees other, other hears other, other speaks to other, other thinks of other, other understands other.[98] Mortality is the cause of otherness and otherness the cause of false duality.

But when he sees that Ātman has become all (*sarvam ātmaivābhūt*),[99] the source and substance, the abode and abider of the world, he is freed from mortality, from the sense of otherness and the false duality. His dealings with the world do not cease but radically change. He sees Ātman abiding everywhere, in himself and in others. The doer is Ātman; everyone else for whom he works is Ātman; and the action itself arises from his Ātman and is a means of giving love and service to Ātman in all.

There is duality, duality between doer and deed, between deed and its result. But this duality brings no bondage to the doer, for he lives and works for the sake of Ātman in him and Ātman in others. All questions raised in this connection by Yājñavalkya[100] are intended to deny the binding influence of all sense of otherness and all false duality. In short, the knower of Ātman is occupied with the good of the world. Hence he is elsewhere called a world-worker (*viśvakṛt*)[101] (one who works for the uplift of the world*). There is the world to be dealt with, but the world is not other. There are instruments for this purpose, but none of them is other. There is the doer, but he does not look upon himself as other. There is the world, there is the work to be done for the world, and there is the doer of the work. But what is not there is the sense of otherness from which arises false duality.

According to Yājñavalkya, a person knows Ātman not for his own sake but for the sake of helping the world through his works. Hence he is called the doer of good works (*brahmavit puṇyakṛt*).[102] This explains why Yājñavalkya concludes his discourse by speaking about the world dealings of a knower of Ātman.

(ii) The Madhu Brāhmaṇa is a logical extension given to the Maitreyī Brāhmaṇa. Dadhyaṅ takes up Yājñavalkya's insight and develops out of it his doctrine of Madhu. Bound by mortality, life is a source of confusion and conflict, grief and pain. His view is that the knowledge of Ātman must be utilised for the sake of freeing life from the bonds of mortality and transforming it into a source of good will and support, sweetness and delight.

The main theme of Madhu Vidyā is the interplay of forces between the two forms of the world, individual (*adhyātmā*) and universal (*adhidaiva*) and the progress achieved through mutual satisfaction and delight. The interplay always takes place on the basis of a common factor that exists in both the forms. Its purpose is to promote progressive development of one by the other. The individual fulfils the good of the universal; and the universal, in the same way, fulfils the good of the individual.

There are, as we have already said, two conditions in which the interplay and mutual development occur, ignorance and knowledge. In the condition of ignorance the progress is achieved through hunger (*aśanā*) and death (*mṛtyu*). Mutually separated, the individual seeks his own growth and satisfaction and the universal its own growth and satisfaction.

One of the common factors in the individual and the universal is the substance of earth. For the individual to grow, more and more substance of earth is needed. Therefore he grows by feeding upon the environment, by absorbing the physical substance of others. As this growth is achieved to the detriment of the growth of others, the individual is eventually destroyed and his physical substance used as food for the growth of the world. By this destruction he is compelled to give what is necessary for the growth of others. Therefore death is the inevitable result of growth through hunger. Just as he destroys others and uses their physical substance as food for his hunger, so too he is eventually destroyed and his corporeal substance used as food for others' hunger. Thus death leads to death.

In the condition of knowledge the law of progress changes. The individual is no longer moved by hunger for growth and no longer compelled to give himself to others. His law now is that of self-giving and fulfilment in the growth and satisfaction of others; in the same way the world gives itself to him and finds its fulfilment in his growth and satisfaction. So runs the first mantra of the Madhu Vidyā: "This earth (in the individual) is *madhu* for all beings and all beings are *madhu* for this earth (in the individual)". As the earth in all beings is given away for the sake of the good of the individual, he is *madhu* for them; in the same way, as the earth in him is given away for the sake of the good of all beings, they are *madhu* for him.

Like earth there are many other factors that serve as the common bond between the individual and the universal — such as water, fire, air, ether, etc. The most important and crowning factor is Ātman. The mantra 2-5-14 goes thus: "For all beings (*sarveṣām bhūtānām*) this Ātman in the individual (*ayam ātmā*) is *madhu*; for this Ātman in the individual (*asya ātmanaḥ*) all beings (*sarvāṇi bhūtāni*) are *madhu*". As he gives himself to Ātman in all, all are *madhu* for him; likewise, as all give themselves to Ātman in him, he is *madhu* for them. In this way both are fulfilled — the individual by the universal and the universal by the individual. Here fulfilment brings fulfilment.

The word *madhu* is used throughout the text in the sense of something which brings good for another — good for the individual or good for the world. Dadhyaṅ gives the above sense to the word because he finds that life in the world has its own delight, the delight of fulfilment through love for others' good. It is distinct from the delight of pure essence in the transcendent Ātman and of perfect extension in the cosmic Ātman. No one who has not won these two forms of delight is entitled to the first, for it is their culmination. While the two arise from the recognition of one's essential identity with Ātman, the delight of fulfilment arises from the effort of fulfilling the evolutionary will of Ātman in the world. This is the highest form of delight proposed to us by Dadhyaṅ.

The whole Madhu Vidyā has been developed on one foundation viz. the metaphysics of Ātman. According to this, Ātman in pure essence has become the lord (*adhipati*) and king (*rājā*) of all beings through cosmic extension; and all, severally and collectively, are fixed or dependent on this Ātman. He supports the universal and individual, even as the hub supports the felly and spokes in a wheel.[103] The suggestion of the analogy is threefold. First, reality is of three grades — highest, higher and lower. The highest reality is Ātman, while the universal and individual are the higher and lower realities. By any stretch of the imagination the latter two cannot give the sense of false appearances of Ātman, as Śaṅkara has stated; second, the universal and individual are involved in forward movement, a movement which is both constant and continuous. Third, their forward movement is made possible by the highest reality of Ātman which is motionless and yet supports all motions. The metaphysics of Ātman has been taken from the previous Brāhmaṇa (2-4) and used as a powerful means by Dadhyaṅ for arriving at a grand result. This is the true significance of the wheel image.

According to Dadhyaṅ, the metaphysics of Ātman must be applied to the interplay of forces between the two essential forms of life, individual and universal, and change the law of hunger and death into that of love and fulfilment (*madhu*). Yājñavalkya speaks about love when he asks Maitreyī to love all for the sake of Ātman in all (*ātmanastu kāmāya savaṃ priyaṃ bhavati*).[104] But he does not develop it into the formula of mutual love and fulfilment between the individual and the universal, as Dadhyaṅ has done. He deals with the knowledge of Ātman and closes his discourse with his teaching how a knower of Ātman sees the world and interacts with it.[105] He does not relate the knowledge of Ātman to the issue of love with which he commenced in 2-4-5. His inconclusive teaching is made conclusive by Dadhyaṅ in his Madhu Vidyā. In this sense Dadhyaṅ is not only indebted to Yājñavalkya but also exceeds him as the teacher of Madhu Vidyā, as one who has upgraded the latter's world-worker into a world-lover.

(iii) Now comes the legend about Dadhyaṅ. There are two mantras 2-5-16 and 2-5-17 which deal with the legend. In fact, they are Ṛk Mantras taken bodily from the Veda.[106] They say three important things: (i) the doctrine of Madhu is taught to the twin gods Aśvins; (ii) the gods put a horse's head on Dadhyaṅ; (iii) Dadhyaṅ teaches the doctrine through the horse's head. The story gives a symbolical account of the circumstances in which the Madhu Vidyā is given to the Aśvins.

Dadhyaṅ has exceeded all conditions of knowledge — knowledge of Ātman in pure essence, of Ātman in cosmic extension and of Ātman serving as the foundation of enlightened action in the world. He has developed himself into a giver of love who fulfils the good of all for the sake of Ātman. In short, the whole world is *madhu* for him: its good is his good; its fulfilment is his own fulfilment. This is the Madhu Vidyā Dadhyaṅ has in his possession, the Vidyā by which he is recognised.

According to Sri Aurobindo, the seers of Veda are spiritual pragmatists who believe that "no salvation should be valued which takes us away from the love of God in humanity and the help we can give to the world ".[107] As one who comes in the line of these seers, Dadhyaṅ is a conscious helper of humanity. He is determined to give away the great possession he has to the world. As humanity is not sufficiently awake, he cannot directly give away his Vidyā to it. But as the cosmic gods represent the highest points of consciousness in humanity, it is easy to transfer the Vidyā to them rather than to humanity itself. The Vidyā thus transferred will be a subconscious possession of the world and shape the world's progress silently but steadily. The best way to do so is to give it to such gods as are full of goodwill for the world and most ready to help it. Dadhyaṅ's choice has naturally fallen upon the Aśvins, because they are known to be full of goodwill for the world (*madhumantaḥ*)[108] and also "the most ready to come to man" and help him (*āgamiṣṭhā devānām*).[109]

In this connection we must note that the two Ṛks (2-5-16 and 2-5-17) are to be regarded as Vedāntic mantras for purposes of exegesis. Hence Dadhyaṅ is a knower and teacher of Madhu Vidyā; and the Aśvins are cosmic gods who have immense goodwill for the world and help all with their noble deeds. Horse's head is the only symbolism that needs to be explained in accordance with the circumstances of Dadhyaṅ's sacrifice for the good of the world.

A sacrifice is given according to rule if it is given without the fault of egoism, otherwise it is not rightly given. Dadhyaṅ's sacrifice of Madhu Vidyā is rightly given (*ṛtāyan*),[110] for it is intended for the good of the world. In the sacrifice there are two important aspects, the gods' cognisance of the sacrifice and Dadhyaṅ's sacrifice to the gods. (a) When the gods take cognisance of Dadhyaṅ's effort to sacrifice, their willingness to receive it has swelled (*aśvat*)[111] into a great satisfaction, for the effort is unique and possessed of great merit. To the seer of the Upaniṣad the word *aśvat* calls up the image of an animal horse (*aśvaḥ*) and the great satisfaction of the gods at the effort looks like an elevated position of the horse's head. Hence he speaks of the willingness and the great satisfaction at Dadhyaṅ's effort as a horse's head placed upon him by the gods. (b) Dadhyaṅ's love for humanity has swelled (*aśvat*) and compelled him to make a great sacrifice to the gods. To the seer of the Upaniṣad the word *aśvat* reminds him again of a horse and its uplifted head and speaks of the love and the great sacrifice of Dadhyaṅ as a sacrifice given through a horse's head to the gods. Thus the whole legend is a symbolical representation of the sacrifice and all other facts associated with it.

(iv) We have pointed out in our study of 2-4 that Ātman is all (*sarvam*) — the source, substance, abode and abider of the world. From this it is seen that for a knower of Ātman neither the world nor the enlightened work performed by him in the world is a falsehood. Further, in our study of 2-5 we have found that the Madhu Vidyā starts from 2-4 and develops the original idea of love of Ātman in the world into a formula of love and fulfilment between the individual (*adhyātmā*) and the universal (*adhidaiva*) aspects of the world. The Madhu Brāhmaṇa is therefore not a reaffirmation of 2-4 or a corrective to it, but a logical culmination thereof.

The teacher of Madhu Vidyā is indeed a sacrificer, but a sacrificer for the good of the world. The word *madhu* can give the sense of an effect but never the sense of a false appearance unless it is given a wrong extension such as the one given by Śaṅkara. Even the sense of an effect, as understood by Śāstry, cannot be given to the word if we remember its original sense of sweetness and delight. Dadhyaṅ uses the word in a sublime sense, in the sense of self-giving love and fulfilment. Love and fulfilment are the characteristics of a knower of Ātman in its completeness. He loves the world and fulfils its good; so too the world loves him and fulfils his good. The world is *madhu* for him; and he is *madhu* for the world.

Neither Śaṅkara nor Śāstry has given us a proper insight into the legend. While it is rejected as a eulogy by Śaṅkara, Śāstry has not said anything significant about it except that the Madhu Vidyā is given to the Aśvins as a sacrifice. But the legend becomes intelligible when it is connected with the word *aśvat*[112] from which the symbolism of horse-head has been created. In short, the legend is rightly interpreted when the light provided by the Upaniṣad is appropriately applied.

(v) The last question to be addressed by us is about the two mantras 2-5-18 and 2-5-19. While the second is a Ṛk from the Veda,[113] the first is not a Ṛk but a passage whose content is as old as the Ṛks. The question is, why does the Madhu Brāhmaṇa close with these mantras? Śaṅkara's answer is that while mantras 2-5-16 and 2-5-17 are about meditation on the Madhu Vidyā, on things that are mutually dependent, mantras 2-5-18 and 2-5-19 are about meditation on the secret aspect of Madhu Vidyā, about the secret Ātman seated behind the world of beings and objects. He relates the last two mantras to the expression *kakṣayaṃ* in 2-5-17 and says that they deal with the secret Ātman. Kapāli Śāstry also agrees with this view about 2-5-18 and 2-5-19. He says that though 2-5-16 and 2-5-17 talk about the Madhu Vidyā, its secret *kakṣayaṃ madhu* is revealed only in 2-5-18 and 2-5-19.[114] He points out that the Upaniṣad affirms through the two mantras that this Madhu "is the Madhu of the Ṛg Veda also."[115]

Before we proceed we shall note what 2-5-18 and 2-5-19 say. The first says: "He created bodies with two feet and bodies with four feet. Having become a bird, he entered into the bodies. He who has thus entered them is that Person who created them. There is no body by which he is not enveloped, no body by which he is not served". The second says: "He became form after form, forms similar and forms dissimilar, in order for us to be near and see his original form — That-Form. Through his Māyā the Lord goes about as the possessor of manifold forms. His horses are a thousand but they are united in their onward movement". Now we shall explain the mantras.

Both the mantras deal with the same theme, the theme of God creating the world of forms for his habitation and for his progress through the habitation. We know that birds build their nests so as to use them as their dwellings and enjoy living in them. In the same way God is shown to be a builder of forms or mansions (*tvaṣṭṛ*) and an enjoyer of life who uses them as his habitations. God the creator of the world and God the enjoyer of the world are one and the same Person. His original form (*tad asya rūpaṃ*) is superior to all forms he has created through his Māyā, because he exceeds them and is immeasurable by them. But still the forms he has created do reveal something of his original form (*praticakṣaṇāya*). This is what God's Māyā does: it measures the immeasurable and reveals a little of that; though a little of the original form, the little is a true representation, a real manifestation of God, otherwise we can never be near and see him. Here the word Māyā cannot be given the sense of a power of illusory creation. It is very clear from the context. Like the word bird (*pakṣi*), the word horses (*harayaḥ*) is very suggestive. With them as the means we travel and move forward. If the bird suggests that God is the builder and enjoyer of mansions, the horses suggest that he is the voyager and the seeker of progressive growth in life. From these mantras it is absolutely clear that though God exceeds the world, the world serves the purpose of fulfilling His Will.

According to Śaṅkara, the secret of Madhu Vidyā is about Ātman of whom the world is a false appearance like the reflected image of the moon.[116] If we grant, for the sake of argument, that this is the secret teaching of Madhu Vidyā, it is not supported by the mantras 2-5-18 and 2-5-19. As we have already explained, they pointedly declare that Ātman is the inhabitant and enjoyer of the world. There is no room at all for Śaṅkara's illusionism in them.

Unlike Śaṅkara, Kapāli Śāstry thinks that the Madhu Brāhmaṇa views the world to be a real manifestation of Ātman. He is right in thinking so. But like Śaṅkara, he makes a distinction between the Madhu Vidyā, on the one hand, and its secret aspect (*kakṣayaṃ madhu*),[117] on the other. For him the Madhu Vidyā deals with the world where everything is interdependent; but the secret aspect of this Vidyā is Ātman, "the root principle of Madhu" which makes interdependence possible in the world. Therefore he thinks that Ātman alone is worthy of attainment. It means that Ātman the creator of the world alone is the object of attainment rather than Ātman the inhabitant and enjoyer of the world. If this is so, then there is no ground for his view that 2-5-18 and 2-5-19 give "a fitting close"[118] to the Madhu Vidyā. For we have already found that the two proclaim not only Ātman to be the creator of the world but also Ātman's creation to be purposeful, the purpose being habitation in the world and enjoyment of the habitation.

If Ātman is worthy of attainment, then the attainment cannot exclude Ātman's purpose in the world. Both are important and both must be accepted. Ātman's purpose can be known only by knowing Ātman. And the purpose can be achieved only by a will united with Ātman's will. From this it does not follow that Ātman alone is important and other things connected with Him are unimportant. A knower of Ātman must know Him in all His aspects.

A knower of Ātman is conscious of the soul in him and the soul in others. The soul develops through the play of forces, forces that meet and mingle from several points in the world. Its ordinary law of development is the law of hunger and death. As long as the law is in operation, the exterior life of the knower of Ātman is subject to confusion and conflict, suffering and pain. He is indeed liberated in his Ātman. But still he is open to these faults, because he is not liberated in his soul which is the secret centre of exterior life. When the soul is liberated and becomes the deepest seat of Ātman, it is freed from the old law of hunger and death, pain and suffering and begins to develop through another law, the law of love and fulfilment (*madhu*). As the law of development is imposed on exterior life from its secret centre namely, the soul, it comes to be known by the name of *kakṣayaṃ madhu*. Śāstry, like his counterpart, has not understood the importance of the soul and its liberation. Dadhyaṅ's mission is to establish that the knowledge of Ātman must culminate in the liberation of the soul from its present law of development and the assumption of the law of love and fulfilment by the liberated soul. By missing this point both Śāstry and Śaṅkara have missed the real teaching of the Madhu Vidyā.

The work of the Upaniṣads is to found the Vedānta on a solid foundation by using the Veda as the starting point. In this process the essence of Veda becomes Vedānta. This is very much in evidence in the Madhu Brāhmaṇa where 2-5-19 is a Ṛk Mantra.[119] The Ṛk says that the Lord is the creator of forms and that the forms are horses on which he rides. He is the voyager who goes forward and enjoys progress through them. The Madhu Vidyā is an expanded version of this original idea. Dadhyaṅ has given prominence to the idea that progress in life must be a free movement whose law is that of love and fulfilment and not a crippled movement whose law is the law of hunger and death. The former law is obscurely suggested by the *united movement* of the horses (*yuktā hyasya harayaḥ*).[120] This is the significance as to why the Madhu Brāhmaṇa closes with this Ṛk Mantra.

SUMMARY AND CONCLUSION

Ātman is to be known in its two aspects, in pure essence and in cosmic extension. In its pure essence Ātman is beyond the world; in its cosmic extension Ātman is the source and substance, the abode and abider of the world. A knower of Ātman knows Ātman in these two aspects, or else his knowledge will be incomplete. He will see Ātman otherwise, not as He is.

A knower of Ātman in its completeness is an enlightened doer of works. He is freed from doing works for ego and its satisfaction. He is freed from all sense of otherness which separates him and others from Ātman. He works for the world, for the world is to be helped to win back its original status, the status of having its origin and substance, its abode and abider in the imperishable Ātman. This is his occupation.

Eventually, the doer of works for the world is a giver of love to the world. In the measure he gives love to the world and finds his satisfaction in the good of the world, the world too gives love to him and finds its satisfaction in his good. Thus the knower of Ātman is both the doer of world-work and the giver of world-love. He does all works and through them expresses his love.

Thus immortality is not only union with Ātman but also union with the world. This is the teaching of the Bṛhadāraṇyaka Upaniṣad. No other Upaniṣad, except the Īśa, has put such a profound content into the concept of immortality as this great Upaniṣad.

The interpretation put forward here is a departure from the beaten track. It has reversed some of the current opinions of scholars about the Upaniṣad. First, that it teaches the falsity of the world. In this connection the words *yatra hi dvaitam iva bhavati tad itara itaram jighrati* etc.[121] are quoted. Actually, they speak about false duality. A false duality is a relation not associated with Ātman. Where the false duality prevails, there everything is seen as other, as separated from Ātman (*itaram*). On the other hand, a real duality is a relation associated with Ātman. Where the real duality prevails i.e. where all duality is a modification of Ātman (*sarvam ātmaivābhūt*),[122] there one smells a thing dependent on Ātman and the means by which a thing is smelled is also dependent on Ātman. Similarly, in all other actions the object of knowledge and the means of knowledge are both dependent on Ātman.[123] Therefore the passage in question speaks about false duality giving place to real duality and not about the falsity of the world (*mithyājagat*). What disappears is the false view of the world and not the world. The questions "what" (*kaṃ*) and "by what" (*kena*) are intended to affirm that both the object and the means are now dependent on Ātman.

Second, that all action for a knower of Ātman ceases. Only actions done for the sake of his ego cease. When the ego disappears, he is engaged in works for the sake of Ātman in the world. Further the Upaniṣad says elsewhere that a knower of Brahman is a doer of good deeds (*brahmavid puṇyakṛt*).[124] Therefore, actions do not cease for a knower of Ātman.

Third, that possessions are to be renounced for the sake of knowing Ātman. The Upaniṣad teaches that only love for the sake of wife, wealth, etc. is to be given up and not the objects of love. Further, Yājñavalkya is a knower of Ātman, but he has not given up his wife or household. Therefore, possessions are not an obstruction to the knowledge of Ātman.

Fourth, that Ātman is acosmic. He is acosmic but not in the rigid sense of the word. He is defined through *neti neti* formula, but this does not mean that he denies the world. He denies only limitation by the world. Hence he is acosmic only in the sense that he exceeds the world. If he denies the world, then the Upaniṣad will not say later that he is the master and king of all beings (*bhūtādhipati*)[125] in the world.

Fifth, that the world is a place of determinism and relative existence and must be rejected through the honey of Ātman. The honey doctrine does not teach that the world is so, but that it is a place of mutual love and fulfilment for a knower of Ātman. When he loves the world for the sake of Ātman, the world too loves him for the sake of the same Ātman. When love meets with love, there is neither determinism nor relative existence for him who has known Ātman.

Sixth, that the world-existence is to be rejected, for otherwise the evil influence of illusory Māyā or insentient Prakṛti on the soul cannot be destroyed. But this is not the view of the Bṛhadāraṇyaka Upaniṣad. It says that in both the individual and the universal aspects the world is the manifestation of the very essence of Ātman (*ātmaivābhūt*)[126] and not caused by anything foreign to Ātman. This is the significance of the particle *eva* in *ātmaiva*. Hence what needs to be rejected is not the world-existence but the wrong view thereof.

Seventh, that the Madhu Brāhmaṇa has no independent teaching apart from the teaching of the Maitreyī Brāhmaṇa. This is not true. As we have found in our reading of it, it has its own teaching, namely, the teaching that for a knower of Ātman life progresses through mutual love and fulfilment. Though this teaching is found in its rudimentary form in the Maitreyī Brāhmaṇa, it is developed and stated as a full-fledged view only in the Madhu Brāhmaṇa.

We may therefore conclude that the Bṛhadāraṇyaka Upaniṣad is most positive in its attitude towards the world and calls upon us to accept the world in full measure and develop it by all means — by knowledge, work and love.

NOTES

1. Bṛhadāraṇyaka Upaniṣad (hereafter Bṛ. Up.), 2-4-5.
2. Ibid., 2-4-6.
3. Ibid.
4. Ibid., 2-4-7, 8,9.
5. Ibid., 2-4-10.
6. Śaṅkara, *Bṛhadāraṇyaka Upaniṣad Bhāṣya* (hereafter Bṛ. Up. B.), 2-4-10.
7. Bṛ. Up., 2-4-11.
8. Śaṅkara, Bṛ. Up. B., 2-4-11.
9. Bṛ. Up., 2-4-12.
10. Ibid.
11. Ibid.
12. Ibid.
13. Ibid.
14. Śaṅkara, Bṛ. Up. B., Tr. Mādhavānanda (1965), p. 379.
15. Ibid., p. 391.
16. Śaṅkara, Bṛ. Up. B., 2-5-15.
17. Ibid., 2-5.
18. Śatapatha Brāhmaṇa, 14-1-1,4, 22 to 24.
19. Ṛg Veda (hereafter RV), 6-47-18.
20. Bṛ. Up., 2-5-15.
21. Ibid., 2-5-16, 17, 19.
22. Kapāli Śāstry, *Lights on the Upaniṣads* (hereafter LU) (1947), p.126.
23. Ibid.
24. Ibid.
25. Ibid.
26. Ibid.
27. Ibid.
28. RV, 1-116-12, 1-117-22.
29. LU, p. 134.
30. Ibid., p.143.
31. Ibid., p. 137.
32. Ibid., p. 138.

33. Ibid.
34. Ibid., p. 130.
35. Ibid., p. 139.
36. Ibid., p. 140.
37. Ibid., p. 143.
38. Ibid., p. 149.
39. Śaṅkara, Bṛ. Up. B., 2-4-12, 14.
40. LU, pp. 149,155.
41. Ibid., p. 155.
42. Ibid., p. 149.
43. Ibid.
44. Bṛ. Up., 2-4-14.
45. Ibid., 2-5-15.
46. Ibid., 2-4-5.
47. Ibid.
48. Ibid.
49. Ibid., 2-4-6.
50. Ibid.
51. Ibid., 2-4-5.
52. Ibid.
53. Ibid., 2-4-6.
54. Ibid., 2-4-5.
55. Ibid., 2-4-7 to 9.
56. Ibid., 2-4-10.
57. Ibid., 2-4-11.
58. Ibid., 2-4-6.
59. Śaṅkara, Bṛ. Up. B., p. 359.
60. Bṛ. Up., 2-4-14.
61. Ibid., 2-4-6.
62. Ibid., 2-5-17.
63. Ibid., 2-5-16.
64. Sri Aurobindo, *The Upanishads* (hereafter TU) (1972), pp. 134,135.
65. Bṛ. Up., 1-2-1.
66. Ibid.
67. Sri Aurobindo, *The Life Divine* (1973), p. 192.
68. Bṛ. Up., 1-3-28.
69. Ibid., 2-5-14.
70. Ibid., 2-4-5.
71. Ibid.
72. Ibid., 2-4-6.
73. Ibid.
74. Ibid., 2-4-5.
75. Ibid.
76. Ibid., 2-4-6.

77. Ibid.
78. Ibid.
79. Ibid., 2-4-7.
80. Ibid.
81. Ibid., 2-4-10.
82. Ibid., 2-4-11.
83. Ibid., 2-4-12.
84. Ibid.
85. Ibid.
86. Ibid.
87. Ibid.
88. Ibid.
89. Ibid.
90. Ibid.
91. Ibid., 3-1-3.
92. Ibid., 2-4-6.
93. Ibid., 2-4-12.
94. Ibid., 2-4-6.
95. Ibid., 4-5-14.
96. Ibid., 2-4-14.
97. Ibid., 1-4-10.
98. Ibid., 2-4-14.
99. Ibid.
100. Ibid.
101. Ibid., 4-4-13. (* *viśvāya sarvakarmakṛt*)
102. Ibid., 4-4-9.
103. Ibid., 2-5-15.
104. Ibid., 2-4-5.
105. Ibid., 2-4-14.
106. RV, 1-116-12, 1-117-22.
107. TU, p. 233.
108. RV, 4-45-3.
109. Ibid., 4-43-2.
110. Bṛ. Up., 2-5-17.
111. Ibid., 1-2-7.
112. Ibid.
113. RV, 6-47-18.
114. LU, p.149.
115. Ibid.
116. Śaṅkara, Bṛ. Up. B., 2-5-15.
117. Bṛ. Up., 2-5-17.
118. LU, p., 148.
119. RV, 6-47-18.
120. Ibid.

121. Bṛ. Up., 2-4-14.
122. Ibid.
123. Ibid.
124. Ibid., 4-4-9.
125. Ibid., 2-5-15.
126. Ibid., 2-4-14.

22

Textual Evidence for the Theory of Māyā

THE EVIDENCE

Māyā is the power of illusion. The world produced by Māyā is illusory. This is a brief statement of the theory of Māyā. There is a debate whether the Upaniṣads support the theory. In answer to it Professor Mahādevan (1911–1983), a distinguished exponent of Advaita, writes thus: "It is true that the doctrine of *māyā* is not to be found in the *Upaniṣads* in its full-fledged form. But the thought itself is not unknown to some of the seers of the *Upaniṣads* ".[1]

In support of his view Mahādevan calls attention to some important Upaniṣads where the notion of Māyā is said to be implicit. (i) "Where verily there is, as it were, a duality, there one knows another" (*yatra hi dvaitamiva bhavati tad itara itaram vijānāti*).[2] The expression "there is, as it were, a duality" implies that "the world of duality is not real, that is illusory, *māyā*". (ii) "[T]he assumption of many shapes by Indra through his illusions (*māyās*) is mentioned ... in the *Bṛhadāraṇyaka* in a context where real difference is denied" (*indro māyābhiḥ pururūpa īyate*).[3] The text says that by his powers of illusion Indra is perceived in many forms. He is the Lord of the world and his forms are the forms of the world. (iii) "By one piece of clay all that is made of clay can be known. The modification is only a name depending on a word. The truth is that it is clay" (*vācārambhaṇaṃ vikāro nāmadheyaṃ mṛttiketyeva satyam*).[4] From this example we are taught that the modification of the Being into the world is to be dismissed as *nāmadheyaṃ*. The word *nāmadheyaṃ* is intended to convey the sense of illusory appearance. (iv) "When we come to the *Śvetāśvatara*, we find the term *māyā* used in the sense of illusion, and the Lord of all beings is described as *māyin*" (*māyinaṃ tu maheśvaram*).[5] Literally, the word Māyin means the Lord of the Illusion, one who creates the illusory world. (v) In another work[6] by Mahādevan he invites our attention to a text which reads as follows: "From death to death he goes, who sees plurality here, as it were" (*mṛtyos sa mṛtyum āpnoti ya iha nāneva paśyati*)[7]. Here he says that the expression "plurality here, as it were" refers to "the world of duality" which is "illusory". We must note that all the five texts mentioned above speak about the illusory world and all the five are indirect references.

THE BṚHADĀRAṆYAKA UPANIṢAD

(a) First comes the text 2-4-14. It develops a point mentioned in the previous text 2-4-12. In this text the process of creation from the great Ātman is set forth. In the process the individual separates himself from Ātman and gradually destroys all his connections with Him (*tāny evānuvinaśyati*). As a result, he is overcome by mortality. Having become a mortal, he is deprived of all consciousness of Ātman (*na pretya saṃjñāsti*).

In the state of mortality the means and ends of the individual are viewed as two separated forms. As this is a false view of the mortal, their duality is declared to be illusory (*dvaitamiva bhavati*). For him the means is other (*itara*) and the end obtained by the means is also other (*itara*). A detailed description of the mortal's view of his means and ends is given by the text: Other smells other; other sees other; other hears other; other speaks to other; other thinks of other; other understands other. This is a state of separation and misery.

However, when the mortal recovers the consciousness of Ātman, he ceases to be a mortal and his false view disappears. Ātman becomes all his means and ends (*sarvamātmaivābhūt*) i.e. they are endowed with the consciousness of Ātman. As a result, there is no duality of means and ends. Now what one should smell and by what? One should smell Ātman by Ātman. What should one see and by what? One should see Ātman by Ātman. What should one hear and by what? One should hear Ātman by Ātman. What should one speak of and by what? One should speak of Ātman by Ātman. What should one think of and by what? One should think of Ātman by Ātman. What should one understand and by what? One should understand Ātman by Ātman. This is a state of oneness and happiness. This is the teaching of Yājñavalkya.

Now we shall state the main points of our discussion. First, duality refers to the duality of the means and the ends possessed by the mortal. Second, their duality is illusory (*dvaitamivabhavati*), because the illusion is caused by the false view of the mortal. Third, when Ātman is recovered by the mortal, the duality disappears, because his false view disappears and his means and ends become endowed with the sense of Ātman. Fourth, the text speaks only about the individual and his possessions. In the beginning he is presented as a mortal. Then he changes and becomes an immortal. Fifth, the word *sarvam* occurs twice in the text. In both places it does not mean the world. On the contrary, it stands for all means and ends possessed by the individual.

Now we are prepared to examine Mahādevan's view on *dvaitamiva bhavati*. We agree with him on two points — (i) duality is an illusory appearance; (ii) it disappears when the mortal becomes a knower of Ātman. From these words it is wrong to conclude that the world is illusory and disappears through the knowledge of Ātman. By duality is meant the dualism of the means and the ends of the mortal. This dualism is illusory. And the knowledge of Ātman removes the dualism and not anything else. Here the topic under discussion is the individual and not the world; he gives up his mortality and becomes an immortal.

(b) Indra has two forms, his original form (*tadasya rūpam*) and the many forms he has assumed (*pururūpaḥ*). The original form is equated with Ātman, the subjective side of Brahman which is not measurable by forms having the qualities of being earlier and later, inside and outside. In this aspect Indra is the all-perceiver (*sarvānubhūḥ*). However, the forms he assumes are very valuable. They are assumed for the sake of apprehending (*praticakṣaṇāya*) his original form (*tadrūpam*) through them.

The exact meaning of *indro māyābhiḥ pururūpa* is to be determined in the light of the above analysis. As Mahādevan says, *māyābhiḥ* cannot mean illusions for two important reasons. First, in relation to the previous word *babhūva*[8] (transformed) it gives the meaning "through the powers of transformation". If the forms of Indra are assumed through the powers of transformation, they are real and not illusory. Second, his forms are said to be assumed for the sake of apprehending his original form. If this is the purpose, then it is not served by illusory forms. Through illusion no fact is ever known. For the fact is veiled and distorted by the illusion. So Indra's forms which are helpful to apprehend his supreme form are necessarily real and not illusory.

As Mahādevan points out, Indra's original form equated with Brahman is not devoid of differences or of forms associated with differences. The original form is rather devoid of *limitation* by the forms he assumes. As the forms are produced through the powers of transformation (*māyābhiḥ*), it is but appropriate to take the original form to be a source of many real forms.

THE CHĀNDOGYA UPANIṢAD

The science of Being (*sadvidyā*) is taught by Uddālaka. The world is a modification of the Being. Therefore all in the world become known by knowing the Being. This is illustrated through examples. One of them is from clay. He says that by knowing a clod of clay (*mṛtpiṇḍena*), all made of clay (*sarvammṛnmayam*) become known (*vijñātaṃ syāt*).

The word clay and the clay belong to two different orders, one is a name and the other is a phenomenon. Though entirely different, they are close to each other, because the first is a name given to the second. Therefore, under certain conditions, confusion between the word and the clay is quite possible. The one condition where this confusion arises is when one is stuck with the word (*stabdhaḥ*). One discriminates between the word and the clay only when one is not obstructed by the word. This is why Uddālaka speaks about the word and the method of escaping the confusion created by the word.

This is his brief observation. When an individual is stuck with the word, he sees that there is an illusory clay begun by the word clay (*vācārambhaṇaṃ vikāraḥ*). But the text says that the illusory clay is but the name clay (*nāmadheyam*) and not the lump of clay. From the name clay, things made of clay do not become known. How are we to be free from the obstruction of the word? By remembering that the phenomenon called clay alone is real (*mṛttiketyeva satyam*). Now the sense of the expression *vācārambhaṇaṃ vikāro nāmadheyaṃ* is absolutely clear. It does not say that the modification of clay is illusory. It rather says that the illusory clay is begun by the word clay and it exists only as the name clay (*nāmadheyaṃ*).

For Mahādevan "all made of clay become known" means that they are known as clay (*mṛttiketi*) and not as the modifications of clay (*vikāra*). If the modifications are merely clay, then why is there a process of creation and the production such as the pot? It is a difficult question to answer.

If the interpretation is to be accepted, then it must agree with the facts connected with clay and its modifications. Let us take the example of a pot made from clay. The clay in the pot is real, because its clayness is unmodified. The pot too is real, because it is a modification of an eternal possibility in the clay. The eternal possibility is referred to as *vyadadhāt śāśvatībhyaḥ samābhyaḥ* in the Īśa. Thus both are real — the clay and the pot made from the clay. When the pot is broken, the clay and the pot are not separated. Their relation is merely reversed: the pot returns to the clay and the clay becomes the continent of the pot. Therefore under no circumstance the pot is illusory: it exists either as an eternal possibility in the clay or as a modification of that possibility. The words "all made of clay become known" mean that they become known as the modifications of the eternal or real possibilities of the clay. As Mahādevan's interpretation does not agree with these facts, it is to be dismissed as unsound.

There is also another reason why his interpretation is not acceptable. There are three propositions in the text 6-1-4 — (1) *ekenamṛtpiṇḍena sarvammṛnmayam vijnātam syāt*;(2) *vācā-rambhaṇaṃ vikāro nāmadheyaṃ*; (3) *mṛttiketyeva satyam*. The first is meant for those who can discriminate between the word clay (*vāk*) and the lump of clay (*mṛtpiṇḍa*), while the second and the third are meant for those who cannot discriminate between the two, who are overcome by the illusory modification begun by the word clay (*vācārambhaṇaṃ vikāraḥ*) and who are therefore advised to discriminate the word clay from the clay (*mṛttiketyeva satyam*).

As long as we are able to discriminate between the two, the second and the third propositions are not relevant to us. All things made of clay are known to be modifications of the lump of clay, for the lump is their material cause. Here the questions of illusory modification (*vikāraḥ*) and reality (*satyam*) have no relevance at all. Mahādevan's attempt is wrong for two reasons: (1) he does not note that the three propositions have two types of *adhikārin* in view; (2) he also does not note that the second and the third propositions speak only about the word clay and the clay and not about the products of clay and the clay. His reading is the cumulative effect of the two mistakes.

The confusion between the word and Ātman is repeatedly mentioned in the Upaniṣads. The Muṇḍaka Upaniṣad says that Ātman cannot be attained through delusion caused by the word (*ayam ātmā labyo na ca pramādāt*).[9] In the same spirit Uddālaka speaks about the delusion begun by the word. From this it is clear that what he has said about the word is definitely not a solitary instruction. The expression *vikāro nāmadheyaṁ,* as Mahādevan claims, does not imply that the world is illusory.

THE ŚVETĀŚVATARA UPANIṢAD

If we go through the Upaniṣad, we come across many references to the creation of the world — (i) *ekam bījam bahudhā karoti*;[10] (ii) *tantunābhaiva tantubhiḥ pradhānajaiḥ svamāvṛṇot*;[11] (iii) *tasmims cānyo ... sanniruddhaḥ*;[12] (iv) *asmān sṛjate viśvam etat.*[13] (i) He makes one seed into many creatures. Here the source of the world is compared to a seed which contains all in an unmanifest state and from which all are released into manifestation. (ii) He covers himself with all born of the original Nature, like a spider which covers itself with the threads drawn from itself. By likening all born of the original Nature to the threads created by the spider from its own being, the world is said to be produced from its previous state of unmanifestation. (iii) Within that the world (the other) is confined. This again says that before its manifestation the world preexists in a state of unmanifestation. (iv) This world is produced from that state. This means that the world comes out of that where it lies in a state of obstruction i.e. envelopment. All these texts clearly prove that the Śvetāśvatara Upaniṣad believes in the theory of transformation (*pariṇāmavāda*). In another text it uses the word transformation itself when it speaks about the creation of the world (*pariṇāmayet*).[14] The theory of Māyā states that the world is produced not from an unmanifest state but from the power of illusion i.e. the power of pure imagination. However, the theory is nowhere presented in the Upaniṣads, including the Śvetāśvatara.

Mahādevan, on the other hand, is of the view that the Upaniṣad upholds the theory of illusion, because the Lord of the world is referred to as Māyin. The word Māyin literally means the Lord of the Illusion. This is surely a solitary evidence. However, it cannot be set aside as of no consequence. By this evidence we are forced to question the validity of the view that the Upaniṣad favours the theory of transformation.

Let us examine Mahādevan's evidence. Though the Lord of Māyā is called Māyin, the descriptions of the Lord do not associate him with the notion of illusion. His Māyā is declared to be responsible for holding the world (the other) confined within the imperishable Ether (*tasmiṃs cānyo māyayā sanniruddhaḥ*)[15] and also for producing it out of that Ether (*asmān māyī sṛjate viśvam etat*).[16] The function of Māyī is thus twofold: (i) to hold the world in an unmanifest state and (ii) to manifest it from this state of unmanifestation. If the Lord of Māyā creates the world from its previous state of unmanifestation, then his Māyā presents itself as the power of transformation rather than that of illusory creation. The Lord is called Māyin, but he produces the world through the power of transformation. This is the crux of the matter.

In 4-10 the Upaniṣad makes Prakṛti (from which all are born through transformation) as the content of Māyā (*māyāṃ tu prakṛtiṃ viddhi*) and recognises the Lord of Māyā as the great Lord who creates all through transformation (*māyinaṃ tu maheśvaram*). From this it is quite evident that the seer of the Upaniṣad tries to bring out the real sense of Māyā without discarding the original word. The point is that he has rejected the sense of illusion from the word Māyā and put into it the sense of transformation. Therefore the word Māyin cannot give the sense of a conjuror but a controller of Māyā which is the power of transformation. This is the unique merit of the Upaniṣad. The difficulty with Mahādevan's contention is that he has caught the word Māyā and completely ignored its context. This is a gross error of omission.

THE KAṬHA UPANIṢAD

The Upaniṣad deals with an important point about the world. The world is characterised by plurality (*nānātva*). It is a creation from the imperishable Ātman which never deviates from its oneness (*ekatva*). Though the two seem to be opposites, they are undivided and present themselves as a harmonious whole.

The Upaniṣad says: whatever is there (in the One), that is here (in the Many); whatever is here (in the Many), that is there (in the One).[17] The power of the One is manifest here as the Many, and the essence of the Many is unmanifest there as the power of the One. Therefore, the wise one sees that here there is absolutely no existence for the Many without the One (*neha nānāsti kiñcana*).[18] (The words "without the One" are to be supplied from the above text 2-1-10.) However, the mind of the mortal sees as if there exist the Many without the One. He who sees thus goes from death to death (*mṛtyos sa mṛtyuṃ gacchati ya iha nāneva paśyati*).[19] (The words "without the One" are to be supplied from 2-1-10.) This means that by holding a false view of the Many one is subject to the evils of transmigration.

Having quoted this text, Mahādevan observes that the word Many qualified by the expression "as it were" means that "the world of duality" is "an illusory appearance." From this he concludes that 2-1-10 contains another evidence which proves the presence of the doctrine of Māyā in the Upaniṣad.

The expression "as it were" (*iva*) surely implies the notion of illusoriness. The Upaniṣad categorically says that the Many here do not exist apart from the One (*neha nānāsti kiñcana).* It is the separation of the Many from the One that is said be illusory, not the Many themselves. The mortal's view of them is certainly illusory, because he sees as if they are independent. But the Many are not so, for they are never separated from the One. This is the underlying import of the declaration that Ātman is indeed this world (*ātmaivedaṃ sarvam*).[20] The text clearly says that "there" and "here", "here" and "there" are harmonious and indivisible. The separation of "here" from "there" is illusory. Unfortunately, Mahādevan has missed this important point.

CONCLUSION

None of Mahādevan's evidences proves his case. He says that the doctrine of Māyā (illusion) is not to be found in the Upaniṣads "in its full-fledged form". We must be quick to add that it is not to be found in them even in its elementary form. It is un-Vedic and not related to Vedānta. He closely follows the great masters like Gauḍapāda and Śaṅkara. They have tried to read the doctrine into the main Upaniṣads and win scriptural support for it by this means.

NOTES

1. T.M.P. Mahādevan, *Upaniṣads* (Selections from 108 *Upaniṣads*), Motilal Banarsidass, New Delhi, 2000, pp.32–33.
2. Bṛhadāraṇyaka Upaniṣad (hereafter Bṛ. Up.), 2-4-14.
3. Ibid., 2-5-19.
4. Chāndogya Upaniṣad (hereafter Ch. Up.), 6-1-4.
5. Śvetāśvatara Upaniṣad (hereafter S. Up.), 4-10.
6. T.M.P. Mahādevan, *Invitation to Indian Philosophy*, Arnold-Heinemann, New Delhi, 1974, p. 359.
7. Kaṭha Upaniṣad (hereafter K. Up.), 2-1-10.
8. Bṛ. Up., 2-5-19.
9. Muṇḍaka Upaniṣad, 3-2-4.
10. S. Up., 6-12.
11. Ibid., 6-10.
12. Ibid., 4-9.
13. Ibid.
14. Ibid., 5-5.
15. Ibid., 4-9, 4-8.
16. Ibid.
17. K. Up., 2-1-10.
18. Ibid., 2-1-11.
19. Ibid.
20. Ch. Up., 7-25-2.

23

The Mortal and the Immortal

THE KNOWER OF TRADITION

Traditional Advaitins claim that they follow the knowers of tradition (*sampradāyavids*),[1] those who know the tradition of right interpretation of the Upaniṣads. To them (Advaitins) the tradition is so insightful and indispensable that without its help a proper comprehension of the scripture is not possible. This is the position of Advaitins. Let us note what according to them is the nature of immortality set forth in the Upaniṣads.

The Upaniṣads point out that a mortal is known by three important characteristics — (i) he sees as if there is a world of plurality (*nāneva paśyati*);[2] (ii) he is under the delusion that he is a non-lord subject to the necessity of works (*anīśa*);[3] and (iii) he is an enjoyer who loves his possessions for their own sake, for the sake of their utility (*sarvasya kāmāya sarvam priyam bhavati*).[4] In fact the three make him triply bound — bound by the world he sees, bound by the works he does, and bound by the enjoyments he seeks. This is, however, not the final word about the mortal. The seers of the Upaniṣads repeatedly affirm that it is possible for him to become absolutely free of the triple bondage through union with the supreme Ātman who is ever-free and without limitations (*asito na vyathate*).[5] He who is thus freed from bondage is referred to as *vimuktaḥ*[6] by the seers. As he is freed from the three evils, the immortal is never a seer of the world, never a doer of works and never an enjoyer of possessions. He is always a knower of Ātman who has abandoned all. For this is the ideal exemplified by those who have attained immortality and become wandering monks (*pravrājinaḥ*).[7]

This, according to the traditional Advaitins, is the nature of immortality outlined in the Upaniṣads. Any other interpretation put on them is not acceptable to them. We shall now go back to the original texts and see how far their account of immortality is supported by the authority of the scripture. If the tradition is a good authority for them, it must be rooted in the authority of the scripture. When they accept it to be so rooted, they must recognise that the scripture is a higher authority than their tradition. By virtue of this, they must also recognise that it is an authority for examining their position as its expounders. They cannot deny the above two roles to it. If they deny them, then their interpretation will automatically lose all its validity.

PERCEPTION OF THE WORLD

The Kaṭha Upaniṣad describes the condition under which a man becomes a mortal or is bound by the law of transmigration. It says: When he thinks that there is this world and none beyond it, he comes under the sway of Death (*ayam loko nāsti para iti mānī punaḥ punarvaśam apadyate me*).[8] So what makes him a mortal is never his thought or perception of the world but the perception that this world alone exists. It means: his mortality is due to his failure to see that there is a higher world of Ātman from which this material world has come into existence. For, as the Upaniṣad says, this is the fact: this world proceeds from Ātman and abides in Ātman.[9] If this is so, then the way to conquer mortality is to recognise the fact and see the world accordingly. Those who see thus, asserts the Upaniṣad, become immortals *(amṛtāste bhavanti)*.[10] So what makes a man an immortal is not his non-perception of the world but his perception that it is derived from Ātman.[11] This is the significance of all creation-texts in the Upaniṣads. They teach not only that the world has been created from Ātman but that the substance of the world is the same as that of Ātman. Hence the Kaṭha Upaniṣad declares "here there is absolutely no existence for the world apart from Ātman" (*neha nānāsti kiñcana*).[12] This is the method of conquering mortality.

Let us try to understand the correct sense of the words *ya iha nāneva paśyati* in the light of their context.[13] These words occur in a verse where the first line runs thus: *yadeveha tadamutra yadamutra tadanviha*[14] (what indeed is here, is there; what is there, is here likewise). A careful study of the line tells us that the world (here) is not only *contained* in Ātman (there) but also *contains* the same Ātman in its bosom. From this the world is proved to be real, real as the essence and the dwelling of Ātman who is real. If this is the nature of the world according to the first line of the above verse, the word *nānā* in the second line cannot give the sense of illusory appearance. Therefore we are compelled to put into *nāneva* a suitable sense.

The words *mṛtyos sa mṛtyum āpnoti*[15] clearly suggest that the perceiver of the world (*paśyati*) is an ignorant individual. He is ignorant of Ātman and so subject to transmigration. He sees as if the world is independent of Ātman. This is the correct sense of *nāneva paśyati*. The mind of a mortal separates the world from Ātman and sees as if the world exists by itself (*iva*).[16] Therefore the world is not illusory, though the perception of the world by the mortal is. It is wrong to say that a knower of Ātman is not a seer of the world; on the contrary, he sees it as a creation from and a dwelling of Ātman.

PERFORMANCE OF WORKS IN THE WORLD

The Muṇḍaka recognises that works done according to the prescribed rules of the Vedas make man a virtuous person. But such works come under the severe criticism of the Upaniṣad. Good deeds prevent him from becoming sinful and, when he is dead, take him to the world where the lord of the gods dwells (*devānām patiḥ*).[17] As these deeds increase the power of *sattva* in him, he becomes fit for godly life and enjoyment in heaven. But by the law of the triple *guṇa* the power of *sattva* attracts its opposite, the power of *tamas*. As a result, *sattva* becomes less and less dominant and it is eventually overcome by *tamas*. When this reversal takes place, man loses his god-form and is compelled to enter the world of mortals. He is reborn, not always as a human being but sometimes as an inferior being also. This is because of the violent turn sometimes[18] taken by the rising *tamas*. It is not enough if one escapes sinful life; it is also necessary that one should escape the evils of transmigratory life. This is the reason why the good deeds are rejected by the Muṇḍaka Upaniṣad.

A doer of good works, as we have found, is indeed good and freed from all sins, but these works do not wipe out his mortality.

For they are done out of desire and attachment[19] which are the sources of mortality. When all the desires of the good man are thrown out of his heart, he is united with Ātman and attains immortality (*yadā sarve pramucyante kāmā ye› sya hṛdi śritāḥ atha martyo amṛto bhavati*).[20] As a knower of Ātman, he is freed from all works, both sinful and virtuous.

But the Muṇḍaka Upaniṣad asserts that a knower of Ātman is also a doer of works (*ātmaratiḥ kriyāvān*).[21] This is indeed an enigmatic teaching. As a knower of Ātman, he cannot have desires; as a doer of works, he must have desires which seek fulfilment through works. The enigma is solved only when we admit that works are of two kinds — (i) those done out of desires (*rāgāt*);[22] (ii) those done for the sake of Ātman in the world i.e. those done without the taint of desires (*parāmṛtam*).[23] A knower of Ātman is indeed free of desires and of works born out of them; but when he accepts works for the sake of bringing freedom to Ātman in the world, he is not bound by them (*na karma lipyate*).[24] He is in full possession of Ātman in himself and yet performs works for the sake of Ātman in other beings. A doer of works for the sake of Ātman in the world is called *ātma-krīḍaḥ*.[25] The Upaniṣad has thoughtfully added this word to its expression *ātmaratiḥ kriyāvān*.[26] By doing so it removes the enigma and makes the expression easy of comprehension.

It is very interesting to note that the enigma is resolved through another means also. The Upaniṣad calls attention to the Lord of the world (*īśam puruṣam*)[27] who is seated in the immutable Ātman (*brahmayonim*)[28] and yet performs works through the mutable Nature (*kartāram*).[29] He does all works through Nature and yet remains well-established in Ātman unaffected and unbound by them. This is the greatness of the Lord. As He is the example to be followed by man, he, like Him, unites himself with Ātman and does works through Nature. Thus he realises Him by attaining to His greatness (*asya mahimānam*).[30] To be great like Him is to be absolutely like Himself (*paramaṃ sāmyam upaiti*).[31] This is another justification for a knower of Ātman to be also a doer of works.

Attention is drawn to a passage in the Bṛhadāraṇyaka Upaniṣad 2-4-14 to show that for a knower of Ātman all works cease. There are two factors on the basis of which all work is done — the doer of works and the object achieved by works. As the doer of works, man smells, sees, hears, speaks, thinks, and understands. As the object achieved by works, something is smelled, something is seen, something is heard, something is spoken of, something is thought of, and something is understood. In this context the above passage raises the point that when all is merged in the Ātman seated in the heart of an individual (*sarvam ātmaivābhūt*),[32] then what should one smell and through what, what should one see and through what, what should one hear and through what, what should one speak of and through what, what should one think of and through what, what should one understand and through what? In other words, this is the teaching contained in the above passage: since all is merged in Ātman, there is a total absence of consciousness of the doer of works and of all things to be obtained by his works. For now all exists as Ātman. If this is the teaching of 2-4-14, then we should agree that for a knower of Ātman works completely cease. Hence he is not a doer of works.

However, this conclusion is not inevitable if we carefully read the passage in question. In the above passage *sarvam ātmaivābhūt* is a crucial statement. The word *abhūt* in it is understood in the sense of dissolution. But it can also give another equally acceptable sense, the sense of self-manifestation. Hence *sarvam ātmaivābhūt* is to be understood to mean "all is a self-manifestation of Ātman". If we accept this interpretation, then the above passage 2-4-14 does not support the traditional view of Advaitins.

When all is a self-manifestation of Ātman, Ātman is united with all. The individual is not a mere doer of works as before, but Ātman expressing its unobstructed will through works. The objects obtained by works are not mere objects as before, but Ātman getting awakened from latency in these objects. As a result, all transaction becomes a transaction between Ātman and Ātman, Ātman awakened in the doer of works and Ātman under the process of being awakened in the objects obtained through works. The questions what and through what, do suggest a sense of denial. What is denied through them is not the doer of works or the objects obtained through works, as interpreted by Advaitins. On the other hand, they deny that the individual is a *mere* doer of works and that the objects obtained through works are *mere* objects. From this we may conclude that for a knower of Ātman works do not cease. They continue as works of Ātman by which Ātman latent in the objects is awakened. This is the teaching of the Bṛhadāraṇyaka Upaniṣad.

ENJOYMENT OF WORLDLY POSSESSIONS

Man is generally greedy. He tries to satisfy his greed through various worldly possessions. According to the Bṛhadāraṇyaka Upaniṣad 2-4-5 his possessions are: wife, sons, brāhmaṇas, kṣatriyas, wealth, worlds, the gods and all beings. He loves them all for the satisfaction he desires to get from them (*sarvasya kāmāya sarvam priyam bhavati*).[33] But they all reject him decisively (*parādhuḥ*).[34] What does it mean? It means that they refuse to give him the satisfaction demanded of them. Now the important question is why his possessions reject him.

Before we proceed further we shall make one point clear. The rejection is spoken of in a context where the possessions are seen elsewhere than in Ātman (*anyatrātmanaḥ*).[35] But the context must be extended to a point already made in the text, namely, the manner in which they are enjoyed. Now the context is this: the possessions are seen elsewhere than in Ātman and they are, therefore, enjoyed in the wrong way. Their rejection is the direct effect of wrong enjoyment which is itself an effect of wrong perception. This is the ultimate cause of their rejection.

Now we shall return to the original question why the enjoyer is rejected by his possessions. The world has been created for habitation and enjoyment by God; accordingly, the world is bound by this true law of existence (*satyadharma*)[36] and abides by it in all circumstances. Compelled by his greed, man declares himself to be the master and enjoyer of the world. He imposes his rule on all things and forces them to obey his dictates. But the world is instinctively aware that he is not its master and it is not his possession. As it remains faithful to its original law of existence, it rejects him and all his attempts to possess and enjoy. This accounts for all struggle and stress he experiences in his life.

We have noted how a mortal conducts himself, especially in regard to his possessions. Now we shall turn to an immortal who is united with Ātman. What is his conduct in the world? Does he keep his possessions and maintain his original connections with the world? The Bṛhadāraṇyaka Upaniṣad says: monks desire this Ātman alone; in order to fulfil their desire, they abandon the world (*etameva pravrājino lokam icchantaḥ pravrajanti*).[37] In other words, they have no possessions and belong to the order of *sannyāsa - āśrama*, and when they attain Him, they renounce even their meagre relations with the world and become wandering monks. Traditional Advaitins cite this text in support of their view that the knowers of Ātman have no possessions and no relations with the world. This text evidently teaches absolute asceticism.

A careful study of the above text brings to light a very important point. The words *etameva icchantaḥ pravrājinaḥ lokam pravrajanti* clearly suggest that a *sannyāsāśramin* was considered fit for seeking Ātman and that he abandoned even this *āśrama* after he realised his goal. But it is very striking that Yājñavalkya, who figures in the Bṛhadāraṇyaka Upaniṣad as the most prominent sage, does not seem to be in favour of either an ascetic being fit for seeking Ātman or his going away as a wanderer after realising Ātman. He clearly points out that if Ātman is an object of desire (*etameva icchantaḥ pravrājinaḥ*), then it is not different from sons, wealth and worlds which are also objects of desire (*ubhe hi ete eṣaṇe eva bhavataḥ*).[38] Desire is exclusive and makes man one-sided: if he desires sons etc., he does not see Ātman; if he desires Ātman, he does not see the world. A householder is attached to the things of the world. Likewise, an ascetic is attached to Ātman. There is basically no difference between the two. For both are bound by attachment. It is for this reason that the Bṛhadāraṇyaka has laid down specifically that Ātman should be seen only as existing together with the world *ekadhaivānudraṣṭavyam etad*.[39] If Ātman and the world are not separated, then there is the conquest of attachment that separates one from the other. Yājñavalkya's own life is a good illustration of his insightful precept. He was a knower of Ātman who was also a householder living with his two wives and having enough wealth to support himself and his family. Therefore the text about *pravrājinaḥ* cannot be considered as representing the Upaniṣad's final view. The Vedānta of Yājñavalkya is that a knower of Ātman does not renounce his possessions or his relations with the world.

A knower of Ātman knows the world in its true perspective. The world is for habitation by God (*īśāvāsyam idaṃ sarvaṃ*).[40] It exists for God and only for God. This is its true law of existence (*satyadharma*).[41] Greed violates the law and is, therefore, the source of all evils. It must be renounced and the whole world surrendered to God, its real master and enjoyer (*māgṛdhaḥ kasyasvid dhanam*).[42] By recovering the true law of the world which he originally abandoned out of greed, he enjoys the world, enjoys by possessing and loving it for the sake of the indwelling God (*tena tyaktena bhuñjīthāḥ*).[43] Thus a knower of Ātman is also an enjoyer of the world.

THE AUTHENTIC VIEW OF VEDĀNTA

To perceive the world is not an evil, but to perceive as if it is independent of Ātman is surely an evil. To perform works in the world is not an evil, but to perform them out of desire is surely an evil. To enjoy possessions is not an evil, but to enjoy them for one's own sake is surely an evil.

Immortality does not destroy but fulfils the essential powers of a mortal. A knower of God is also a seer of the world, for he sees it to be a creation from Him. He is also a doer of works, for through works he helps the world to realise Him or attain equality with Him. Above all, he is also an enjoyer of the world, for he possesses and loves all things for His sake. Immortality destroys only one thing and it is man's mortality. The whole method of Vedānta (*vidhiṃ kṛtsnam*)[44] may be summed up thus: affirmation and not negation except that of limitation.

It is a wrong view that Ātman alone is good and the world is an evil. This is the reason why traditional Advaitins speak only of the attainment of Ātman and neglect the other equally important attainments mentioned in the Upaniṣads. Ātman is good. And the world too is good, for it is the self-extended Ātman. We must always bear in mind the Upaniṣad's dictum *yadamutra tadanviha* (what is there, that is here).[45] It teaches that there is no dichotomy between Ātman and the world, that Ātman is really the world (*ātmaivedaṃ sarvam*).[46]

The account of immortality given by the Advaitins is one-sided and not faithful to the scripture. For the *advaita* of the Upaniṣads holds that an immortal is united not only with Ātman but also with the world.

NOTES

1. Śaṅkara, *Gītā Bhāṣya*, 13-13.
2. Kaṭha Upaniṣad (hereafter K. Up.), 2-1-10.
3. Muṇḍaka Upaniṣad (hereafter M. Up.), 3-1-2.
4. Bṛhadāraṇyaka Upaniṣad (hereafter Bṛ. Up.), 2-4-5.
5. Ibid., 3-9-26.
6. K. Up., 2-2-1.
7. Bṛ. Up., 4-4-22.
8. K. Up., 1-2-6.
9. Ibid., 2-3-1.
10. Ibid., 2-3-2.
11. Ibid.
12. Ibid., 2-1-11.
13. Ibid., 2-1-10.
14. Ibid.
15. Ibid.
16. Ibid.
17. M. Up., 1-2-5.
18. Ibid., 1-2-10.
19. Ibid., 1-2-9.
20. K. Up., 2-3-14.
21. M. Up., 3-1-4.
22. Ibid., 1-2-9.
23. Ibid., 2-1-10.
24. Īśa Upaniṣad (hereafter Īś. Up.), Mantra 2.
25. M. Up., 3-1-4.
26. Ibid.
27. Ibid., 3-1-3.
28. Ibid.
29. Ibid.
30. Ibid., 3-1-2.
31. Ibid., 3-1-3.
32. Bṛ. Up., 2-4-16.

33. Ibid., 2-4-5.
34. Ibid., 2-4-6.
35. Ibid.
36. Īś. Up., Mantra 15.
37. Bṛ. Up., 4-4-22.
38. Ibid.
39. Ibid., 4-4-20.
40. Īś. Up., Mantra 1.
41. Ibid., Mantra 15.
42. Ibid., Mantra 1.
43. Ibid.
44. K. Up., 2-3-18.
45. Ibid., 2-1-10.
46. Chāndogya Upaniṣad, 7-26-2.

24

Two Forms of Synthesis of Yoga*

THE TITLE OF VEDĀNTA

The Upaniṣads are known by the title of Vedānta. The word *vedānta* gives two meanings — (i) that which forms the final portion of the Vedas; (ii) that which sets forth the inner essence of the Vedas. The title is generally applied to the Upaniṣads in both of these senses as if this double application is justifiable.

The Vedas fall into three broad divisions — Mantras, Brāhmaṇas, and Upaniṣads. Scholars equate the Vedas sometimes with the Mantras, sometimes with the Mantras and Brāhmaṇas, sometimes with the Upaniṣads, and sometimes with all the three divisions. According to the threefold division, the Upaniṣads come at the end of the Vedas. Hence they are known by the name of Vedānta. When we examine the contents of the Upaniṣads, we note that they try to expound the inner sense of the Vedas (Mantras). This is evidenced by the texts like the Bṛhadāraṇyaka (2-5), the Muṇḍaka (3-1), and the Śvetāśvatara (4-8). This is another reason why the Upaniṣads are given the title of Vedānta.

We know that the Upaniṣads are generally found to be parts of the Brāhmaṇas. If this is the case, the Brāhmaṇas must be regarded as really the final portion of the Vedas. But still the title of Vedānta would be reserved for the Upaniṣads alone. This means that the title is given not on the basis of where they stand but on the basis of what they teach. From this we are forced to conclude that the title is justifiable only in one sense of the word *vedānta*, namely, in the sense that the Upaniṣads represent the inner sense of the Vedas (Mantras).

THE YOGA OF THE UPANIṢADS

Let us begin with the Vedas and note what their Yoga stands for. It stands for two things. First, union with the immortal and imperishable Person; second, the means of union designed for this purpose. As the means of union, the Yoga has three elements — the mind (*manas*); [1] the god Agni hidden in the heart of the mortal (*guhā santaṃ*);[2] and the general gods active in the world (*viśvedevāḥ*).[3] The mind in the Vedic society has no direct access to this inner god. For he is too dormant or too deeply hidden in the heart of the seeker of immortality. However, it does not prevent the seeker from attaining his goal, namely, union with the immortal Puruṣa. As his mind opens easily to the gods in the world, he seeks their help and action through his prayers and supplications. With the strength and support provided by them the hidden god Agni is brought to birth (*amartyam marteṣvā janata*),[4] and made into a powerful means for reaching the immortal Person. As this god knows his way of submission to the gods (*sa veda deva ānamaṃ devāṃ*),[5] he works for the realisation of immortality and gives the mortal the fruit of his work. In other words, the mortal becomes immortal through the work of Agni.

It is necessary to note the manner in which the mind of the seeker of immortality operates. It operates as an externalising instrument, for it sees all to be placed or to be working, externally. Therefore it looks upon the general gods as the gods abiding in the ether of the world (*vyoman yasmin devā adhi viśve niṣeduḥ*);[6] the secret god Agni as a god who enters the human body (*āviśan*)[7] and is domiciled there (*vivāsanti*);[8] this god's release from the darkness of the body (*tamasaḥ*)[9] as a birth effected by the gods (*janata*);[10] this one as a ship that travels over the waters (*parṣannāveva*),[11] a ship that carries man to his destination; again, this one as "the doer of the Yoga" or "the effecter of perfection" for man (*sādhu*);[12] the realisation of the goal of immortality as the getting of a place in the immortal and imperishable world (*tasminmām dhehi amṛte loke akṣite*)[13]. Though the mind thus externalises all, it is not a crippled instrument. For it sees all that needs to be seen — the gods in the world, the god in the body, and the highest Godhead beyond the world — and obtains all that needs to be obtained. Such is the Yoga developed by the Vedas.

Though the Upaniṣads are generally inspired by the teachings of the Vedas, they differ from them when there is a need to assert their independence. Their view about the gods of the Vedas is one such example. They do not consider the gods to be really helpful to men. For the gods are displeased with men who seek higher wisdom. Rather they look upon them as cattle to be kept and used by the celestial. They are capable of even preventing them from getting the higher wisdom.[14] Like men, they do not possess the knowledge of Brahman; like them, they are the seekers of Brahman.[15] Though they seek Him, they hardly succeed in their attempt (*nainad devā āpnuvan*).[16] They have been even classed as one of the many possessions given to men for their use and enjoyment.[17] This is a complete reversal of the position given to the gods in the Vedas. From this it is clear that the gods have no value for the seekers of immortality. This explains why prayers and supplications addressed to the gods do not occur in the texts of the Upaniṣads.

In the Upaniṣads the secret god Agni is removed by the secret Ātman (*antarātmā*). There are frequent references to the existence of this Ātman in mortals.[18] It is seated in all beings (*sarvabhūtāntrātmā*).[19] Its location is in the middle portion of the body (*madhye asīnam*).[20] The heart forms the middle portion of the body and so it is said to be abiding in the heart (*hṛdaye samniviṣṭaḥ*).[21] As it is deeply hidden (*guhā hitaṃ gahvareṣṭham*)[22] and does not shine forth (*na prakāśate*),[23] it is not seen by mortals. However, it is pointed out that if the mind, precisely the intellect, becomes sharp and subtle, the Ātman can be surely seen by it (*dṛśyate buddhyā sūkṣmayā*).[24] It is seen by those whose intellect is thus developed through rigorous disciplines.

The senses called the doors of the body face always outwards. Therefore a mortal sees the outer things and not the inner Ātman (*paśyati na antarātman*).[25] If the Ātman is to be seen, then the mind must be freed from the dominating influence of the senses and endowed with discrimination. Discrimination consists in recognising the existence of another reality deeper and greater than the reality of the world. He who is endowed with a discriminating mind (*vijñānavān*)[26] turns his attention away from the world and penetrates into the secret place of the heart where the inner Ātman is seated. As a result, he sees what he was not able to see under the spell of the senses — the deeper reality in him. Though now the senses operate, they cannot prevent him from seeing this deeper reality, for they are kept under perfect control (*sthirām dhāraṇām*).[27] The conclusive view of the Upaniṣad is that nobody can attain this secret Ātman without a proper self-control (*nāsamāhitaḥ enamāpnuyāt*).[28] There is an important reason why the discovery of this Ātman is so hard and so demanding. The Ātman is so deeply hidden in the heart that it has become almost non-distinct from the body. As a result, it should be separated from the body through a difficult process. The Upaniṣad says that one should separate it from one's body with boldness (*taṃ svāt śarīrāt pravṛhet dhairyeṇa*),[29] with the strength acquired by a well disciplined mind.

When the inner Ātman is realised, it becomes the right means for attaining the immortal Puruṣa, the highest goal of the mortals. There is a process of gradually rising from level to level till it culminates in the highest. It begins with the senses. They are merged into the mind, the mind into the conscious Ātman,[30] the conscious Ātman into the great Ātman, the great Ātman into the silent Ātman also called the unmanifest Ātman,[31] and eventually the unmanifest Ātman is exceeded by the Puruṣa. The yogic effort ceases when the silent or the unmanifest Ātman is attained. As a result, the process of successive merger stops here. Though the Puruṣa beyond the unmanifest Ātman cannot be attained through the yogic effort, He is attained when He himself reveals his form to the seeker of immortality (*vivṛṇute tanūm svām*).[32] He is the highest of all forms of Ātman, for there is nothing higher than Him.

If the conscious Ātman (*jñānātmā*) is equated with the inner Ātman (*antarātmā*), we may say that the former is the means of reaching the highest Puruṣa. If this Puruṣa is equated with the highest Ātman, we may speak of attaining Ātman with Ātman. As the Māṇḍūkya Upaniṣad puts it, it is entering Ātman with Ātman (*saṃviśaty ātmanā ātmānaṃ*).[33]

Here we must note an important point. Just as the secret god Agni of the Vedas is replaced by the secret Ātman of the Upaniṣads, so also the role played by the gods (*agni* and *viśvedevāḥ*) in the Vedas is superseded by the one assumed by the mind in the Upaniṣads. While in the Vedas the gods act and accomplish all for the sake of the mind, the mind in the Upaniṣads is capable of self-action and self-accomplishing effort.

The role given to the teachers (*ācāryas*) in the Yoga of the Upaniṣads bears some resemblance to the role played by the gods in the Vedas. For both of them offer external support to the seekers of immortality. But they differ with regard to the measure of support given to the seekers. While the gods perform the whole yoga for their sake, the teachers leave their yoga to themselves and help them only through personal example and important instructions. They do influence their efforts, but this is done as a special help.

Before we proceed further there are two important things to be noted about the teacher. First of all, the words by which he is referred to — *guru*,[34] *bhagavantaḥ*,[35] *ācārya*[36] and so on. Second, the different classes to which he belongs — sometimes he is a husband,[37] sometimes he is a father,[38] sometimes he is a child,[39] sometimes he is a seer,[40] sometimes he is just a wise man,[41] and sometimes he is a god.[42] These help us to understand how the teachers are regarded in the Upaniṣads. First, they are treated with great respect and admiration. Second, their help is readily accepted irrespective of what position they hold in the society or where they come from. They hold almost all positions in the society; they hail not only from this world but also from the world of the gods.

There is a passage in the Chāndogya Upaniṣad[43] which clearly defines the kind of help given by the teacher to the seeker of immortality. It also points out to the type of effort made by the latter. The seeker is compared to a person who belongs to a country called Gandhāra but finds himself abandoned in a solitary place far away from his country. He is unable to return to his country, because he is blindfolded and does not know the direction in which his country lies. Like the seeker, the teacher is compared to a person who releases his bandage and tells him the way in these words, "in that direction are the Gandhāras, go in that direction". Upon this the other person arrives at Gandhāra by asking his way from village to village. From this it may be seen that the teacher's part is to remove the obstruction and give the necessary instructions, and the seeker's part is to reach his goal through personal effort.

In another place the same Upaniṣad draws our attention to the order in which the teacher's assistance and the seeker's personal effort stand. Accordingly, first comes the personal effort of the seeker (*prathamaḥ*)[44] and next comes the assistance given by the teacher (*dvitīyaḥ*).[45] Therefore in the Yoga of the Upaniṣads the teacher's help, though very valuable, is graded as of secondary importance.

In this connection the command of the Kaṭha Upaniṣad is noteworthy — arise, awake, having attained the great ones learn of them.[46] It is a command given particularly to those who have to search for their teachers and find them through personal effort. It is a call to make up one's mind to become a seeker of Ātman, to awake to the need for getting help from the great ones who have already attained Ātman, to find them and be satisfied of their worth. It is a practical teaching, for it is not easy to know who the really great ones are from the vast multitude of men. Where to go to find out the great ones (*varān*) and how to understand their real worth (*nibodhata*)? The seeker should go to a place where the Brāhmaṇas and the Kṣatriyas live. For by both temperament and training they are known to be serious seekers of Ātman. It will be fruitful to go to them rather than to others who are unlike them in their temperament and training. Having gone there, the seeker should note if they possess the marks of a genuine knower of Ātman. What are these marks? They are: (i) A knower of Ātman is food (*odanaḥ*)[47] for Ātman; (ii) originally, he was food for Death (*mṛtyuḥ*),[48] but now as he has become food for Ātman, this Death becomes a supplementary food for the same Eater-Ātman (*upasecanam*).[49] In other words, the two marks are: (i) A knower of Ātman has given up his whole life to Him and shines like a god (*taijasaḥ*);[50] (ii) a knower of Ātman has given up mortality, hates none (*na tato vijugupsate*)[51]and looks upon himself as the whole of mankind (*sa u loka eva*).[52] Any one who possesses these two marks, let him be a Brāhmaṇa or a Kṣatriya, is to be understood as a real knower of Ātman (*varan*). If we leave out the Brāhmaṇas and the Kṣatriyas and the marks they possess, who can know in this way where Ātman stands revealed (*ka itthā veda yatra saḥ*)?[53] That is to say, the attempt at finding *varan* by the seeker will surely fail.

If we place the two Yogas side by side, the Yoga of the Vedas and the Yoga of the Upaniṣads, we are able to see one in the light of the other. In both, union with the immortal Puruṣa is the ultimate goal of the mortals. Again, in both, the means of union has three elements.

The three in the Yoga of the Vedas are: the mind, the general gods in the world, and the secret god Agni in the body. And the three in the Yoga of the Upaniṣads are: the mind, the teacher, and the secret Ātman. Though they are similar to each other in the these two respects, they mutually differ in their conceptions of the three elements on which each of them is founded. If we go by their striking similarities, we may conclude that the Yoga of the Upaniṣads has developed itself out of the earlier roots in the Vedas.

Our account of the Yoga of the Upaniṣads will be incomplete if we do not discuss the relevant points mentioned in the Kena. Though it shares the general character of other Upaniṣads, its view of Yoga or winning immortality is unique. The mind seeks immortality not through the independent action of the gods, as in the Vedas, but through its own power of reflection and enquiry (*mīmāmsā*).[54] In this respect it is one with the other Upaniṣads. But in another more important respect it differs entirely from them. It looks upon the gods as powers inherent in the mind and its two other instruments, the life and the senses (*adhyātmā*).[55] It discovers that there are really two means for realising the form of Brahman (*brahmaṇo rūpam*)[56] — the little means (*dabhram*) in the inner Ātman (*tvam*)[57] and the little means (*dabhram*) in the divine powers (*deveṣu*)[58] working in and through the three instruments — Indra in the mind, Vāyu in the life, and Agni in the senses. Therefore, immortality is attained by both, by the knowledge of the inner Ātman (*vidyayā vindate amṛtam*)[59] and by the divine powers inherent in the powers of mind, life and senses (*amṛtatvam hi vindate ātmanā*).[60] Unlike the other Upaniṣads, the Kena does not set aside the gods but assimilates them as divine powers inherent in our mind, life and senses. Freed from mortality, they arrive at fulfilment in the supreme God — the mind becomes the Mind of God, the life becomes the Life of God, and the senses become the Senses of God.[61] Indeed this is a larger Yoga, a larger path to immortality than the one offered by the other Upaniṣads. This makes the Kena a unique Upaniṣad.

THE YOGA OF KNOWLEDGE

The Kaṭha Upaniṣad has declared that the goal of the mortals is the highest imperishable Brahman (*akṣaram brahma param*).[62] But it points out that the Brahman is not truly comprehended by the human mind. On this point the words of Yama are noteworthy. He says that even the gods entertained doubt in days of yore about truly comprehending the nature of Brahman (*na hi suvijñeyam*).[63]

What makes the comprehension doubtful is that the object of knowledge is the highest imperishable Brahman. It means that there are other imperishable forms too and they are to be known and exceeded in order to know the highest imperishable form of Brahman. What are the other imperishable forms? According to the Muṇḍaka Upaniṣad, there are three forms and the highest of them (*paraḥ*) is preceded by two others, the imperishable (*akṣaraḥ*) and the higher imperishable (*akṣarāt parataḥ*).[64] In other words, the highest imperishable form of Brahman is known when the other two forms, the imperishable and the higher imperishable, are known and exceeded. This means that Brahman is comprehended not in one but in three connected forms. Hence Brahman is elsewhere declared to be threefold (*trividham brahmam*).[65]

Brahman is thus possessed of three forms. Apart from this, the forms differ in the degree of their subtlety. This is why they are arranged according to an ascending order.[66] One is more subtle than the other. The highest imperishable Brahman is the most subtle in form (*susūkṣmaṃ*).[67] Keeping the order in view, He is described as subtler than the subtle, greater than the great (*anoranīyān mahato mahīyān*).[68] This is another reason why a true comprehension of Brahman is doubtful.

The true comprehension is further complicated by the fact that the instrument by which the mortals try to know Brahman, namely, the mind (*buddhi*),[69] is not subtle but conditioned by its association with the material body and the material world. Their mind is controlled by the senses and it measures all by the measure of the world. This is the significance of the teaching that the mind of the mortals is turned outward (*parāṅpaśyati*).[70] In other words, their mind is bound by the most gross forms and, therefore, incapable of seeing the most subtle Brahman.

The important issue before the Yoga of Knowledge is how to know Brahman through an instrument which is unlike Brahman. The only instrument given to the mortals is their mind, but the instrument is unfit to perceive the supremely subtle Brahman. If it is bound by the senses and the material world, we must know how it comes to be bound in this way. If we discover its real source of bondage, it is possible to liberate it from the senses and the outer world and make it a powerful instrument of knowledge. The Upaniṣads proclaim in one voice that desires (*prācaḥ kāmān*)[71] are the real source of bondage and that the ineffectiveness of the mind is merely a result of their influence.

The mind of the mortal is an abode of desires. As long as it continues to be their abode, it is ruled by them and their rule is interminable under any circumstance. But there is a way to destroy them and their rule. It is by expulsion and renunciation. By expelling them, the mind is kept free and perfect; by renouncing all attachments born of the desires, it is completely detached from its old habits. When the mortal is free of the desires (*akṛatuḥ*),[72] he is freed from the senses and the material objects of the world (*vimuktaśca vimucyate*).[73]

Expulsion of desires and renunciation of attachments are the two methods with which the Yoga of Knowledge begins. Through them the mind becomes pure and free of desire and develops into an instrument of subtle perceptions. Those endowed with this mind are called the seers of subtle realities of the world (*sūkṣmadarśibhiḥ*).[74] Now the seeker of immortality has acquired the full qualification to walk steadily in the path of Yoga.

The mind originally turned outside is now turned inside. Through constant meditation (*upāsanā*) and concentration (*tapas*) the purified mind rises gradually from form to form till the rising culminates in the attainment of the highest imperishable form of Brahman. For this purpose the Yoga uses the famous method referred to by the Upaniṣad as "Not-this, Not-this, Instruction" (*ādeśaḥ na iti na iti*).[75] (i) The mind merges into the imperishable Brahman who is seated in the secret cave of the heart (*gahvareṣṭham*).[76] Having merged into this form of Brahman, it is seen that Brahman is limited by this form. Therefore, this attainment is denied, *na iti*. (ii) Through the denial the mind merges into the higher imperishable Brahman who is seated above but within the world. It is seen that Brahman is limited even by this higher form. Therefore, this attainment too is denied, *na iti*. (iii) Through the denial the mind merges into the highest imperishable Brahman who is seated beyond the world. As this is the highest form of Brahman and as there is no form higher than this one, the process of gradual ascent by the mind becomes complete and no further ascent is possible.

We must note that in this process the forms of Brahman unfold themselves one after another. When the lower is denied, the higher manifests itself. The higher arises not by eliminating the lower. What is really eliminated is limitation by the lower. This is the true significance of the method Not-this, Not-this. Therefore, when the highest imperishable Brahman (beyond the world) is attained, He is seen to embrace the other two (within the world) as His own forms. Keeping this harmonious totality of Brahman in view, the Muṇḍaka says that He is possessed of the forms within the world and of the form beyond the world (*sabāhya-ābhyantaraḥ*).[77]

Another important point to be noted is that in the Yoga of Knowledge the imperishable is attained only by the imperishable, or Brahman is attained only by Brahman. This is the true significance of the famous statement of the Taittrīya Upaniṣad — the knower of Brahman attains the highest Brahman (*brahmavid āpnoti param*).[78]

THE YOGA OF WORKS

Extensive discussion on works is found in no other Upaniṣad except the Muṇḍaka. In this respect it is a unique Upaniṣad. It holds two opposite views about works. According to one view, mortality can never be overcome through them. Prescribed works make man virtuous here and take him to the world of the gods at the end of his embodied life. There he lives and enjoys like the gods. But he cannot get rid of the law of transmigration. When the merit acquired through good works is exhausted, he is deprived of his god-form and god-life. He is compelled to take birth in the world of mortals. In some cases even inferior births are inevitable (*hīnataram*).[79] Deluded men alone think that good works are capable of making them immortals. All good works are done out of desire and attachment (*rāgāt*).[80] As a result, the doers of these works can never become immortals. To them immortality is a mere delusion.

A seeker of immortality should know that his unaccomplished goal (*akṛtaḥ*) is not accomplished through work (*nāsty kṛtena*).[81] Hence he should arrive at complete indifference to works (*nirvedamāyāt*).[82] Freedom from works brings freedom from passions. Freed from works and passions, the seekers of immortality become calm and conscious of all factors that firmly keep them in this state (*śāntā vidvāṃso bhaikṣyacaryāṃ carantaḥ ... virājaḥ*).[83] From this state they go to the world where lives the imperishable Ātman, the immortal Puruṣa (*yatrāmṛtaḥ sa puruṣaḥ*).[84] Into that divine Puruṣa they disappear, very much like the rivers that flow into the sea and disappear there (*samudre astam gacchanti*).[85] This is the Yoga of Renunciation of Works (*saṃnyāsa yoga*).[86]

Now we shall discuss the other view about works. In support of this view God himself is given as an example. The divine Person (*īśam puruṣam*),[87] according to the Upaniṣad, is extended in the immutable Brahman beyond Nature as his higher seat (*brahmayonim*)[88] and in the mutable Nature as the Doer of Works (*kartāram*).[89] Man is originally united with Him in these two aspects. In the first, he is one with the immutable Brahman (*sayujā*);[90] in the second, he is equal to the Doer of Works (*sakhāyā*).[91] But somehow he is separated from Him, and his law of action has become unlike His law. He is separated from Him, because he is not one with the immutable Brahman who is the non-doer (*anaśnan*).[92] His law of action is unlike God's law, because he is not an onlooker (*abhicākaśīti*)[93] of Nature and all her works like God. Rather he is attached to works and enjoys doing them out of attachment (*pippalaṃ svādvatti*).[94] God is great, because He is one with Brahman and not attached to the works of Nature. But the mortal man is not possessed of this greatness, because he is separated from Brahman and attached to the works of Nature as if he is their source and not Nature. In short, the mortal is unlike God. And this is the cause of all his misery and grief (*anīśayā śocati*).[95]

When the mortal gives up his wrong law and performs all works according to God's law, all attachment for them disappears. He gradually becomes an onlooker of Nature and her works and realises his oneness with the immutable Brahman. Eventually, he attains absolute likeness to God (*paramaṃ sāmyamupaiti*)[96] and becomes freed from grief (*vītaśokaḥ*).[97]

If we examine the above view of works as expounded by the Upaniṣad, we may note the following important points. (i) Works are done by God's Nature. Hence He is the doer of works through his Nature (*kartāram*). (ii) He is not bound by works because he is seated in the immutable Brahman (*brahmayonim*) as the unattached witness of Nature and her works (*abhicākaśīti*). This reveals his greatness. (iii) In his real or original nature man is like God (*sayujā, sakhāyā*). He suffers because he is unlike God and his law of works is unlike God's law. (iv) He is freed from grief when he attains absolute likeness to God and does all works in accordance with God's law.

From all these points it becomes clear how here works are viewed by the Upaniṣad. Works are surely a powerful means for immortality. Immortality consists in attaining absolute likeness to God (*īśam puruṣam*). Man is a mortal not because he is a doer of works but because he has forgotten God's example and abandoned God's law of works in the world. Works do not bind, for God himself is the doer of works and remains unbound by them. They bind only when they are done according to the wrong law, i.e., when they are done out of desire and attachment. Therefore, mortality is not due to works but due to desire and attachment. When they are done according to God's example or God's law, mortality is destroyed and immortality attained. This is the Yoga of Fulfilment through equality with God.[98]

Thus we have two views about works as set forth by the Muṇḍaka Upaniṣad. According to the first, immortality is gained by renouncing all works; according to the second, immortality is won by doing all works in consonance with God's law. Both are supported by the authority of scriptures. In the case of the first the Muṇḍaka very clearly says that it is rooted in the Vedānta;[99] in the other case the Upaniṣad simply discusses a Mantra taken from the Veda[100] and makes us understand that it is derived from a source anterior to the Vedānta, namely, the Veda. Though both the Yogas, renunciation and fulfilment, are recognised to be valid means of attaining immortality, the Muṇḍaka seeks to throw its weight behind the second. This becomes evident from its pronouncement on the position of *brahmavids*.

A *brahmavid* is one who has known Brahman and attained immortality. Even if there are many who have become *brahmavids* through the path of renunciation, outnumbering a solitary one who has risen to this position through the path of fulfilment or works, this solitary one, the Upaniṣad seems to say, is the highest of them (*eṣa brahmavidām variṣṭhaḥ*).[101] This means that the Yoga of Works is considered to be superior to the Yoga of Renunciation. What is the justification for this pronouncement? Is it because that the authority of Veda is much earlier than the authority of Vedānta?

The Gītā is one of the three main authorities of Vedānta (*prasthānatraya*). In keeping with this view we find that there are many striking parallels between the Gītā and the Muṇḍaka. Look at the following lines from the Gītā.

1. Know Me for the doer of this who am yet the imperishable non-doer.[102]
2. They have become of like nature and law of being with Me.[103]
3. Renunciation and Yoga of Works both bring about the soul's liberation, but of the two the Yoga of Works is superior. [104]

From these lines it is clear how the Gītā closely follows the views expressed in the Muṇḍaka Upaniṣad. In another place the Gītā's denouncement of *saṃnyāsayoga* is stated in powerful terms without prejudice to its remark in 5-2. The author of the Gītā says:

> Were I not to do works, then all these worlds would sink to destruction.[105]

Sri Aurobindo's comment on this passage is noteworthy. He explains it by saying that the ascetic ideal of renunciation "contains in itself the very principle of world-destruction". [106] That is to say, the ideal is "destructive of the principle of human life and disturbing to the settled line of its advance".[107] The above passage 3-24 is relevant to us because it explains why the Yoga of Works is accorded a higher position than the Yoga of Renunciation not only in the Gītā but also in the Muṇḍaka Upaniṣad.

THE YOGA OF LOVE

Love is the delight of union. It is of two kinds, love of the world and love of Ātman. Wife, husband, sons, members of the society like the Brāhmaṇas and Kṣatriyas, worlds, the gods, and the beings — all these come under the category of the world. To love them is to love the world. On the other hand, the inmost in the world (*antarataram*)[108] is Ātman. To love the inmost in the world is to love the imperishable Ātman.

The Upaniṣad says that Ātman is dearer than the world because love of Ātman, unlike love of the world, never perishes (*na priyam pramāyukam bhavati*).[109] If this is so, Ātman alone is to be loved and not the world which is other than Ātman (*anyamātmanaḥ*).[110] This is the significance of the imperative that one should meditate upon Ātman alone as dear (*ātmānameva priyamupāsita*).[111]

In olden days ascetics (*pravrājinaḥ*) abandoned the world and desired Ātman. For them Ātman and the world present themselves as two different objects of desire (*eṣāṃ naḥ ayam ātmā ayaṃ loka iti*).[112] This Ātman is desired when there is no desire for the world; this world is desired when there is no desire for Ātman.

The desire for the world expresses itself mainly through three desires — desire for sons (*putraiṣaṇā*), desire for wealth (*vittaiṣaṇā*), and desire for worlds (*lokaiṣaṇā*).[113] They are inseparable and connected with one another. One leads to the other — the desire for sons to the desire for wealth, the desire for wealth to the desire for worlds (*ya hy eva putraiṣaṇā sa vittaiṣaṇā ya vittaiṣaṇā sa lokaiṣaṇā*).[114] The ascetics rise against the three desires (*vyutthāya*)[115] and eventually abandon the world (*lokam pravrajanti*).[116] Having done so, they desire this great unborn Ātman (*etameva pravrājinaḥ icchantaḥ*).[117] Otherwise the desire for Ātman cannot arise nor can He be attained.

According to the ascetics, the Yoga of Love demands two things. (i) Desire for the world should be renounced by renouncing the world. (ii) Ātman should be attained by making Him as the sole object of desire. But Yājñavalkya does not think that the Yoga makes such demands. In this connection he makes two significant remarks. (i) Desire for the world and desire for Ātman are both desires only (*ubhe hyete eṣaṇe eva bhavataḥ*).[118] (ii) All is dear not for the sake of all, but for the sake of Ātman (*na sarvasya kāmāya sarvam priyam bhavati, ātmanastu kāmāya sarvam priyam bhavati*).[119] Both these remarks aim at disputing the views of the ascetics.

Desire is the cause of attachment. Therefore desire for the world produces attachment for the world; desire for Ātman produces attachment for Ātman. As attachment is the cause of separation, it separates one from the other — attachment for the world separates it from Ātman, even as attachment for Ātman separates Him from the world. This explains why the ascetics rise against the three desires and, subsequently, renounce the world. On the other hand, if Ātman is loved, the world too is loved for the sake of Ātman. The world has no separate existence from Ātman (*anyamātmanaḥ*).[120] In fact, in the world is Ātman as its dweller (*ātmā sarvāntaraḥ*).[121] Like desire, love does not generally saparate one from the other.

It is said that love of the world perishes (*pramāyukam bhavati*). For the love arises from the world which is perishable by nature. But love of the world can be made imperishable like love of Ātman. If the world is loved for the sake of Ātman, then surely love of the world becomes imperishable. For the love arises not from the perishable world but from the imperishable Ātman. In other words, the source of real love is Ātman and not the world. When it is said that Ātman alone is to be meditated upon as dear,[122] it does not mean that the world or love of the world is to be abandoned. It means that the source of real love, as we have already said, is Ātman and love of all other things must arise only from the love of Ātman.

Strictly speaking, the Yoga of Love is accomplished when love (*priyam*) is not mistaken for desire (*eṣaṇā* or *icchā*), when Ātman is regarded as the object of love and not desire, and when the desire for the world is renounced by renouncing merely the desire and not the world. Keeping these things in his mind, Yājñavalkya has restated the Yoga in his own terms.

We are surrounded by many things — husband, wife, sons, wealth, members of the society such as the Brāhmaṇas and Kṣatriyas, beings in general, worlds, and the gods. This is the kind of world in which we live, seek possessions and enjoy them. How should a seeker of immortality proceed through the Yoga of

Love? How should he find himself in the world after completing the Yoga successfully?

He should understand a few things about the object of love, before he actually begins the Yoga. Love of the world for its own sake perishes, whereas love of Ātman does not. For Ātman is imperishable (*akṣaram*)[123] and does not perish like the things of the world. Though love for the world perishes, it becomes imperishable when the world is loved for the sake of Ātman. This is taught by Yājñavalkaya in elaborate terms in the Upaniṣad. He himself has summarised his teaching in these words:

> *na vā are sarvasya kāmāya sarvam priyam bhavati, ātmanastukāmāya sarvam priyam bhavati* (not for the sake of all is all dear but all is dear for the sake of Ātman).[124]

Now the seeker is qualified to begin the Yoga. It consists of two major steps. (i) Ātman is to be seen in all things of the world revealed to us by the senses (*draṣṭavyaḥ*).[125] Having seen thus, His relation to the world is to be studied with the help of the scriptures (*śrotavyaḥ*).[126] Having studied thus, the relation is to be precisely determined through reflection and reasoning (*mantavyaḥ*).[127] Finally, after determining Ātman to be dearer than everything else (*preyaḥ anyasmāt sarvasmāt*),[128] He is to be meditated upon accordingly (*nididhyāsitavyaḥ*).[129] (ii) By meditating on Ātman all this is known from Ātman (*ātmanaḥ darśanena śravaṇena matyā vijñānena idaṃ sarvaṃ viditam*).[130] For Ātman is the world (*ātmaivedaṃ sarvam*).[131] Since all is known in this way, all is dear for the sake of Ātman and the seeker of immortality becomes a devotee of Ātman, one full of love for Ātman and the world known from Ātman.

Yājñavalkya's contribution to Vedānta is that the Yoga of Love makes a seeker of immortality a true lover of the world, not an ascetic who renounces the world and becomes a wandering monk (*pravrājinaḥ*).[132] Some scholars point out that this Yoga is taught by Yājñavalkya to his wife Maitreyī on the point of his going to the forest and embracing monastic life. Through his remark on the two desires he has opened the eyes of the ascetics to the startling truth that they abandon the world because they are bound by their attachment for Ātman. Is it possible for such a person to become a monastic and live in the forest? The words such as *antam karavāṇi*[133] in the Upaniṣad are considered to be supportive of the claim of these scholars. But their claim can be disputed by reading the words differently without implying asceticism. Yājñavalkya's own life is sufficient proof that the scholars are wrong.

THE TWO FORMS OF SYNTHESIS

(1) In our study of the Vedas and Upaniṣads we have focussed on five systems of Yoga — the Yoga of the Vedas, the Yoga of the Upaniṣads, the Yoga of Knowledge, the Yoga of Works and the Yoga of Love. Each system of Yoga is a synthesis in its own way. Each contains its own elements, and each produces its own characteristic result by combining them harmoniously and imposing on them a law of orderly operation.

In the Yoga of the Vedas there are three elements — the mind of the seeker of immortality, the gods of the world, and the secret god Agni seated in the heart of the seeker. All the three function harmoniously and effectively. The aspiration for immortality is expressed through the intense prayers of the mind. It is fulfilled by the powerful action of the gods who use Agni as the effective means of realisation. In other words, the whole Yoga is done by them for the sake of the mortal. It is significant to note that Agni is addressed as the doer of the Yoga (*sādhu*).[134] He does the Yoga for the sake of man. He is frequently referred to as a god who works for the sake of man — *naskridhi*,[135] *āryāya*,[136] *martyāya*,[137] and so on The above Yoga corresponds to the system of Yājña developed by the Vedas (Brāhmaṇas). According to it, the whole sacrifice (*yajña*) is conducted by a chief priest (*ṛtvij*); he is assisted by other priests who are his companions; all of them work for the sake of Yajamāna who commissions the sacrifice and to whom goes the fruit of sacrifice. Therefore the priests do the work and give the fruit of work to the Yajamāna. In exactly the same way, here the fruit of Yoga is given to the mortal who seeks immortality, but the Yoga itself is done by the gods. The characteristic feature of the Yoga of the Vedas is that it is other-dependent, making the mortal entirely dependent on the gods, their power and action.

Like the Yoga of the Vedas, the Yoga of the Upaniṣads is a synthesis, but a new synthesis. Here too there are three elements — the mind of the seeker of immortality, the teacher who is a knower of Ātman and a giver of instructions on Ātman, and the inner Ātman deeply hidden in the heart of the seeker. They operate smoothly and systematically. Man is a mortal, because he is not possessed of the higher knowledge by which he can realise immortality. The burden of escaping mortality and realising the immortal Ātman is on his shoulders. Therefore he wins immortality through intense and hard work. He receives no help from the gods, for immortality cannot be given by anyone else, even by the gods. If he were to approach a god for getting some help from him, as in the case of Naciketas, he would look upon him mainly as a teacher who would not do Yoga on his behalf but stand apart and show the way. As the Yoga is hard to practise (*durgam*), he may occasionally need external help for removing his psychological obstructions. This the teacher offers willingly and removes the obstructions. Otherwise he helps with his instructions alone. When the mortal succeeds in discovering the inner Ātman in the secret cave of his heart, his success is the result of his personal strength and personal effort. He sees the inner Ātman as his own hidden being and merges himself with it. When he attains the highest Person through the inner Ātman, he sees that Person to be no other than his own highest Ātman. In this way the Yoga of the Upaniṣads, as distinguished from the Yoga of the Vedas, is raised on the edifice of self-dependence and self-effort. In spite of these major differences, the old synthesis, as we have already said, should be considered as the source of the new synthesis. From the broad agreement that exists between the two Yogas, we are compelled to come to this conclusion.

Now we shall turn to the three systems of Yoga — Knowledge, Works and Love. They are so called because they are founded upon the three divine powers of the indwelling Ātman — Knowledge, Will and Love. In the mind of the mortal they express themselves as the inferior powers of thought, desire, and sense-attachment. When the mind gives up its confused thoughts and seeks the power of knowledge, the inner Ātman manifests this original power behind the thoughts; when the mind gives up its obscure desires and seeks the power of will, the inner Ātman manifests this original power behind the desires; when the mind gives up its unruly sense-attachments and seeks the power of love, the inner Ātman manifests this original power behind the sense-attachments. The immortal Puruṣa is attained when the mind is merged into the inner Ātman and the Ātman becomes the means for this attainment. In each system of Yoga there is thus a definite synthesis. The synthesis varies according to the original power of inner Ātman which is chosen by the mind as the point of its merger. The word *yoga* itself means a union, a synthesis. And each system is known by the name of Yoga because each is a synthesis, a synthesis of the mind and the inner Ātman.

(2)We shall now discuss another form of synthesis — the synthesis of the Yogas themselves, particularly the Yogas of Knowledge, Works and Love. By themselves they are three separate means and produce three separate results. But the point under consideration is this: is it possible to use them as a unified means and produce a grand result? Let us turn to the Upaniṣads and note whether they have thrown light on this important point.

The Upaniṣads speak of three principal aspects of God corresponding to the three Yogas — He is the Knower (*boddhā*),[138] He is the Doer (*kartā*),[139] and He is the Object of Love (*priyam*).[140] They also speak of attaining immortality by becoming of like knowledge (*pratibodhaviditam*),[141] of like law of action (*paramaṃ sāmyam*)[142] with God. From these texts two things may be inferred. (i) Man can attain a supreme state where he becomes of like nature with God, God in His completeness as the Knower, the Doer, and the Object of Love, God from whom none of the aspects is excluded. (ii) All the three Yogas can be unified into a complete means for realising God in His entirety. Without supporting evidence from the scripture the two inferences will be dismissed as mere conjectures.

The author of the Gītā seems to confirm our surmises when he says that he who knows God in His completeness (*sarvavid*)[143] worships Him in all ways of his natural being (*sarvabhāvena*).[144] And the result assured by this worship is that the devotee becomes a "man of wisdom and fulfilment" (*buddhimān syātkṛtakṛtyaḥ*).[145]

The words *sarvavid* and *sarvabhāvena* are very significant. The first refers to a man who has attained God in all His main aspects; the second to the whole series of means provided by his natural being (note that the word *sarvabhāvena* is in the instrumental case), the means by which he rises to God — knowledge, works and love. This gives us sufficient proof that the three Yogas can be unified into a supreme means of realising God in His integrality. But we wait for the final proof to come from the Upaniṣads themselves, for the Gītā's words are generally restatements of the original teachings of the Upaniṣads by which its author is greatly influenced.

We shall now turn to the Upaniṣads. Of them one seems to be of special interest, namely, the Muṇḍaka Upaniṣad. There are two reasons why it is so. (i) Its closeness to the Gītā, as we have found in the beginning; (ii) the title by which it is known, Head-Scripture, the foremost text of Vedānta (*muṇḍakam*). The much needed proof is there to be found in this Upaniṣad. It says that Ātman is to be realised through the means of complete knowledge (*labhyaḥ hy eṣa ātmā samyagjñānena*).[146] What is the means referred to here? It refers to man himself as a possessor of the threefold means — he whose mind is in union with Ātman (*ātmaratiḥ*); he whose works are the works of Ātman (*kriyāvān*); he whose heart of love has become an eternal garden of love-play — I take "play" to be "love-play" because in the previous verse 3-1-2 God is referred to as the Beloved (*juṣṭam*) — with Ātman (*ātmakrīḍaḥ*).[147] In other words, Ātman in his completeness is realised through knowledge, works and love.

There are many knowers of Brahman (*brahmavids*). They have attained Him through the separated means of knowledge, works and love. Among them (*brahmavidām*) this one (*eṣaḥ*) is declared to be the best (*variṣṭhaḥ*),[148] this one who has attained union with Him through all the three means together — knowledge, works and love.

If the three Yogas are synthesized into a higher and comprehensive Yoga, what is the underlying principle of their synthesis? It is this: Each is an independent and effective means of liberation but incomplete without the other two. Fitness for one Yoga is not the same as the fitness for another. Therefore no single individual can practise all the Yogas one and the same time. This is the argument put forward by those who do not favour the synthesis. This is due to thinking with words not related to reality (*ativāda*). A wise man does not think so (*na ativādi*).[149] What does he do then? He sees life and understands all from it. In all beings life shines forth variously (*prāṇaḥ vibhāti*)[150] — as the powers of knowledge, will and emotion. Knowing the *prāṇa* completely (*vijānan*),[151] the wise man (*vidvān*)[152] understands that its powers are not opposed to one another, rather they are complementary. For they are the expressions of the same *prāṇa.* As a result, he sees that it is possible for a single individual to use the powers simultaneously and be a knower of Ātman, a doer of Ātman's work, and an enjoyer of love-play with Ātman, without facing opposition from any side. The word *samyagjñāna* is intended to convey the point that in *prāṇa* all the three powers of knowledge, will, and emotion are naturally synthesized. This is the highest Yoga we have found in the teachings of Muṇḍaka Upaniṣad.

From the above discussion three important things become clear to us. (i) The Muṇḍaka stands for a synthesis of the three Yogas — Knowledge, Works and Love. (ii) It recommends this Yoga as the best of all Yogas pursued as mutually separate and independent methods. (iii) The Gītā's conception of the synthesis of the Yogas has its unmistakable origin in the Muṇḍaka Upaniṣad. Or, the author of the Gītā has put his royal seal of approval on the unique Yoga developed by this Upaniṣad.

NOTES

1. Ṛg Veda (hereafter RV), 1-171-2.
2. Ibid., 5-8-3.
3. Ibid., 6-9-5.
4. Ibid., 4-1-1.
5. Ibid., 4-8-3.
6. Ibid., 1-164-39.
7. Ibid., 5-25-4.
8. Ibid., 4-11-5.
9. Ibid., 5-1-2.
10. Ibid., 4-1-1.

11. Ibid., 5-25-9.
12. Ibid., 1-77-3. Vide Sri Aurobindo, *The secret of the Veda* (1971) pp.263,270.
13. Ibid., 9-113-7.
14. Bṛhadāraṇyaka Upaniṣad (hereafter Bṛ. Up.), 1-4-10.
15. Ibid.
16. Īśa Upaniṣad, Mantra 4.
17. Bṛ. Up., 2-4-5.
18. Kaṭha Upaniṣad (hereafter K. Up.), 2-2-9; Muṇḍaka Upaniṣad (hereafter M. Up.), 2-1-4; Śvetāśvatara Upaniṣad (hereafter S. Up.), 3-13.
19. K. Up., 2-2-10.
20. Ibid., 2-2-3.
21. Ibid., 2-3-17.
22. Ibid., 1-2-12.
23. Ibid., 1-3-12.
24. Ibid.
25. Ibid., 2-1-1.
26. Ibid., 1-3-6.
27. Ibid., 2-3-11.
28. Ibid., 1-2-24.
29. Ibid., 2-3-17.
30. Ibid., 1-3-13.
31. Ibid., 1-3-11.
32. Ibid., 1-2-23.
33. Māṇḍūkya Upaniṣad, Mantra 12.
34. Chāndogya Upaniṣad (hereafter Ch. Up.), 8-15-1; M. Up., 1-2-12.
35. Ibid., 6-1-7; 7-1-3.
36. Ibid., 2-3-11; 2-23-13; 4-9-3; 4-14-1; 6-14-2.
37. Bṛ. Up., 2-4-5.
38. Taittrīya Upaniṣad (hereafter T. Up.), 3-1-1.
39. Ch. Up., 7-1-1.
40. Bṛ. Up., 2-5.
41. Ch. Up., 4-4-3.
42. K. Up., 1-2-13.
43. Ch. Up., 6-14-2.
44. Ibid., 2-23-1.
45. Ibid.
46. K. Up., 1-3-14.
47. Ibid., 1-2-25.
48. Ibid.
49. Ibid.
50. Bṛ. Up., 4-4-9.
51. K. Up., 2-1-5.
52. Bṛ. Up., 4-4-13.
53. K. Up., 1-2-25.

54. Kena Upaniṣad (hereafter Ke. Up.), 2-1.
55. Ibid., 4-5.
56. Ibid., 2-1.
57. Ibid.
58. Ibid.
59. Ibid., 2-4.
60. Ibid.
61. Ibid., 1-1.
62. K. Up., 1-3-2.
63. Ibid., 1-1-21.
64. M. Up., 2-1-2.
65. S. Up., 1-12.
66. M. Up., 2-1-2.
67. Ibid., 1-1-6.
68. K. Up., 1-2-20.
69. Ibid., 1-3-12.
70. Ibid., 2-1-1.
71. Ibid., 2-1-2.
72. Ibid., 1-2-20.
73. Ibid., 2-2-1.
74. Ibid., 1-3-12.
75. Bṛ. Up., 2-3-6.
76. K. Up., 1-2-12.
77. M. Up., 2-1-2.
78. T. Up., 2-1-1.
79. M. Up., 1-2-10.
80. Ibid., 1-2-9.
81. Ibid., 1-2-12.
82. Ibid.
83. Ibid., 1-2-11.
84. Ibid.
85. Ibid., 3-2-8.
86. Ibid., 3-2-6.
87. Ibid., 3-1-3.
88. Ibid.
89. Ibid.
90. Ibid., 3-1-1.
91. Ibid.
92. Ibid.
93. Ibid.
94. Ibid.
95. Ibid., 3-1-2.
96. Ibid., 3-1-3.
97. Ibid., 3-1-2.
98. Ibid., 3-1-3.
99. Ibid., 3-2-6.

100. RV, 1-164-20.
101. M. Up., 3-1-4.
102. Gītā, 4-13.
103. Ibid., 14-2.
104. Ibid., 5-2.
105. Ibid., 3-24.
106. Sri Aurobindo, *Essays on the Gita* (1970), p.135.
107. Ibid.
108. Bṛ. Up., 1-4-8.
109. Ibid.
110. Ibid.
111. Ibid.
112. Ibid., 4-4-22.
113. Ibid.,
114. Ibid.,
115. Ibid.,
116. Ibid.,
117. Ibid.,
118. Ibid.,
119. Ibid., 2-4-5.
120. Ibid., 1-4-8.
121. Ibid., 3-4-2.
122. Ibid., 1-4-8.
123. Ibid., 3-8-8.
124. Ibid., 2-4-5.
125. Ibid.
126. Ibid.
127. Ibid.
128. Ibid., 1-4-8.
129. Ibid., 2-4-5.
130. Ibid.
131. Ch. Up., 7-26-2.
132. Bṛ. Up., 4-4-22.
133. Ibid., 2-4-1.
134. RV, 1-77-3.
135. Ibid., 1-127-11.
136. Ibid., 7-5-6.
137. Ibid., 7-5-8.
138. Praśna Upaniṣad, 4-9.
139. Ibid.
140. Bṛ. Up., 1-4-8.
141. Ke. Up., 2-4.
142. M. Up., 3-1-3.
143. Gītā, 15-19.
144. Ibid.

145. Ibid.
146. M. Up., 3-1-5.
147. Ibid., 3-1-4.
148. Ibid.
149. Ibid.
150. Ibid.
151. Ibid.
152. Ibid.

* Article contributed to *Synthesis of Yoga* Edited by Kireet Joshi (2011).

25

The Upaniṣads: A Survey of their Teachings

It is said that the Upaniṣads are heterogeneous and cannot lend themselves to be organised into a harmonious system. But this is not the traditional view. The traditional commentators point out that they set forth a cogent perspective. Sri Aurobindo says that they speak from a highly synthetic point of view. Therefore we cannot deny that a unified system of ideas is implicit in them. If this is so, it is necessary to make an attempt to develop the system. This is done through discussions on seven important topics under which come all relevant ideas.

NATURE OF ĀTMAN

The Kena Upaniṣad teaches that Brahman is threefold — (i) the known, (ii) the unknown and (iii) the supreme. First of all, there is a Brahman by which the word is expressed, the mind is thought, one sees the eye's seeings, the ear's hearing is heard, and the life-breath is led forward. Secondly, there is another Brahman which is not expressed by the word, not thought by the mind, not seen with the eye, not heard with the ear and does not breathe with the breath. Thirdly, there is a supreme Brahman which goes beyond the known and the unknown. It is other than the known (*anyadeva tadviditāt*):[1] It is Hearing of our hearing, Mind of our mind, Speech of our speech, Life of our life-breath and Sight of our sight. In like manner, It is above the unknown (*aviditādadhi*):[2] There sight travels not nor speech nor mind; we know It not; nor can we distinguish how one should teach of It. Though the supreme Brahman exceeds the known and the unknown, It is not external to them, for It holds them together in Its bosom: It is at once the unexpressed and the expressed; at once thought not by the mind and thought by the mind; at once sees not with the eye and sees the eye's seeings; at once hears not with the ear and hears the ear's hearing; at once breathes not with breath and leads forward the life-breath. In this supreme aspect is revealed the true form of Brahman; and it is this Brahman that one should know (*tadeva brahma tvaṃ viddhi*).[3]

The same conception of Ātman is found everywhere in the Upaniṣads. In this connection three instances may be cited — the Īśa, the Muṇḍaka, and the Māṇḍūkya. (i) The Īśa speaks about the extension of the Lord (*saparyagāt*)[4] in the mutable Nature (*ejati*)[5] and in the immutable Self (*naijati*).[6] In the immutable Self the Lord is bright, bodiless, woundless, sinewless, pure, and without evil; in the mutable Nature the Lord looses forth the world through his threefold appearance — the Seer, the Thinker, and the Realiser.[7] As the Seer, he sees the truth of things in his immutable Self; as the Thinker, he thinks out their possibilities and conceives the world; and as the Realiser, he transforms his conception into an objectified reality. The Lord, the immutable Self, and the mutable Nature are, therefore, the three forms of the same reality of the Īśa Upaniṣad.

(ii) The Muṇḍaka speaks of That (*tad*) being perceived by the wise as both the immutable Self and the mutable Nature which is the source of beings (*tad avyayam yadbhūtayonim*).[8] The immutable Self is eternal, invisible, ungraspable, without family, without caste, without eyes, ears, hands and feet. On the other hand, Nature creates through the law of manifold becoming (*vibhuṃ*)[9] and is, therefore, the source from which the world of beings appears. In relation to Nature the immutable Self is subtle; in relation to the Self That is exceedingly subtle (*susūkṣmaṃ*).[10] However, That is not external to them, for the same That is extended in them (*sarvagatam*).[11] Thus the three realities are indivisible and one according to the Muṇḍaka Upaniṣad.

(iii)Unlike the foregoing Upaniṣads the Māṇḍūkya defines Ātman as four-footed (*catuṣpāt*)[12] — the Viśva Ātman, the Taijasa Ātman, the Prājña Ātman, and the Caturtha Ātman. The first three belong to the order of the world. The world is of three levels — gross, subtle, and causal. They are represented respectively by the Viśva, the Taijasa, and the Prājña. Each one is conscious of the world he represents — the Viśva is conscious of the external world (*bahiṣprajña*);[13] the Taijasa is conscious of the internal world (*antaḥprajña*);[14] the Prājña is conscious of the causal world where all exists as a mass (*prajñānaghana*).[15] These are descriptions of the triple Ātman. The descriptions given of the Caturtha Ātman tell us that he is devoid of the world — not inwardly conscious, not outwardly conscious, not conscious of the mass in the causal world, not seen by the eyes, not involved in actions, not grasped by the organs of action, not possessed of mark, not thought by the mind and not possessed of name.[16] If the Upaniṣad gives two opposite accounts about Ātman, then Ātman cannot be considered four-footed. For by this expression Ātman is considered to be harmonious. How are we to resolve this conflict?

In the Māṇḍūkya there are two significant expressions that come to our help — *ekātma-pratyaya-sāraṃ* and *prapañcopaśamaṃ*.[17] By the first is affirmed that the Caturtha Ātman is he who is of the same nature (*ekātmā*) and whose essence is of the nature of cause (*pratyayasāram*); by the second is told that in the essence of Ātman the world is stilled (*prapañcopaśamaṃ*) i.e. the world is made to stay in a condition of stillness or non-manifestation. From this we understand the correct relation between Ātman and the world — Ātman exceeds and does not deny the world. He does not deny the world, because the world is his essence expressed in a small measure; he exceeds the world, because his own essence is infinitely more than the essence actually expressed in the world. If he exceeds and does not deny the world, then all negative expressions applied to him must be suitably explained. They do not deny his expression in the world but his limitation by expression. This removes the apparent conflict between the Caturtha Ātman and the world and helps us to grasp the definition of Ātman as four-footed (*catuṣpāt*). As the four-footed, Ātman is the undivided whole (*advaitam*),[18] for he is the world and also that which exceeds the world.

The dichotomous division of Ātman as the qualified (*saguṇa*) and the unqualified (*nirguṇa*), the formed (*mūrta*) and the formless (*amūrta*), the cosmic (*saprapañca*) and the acosmic (*niṣprapañca*) does not exist in the Upaniṣads. It is an invention of the later Vedāntins. Everywhere the Upaniṣads teach the same doctrine that Ātman is one and indivisible .

NATURE OF THE WORLD

The Īśa defines Ātman as *svayambhūḥ*,[19] as he who exists by himself and becomes by himself. The law by which Ātman creates the world is the law of self-becoming. He is both the efficient and material cause of the world. He is the force that shapes the world and the material by which the world is made. There are three steps in the process of self-becoming — seeing, conceiving, and realising.[20] The Īśa points out that there are three forms of Ātman and they correspond to the three steps of creation. As the Seer (*kaviḥ*), he visualises the truths of things hidden in his eternal consciousness. As the Thinker who conceives (*manīṣī*), he forms his conception after studying the possibilities presented to him. As the Realiser (*paribhūḥ*), he eventually shapes the world according to his original conception. As the creation of the world is accomplished through a faultless process, the world thus created is declared to be well-made (*sukṛtam*).[21]

If the world is well-made, how then do we see faults in the world, faults such as ignorance, delusion, and misery? In answer to the question a twofold Nature is mentioned, an effulgent Nature of Ātman (*devātmaśakti*)[22] and a Nature of Guṇas (*svaguṇāḥ*).[23] The latter Nature is derived from the former Nature. But the former is hidden by the latter by her Guṇas (*devātma śaktiṃ svaguṇair nigūḍhām*).[24]

Originally, the world is the creation of the effulgent Nature. The world, not separated from Ātman, is conscious that Ātman is its source and substance, abode and abider. As a result, the pluralistic world is a plurality of conscious beings. When a lump of salt is dissolved in water, the entire volume of water is pervaded by the salt. There is not a single particle of water that does not taste saline.[25] Likewise, the world created by the effulgent Nature is a conscious mass (*vijñānaghana*)[26] where everything is pervaded by Ātman and appears like the image of Ātman. As the world is saturated with the consciousness of Ātman, no fault of any description can ever appear here. This is why it is called the ever-illumined Brahman-world.[27]

Somehow from the action of the higher Nature the lower Nature of Guṇas appeared. Her Guṇas (*sattva*, *rajas* and *tamas*) are obscure and operate through conflict and confusion, struggle and opposition. As a result, the original world of conscious beings was separated from Ātman and bound by her evils — ignorance, delusion and misery. This is how faults intervened and the world was overtaken by death (*mṛtyunābhipannam*).[28] So, how are we to escape the evil of death and recover the original world of immortal light and consciousness?

Traditional Advaitins argue that death can be crossed over only under one condition viz. when the whole world of plurality is ascertained to be an illusory appearance and when it is completely dissolved into Ātman. In this connection they cite two texts — (1) He who sees plurality (*nānā*) here, as it were, goes from death to death;[29] (2) all modification has speech as its origin and exists merely as name; and clay alone is real.[30] If death is bound up with the sense of plurality, it can be crossed over by dissolving not only this world but also the world of Brahman. For even the world of Brahman is of the nature of plurality and it is to be dissolved into Ātman. Whether or not the argument of the traditional Advaitins is acceptable depends on the interpretations given to the above texts.

Let us examine the interpretations of the above two texts. We know that the first one is from the Bṛhadāraṇyaka. The same text occurs in the Kaṭha Upaniṣad also where the ideas not mentioned explicitly by the Bṛhadāraṇyaka are mentioned very clearly. It speaks about the actual connection between the world (here) and Ātman (there): whatever is in the world is also in Ātman; whatever is in Ātman is also in the world (*yad eveha tad amutra yad amutra tad anviha*).[31] It means that both are inseparable and exist together. This is why the Chāndogya says that Ātman is really the world (*ātmaivedaṃ sarvam*).[32] If in the world Ātman exists as the world, in Ātman the world exists as Ātman. Having seen this mutual oneness, the wise have declared that here there is absolutely no world independent of Ātman (*na iha nānāsti kiñcana*).[33] However the mortals see otherwise. Not only do they not see Ātman but they see as if the world exists by itself (*iha nāneva paśyati*).[34] As a result, they go from death to death (*mṛtyos sa mṛtyum āpnoti*).[35] The point to be noted here is that the world is overtaken by death only when it is seen as if it is independent of Ātman. If the world is seen as it is, as having no existence apart from Ātman, it is absolutely free of death. They who see the world in this way escape the evil of death and become immortals (*amṛtāste bhavanti*).[36] It is wrong to think that the world is the cause of death and death is removed by removing the world. Death is caused by the false view of the world. It is removed when the false view is removed.

We shall now come to the Chāndogya text 6-1-4. It is a teaching given to Śvetaketu by his father Uddālaka. Uddālaka says that all becomes known by knowing the one. This is the original proposition (*pratijña*). It is illustrated through examples. One of them is a clay-example. It is said that by one clod of clay all that is made of clay becomes known. In this connection occur the words *vācārambhaṇaṃ vikāro nāmadheyaṃ mṛttiketyeva satyam* (all modification has speech as its origin, and clay alone is real). The above words are explained as follows: Since all modifications such as pots, jars, etc. exist as mere words, they are unreal. Clay alone is real, because it remains unmodified. If this is so, what is the implication for the original proposition (*pratijña*)? It implies that by knowing the One all here become illusions.

But this does not seem to be the right sense of Uddālaka's teaching. For, as he has said in 6-2-2, the real (*sat*) comes from the real (*sat*). It follows from this statement that the modifications of clay such as pots must be real entities, because they come from clay which is real. As the interpretation of 6-1-4 does not agree with the teaching of 6-2-2, it must be set aside conclusively as unscriptural.

What then is the correct meaning of the *vācārambhaṇa* text? Śvetaketu returns home after studying the Vedas for twelve years with his teacher. He is proud that he has known Ātman by learning the words of scripture (*mahāmanāḥ*).[37] But his father knows that his son is under a delusion. So he tries to speak to him about the real nature of Ātman. He says that a true knowledge of Ātman leads to the knowledge that all here (*idam sarvam*) are Ātman's manifestations. It implies that from the word Ātman no knowledge of Ātman's manifestations is possible. His clay example is intended to illustrate this important point. If the word clay is mistaken for the clay, it is an illusory modification. The illusory modification is begun by the word clay (*vācārambhaṇaṃ vikāraḥ*) and what is thus begun is certainly the name clay (*vācārambhaṇaṃ nāmadheyaṃ*). From the word clay all that is made of clay can never be known. They can be known only from the original clay. For the original clay alone is real (*mṛttiketyeva satyam*).[38] By speaking about the illusory modification created by the word, Uddālaka tells his son that he is deluded by the word Ātman and does not know the real Ātman. We must note here that the Upaniṣads now and then warn against this delusion — (i) Ātman cannot be known by studying many scriptures;[39] (ii) Ātman cannot be attained through many scriptures;[40] (iii) all the Vedas studied through the six aids deal with the lower knowledge[41] of the imperishable Ātman obtainable from the words of the Mantras; (iv) Ātman cannot be attained through delusion (*na ca pramādāt*).[42] So Uddālaka's instruction is perfectly in line with the teachings of other Upaniṣads. This is the correct significance of the *vācārambhaṇa* text. It is far from suggesting that the world is a false appearance of Ātman. All it says is that if the word Ātman is not mistaken for Ātman, then by knowing Ātman all becomes known i.e. all is known to be the manifestation of Ātman.

From the foregoing discussions it is absolutely clear that the way to escape death is not through rejection of the world as an illusory appearance. But then what is the way to escape death? We have fallen into death only by separating the world from Ātman and seeing it elsewhere (*anyatrātmanaḥ*).[43] This is what the Upaniṣads say. If this is so, then escape from death must be worked out both negatively and positively. Negatively, we must deny that the world is independent of Ātman (*na iha nānāsti kiñcana*).[44] Positively, we must realise with all our heart that the very essence of Ātman has become the world (*sarvam ātmaiva-abhūt*).[45] To think that Ātman is devoid of the world is to enter into a great darkness (*bhūyatamaḥ*).[46] In this connection we must remember the important instruction that Ātman is to be realised only as existing together (with the world) (*ekadhaiva-anudraṣṭavyam etad*).[47] We must cross over death through the knowledge of the many not separated from the One (*avidyayā mṛtyuṃ tīrtvā*)[48] and attain immortality through the knowledge of the One not sought as devoid of the many (*vidyayā amṛtam aśnute*).[49]

To return to the main point, namely, the action of the lower Nature of Guṇas and the appearance of faults in the world, we must remember that she may hide Ātman and separate the world from Him, but, however, she is not outside His control. In fact, she is the inferior action of Ātman's original Nature. This is the significance of the expression *svaguṇāḥ* (own modes). To put it otherwise, the Guṇas are not independent but subject to the will of Ātman. Hence He is called the Lord of the Guṇas (*guṇeśaḥ*).[50] Therefore, by gradually subordinating the world to the Lord's will, the Guṇas will be compelled to disappear into their source and the world helped to return to its original position as a mass consisting of only conscious individuals (*vijñānaghana eva*).[51] This will bear testimony to the assertion that there is absolutely no existence of the world independent of Ātman (*na iha nānāsti kiñcana*). As we have already remarked, the Kaṭha Upaniṣad takes the assertion only in the above sense.

NATURE OF THE INDIVIDUAL

(i) Originally, the individual is not separated from the imperishable Lord. He is one in essence of being and consciousness with Him (*sayujā*).[52] He is also equal to Him (*sakhāyā*)[53] in his law of action. The original law of the Lord consists in being seated in the immutable Ātman and, at the same time, witnessing the works done by Nature (*anaśnan anyo abhicākaśīti*).[54] Thus He is both a non-doer and a doer of works (*kartāram*).[54] He is always free and works do not bind him. But somehow the individual forgot his oneness with the Lord and lost the divine law of action. His law of action is now contrary to the original law (*anyaḥ pippalaṃ svādvatti*).[55] Therefore he is a non-lord bound by works and grieves on account of the bondage (*anīśayā śocati*)[56] created through his works.

(ii) There is another view of the individual. The Lord (*īśa*) has created the world with a view to be the dweller and enjoyer of the world. The world cannot be otherwise, because it is bound by the law of the Lord called *satyadharma*.[57] Somehow greed has overtaken the individual and made him a dweller and enjoyer of the world. As this is evidently against the law of the Lord, he is compelled to struggle in a blind darkness (*andham tamaḥ*)[58] which causes delusion and grief.

(iii) There is yet another view of the individual. Ātman has extended himself to be a huge form, an infinite in space, a limitless mass of conscious beings (*mahadbhūtam anantam apāram vijñānaghanaeva*).[59] Somehow the individual destroys (*anuvinaśyati*)[60] his original connections with Ātman and becomes a separate entity. As a result, he is overcome by death (*mṛtyunābhipannam*).[61] Having passed into the state of death, all consciousness of Ātman has disappeared from him (*na pretya saṃjñāsti*).[62] Now he is no longer himself but has become other (*anya*) and the world is no longer itself but has become a mass of others (*anyāḥ*). This is how man has become a mortal among mortals in the world.

If we examine the above three views, all three affirm in one way or other that man's present state is a state of grief (*śoka*), darkness (*tamas*), and mortality (*mṛtyu*). But this is not ineradicable, because this is not his natural state (*svabhāva*). How to win back the original state of freedom? Three solutions are offered, depending upon how the present state of man has been brought about according to the Upaniṣads.

(i) If the individual grieves on account of the delusion that he is a non-lord and if he is, therefore, compelled by his works, the delusion and compulsion should go, for they are not natural to him. When do they go? When he sees the other side of existence (*anyam*)[63] where bondage and grief do not exist, where the Lord is worshipped (*īśam juṣṭam*)[64] as the eternal abode of all beings, and where his own greatness is revealed and it is found to be the same as the greatness of the Lord (*asya mahimānam*),[65] they go away. He becomes freed and attains absolute likeness with the Lord (*paramaṃ sāmyam upaiti*).[66]

(ii) If the world is created for the sole purpose of habitation and enjoyment by the Lord (*īśāvāsyam idam sarvam*),[67] any deviation from this law causes mortality. As greed compels us to deviate from this original law and possess the world as our own, we become mortals. The way to overcome mortality is to give up the greed (*māgṛdhaḥ kasyasvid dhanam*)[68] and surrender the world to the Lord. Immortality consists in upholding the law of the Lord and finding all satisfaction through the law (*tena tyaktena bhuñjīthāḥ*).[69] When we do so, we no longer struggle in a blind darkness, no longer live in delusion (*moha*) and grief (*śoka*)[70] but put an end to all mortality.

(iii)If we are dead to Ātman and become strangers in the world of mortals groping for light and joy, the way out is to become conscious of Ātman. Instead of seeing the world elsewhere than in Ātman (*anyatrātmanaḥ*)[71] we learn to see Ātman as the source and substance, abode and abider of the world (*sarvam ātmaivābhūt*).[72] When we do so, we overcome mortality and become knowers of Ātman. Union with Ātman naturally culminates in the realisation of union with all, for Ātman is extended in all. Perception of Ātman completely dispels the sense of otherness (*anyatva*), whether the sense is related to the perceiver or to the world perceived by him. Where the sense of otherness is abolished, there the sense of immortality prevails.

From our discussions we may notice one important thing common to the three views about the individual. There is a fall from the state of immortality and the fall is rectified by returning to the original state. Now two questions arise, (i) what is the reason for the individual to become a mortal even though his state is free of mortality and (ii) does he depend entirely on personal effort to get rid of mortality?

We know that the three views set forth above are based mainly upon three Upaniṣads — the Muṇḍaka, the Īśa, and the Bṛhadāraṇyaka. So if we look for answers from them to the above questions, they simply state the issue without throwing any light on the points connected with it. We do not know how the individual becomes a non-lord and comes to grief. Nor do we know how the greed for possessions intervenes and the Lord's law comes to be abandoned. Nor again do we know how the individual separates himself from Ātman and becomes a mortal. We do not also know whether personal effort is sufficient for his escape from mortality. The above Upaniṣads seem to say that the individual is responsible for his fall and so he rises by himself. Beyond this point they offer no help.

In this context the help we get from the Śvetāśvatara is unique. For it throws sufficient light on the important question how the immortal individual becomes a mortal. It says that there are two Māyās, original and derived. The original Māyā is the source of all individual beings. It does not separate them from the Lord of whom they are manifestations. They are conscious of the Lord and exist as His immortal expressions. But in the process of creation another Māyā (*anyaḥ*)[73] comes into play. Its role is to equip them with the instruments such as the mind. As it is a Māyā of three *guṇas* — *sattva*, *rajas*, and *tamas*,[74] it binds all with mortality. However, it cannot always keep the individuals under its control. For, if they are determined to get rid of this Māyā, the Lord comes to their help and, as a result, it is obstructed by the original Māyā (*anyo māyayā saṃniruddhaḥ*).[75] From this it clear that the Lord is the controller of the original Māyā as well as the Māyā of the three *guṇas*. In relation to the first he is the Lord of Māyā (*māyī*).[76] In relation to the first and the second (which is known by the name of Prakṛti) the Lord of Māyā is redesignated as the great Lord (*māyinaṃ tu maheśvaram*).[77] If the Lord controls both Māyā and Prakṛti, then man's fall from his original state is surely due to the action of Prakṛti and, therefore, due to the Lord himself who brings about his fall through the three *guṇas*.

If the fall is brought about by the Prakṛti, then man is not entirely responsible for this consequence. The Lord is the main cause of his fall. If He causes his fall, He also helps him to rise. Therefore man's effort to overcome his fall is not unaided. The Lord comes to his help and saves him through the force of Māyā and reveals Himself as the saviour (*mokṣa hetuḥ*).[78] If this is so, then by the liberation of one individual and by his being the chosen instrument of the Lord the whole world can return to its original state of perfection and freedom. This should be the justification of his role as the world-worker (*viśvakṛt*)[79] (a doer of works for the world). The crucial point is that the liberated individual must be accepted by the Lord as his chosen instrument. Otherwise he can bring good to the world as much as is possible for him. In the Upaniṣads the individual liberation is given the utmost importance. However, it does not mean that the good of the world is neglected. For the world first develops the individuals. Then alone it develops itself through them.

IMMORTALITY AND RENUNCIATION

Immortality is the goal of life and renunciation is the means therefor. What are to be renounced? Domestic life, possessions and works. They are interconnected with one another. We win possessions through works and, having won them, protect them through works. Therefore without works no one can get possessions or preserve them. Domestic life is built on the twin foundations of possessions and works. All the three are the sources of mortality. Possessions make us mortals because they keep us ever attached to them; works also make us mortals because they are done out of attachment for possessions; domestic life being an institution dependent on both possessions and works is an organised way of living as mortals. Therefore a seeker of immortality is called upon to renounce all the three sources of mortality — works, possessions, and domestic life. The word *bhikṣācaryaṃ* symbolises a life of complete renunciation.

Renunciation is practised by going away from family and thus giving up both possessions and works and living in the forest *(upavasanty araṇye)*.[80] Those who do so become tranquil knowers of the imperishable Ātman *(śāntā vidvāṃso bhaikṣyacaryāṃ carantaḥ)*[81] and escape the bonds created by possessions and works.

In this connection we may note that there is a passage bearing on the life of those who have completely renounced. This occurs in the Bṛhadāraṇyaka Upaniṣad. It is as follows: "Seeking this world (of the Self) alone [*lokmicchantaḥ*] monks [*pravrājinaḥ*] give up their homes [*pravrajanti*]. (The reason for) this is this: The ancient knowers, it is said, did not desire progeny, thinking, 'what shall we do with progeny — we who have realised this world, this Self [*kiṃ prajāya kariṣyāmo eṣām no ayamātmāyaṃ loka iti*]?' Giving up the desire for sons, for wealth and for worlds [*vyutthāyātha*], they took up a wandering medicant's life [*bhikṣācaryaṃ caranti*]. That which is the desire for sons is the desire for wealth, and that which is the desire for wealth is the desire for worlds, for both these are but desires".[82]

The view contained in the final portion of the passage is held by the sage Yājñavalkya. From the famous discourse given to his wife Maitreyī[83] he is depicted as a symbol of absolute renunciation. It is pointed out that the discourse takes place on the eve of his renunciation of domestic life and departure into the forest as an ascetic.[84] But if we closely observe Yājñavalkya's life as presented in the original text, we have a serious doubt whether he is an advocate of renunciation. First, though he is a householder wedded to two women, Maitreyī and Kātyāyanī, and possessed of a considerable amount of wealth, he is not a mere householder but a knower of Ātman also.[85] Second, his readiness to contest and win more wealth through the contest.[86] From these it is clear that Yājñavalkya does not consider that domestic life and possessions are to be renounced in order to be a knower of Ātman. If this is so, how do we reconcile the final portion of the above passage 4-4-22 with Yājñavalkya's own life-style?

Let us go back to the original passage 4-4-22 and try to understand it carefully. For the wording of the text is difficult to comprehend. Hence we shall, here and there, supply the missing ideas and state the text according to our reading: " [1] The renouncers desire this Ātman alone (*etameva icchantaḥ pravrājinaḥ*). So desiring they renounce the world (*lokam pravrajanti*). [2] [That is due to what they have heard about the sages of the past.] Certainly the ancient knowers of Ātman did not desire children and thought, 'what shall we do with children, we to whom this Ātman and this world (*yeṣāṃ no'yamātmāyaṃ loka iti*) [are in two opposite directions]?' [In both cases children are of no use. They are needed only for those who do not seek Ātman but only the world]. They [the ancients], rising up in the opposite direction (*vyutthāyātha*) to the desire for children, for wealth and for worlds, embrace the life of the renounced (*bhikṣācaryaṃ caranti*). [3] [We admit that] the desire for children is the desire for wealth, and the desire for wealth is the desire for worlds. [But even to rise against them and desire Ātman is a desire.] [Thus] both are desires only (*ubhe hyete eṣaṇe eva bhavataḥ*) [— the desire for children, etc., on the one hand, and the desire for Ātman, on the other]."

There are three parts in the above passage — 1, 2 and 3. Part 1 is about the current renouncers; part 2 is about the ancients who embraced the life of the renounced; part 3 is about the observation made by Yājñavalkya on renunciation. Here the key word *ubhe* (both) cannot mean the above three desires — desires for children, wealth, and worlds. This is patent. The word means the two categories of desire, the first containing the three mundane desires and the second containing the desire for Ātman mentioned in the very beginning of the passage.

Through renunciation the world is abandoned but not the desire. The desire gets transferred to Ātman and becomes the desire for Ātman. As the object of desire, Ātman is revealed. But the world not being desired passes into oblivion. In consequence, one may reach self-extinction in Ātman and enter a greater darkness (*tato bhūya tamaḥ*).[87] The Muṇḍaka text 3-2-8 is a case in point. It says that the knower of Ātman reaches the highest of the high Person like the rivers which disappear in the ocean giving up their name and form (*astam gacchanti nāmarūpe vihāya*). Further, there is a violation of the instruction that Ātman should be seen only as being together with the world (*ekadhaiva-anudraṣṭavyametat*).[88] This is the reason why renunciation is not favourably viewed in 4-4-22. If this is so, then Yājñavalkya is consistent in all circumstances.

The renunciation is surely a means to immortality. But it is best when desire alone is renounced and not the object of desire; it does not matter whether the object is the world or Ātman. The desire for the world makes one a loser of Ātman, whereas the desire for Ātman makes one a loser of the world. When desire alone is renounced, Ātman and the world are seen and possessed together (*ekadha*) by the individual.

IMMORTALITY AND FULFILMENT

Fulfilment consists in raising all to their divine counterparts and rejecting none as unfit for divine perfection. It rejects only the limitations imposed by death. We may speak of four forms of Ātman — (i) the inner Ātman (*antarātmā*);[89] (ii) the outer Ātman connected with mind and senses (*śārīrātmā*);[90] the world-Ātman extended in all creatures (*sarvabhūtāntrātmā*);[91] the Deva-Ātman who is the source of the world (*īśaḥ*).[92] One may find fulfilment in any of these four forms of Ātman: one may go beyond himself and the world and be united with the Deva-Ātman, as in the Śvetāśvatara;[93] or one may be united with the inner Ātman, as in the Kaṭha;[94] or one may be united with the outer Ātman, as in the Kena;[95] or one may be united with the world-Ātman, as in the Kaṭha.[96] Does this mean that the Upaniṣads offer four alternative forms of fulfilment to the seeker of Ātman? It is quite possible to look upon them as four different alternatives given to him and seek Ātman in any of these forms.

There is another possibility also. We know that the Deva-Ātman is the ultimate source of the world and all the other three are the very forms of this original Ātman. If this is so, it is possible for the seeker of Ātman to fulfil himself in all the four forms successively and simultaneously. This seems to be the underlying intention of the Upaniṣads. For there is a declaration in the Muṇḍaka Upaniṣad to this effect. It says: Ātman is attainable through complete knowledge (*labhyaḥ ... eṣa ātmā saṃyag-jñānena*).[97] This is a dominant note to be preserved by all knowers of Ātman. But then there is this question, why do the Upaniṣads speak of four forms of Ātman as if they are four separate forms and meant for four separate fulfilments? They do so because they want to emphasise that fulfilment in Ātman may begin anywhere. If it is begun at one point, it is possible to move to the other points also. The extension may be initially successive but eventually simultaneous. Therefore the four forms of Ātman spoken by the Upaniṣads are not meant for four exclusive realisations. In this context the note given by the Muṇḍaka Upaniṣad should be regarded as revealing the most authentic side of the Upaniṣadic tradition.

If one reaches complete fulfilment in Ātman, one may, among other things, be united with the world-Ātman. He may find Ātman in all beings and all beings in Ātman[98] or Ātman as all beings.[99] But, strictly speaking, this is a fulfilment for the individual and not for the world at large. In other words, the knower of Ātman may be united with the world but this union is personal and not trans-personal. For the world, from its side, remains steeped in ignorance and, therefore, not united with Ātman. If this is so, then his personal fulfilment must lead to a trans-personal fulfilment. Such a trans-personal fulfilment will be a fulfilment for the world. It is therefore necessary that the liberated individual must work for the world-liberation. This is the significance of the word *viśvakṛt* in the Bṛhadāraṇyaka Upaniṣad.[100]

The idea of a liberated individual engaged in the work of liberating the world occurs in the Muṇḍaka[101] and the Chāndogya[102] Upaniṣads. But the idea occurs as a mere hint rather than as a clearly expressed statement. The Muṇḍaka says that the liberated (*ātmaratiḥ*) works for the world (*kriyāvān*) by being at play with Ātman in all beings (*ātmakrīḍaḥ*). Since he works for the world's fulfilment, for the emergence of Ātman in the world, he is aptly called the best knower of Brahman (*variṣṭhaḥ*) by the Upaniṣad.[103] In him fulfilment is perfect in every respect. Thus immortality is not an exclusive fulfilment in Ātman. It is a complete fulfilment, complete in all essential aspects of the liberated individual.

AN IDEAL WORLD

The seers of the Upaniṣads uphold the view that Ātman is the sole reality. It is one of the many important insights they have received from the great sages of the Vedas. Ātman is taught both negatively (*neti*) and affirmatively (*iti*) by them. This does not mean that He is a composite of two forms, the indefinable and the definable. For He is the supreme reality exceedingly subtle (*susūkṣmam*)[104] and indivisibly extended everywhere — in the indefinable and the definable (*sarvagatam*).[105] We may therefore say that He is threefold (*trividham*). If the third and supreme aspect is not taken into consideration, then we cannot grasp the secret of the indivisible oneness (*advaitam*)[106] of His two fundamental forms described in the Upaniṣads.

The world is a manifestation of Ātman (*sarvam ātmaiva-abhūt*).[107] But what is the kind of world that comes out of Ātman? It is a mass of beings made of consciousness alone (*vijñāna-ghanaeva*).[108] It is a world where all is bright, free and blissful, for all is conscious of Ātman and not separated from Ātman. But the power of creation can assume a dominant role and carry the process of manifestation to its logical end, that is, it can develop the world as if it is independent of Ātman. When Māyā operates in this way, it is called the inferior Māyā or Prakṛti. The world created by Prakṛti is a mass of mortals in whom there is no consciousness of Ātman (*na saṃjñāsti*).[109]

If the extreme and inferior action of Māyā produces the world of mortals, then the inferior action is compelled to reverse itself. For all extremes reverse themselves. This reversal occurs first in the individuals. They become seekers of Ātman and realise Him. By doing so they conquer mortality and become immortals. From them the reversal is extended to the world at large. A knower of Ātman (*ātmaratiḥ*) is engaged in the work of helping the world to win immortality like him (*ātmakrīḍaḥ kriyāvān*).[110] This work is called a play (*krīḍa*) because it is done by him from delight and for bringing delight to the world. Such an individual is referred to as the best knower of Ātman (*variṣṭhaḥ*),[111] because he works for the uplift of the world.

There are two factors which obstruct the passage from mortality to immortality — desire and attachment for the world. When they are abandoned, a mortal becomes an immortal. He attains Ātman not only in his soul and body but also in the world and beyond the world. Having attained Ātman everywhere, he works for the liberation of mankind. When the mankind is liberated, all forms of death such as ignorance, delusion and misery disappear from the face of the earth. This means that the action of Prakṛti has been completely reversed by the work of the wise. Then the world becomes an ideal world (*sukṛtam*), to use an expression of the Taittrīya Upaniṣad. The ideal world not separated from Ātman is also known by the Chāndogya Upaniṣad as the Brahman-World.[112]

THE UPANIṢADS AND THE TITLE OF VEDĀNTA

The Upaniṣads are known by the title of Vedānta. The word *vedānta* has two components *veda* + *anta*. The second one gives two meanings — (i) that which comes at the end; (ii) that which is the inner essence. Thus the compound may be interpreted in two ways — (i) that which comes at the end of the Veda compilation; (ii) that which represents the inner essence of the Vedas.

Of the two interpretations, the first is more popular than the second. It is held by scholars that the Vedas and the Upaniṣads have two different subject-matters: while the former deal with *karma*, the latter deal with *jñāna*. As there is no common basis between the two, they contend that the title of Vedānta given to the Upaniṣads is justifiable only in the sense that they are placed as the concluding portion of the Vedas. This view is set forth by the traditional teachers of Vedānta.

If the Vedas refer to the Ṛk Mantras and not the Brāhmaṇas, then they cannot be considered as dealing with *karma*. As the Mantras certainly contain germs of *jñāna*, it is quite conceivable that the Upaniṣads try to bring out their essence in clear terms. This is supported by the Upaniṣads themselves. The Muktikā Upaniṣad says that "like oil in the sesamum seed Vedanta is well-established in Vedas" (*tileṣu tailavat vede vedāntaḥ supratiṣṭhitaḥ*).[113] If in the Vedas the Upaniṣads are contained, then what is stated in the Upaniṣads is the inner sense of the Vedas, the original Vedānta.

If we carefully read the Upaniṣads, we find that there are three evidences in support of the above view. The Muṇḍaka Upaniṣad gives the first evidence. There are four mantras in its third chapter.[114] They deal with a Ṛk taken from the hymns of Ṛṣi Dīrghatamas. The Ṛk says that man has fallen from his original divine status and does works through a law contrary to the law of the Lord who is a non-doer (*anaśnan*) and yet a witness of works done by Nature (*abhicākaśīti*). The Muṇḍaka elucidates the Ṛk in these words. Man grieves (*anīśayā śocati*) by doing works in the wrong way i.e. by being a doer bound by his attachment for works. He escapes the grief when he sees the Lord and His divine law of action which reveals His greatness (*īśam asya mahimānam*). Having overcome his personal grief, he works for the removal of grief from the world. This is the significance of *ātmakrīḍaḥ* in the Upaniṣad.

The second evidence is provided by the Śvetāśvatara Upaniṣad.[115] The same Ṛk of Dīrghatamas appears here also. The Upaniṣad accepts the light thrown on the Ṛk by the Muṇḍaka. But it goes farther than the latter and points out that the Lord is the controller of two Natures, Māyā and Prakṛti. As He controls the two, He is called the great Lord (*maheśvaram*). The Upaniṣad suggests that man's fall is really due to Prakṛti and his fall is overcome when Māyā intervenes and overcomes the action of Prakṛti. This explains the two important points left out by the Muṇḍaka, (i) how an immortal becomes a mortal and (ii) how man comes out of his fall. The elucidation of the Ṛk by the Śvetāśvatara is more insightful and comprehensive than the one given by the Muṇḍaka.

The last and the third evidence is offered by the Bṛhadāraṇyaka Upaniṣad.[116] This mantra is also a Ṛk which describes the Lord as a voyager who uses a large number of horses for his voyage (*asya harayaḥ śatā daśa*). As the horses are united (*yuktāḥ*), their movement is harmonious. This symbolises that for the Lord life progresses through love and fulfilment (*madhu*). The entire Madhu Vidyā is a detailed account of how life develops through *madhu*. By quoting the above Ṛk the Upaniṣad points out that the Honey Doctrine (Madhu Vidyā)[117] is an expanded version of an idea taken from the Veda. These three evidences are sufficient to prove that the essence of the Vedas has been developed and stated in clear terms by the Upaniṣads. From this it may be seen that the Upaniṣads are not mere additions but elucidations of the original ideas of the Vedas. Here it is worthwhile to remember the words of Sri Aurobindo who says that the Upaniṣads represent the soul of the Vedas.

NOTES

1. Kena Upaniṣad, 1-4.
2. Ibid.
3. Ibid., 1-5.
4. Īśa Upaniṣad (hereafter Īś. Up.), Mantra 8.
5. Ibid., Mantra 4.
6. Ibid.
7. Ibid., Mantra 8.
8. Muṇḍaka Upaniṣad (hereafter M. Up.), 1-1-6.
9. Ibid.
10. Ibid.
11. Ibid.

12. Māṇḍūkya Upaniṣad (hereafter Ma. Up.), Mantra 2.
13. Ibid., Mantra 3.
14. Ibid., Mantra 4.
15. Ibid., Mantra 5.
16. Ibid., Mantra 7.
17. Ibid.
18. Ibid.
19. Īś. Up., Mantra 8.
20. Ibid.
21. Taittrīya Upaniṣad, 2-7-1.
22. Śvetāśvatara Upaniṣad (hereafter S. Up.), 1-3.
23. Ibid.
24. Ibid.
25. Bṛhadāraṇyaka Upaniṣad (hereafter Bṛ. Up.), 2-4-12.
26. Ibid.
27. Chāndogya Upaniṣad (hereafter Ch. Up.), 8-4-2.
28. Bṛ. Up., 3-1-3.
29. Ibid., 4-4-9.
30. Ch. Up., 6-1-4.
31. Kaṭha Upaniṣad (hereafter (K. Up.), 2-1-10.
32. Ch. Up., 7-26-2.
33. K. Up., 2-1-11. See footnote 18 on page 301.
34. Ibid.
35. Ibid., 2-1-10.
36. Ibid., 2-3-2.
37. Ch. Up., 6-1-2.
38. Ibid., 6-1-4.
39. M. Up., 3-2-3.
40. K. Up., 1-2-23.
41. M. Up., 1-1-5.
42. Ibid., 3-2-4.
43. Bṛ. Up., 2-4-6.
44. Ibid., 4-4-19.
45. Ibid., 2-4-14.
46. Īś. Up., Mantra 9.
47. Bṛ. Up., 4-4-20.
48. Īś. Up., Mantra 11.
49. Ibid.
50. S. Up., 4-16.
51. Bṛ. Up., 2-4-12.
52. M. Up., 3-1-1.
53. Ibid.
54. Ibid., 3-1-1; 3-1-3.
55. Ibid.
56. Ibid., 3-1-2.

57. Īś. Up., Mantra 15.
58. Ibid., Mantra 9.
59. Bṛ. Up., 2-4-12.
60. Ibid.
61. Ibid., 3-1-3.
62. Ibid., 2-4-12.
63. M. Up., 3-1-3.
64. Ibid.
65. Ibid.
66. Ibid.
67. Īś. Up., Mantra 1.
68. Ibid.
69. Ibid.
70. Ibid., Mantra 7.
71. Bṛ. Up., 2-4-6.
72. Ibid., 2-4-14.
73. S. Up., 4-9.
74. Ibid., 5-7.
75. Ibid., 4-9.
76. Ibid.
77. Ibid., 4-10.
78. Ibid., 6-16.
79. Bṛ. Up., 4-4-13.
80. M. Up., 1-2-11.
81. Ibid.
82. Śaṅkara, *Bṛhadāraṇyaka Upaniṣad Bhāṣya*, Tr. Madhavananda, (1965), 4-4-22.
83. Bṛ. Up., 2-4.
84. Ibid., 4-5-2.
85. Ibid., 3-7-1.
86. Ibid., 3-1-2.
87. Īś. Up., Mantra 9.
88. Bṛ. Up., 4-4-20.
89. S. Up., 3-13.
90. Bṛ. Up., 4-3-35.
91. K. Up., 2-2-10.
92. S. Up., 1-8.
93. Ibid.
94. K. Up., 1-2-12.
95. Kena Upaniṣad, 1-2.
96. K. Up., 2-2-12.
97. M. Up., 3-1-5.
98. Īś. Up., Mantra 6.
99. Ibid., Mantra 7.

100. Bṛ. Up., 4-4-13.
101. M. Up., 3-1-4.
102. Ch. Up., 7-25-2.
103. M. Up., 3-1-4.
104. Ibid., 1-1-6.
105. Ibid.
106. Mā. Up., Mantra 7.
107. Bṛ. Up., 2-4-14.
108. Ibid., 2-4-12.
109. Ibid.
110. M. Up., 3-1-4.
111. Ibid.
112. Ch. Up., 8-4-2.
113. Muktikā Upaniṣad, 1-9.
114. M. Up., 3-1-1, 2,3,4.
115. S. Up., 4-6,7,8,9,10.
116. Bṛ. Up., 2-5-19.
117. Ibid., 2-5.

26

Yoga: A Means to Fulfilment*

The word *yoga* gives the sense of union. From this, *adhyātmayoga*[1] means union with the supreme Ātman. By this union a mortal becomes an immortal. A mortal has three major powers — cognition, volition and emotion. All the three are lifted, enlarged and fulfilled when he becomes an immortal. For union with Ātman does not destroy but fulfils. In it nothing is destroyed except mortality. This is the whole method of yoga used in the Upaniṣad (*yoga vidhimca kṛtsnam*).[2] If we carefully read the Upaniṣads, we may find that they are a record of unique yogic realisations. They do not give descriptive accounts of inner experiences but state their settled realisations in objective terms. Broadly speaking, their realisations fall into three distinct categories — (a) those related to man as a knower (*jñātā*); (b) those related to him as a worker (*kartā*); and (c) those related to him as an enjoyer (*bhoktā*). They are the three sides of an immortal being.

THE GREAT KNOWER

Man is a knower, but his knowledge is that of a mortal, one who is not united with Ātman. He sees only the world outside, the material world. Besides this he does not see any other world. From this he concludes that no other world exists (*nāsti para iti*).[3] According to another version, he sees as though there is separation between the world and Ātman (*nāneva paśyati*).[4] A third version says that he sees all elsewhere than in Ātman (*anyatrātmanaḥ*).[5] Thus the knowledge possessed by a mortal is exclusive of Ātman and limited to the world. In the Upaniṣad this knowledge is referred to as *avidyā*,[6] as that which is other than *vidyā*. From *avidyā* arise man's transmigratory existence and all attendant evils such as delusion, grief and suffering.[7]

By union with Ātman the exclusive and limited knowledge of the mortal is enlarged and made perfect and complete (*sujñāna*).[8] He sees not only this world more clearly than before but many other higher worlds. Not only does he know of these worlds but he notices that this and all the others proceed from and abide in the immortal Ātman. That Ātman is their ultimate cause and support is conveyed through the figure of the *aśvattha* tree whose roots are above and branches are down below (*ūrdhvamūlo' vākśākha*).[9] Further, the Upaniṣad draws our attention to the fact that what is here in the world, is there in Ātman also; likewise, what is there in Ātman, is also here in the world (*yadeveha tadamutra yadamutra tadanviha*).[10] From the fact of this mutual oneness it conclusively shows that here there is no separation whatsoever from Ātman (*neha nānasti kiñcana*).[11] The same truth is reaffirmed in the Bṛhadāraṇyaka Upaniṣad which says that all this is the Ātman (*idaṃ sarvaṃ yad ayam ātmā*).[12] Hence the world and Ātman are one and indivisible. With this realisation the mortal becomes immortal and freed from the law of transmigration and its evils.

If man sees the world and not its oneness with Ātman, what is it that makes him see the world in the wrong way? It is his mind dominated by the outgoing senses, says the Upaniṣad. The senses see only the outer things. Under their domination the mind too sees only the gross things. As a result, the world's oneness with Ātman, which actually belongs to the domain of subtle existence, cannot be grasped by our mind. When the mind overcomes the domination of the senses, it becomes pure and fit for seeing subtle things. They in whom the mind sees thus are called the seers of subtle realities (*sūkṣmadarśibhiḥ*).[13] Having acquired the subtle vision, it sees that the world is really one with Ātman. It also sees that the world's separation from Ātman is an illusion created by the senses. It is for this reason that the mind is said to be solely responsible for removing the wrong vision of the world (*manasā eva*).[14] If the mind errs, then the error is to be eliminated only through the mind. From this it is clear that unless the mind is properly disciplined, it will see merely the world and not its subtle connection with Ātman.

Ātman is both beyond the world and self-extended as the world. In the latter aspect he is called the universal Puruṣa. The Bṛhadāraṇyaka Upaniṣad speaks of two perceptions of this cosmic Ātman — the experience of Ātman in all beings (*ātmani evātmānam paśyati*)[15] and the experience of Ātman as all beings (*sarvam ātmānam paśyati*).[16] To these two the Īśa Upaniṣad adds one other experience and speaks of triune experience of Ātman. First, the experience of Ātman in whom all beings exist (*sarvāṇi bhūtāni ātmany eva*).[17] He contains all within his being and consciousness. He holds them "as the infinite ether contains in itself all objects". Second, the experience of Ātman who dwells within all beings (*sarvabhūteṣu cātmānam*).[18] He controls all by controlling their motion from within. Though he is seated inside all, he is not imprisoned by them. He is absolutely free and all-blissful. He contains and inhabits all existences "not in a physical but in a spiritual sense". Third, the experience of Ātman's oneness with all existences (*sarvāṇi bhūtāni ātmaivābhūt*).[19] He not only contains and inhabits all but is also united with them. For they are his own becomings. This is the crowning experience of the cosmic Ātman. For it abolishes all division, all opposition between the world and the self-extended Ātman.

Sri Aurobindo frequently refers to this triune experience of Vedāntins. His comments on it are noteworthy. He says: " the Self becoming all existences is the basis of our oneness with all; the Self containing all existences is the basis of our oneness in difference; the Self inhabiting all is the basis of our individuality in the universal".[20] From this we understand the spiritual significance of these unique experiences for us. In another comment on them he points out that they are traceable to the experiences of the seers of the Veda. "In the Veda", he says, "all these . . . are asserted of the gods. In essence the gods are one existence which the sages call by different names; but in their action founded in and proceeding from the large Truth and Right Agni or another is said to be all the other gods, he is the One that becomes all; at the same time he is said to contain all the gods in himself as the nave of a wheel contains the spokes, he is the One that contains all; and yet as Agni he is described as a separate deity, one who helps all the others, exceeds them in force and knowledge, yet is inferior to them in cosmic position and is employed by them as messenger, priest and worker, — the creator of the world and father, he is yet the son born of our works, he is, that is to say, the original and the manifested indwelling Self or Divine, the One that inhabits all."[21] We are indeed indebted to Sri Aurobindo for giving us this profound insight into the Vedānta. It is striking that the experiences of the seers of Vedānta are the same as those of the seers of Veda.

When the universal Ātman is realised, one has to rise to the level of the transcendent Ātman called the highest of high Person (*parātparam puruṣam*).[22] But the ascension into the highest Ātman is a difficult achievement, for, as the Upaniṣad says, the spiritual path, like a razor's edge, is difficult to tread on (*durgam pathas*).[23] One who is established in the realisation of the universal Ātman is generally limited to that realisation. For he thinks that this is the highest form of Ātman. In order to ascend further he has to remove this limitation. When the limitation is completely removed, the transcendental form of Ātman is immediately revealed to the individual (*tattva bhāvaḥ prasīdati*).[24]

Here an error is possible. If the transcendent Ātman is attained by a radical dissolution of the world of names and forms without which his universal existence is inconceivable, then one enters the highest of the high as if into a great darkness (*bhūya tamaḥ*).[25] In fact, another Upaniṣad recognises this possibility when it says that just as the flowing rivers disappear in the sea giving up name and form, even so the knower, freed from name and form, attains (*upaiti*) the supreme divine Being.[26] Here the word *upaiti* conveys the sense of disappearing into the Being. Therefore, with a view to protect the seeker of the transcendent Ātman from the dissolution of his individuality, the Kaṭha Upaniṣad categorically states that Ātman must be apprehended only as having both of his forms, the universal and the transcendental (*eva ... ubhayoḥ*)[27] and not otherwise. It is a condition of yoga laid down everywhere in the Upaniṣads (*yogavidhi*)[28] — the Īśa, Kena, Muṇḍaka, Māṇḍūkya, and Bṛhadāraṇyaka, to mention a few of them.

Man is a mortal knower, but he is not destined to be so. He is to fulfil himself, through union with Ātman, as a great knower to whom the whole reality of the world is revealed.

THE GREAT WORKER

Man is a worker, but his works are those of a mortal, one who is not united with Ātman. The Upaniṣad speaks of his works as the inferior ones (*avaram karma*).[29] The inferior works are of two kinds — (i) those done for the sake of fulfilling one's desires; (ii) those done according to an inferior law of action.

(i) The Bṛhadāraṇyaka Upaniṣad speaks about three important desires — (a) desire for sons (*putraiṣaṇā*);[30] (b) desire for wealth (*vittaiṣaṇā*);[31] and (c) desire for worlds (*lokaiṣaṇā*).[32] They are fulfilled according to the law of the scriptures. In other words, they are fulfilled through works prescribed by the scriptures (*vidhi*). Those who mould their life according to these works tread on the path of virtuous men. When they die, they go to the world of good deeds (*sukṛtasya loke*)[33] where the lord of the gods abides (*devānām patiḥ*).[34] They live there like the gods and obtain all enjoyments like them. When the merits of their deeds are exhausted, they are forced to return to this mortal world (*imam lokam . . . viśanti*).[35] This is one of the important insights of Vedānta. The Lord of Yoga reiterates it in the Gītā.[36] The relevant verse runs thus:

te tam bhuktvā svargalokam viśālam
kṣīṇe puṇye martyalokam viśanti.

Even though the works are prescribed by the scriptures, they are inferior, because they fulfil desires and do not wipe out mortality.

(ii) The Lord, according to the Muṇḍaka Upaniṣad, is at once the immutable Ātman (*anaśnan*) and the mutable Nature of whom Ātman is the witness (*abhicākaśīti*), the Non-Doer and the Doer of works.[37] In him is contained the wonderful Law of Action which brings out most appropriately his eternal greatness and glory. Somehow man has forgotten his essential oneness with God and lost God's Law of Action. As a result, he is deluded. He becomes a non-lord (*anīśa*)[38] and is bound by the works of Nature. He acts according to his own law, the law that promotes personal interest in all works, and enjoys the good and bad born of his works (*anyaḥ pippalaṃ svādvatti*).[39] Thus delusion and bondage throw him into a life of grief and suffering.[40] The works of the mortal are certainly inferior, because they are done not according to God's law.

(i) The Vedāntins, whose main aim is the attainment of union with the supreme Ātman (*avyaktātpuruṣaḥ paraḥ*),[41] teach that immortality is attained not by satisfying the desires but by totally eradicating them from one's heart (*yadā sarve pramucyante kāmā ye'sya hṛdi śritāḥ atha martyo amṛto bhavati*).[42] For the desires are the very sources of mortality. However, it is absolutely wrong to conclude that with the disappearance of desires all works disappear from the individual. What actually disappears is the fault of mortality from works and not works themselves. An immortal is not crippled by ceasing to be a mortal. He does all works without being bound by mortality (*na karma lipyate*).[43] In him mortal works have turned themselves into works not tainted by mortality (*parāmṛtam*).[44] When he is thus delivered from inferior works, he attains deliverance from all grief and suffering (*vimuktaśca vimucyate*).[45]

(ii) Now we shall turn to the other category of inferior works. A mortal grieves, because that is the inevitable outcome of works done from his personal law of action. In other words, his grief is the direct consequence of his inferior works. But when he sees the other side of his mortal existence (*paśyati anyam*),[46] all change drastically. There he sees the Lord in his native majesty and glory, the One who is eternally the Non-Doer and the Doer of works. There he sees that he is one with God in essence of being and consciousness (*sayujā*);[47] that in his original law of action he possesses, as an eternal companion (*sakhāyā*),[48] the majesty and glory of God (*asya mahimānam*),[49] that is, God's Law of Action. As a result of this profound vision, his personal law of action ceases. He gets back to the original law and becomes God's best companion (*paramaṃ sāmyam upaiti*).[50] In the language of the Gītā this attainment is referred to as likeness to God's Dharma (*sādharmya*).[51] All his inferior works tainted by *pāpa* and *puṇya* disappear from him. By doing works according to God's Law, he is freed from all grief (*vītaśokaḥ*).[52] Here too, as in the previous case, when a mortal becomes an immortal, his works do not disappear; what disappears is his personal law of works. An enjoyer of union with Ātman is also an accomplisher of works (*ātmaratiḥ kriyāvān*).[53] His works are necessary because with them he tries to help the world and liberate it from bondage and suffering (*ātmakrīḍaḥ*). The idea of *ātmakrīḍaḥ* develops itself logically from the expression *ātmaratiḥ kriyāvān*.

Desire demands exclusive satisfaction. Therefore it is fit to be abandoned. If this is the rule, it applies to all desires, including the desire for Ātman. Yājñavalkya rightly says that the desire for mundane objects and the desire for Ātman are both desires only (*ubhe hy ete eṣaṇe eva bhavataḥ*).[54] Generally, desire for Ātman ends as a desire for personal liberation. Though personal liberation is recognised in the Upaniṣads, the Muṇḍaka particularly insists that the desire of personal liberation is to be exceeded by working for world-liberation. Such an individual is referred to as the best one (*variṣṭhaḥ*).[55] For he is at play with others in the world and removes their grief through the play. This is the significance of the expression *ātmakrīḍaḥ*.[56]

If an immortal is an accomplisher of works, the one purpose of his works is to bring enlightenment to the world and to raise it beyond all bondage and suffering. He is asked to live a hundred years in the world (*jijīviṣet śataṃ samāḥ*)[57] and do all appointed works (*karmāṇi*)[58] just for this higher purpose.

Man is a mortal worker, but he is not destined to be so. He is to fulfil himself, through union with Ātman, as a great worker of the whole world.

THE GREAT ENJOYER

Man is an enjoyer of possessions, but his enjoyments are those of a mortal, one who is not united with Ātman. His possessions are manifold. The Bṛhadāraṇyaka Upaniṣad gives a long list of these possessions — wife, sons, brāhmaṇas, kṣatriyas, wealth, worlds, the gods and all beings.[59] He thinks that the world exists for his utility and satisfaction. Therefore he loves all for their own sake, for the satisfaction they give to his ego (*sarvasya kāmāya sarvam priyam bhavati*).[60] This is but a violence committed upon the world. The world is instinctively aware that he is not its master and it is not his possession. As the Upaniṣad says, all in the world reject him, reject his domination and oppression (*parāduḥ*).[61] Thus there is an underlying discord between him and the world. From this hidden opposition which is rooted everywhere all evils arise. As a result, his enjoyments fail to give him satisfaction or happiness. This is the fate of all mortal enjoyments.

If man is not the ruler of the world, who else is its ruler? If the world is not his possession, whose possession is it then (*kasyasvid dhanam*)?[62] According to the Īśa Upaniṣad, the real ruler and possessor of the world is God (*īśaḥ*).[63] From this we may understand that the world has been created for God's habitation, for His utility and enjoyment; that the existence of the world is, therefore, bound by this eternal law (*satyadharma*).[64] If, for any reason, the law is disregarded, the world registers its protest through powerful resistance. We owe this insight to the wise sage Yājñavalkya.

When man renounces his greed for possessions (*mā gṛdhaḥ*)[65] and sees that God is to be seated as the ruler and inhabitant of the world (*īśāvāsyam idaṃ sarvaṃ*),[66] he goes beyond mortality and becomes an immortal (*mṛtyuṃ tīrtva . . . amṛtam aśnute*).[67] By becoming so he loses neither the world nor the right of enjoying the world. By returning to the eternal law of the world which he originally abandoned out of greed, his possessions are rightly held and his enjoyments are rightly determined. This is the true sense of the command *tena tyaktena bhuñjīthāḥ*.[68] The verb is used in the sense of not only a call to enjoy but also a call to possess. The immortal person possesses all (*tasya lokaḥ*),[69] for they are the habitations of God; he enjoys all, for that is the result of helping them to realise the indwelling God (*sarvasya kartā*).[70] In short, he loves all for the sake of Ātman (*ātmanas tu kāmāya sarvam priyam bhavati*).[71]

Yājñavalkya has said that the world rejects him who disregards its law of existence and imposes on it his rule. If he renounces his offensiveness and sees the necessity of loving the world, what will be its response to him? The individual and the world are two interdependent realities. Hence one influences the other. If the individual hurts the world, the world returns the hurt to him in suitable terms. To give another instance, he uses the world as food for his growth; in the same way, the world uses him, when he is dead, as food and maintains its parallel growth.

From this it is clear that his love for the world will surely generate love from the world. This is precisely the view of the Bṛhadāraṇyaka Upaniṣad. It says, this self is honey for all beings and all beings are honey for this self (*ayam ātmā sarveṣām bhūtānām madhu, asyātmanaḥ sarvāṇi bhūtāni madhu*).[72] Here the term honey (*madhu*) is used as a figure for love which is sweet and delightful like honey. The individual gives love to all (*asyātmanaḥ sarvāṇi bhūtāni madhu*) and all give love to the individual (*ayam ātmā sarveṣām bhūtānām madhu*). This is called the science of Madhu (*madhu vidyā*) of the seer Dadhyaṅ. It wipes out all mortal enjoyments and delivers from the necessity of transmigration (*saṃsāra*). When love brings about love, all evils disappear from man's life and all his enjoyments culminate in utter sweetness and delight. By this he wins immortality for himself and for the world. This is the message of Madhu Vidyā.

Mortality is never due to possessions. There is no doubt about it. Just as it is not due to perceiving the world or performing works in the world, so too it is not due to enjoying the possessions. What causes mortality is attachment — attachment for the world, attachment for works and attachment for possessions. The three attachments are the three forms of death (*mṛtyo rūpāṇi*)[73] by which man is bound.

Man is a mortal enjoyer, but he is not destined to be so. He is to fulfil himself, through union with Ātman, as a great enjoyer of the world like Dadhyaṅ.

THE ĪŚA UPANIṢAD

The seer's *yoga* with the supreme Ātman has been stated in three broad outlines in the Īśa Upaniṣad. There stand three distinct self-experiences. First, the experience of how one sees all aspects of Ātman and rises to the status of a supreme knower (*vijānataḥ*).[74] Second, the experience of how one performs all appointed works without attachment (*na karma lipyate*)[75] and becomes a great worker. Third, the experience of how one repossesses the true Law and becomes a great enjoyer through this Law (*bhuñjīthāḥ*).[76] They represent the essence of the yoga of the entire Vedānta. This is perhaps the reason why the Īśa is made to stand at the head of the traditional enumeration of the Upaniṣads which are twelve in number.

NOTES

1. Kaṭha Upaniṣad (hereafter K. Up.), 1-2-12.
2. Ibid., 2-3-18.
3. Ibid., 1-2-6.
4. Ibid., 2-1-10.
5. Bṛhadāraṇyaka Upaniṣad (hereafter Bṛ. Up.), 2-4-6.
6. K. Up., 1-2-4.
7. Ibid., 1-2-6.
8. Ibid., 1-2-9.
9. Ibid., 2-3-1.
10. Ibid., 2-1-10.
11. Ibid., 2-1-11.
12. Bṛ. Up., 2-4-6.
13. K.Up., 1-3-12.
14. Ibid., 2-1-11.
15. Bṛ. Up., 4-4-23.
16. Ibid.
17. Īśa Upaniṣad (hereafter Īś. Up.), Mantra 6.
18. Ibid.
19. Ibid., Mantra 7.
20. Sri Aurobindo, *The Life Divine* (2001), p. 168.
21. Ibid., pp. 168-169.
22. Muṇḍaka Upaniṣad (hereafter M. Up.), 3-2-8.
23. K. Up., 1-3-14.
24. Ibid., 2-3-13.
25. Īś. Up., Mantra 9.
26. M. Up., 3-2-8.
27. K. Up., 2-3-13.
28. Ibid., 2-3-18.
29. M. Up. 1-2-7.
30. Bṛ. Up., 4-4-22.
31. Ibid.
32. Ibid.
33. M. Up., 1-2-1.
34. Ibid., 1-2-5.
35. Ibid., 1-2-10.
36. Gītā, 9-21.
37. M. Up., 3-1-1.
38. Ibid., 3-1-2.
39. Ibid., 3-1-1.
40. Ibid., 3-1-2.
41. K. Up., 1-3-11.
42. Ibid., 2-3-14.

43. Īś. Up., Mantra 2.
44. M. Up., 2-1-10.
45. K. Up., 2-2-1.
46. M. Up., 3-1-2.
47. Ibid., 3-1-1.
48. Ibid.
49. Ibid., 3-1-2.
50. Ibid., 3-1-3.
51. Gītā, 14-2.
52. M.Up., 3-1-2.
53. Ibid., 3-1-4.
54. Bṛ. Up., 4-4-22.
55. M. Up., 3-1-4.
56. Ibid.
57. Īś. Up., Mantra 2.
58. Ibid.
59. Bṛ. Up., 2-4-5.
60. Ibid.
61. Ibid., 2-4-6.
62. Īś. Up., Mantra 1.
63. Ibid.
64. Ibid., Mantra 15.
65. Ibid., Mantra 1.
66. Ibid.
67. Ibid., Mantra 11.
68. Ibid., Mantra 1.
69. Bṛ. Up., 4-4-13.
70. Ibid.
71. Ibid., 2-4-5.
72. Ibid., 2-5-16.
73. Ibid., 4-3-7.
74. Īś. Up., Mantra 7.
75. Ibid., Mantra 2.
76. Ibid., Mantra 1.

* Article contributed to *Streams of Yogic and Mystic Experience* Edited by Manoj Das (2010).

27

Two Types of Devotees

TWO TYPES OF WORSHIP

The Gītā is basically a treatise on the philosophy and practice of a yoga which divinizes the human soul. Most of its important ideas appear in the second six chapters — chapters 7 to 12. In the twelfth the idea of Bhakti, alluded to from the very beginning, is fully developed into a firm foundation for the rest of the chapters — chapters 13 to 18. Here its unique merit in the yoga of the Gītā is enunciated in terms at once concise and conclusive. Of the twenty verses of this chapter, we are mainly concerned with the first five where Krishna gives his views on the relative merits of the two forms of worship known to and supported by the Vedāntins — (i) worship of the unmanifest Imperishable (*avyaktam akṣaram*)[1] and (ii) worship of the supreme Lord of the world (*lokamaheśvaram*).[2]

THE TEXT

Arjuna Said: Those devotees who thus by a constant union seek after Thee, and those who seek after the unmanifest Imperishable,—which of these are the accomplished knowers of Yoga?[3]

Śrī Bhagavān Said: Those who found their mind in Me, ever-united and endowed with a supreme faith, and seek after Me — these I hold to be perfectly united.[4]

But those who seek after the Unmanifest as the indefinable, the imperishable, the all-pervading, the unthinkable, the high-seated, the immobile, the eternal, they by restraining all their senses, by making their understanding equal and by engaging themselves in doing good to all beings, arrive to Me only. [5]

With difficulty is reached the goal of the Unmanifest by embodied souls; greater is the difficulty of those who are attached to their exclusive realization of the Unmanifest.*[6]

TEXTUAL PROBLEMS

Before we proceed to expound the teachings of the Gītā in these five verses we shall have to set the direction very clearly and show why this interpretation has become necessary.

Generally, Vedāntic interpretation is a difficult venture. One of the reasons why it is so is that it has to deal with problems arising from the style of textual compositions. And the interpretation of the Gītā is no exception to this rule. There are two textual problems in the above five verses which stand in the way of a proper comprehension of the Gītā's teachings. The first one concerns the word *yuktatamāḥ* in the second verse[7] and the next one concerns the whole of the fifth verse.[8]

(i) In 12-2 the word *yuktatamāḥ* is correlated with the seekers of the Īśvara. It implies that the seekers of the Avyakta cannot be correlated with the word. But in 12-4 this implication is not upheld; at the same time they are not openly correlated with the word as in 12-2. This makes the Gītā's teaching uncertain. (ii) The same uncertainty prevails in 12-5 also, but in a different form. One line says that the goal of the Avyakta is difficult; in another line the same goal is said to be very difficult. Does this imply that the Gītā is not in favour of the seekers of the Avyakta? If so, it is not clear why it should try to abandon in 12-4 the distinction made between the two groups of seekers in 12-2, as if it favours both of them.

As these problems arise out of the style of composition and not out of the obscurity in the ideas of the teacher of the Gītā, we are sure of solving them successfully. But the way to solve them is to read the original texts again and again till we find the solution. At the same time we must not forget the fact that repeated readings pay only when we are already in possession of the master-idea of the main text.

EXPOSITION

Having had the vision of the Īśvara and having realized that Krishna is verily the great Lord of the world (*lokamaheśvaram*)[9] answering to all descriptions of the Lord given previously by Krishna himself, Arjuna sees two possibilities of worship. First, worship of the Īśvara with his three dominant characteristics — (i) the Imperishable (*tvam akṣaraṃ*);[10] (ii) the original Doer or the original Nature which does works (*tvam ādikartre*);[11] and (iii) the supreme Imperishable (*tvam akṣaraṃ paramaṃ*).[12] Secondly, worship of the limited form of the Imperishable exclusive of the other characteristics. They correspond to the two types of seekers with which Arjuna is familiar — those who worship the Īśvara and those who worship the unmanifest Akṣara. Now he asks Krishna: Which of them are to be considered as the accomplished knowers of Yoga (*yogavittamāḥ*)?

Krishna's answer to this question is direct and decisive. He uses the word 'Me' to refer to the Īśvara-form as distinguished from the other form of the unmanifest Imperishable. He says, 'Those who found their mind in Me, ever-united and endowed with a supreme faith, and seek after Me are perfectly united'.

A *yukta* is one who is united; so a *yuktatama* is one who is perfectly united. According to Krishna, the seekers of the Īśvara excel in union, whereas the seekers of the Avyakta do not. Though excellence in union differentiates the two types of seekers, we do not know how the excellence is measured by Krishna.

The words Īśvara and Avyakta are used in two distinct senses: While the first stands for Brahman in its integrality—the supreme Imperishable with the unmanifest Imperishable and Nature as its two inseparable aspects, the second refers to the same Brahman exclusively identified with the aspect of the unmanifest Imperishable. To be united with the exclusive Brahman or the Avyakta is to be a *yukta*; to be united with the integral Brahman or the Īśvara is to be a *yuktatama*. To put the distinction differently, a *yukta* is one who is united with the Avyakta and whose union is exclusive or imperfect; a *yuktatama* is one who is united with the Īśvara and whose union is integral or perfect. The Gītā always insists on knowing the integral Brahman and attaining perfect union — *brahma tadviduḥ kṛtsnam,*[13] *mām vetti tattvataḥ.*[14] Hence its emphasis on *yuktatama.*

Now we understand why the seekers of the Īśvara excel the seekers of the Avyakta. The former excel, because they are united with the integral Brahman; the latter do not, because they are not united with this Brahman but with the exclusive Brahman.

Owing to their exclusiveness the seekers of the Avyakta are generally insistent and do not go beyond what they have attained. Therefore they see the unmanifest Brahman purely in its own terms[15]— as the indefinable, the imperishable, the all-pervading, the unthinkable, the high-seated, the immobile, the eternal and so on. But if they give up their exclusiveness, they also can become perfectly united (*yuktatamas*).[16] This is the significance of the two indeclinables used in the third and fourth verses — *tu* and *eva.*[17]

If they drop their insistent attitude and admit that the unmanifest Imperishable does not exclude but is the very source and foundation of Nature, then they see that Nature manifests all beings here (*sarvāṇi bhūtāni*) and works out in them the Will of the supreme Imperishable or the Īśvara. Hence, instead of resorting to mortification of their personal nature, they restrain their senses (*saṃniyamya indiriyagrāmaṃ*),[18] develop their understanding into a faculty which perceives everywhere the same impersonal Will being worked out by Nature (*samabuddhayaḥ*)[19] and, with the instruments thus upgraded, engage themselves in doing good to all creatures (*sarvabhūtahite ratāḥ*),[20] that is, in fulfilling that Will in all. By doing so they too become the seekers of the Īśvara and attain perfect union (*te prāpnuvanti māmeva*).[21] There is therefore only one way for the seekers of the Avyakta to overcome their limitation and become *yuktatamas* and this is by becoming the seekers of the Īśvara (*madbhaktaḥ*).[22] Other than this, there is no way.

The way of the Avyakta is hard and painful (*avyaktā hi gatirduḥkham*)[23] unlike the other way which is very easy (*susukham*).[24] For in this way the seeker faces many difficulties, difficulties in realizing the Unmanifest and greater difficulties in overcoming the limitation in the realization. In the first he must pass from the manifest to its opposite side where abides the Unmanifest; in the second he must release himself from the limitation of exclusive realization of the Unmanifest. In the other way these difficulties do not exist. For the seeker does not have to pass out of the manifest order; nor is his realization of the Unmanifest exclusive. By passing beyond the three Guṇas (*guṇān etān atītya trīn*)[25] and yet remaining within the order of becoming of Nature, he realizes the Unmanifest without exclusiveness. This means that his realization takes place in the very conditions of the manifest (*ihaiva*)[26] (even here), which makes the goal of the Īśvara easily attainable.

In the ultimate analysis the difficulties in the way of the Unmanifest result from the fact that the faith of the seeker is in his personal effort and personal strength and achievement. But in the other way the seeker puts his whole faith in the impersonal Nature (*daivīmprakṛtiṃ*),[27] which takes him easily to the supreme Imperishable. This is its greatest merit and this is why the Gītā speaks of the seekers of the Īśvara as being endowed with a supreme faith (*śraddhayā parayopetāḥ*).[28] Here the seeker progresses only by the strength of the impersonal Nature of the Īśvara. Therefore he faces no difficulties, as in the other way, the way of the Unmanifest .

Embodied souls are souls manifest in Nature (*dehavatbhiḥ*).[29] In them Nature is at work, fulfilling the Will of the Īśvara through personal nature. Since the manifest is considered to be the opposite of the Unmanifest, no embodied soul, without ceasing to accept the conditions of embodied life, can reach the opposite side, for to be embodied is to accept and remain committed to the manifest—personal nature and the works of Nature. Therefore an embodied soul can pass out of the manifest only by mortification of its personal nature and eventually by resisting and setting aside the mighty Will of the impersonal Nature. This is really an uphill task very difficult to accomplish (*duḥkham dehavatbhiravāpyate*).[30] However, success in this way is surely possible, but it is gained by breaking all the powerful laws of development by which Nature does works in the embodied souls.

There are three distinct stages in the way of the Unmanifest: first of all, the seekers discriminate between the manifest and the Unmanifest, the manifest in which they grow by the inexorable laws of Nature and the Unmanifest which they have to conquer by leaving aside the manifest; second, they escape into the Unmanifest by systematically severing all connections with the manifest; third, having thus entered, they keep their whole consciousness fixed upon the Unmanifest (*avyakta-āsakta-*

cetāmsi).[31] But this is an exclusive realization, because they have realized Brahman to be exclusively the Unmanifest. Given the exclusiveness, they become attached to their realization (*avyakta-āsakta-cetāmsi*)[32] because they cannot come out of their realization and see that Brahman is the supreme Imperishable, the Īśvara who exceeds the unmanifest Imperishable and manifests all by his original Nature. As long as they are attached to their exclusive realization, they are *yuktas* and not *yuktatamas.*

From the point of view of the integral Brahman, there is really no opposition between the Īśvara and the Avyakta. Therefore, is it not possible for the *yuktas* to develop into the *yuktatamas,* the united to become the perfectly united? It is certainly possible, but they must be prepared to face hurdles much more difficult to overcome than those they faced while entering the unmanifest Imperishable (*kleśo 'dhikatarah teṣām*).[33]

The first and foremost step in this direction is to understand that perfect union with Brahman is not possible unless they are willing to abandon their attachment for the exclusive realization of the Unmanifest. This takes them to the next step where they become totally unattached to this exclusive realization (*avyakta-asakta-cetāmsi*).[34] In the third and final step they abandon their exclusive realization by accepting all that they originally abandoned for the sake of winning the Unmanifest. They now admit that the unmanifest Imperishable is the eternal foundation upon which Nature works out the Will of the supreme Imperishable in all beings (*sarveṣu bhūteṣu*). They also admit that their main occupation is to do good to all creatures and take delight in promoting the upward movement of Nature in them. These are immense difficulties, unlike those confronted while conquering the Unmanifest, because at every step the *yuktas* have to reverse their original position and abandon all that they considered to be advantageous and good in reaching this position.

On passing through these difficulties the *yuktas* become the *yuktatamas* and arrive at the grand realization of the integral Brahman, the Īśvara (*te prāpnuvanti māmeva*).[35] However, they are not declared to be *yuktatamas* in the words of the Gītā. We must understand why they are not so declared by the Gītā.

The reason why the title of *yuktatamaḥ* is withheld from the seekers of the Avyakta is that they do not fulfil the requirements demanded of a *yuktatama*. In the Gītā's view a *yuktatama* excels in union as well as in the means of union. The seeker of the Īśvara is declared to be a *yuktatama* because he excels in both. But the seeker of the Avyakta in verse 12-4 excels only in union and not in the means of union. Unlike the direct and easy means of the seeker of the Īśvara, the means adopted by him are tortuous and very difficult.[36] Hence the Gītā does not confer the title of *yuktatamaḥ* on him.

CONCLUSION

Now we have two categories of the seekers of the Avyakta, *yuktas* and *yuktatamas*. As *yuktas,* they seek the unmanifest Brahman purely in terms proper to its position—as *akṣaram, anirdeśyam, sarvatragam, acintyam, kūtastham, acalaṃ, dhruvam,* etc.[37] When the seeking develops fully, they are united with the Unmanifest and get attached to its exclusive realization. And the path leading to their realization is hard and painful (*duḥkham*).[38] As *yuktatamas*, they get rid of attachment for the exclusive realization of the unmanifest Brahman and resolve to seek the integral Brahman, the Īśvara. In the end they are united with the Īśvara. But on account of the great difficulty (*kleśo' dhikataraḥ*)[39] associated with their means the Gītā whitholds from them the title of *yuktatamāḥ*.[40]

In contrast to the two categories of the seekers of the Avyakta, the seekers of the Īśvara are unique. For they alone win the title of *yuktatamāḥ*. The seekers of the Avyakta come closer to them by uniting themselves with the Īśvara, but miss the title by using a means of union which is very difficult and tortuous. But when they unite themselves with the unmanifest Brahman through a similar means but less arduous, they become attached to its exclusive realization. As a result, they move farther away from the seekers of the Īśvara and miss not only the title but the very realization of the Īśvara. Among the three categories of seekers, the second one is very rare and exceptional. So we may leave it aside and consider as if the first and the last alone exist. If we try to grade them according to merit, we find the seekers of the Avyakta occupy a position much lower than that of the seekers of the Īśvara.[41] The Gītā's choice, therefore, falls naturally on the latter. It speaks approvingly of *mayyāvesita-cetāmsi* (those who have lodged their whole consciousness in the Īśvara),[42] as opposed to *avyaka-āsakta cetāmsi* (those who are attached to their exclusive realization of the Avyakta),[43] and declares that in the case of the former the Īśvara himself becomes the liberator of the souls (*teṣāmaham samuddhartā mṛtyu samsāra-sāgarāt bhavāmi*).[44]

We know that ascetics seek the unmanifest Imperishable. They look upon that as the highest desirable object besides which nothing exists. As embodied souls are on the side of the manifest (*vyakta*) they hold that the goal of the Unmanifest must be reached by renunciation of all to be found on this side (*sannyāsa*). By bringing out the inferior position the seekers of the Avyakta occupy in comparison with the seekers of the Īśvara, the teacher of the Gītā plainly tells us that the support he offers to the ascetics and their view of renunciation is not unqualified. Arjuna's question about the relative merits of the two forms of worship implies that he is under the influence of the current view that asceticism is the ultimate teaching of the Vedānta. Krishna's decisive answer clinches the issue by assigning an inferior position to the ascetics. Therefore asceticism cannot be the dominant view of the Vedānta or of the Gītā for that matter. The stern opposition from the ascetic tradition to this conclusion pales into insignificance before the authority and assertion of no less a person than Krishna. This perhaps is the true message of the opening verses of the twelfth chapter.

There is a good deal of metaphysics in the Gītā, yet it is not a metaphysical pronouncement made in logically perfect and flawless terms. Because it is preeminently a metaphysical poetry. If the sense of its terms is uncertain in some places, it is not a fault that has crept into its texture inadvertently, but a merit that makes metaphysical poetry possible. Deliberate uncertainty in expression is used as a device to break the rigidity of words and create out of them a highly suggestive and rich poetry. In this the Gītā is without a match among the works of its kind. In the opening verses of its twelfth chapter we see a little bit of this poetry emerging out of words into which a doubtful sense is put by the text.

NOTES

1. Gītā, 12-1.
2. Ibid., 5-21.
3. Ibid., 12-1.
4. Ibid., 12-2.
5. Ibid., 12-3,4.
6. Ibid., 12-5.
   * I have split the compound *avyaktāsaktacetāmsi* into *avyakta* + *āsakta cetāmsi* and rendered the second word as 'those who are attached to their exclusive realization', because all attachments without exception imply exclusiveness.
7. Ibid., 12-2.
8. Ibid., 12-5.
9. Ibid., 5-29.
10. Ibid., 11-37.
11. Ibid.
12. Ibid., 11-18.
13. Ibid., 7-29.
14. Ibid., 7-3.
15. Ibid., 12-3.
16. Ibid., 12-2.
17. Ibid., 12-3,4.
18. Ibid., 12-4.
19. Ibid.
20. Ibid.
21. Ibid.
22. Ibid., 12-14.
23. Ibid., 12-5.
24. Ibid., 9-2.
25. Ibid., 14-20.
26. Ibid., 5-19.
27. Ibid., 9-13.
28. Ibid., 12-2.
29. Ibid., 12-5.
30. Ibid.
31. Ibid., 12-4.
32. Ibid.
33. Ibid., 12-5.
34. Ibid.
35. Ibid., 12-4.

36. Ibid., 12-5.
37. Ibid., 12-3.
38. Ibid., 12-5.
39. Ibid.
40. Ibid., 12-4.
41. Ibid., 12-2.
42. Ibid., 12-7.
43. Ibid., 12-5.
44. Ibid., 12-7.

28

The Śāstra and the Brahmasūtra

BĀDARĀYAṆA AND ŚAṄKARA

One of the *sūtras* of the Brahmasūtra runs as follows: *śāstra yonitvāt* (1-1-3). Evidently it is a declaration about Brahman already defined as the ultimate source of the world (1-1-2). Śaṅkara has given two interpretations to the *sūtra* 1-1-3. According to the first, Brahman is the source of the Vedas; according to the second, the Vedas are the sources from which Brahman is known. Though the *sūtra* lends itself to be interpreted in two different ways, it is doubtful whether it is intended to be so understood by the author of the *sūtra*. The *sūtra* which follows immediately 1-1-3 goes thus: *tat tu samanvayāt* (1-1-4). The text is very clear. It affirms that the Upaniṣad passages, when fully reconciled, give us the knowledge of Brahman. If this is the view of Bādarāyaṇa, then 1-1-3 cannot be given the interpretation that Brahman is the source of the Vedas. But then how does Śaṅkara think that this interpretation can be given to 1-1-3? The reason is obvious. He thinks that within the scope of 1-1-3 the Bṛhadāraṇyaka text 2-4-10 is included as one of the *viṣayavākyas*. According to him, the text speaks about the appearance of the Vedas from Ātman (Brahman). Thus we have two conflicting views about the *sūtra* 1-1-3.

From the teaching of the *sūtra* 1-1-4 the previous *sūtra* 1-1-3 can only affirm that the Vedas are the sources from which Brahman is known. On the other hand, the passages of the Upaniṣads suggest that the word *yoni* in 1-1-3 admits of two interpretations, one supporting the view that the word means Brahman and another favouring the view that by the word is meant the Vedas. The question is therefore how to determine the import of 1-1-3. Is it to be determined by reference to the *sūtra* 1-1-4 or the relevant passages of the Upaniṣads?

THE SUPPORTING PASSAGES OF THE UPANIṢADS

According to Śaṅkara, there are passages in the Upaniṣads equally supportive of the two interpretations given to the *sūtra* 1-1-3. In the Bṛhadāraṇyaka Upaniṣad the text 2-4-10 speaks of the great Ātman as the source of the Ṛg Veda, etc. The text is rendered thus: "As from a fire kindled with wet faggot diverse kinds of smoke issue, even so, my dear, the Ṛg Veda, Yajur Veda, Sāma Veda, Atharvāṅgirasa, history, mythology, arts, Upaniṣads, pithy verses, aphorisms, elucidations and explanations are (like) the breath of this infinite Reality. They are like the breath of this (Supreme Self)."[1] Śaṅkara cites this text as the evidence of his first interpretation.

There are many other passages in the Upaniṣads which reveal that Brahman is the highest reality. Śaṅkara invites our attention to the following passages: "O amiable one, this universe, before its creation, was but Existence, one without a second";[2] "Before its creation this universe was but the Self that is one";[3] "That Brahman is without prior or posterior, without interior or exterior (i.e. homogeneous without a second)"; "This Self, the perceiver of everything, is Brahman";[4] "All that is in front is Brahman, the immortal."[5] These, according to him, support the second interpretation of the *sūtra* 1-1-3.[6]

Thus the two interpretations given to 1-1-3 are shown to be valid with the help of the relevant passages from the Upaniṣads. Though the *sūtra* can be so explained, *sūtra* 1-1-4 strongly suggests that the former be explained only in one sense. Therefore a decision becomes necessary as to what exactly is meant by the *sūtra* 1-1-3. In this regard we must bear in mind that Śaṅkara is a commentator and his business is to bring out the sense intended by the author of the *sūtras*, Bādarāyana. He is not free to go to the original sources, namely, the Upaniṣads which form the basis of the *sūtras,* and offer independent interpretations. Further, when the *sūtras* clearly indicate the sense intended by their author, he has no choice but to abide by the indication. The author's view alone is final and not the one held by the commentator. We are therefore compelled to decide in favour of Bādarāyana's indication and reject the first interpretation given to 1-1-3 by Śaṅkara.

Though we are perfectly justified in adopting this line of argument in determining the true import of the *sūtra* 1-1-3, we shall allow for the sake of argument that the word *yoni*, as explained by Śaṅkara, is intended to give also the sense of Brahman who is the source of the Vedas, and note the consequences.

THE BṚHADĀRAṆYAKA UPANIṢAD (2-4-10) AND ŚAṄKARA

Let us take a close look at the above text 2-4-10 as interpreted by Śaṅkara. He gives two interpretations to the text of which one is based on secondary sense and the other on primary sense. His followers have accepted both the interpretations unquestioningly.

(i) The original text speaks about the great Bhūta manifesting the Vedas like breath. According to Śaṅkara, the great Bhūta is the great Ātman. It is the highest cause and all Vedas appear out of it. In their secondary sense the Vedas are but names and the names suggest the names and forms by which the world is characterised. Hence the text is regarded as speaking about the appearance of the world of names and forms from the great Ātman. Names and forms are compared to breath because they come out without any effort from Ātman like breath.

(ii) In the next interpretation the Vedas are taken in their primary sense. In them there are different parts which fall into two broad categories, Mantras and Brāhmaṇas. With the two categories the Vedas come out like breath from the great Ātman. Śaṅkara points out that the word breath (*niḥśvasitam*) indicates that the Vedas belong to a special category. Unlike the compositions produced through human effort (*pauruṣeyam*), they are produced effortlessly, like breath, from the great Ātman. The text is therefore considered as revealing the greatness of the Vedas.

Thus the import of 2-4-10 is twofold. According to one, it is about the appearance of the world from the great Ātman. This evidently cannot be a *viṣayavākya* of the *sūtra* 1-1-3 which, as interpreted by Śaṅkara, says that Brahman (Ātman) is the source of the Vedas. According to the other import of 2-4-10, it is concerned with the idea that the Vedas are the effortless creations of the great Ātman. Even according to this import, the text cannot be a *viṣayavākya* of the *sūtra* 1-1-3. For the text and the *sūtra* deal with two different aims. We are told by Śaṅkara that while the aim of the former is to establish the greatness of the Vedas, the aim of the latter is to prove the greatness of Brahman who is both omniscient and omnipotent.[7] As they do not have the same import, it is not possible to relate one to the other. So from his own accounts of the text 2-4-10 and the *sūtra* 1-1-3 we are forced to conclude that Śaṅkara cannot consider the former as the *viṣayavākya* of the latter. In other words, the first interpretation given by him to the *sūtra* 1-1-3 is inadmissible.

THE GREATEST OF THE BHŪTAS

The Taittrīya Upaniṣad (2-1-1) speaks of five *bhūtas*: ether (*ākāśa*), air (*vāyu*), fire (*agni*), water (*āpaḥ*) and earth (*pṛthivī*). They are the elements from which all objects in the world arise. They are combined in different ways and from these combinations different objects come into existence.

If we start from *pṛthivī*, it exists in *āpaḥ*, for *āpaḥ* is its cause; *āpaḥ* exists in *agni*, for *agni* is its cause; *agni* exists in *vāyu*, for *vāyu* is its cause; finally *vāyu* exists in *ākāśa*, for *ākāśa* is its cause. According to this gradation, the greatest of the *bhūtas* is *ākāśa*. On account of this supreme position, it has come to be known by the name of Mahad Bhūta.

From the point of view of beings (*sarvāṇi bhūtāni*), *ākāśa* is their essence.[8] For all beings, mobile and immobile, arise from *ākāśa* and dissolve into the same *ākāśa*. It is not only their essence but also their abode. When the beings come out of *ākāśa*, they do not have independent existence but exist in the same *ākāśa*. In short, *ākāśa* is greater than all beings (*jyāyān*).[9]

When *vāyu* becomes active, it is extended in *ākāśa*, its mother element; hence its name *mātariśvan*.[10] Through the force of *vāyu*, the world which remains unmanifest in *ākāśa* passes into manifestation.

Another important feature of *ākāśa* is that *śabda* is its essence. Therefore all objects originally exist in *ākāśa* as *śabda*. When *śabda* is endued with *rūpa* through the force of *vāyu*, all objects come into existence and are in possession of gross forms. As every object is *śabda* in origin and *rūpa* in manifestation, it is called *nāma-rūpa*. It is significant to note that since all name comes out with its form from *ākāśa*, *ākāśa* is described as the accomplisher of name-and-form association (*nāmarūpayor-nirvahitā*).[11]

ĀTMAN AS THE EXAMPLE

We shall now examine the text 2-4-10 in the Bṛhadāraṇyaka in some detail and note what it says. First of all, the text occurs as an illustration of a teaching of Yājñavalkya embodied in 2-4-6. He has taught there that the world (*idam sarvam*) is Ātman (*ayam ātmā*). Second, the question how the world is Ātman is answered through several examples. Third, in 2-4-10 two examples are found, fire and *mahad bhūta*. Fourth, as smoke-forms come out from fire, so the Vedas, etc. come out from *mahad bhūta.* Fifth, we are made to understand that the world is Ātman in the same way as smoke-forms are fire, in the same way as the Vedas, etc. are *mahad bhūta.*

From the analogy of fire we may understand how the world is Ātman. Fire is a homogeneous entity, but smoke-forms that appear out of it are varied. In spite of their variety they are fire, because they are the expressions of fire. Like this, the world is a plurality of names and forms and appears out of Ātman; even though it is a plurality, it is still Ātman because it is the manifestation of Ātman. But from the analogy of *mahad bhūta* we are unable to draw parallel ideas about Ātman and the world's oneness with Ātman, because, unlike the analogy of fire, this analogy is not easy to comprehend. The expression *mahad bhūta* is capable of giving two different meanings — (i) the great Being or Ātman; (ii) the great Element. And its correct sense is a matter of interpretation. So we shall now determine what particular object is denoted by the analogy, Ātman or Bhūtākāśa.

Śaṅkara reads *mahad bhūta* as the great Ātman. There are two strong reasons for so reading it. First, the same Bṛhadāraṇyaka text 2-4 uses the expression *mahad bhūta* in another place (2-4-12) in the sense of the great Ātman; even if it is to be understood in the sense of *bhūtākāśa,* it is used everywhere as a synonym of Ātman. For example, the Chāndogya Upaniṣad (8-14-1) equates it with Ātman. Though Śaṅkara's reading is supported by strong evidences, there is another more valid reason why his reading should not be accepted.

In determining the precise sense of *mahad bhūta* we must be guided mainly by the context of the text 2-4-10. Other considerations, if they go against the context, cannot be decisive. As the context shows, the underlying purpose of the text is to serve as an illustration of a teaching about Ātman and the world's oneness with Ātman mentioned in the preceding text 2-4-6. The teaching, as we have already found, is illustrated through two examples, fire and *mahad bhūta*.

As an example, fire has two characteristics: (i) it is an object known to us in experience; (ii) it is a homogeneous entity similar to Ātman. From our experience we know that fire is a homogeneous entity and all smoke-forms that come out of it are still fire because they are its expressions. Analogically, we come to the following conclusions: Ātman is homogeneous consciousness; the world is a product of Ātman and, as a product, it is Ātman and not different from Ātman, because it is the manifestation of consciousness. This is how the fire analogy helps us to grasp the significance of the teaching that the world is Ātman. Without the analogy the teaching will be obscure.

Like fire, *mahad bhūta* is another example. As an example, this too must possess the two characteristics: (i) it must be something knowable through experience; (ii) it must be something homogeneous and similar to Ātman. If *mahad bhūta* has to have these characteristics, then it cannot be equated with Ātman, as Śaṅkara has equated it. If, on the contrary, *mahad bhūta* is so equated, it can neither be an object of experience nor something similar to Ātman. Further, this equation reduces reasoning through analogy itself to an absurdity, because Ātman is given as the analogy of Ātman. It follows from this that *mahad bhūta* is to be understood as referring to *ākāśa*, the highest of the five *bhūtas*. As *bhūtākāśa*, it is both an object of experience and a homogeneous substance similar to Ātman. As in the case of the fire example, *mahad bhūta* with its two characteristics is now quite illuminating. For it opens our eyes to the underlying significance of the original teaching that the world is Ātman.

From the context we find that 2-4-10 does not speak about Ātman but about *bhūtākāśa* as the source of the Vedas. This gives an important clue about the correct sense of 2-4-10. Now the clue has to be justified by reading the whole text 2-4-10 in its light. Once the justification is given, we may bring out its implications for 2-4-6 with the help of the analogy of *bhūtākāśa*.

THE MAHAD BHŪTA AS THE BHŪTĀKĀŚA

Let us use the above clue and try to understand the Bṛhadāraṇyaka text 2-4-10. We know that the above text is an illustration of the previous text 2-4-6. It illustrates through the examples of fire and *mahad bhūta*.

The view that *mahad bhūta* is an example like fire may be challenged. First, it may be said that 2-4-10 does not have two examples. For it begins with the example of fire and proceeds to draw a conclusion about *mahad bhūta* or Ātman. The word *evam* here is indicative of this conclusion. Second, *mahad bhūta* is to be equated with Ātman, because it is so equated in the subsequent mantra 2-4-12. But the challenge can be met in this way. First, the word *evam* also indicates likeness of something to something else mentioned previously, as in the mantra 2-4-11. It does not always indicate a conclusion drawn from a previous proposition. Second, in 2-4-10 the word *mahad bhūta* is not to be understood as Ātman. For if we go strictly by 2-4-10, as we have already observed, the word means something else and its correct sense has to be determined accordingly. Third, here the word *evam* gives merely the sense of likeness. Therefore *mahad bhūta* must be regarded as another example like *agni*.

Fire is one of the five *bhūtas*. Like fire, *mahad bhūta* is another but a fundamental *bhūta* in the same category. It refers to *bhūtākāśa*. As it is fundamental to all *bhūtas*, it is called *mahad bhūta*. It is given as an example for Ātman. The purpose is that Ātman is to be understood by working out the parallels between itself and *bhūtākāśa*, as in the case of the fire example.

The *bhūtākāśa* has two characteristics: first, it is a homogeneous entity possessing *śabda* as its essence; second, from this all words arise, for they are sound-formations (*śabdarūpas*). The sound-formations are of two kinds, *śrutis* and *smṛtis*. While the four Vedas and the Upaniṣads come under the category of *śrutis*, other forms of literature such as verses (*ślokas*), aphorisms (*sūtras*) etc. fall under the category of *smṛtis*. Though sound-formations are multifarious, they are essentially *bhūtākāśa*, for they are the expressions of *śabda*. Using these two characteristics as parallels to Ātman, we may say that Ātman is homogeneous consciousness (*cinmātra*) and from this the world appears as a mass of conscious forms (*vijñānaghana*).[12] We may further say that though the world is a mass of forms, it is essentially one with Ātman, for it is the manifestation of the original consciousness. Stated otherwise, we may say that the world is not to be regarded as having come from elsewhere than from Ātman and as having an essence of its own which is otherwise than that of Ātman (*anyatrātmanaḥ*).[13] This is what Yājñavalkya proposes to tell us through the analogy of *mahad bhūta*. This perfectly agrees with what he has already told us through the analogy of fire. (vide section 5 above).

There are now three questions incidental to our interpretation of 2-4-10. First, can we say that the Vedas arise from *bhūtākāśa*? For we have only heard that beings (*bhūtas*) arise from it and not the Vedas. Second, can we say that the word *niḥśvasitam* is used in the sense of effortless creation and indicates that the Vedas appear from *mahad bhūta* without any effort? Third, as the word in the above sense cannot be applied to the appearance of *smṛtis* which are produced through effort, can we conclude that it must be understood in some other sense?

As for the first question, we must note that the Ṛg Veda[14] has said that the supreme Vyoman (*ākāśa*) is the seat of the gods and the words of the Vedas. As regards the next question, Śaṅkara thinks that the word *niḥśvasitam* is used in the sense of effortless creation. As the word can be applied only to the Vedas and not to other works, he reinterprets *ślokas*, *sūtras*, etc. in such a way that they give up their original senses and denote different aspects of the Brāhmaṇas which explain the Mantras. According to this interpretation, 2-4-10 speaks only about the two portions of the Vedas — Mantras and Brāhmaṇas; and the application of the word *niḥśvasitam* to both of them is quite admissible. But, since Śaṅkara's interpretation mutilates the original text, it must be given up and the words *ślokas*, *sūtras*, etc. must be taken in their accepted senses. If we do so, then the word *niḥśvasitam* cannot be given the sense of effortless creation.

The original text (2-4-10) says that both *śrutis* and *smṛtis* appear from the same source through the force of breath. Here Yājñavalkya is concerned with making only one point, namely, the affirmation that *mahad bhūta* is the source of all compositions, *śrutis* as well as *smṛtis,* regardless of whether they are effortlessly produced or produced through effort. Hence our answer to the third question is that the word *niḥśvasitam* can only mean the appearance of *śrutis* and *smṛtis* through an *inherent force* of *mahad bhūta.* This is another way of saying that the words of *śruti* and *smṛti* appear from *bhūtākāśa* through the force of *vāyu.*

From the above discussion it is clear that the text 2-4-10 in the Bṛhadāraṇyaka Upaniṣad has been misunderstood by Śaṅkara. In section 2 we have proved from the context that the *sūtra* 1-1-3 is intended to give this sense alone — that *śāstra* is the source (*yoni*) from which Brahman is known. However, we have allowed the view of Śaṅkara, which says that Brahman is the source (*yoni*) of *śāstra*, and then proved that the *sūtra* 1-1-3 cannot be given this sense by relating it to the Bṛhadāraṇyaka text 2-4-10.

There is another more important point why the above text 2-4-10 or any other text which speaks of Brahman as the source of the Vedas, is not relevant to the *sūtra* 1-1-3. For the *sūtra* uses the word *yoni* not in the sense of a cause (*kāraṇa*) which produces an effect (*kārya*), but in the sense of a means of knowledge (*pramāṇa*). This is confirmed by the *sūtra* 1-1-4. In this sense *yoni* cannot refer to Brahman which is *prameya.* It actually refers to a means of knowledge (*pramāṇa*) from which Brahman is known (*prameya*). In other words, *śāstra yonitvāt* means *śāstra* which is *yoni* for knowing Brahman. No other meaning can be given to the above *sūtra.*

NOTES

1. Śaṅkara, *The Bṛhadāraṇyaka Upaniṣad Bhāṣya,*Tr. Swāmī Mādhavānanda, Advaita Ashram, 1965, p. 361.
2. Chāndogya Upaniṣad (hereafter Ch. Up.), 6-2-1.
3. Aitareya Upaniṣad, 1-1-1.
4. Bṛhadāraṇyaka Upaniṣad (hereafter Bṛ. Up.), 2-5-19.
5. Muṇḍaka Upaniṣad, 2-2-11.
6. *Brahmasūtra Bhāṣya of Śaṅkarācārya,* Tr. Swāmī Gambhīrānanda, Advaita Ashrama, 1972, pp. 21-22.
7. Ibid., 1-1-3.
8. Ch. Up., 1-9-1.

9. Ibid.
10. Īśa Upaniṣad, Mantra 4.
11. Ch. Up., 8-14-1.
12. Bṛ. Up., 2-4-12.
13. Ibid., 2-4-6.
14. Ṛg Veda, 1-164-39. Cf. Sri Aurobindo: "All Shabda (*vāk*)... manifests out of *ākāśa* by the force of *mātariśvan,* the great active and creative energy..." *Hymns to the Mystic Fire,* Sri Aurobindo Ashram, 1998, p.506.

29

Philosophy of the Upaniṣads: A Study by Sri Aurobindo

THE CENTENARY YEAR

Sri Aurobindo's birth centenary was celebrated in the year 1972. On this occasion all his writings were collected and brought out in 30 large volumes. It is a fitting tribute to a great seer and poet, an equally great scholar and writer who has expounded his unique philosophy of evolutionism and announced the advent of a new world-order. One of the volumes has the title *The Upanishads* (volume 12). The opening section in the above volume is on the subject *Philosophy of the Upanishads.*[1] It develops the philosophical content of the Upaniṣads as understood by Sri Aurobindo. There are six parts in it and the last one bearing the title *The Triple Brahman* is left incomplete by him. As the bibliographical note in that volume says, it was written by the author during the Baroda period.

THE TEXTS OF THE UPANIṢADS

The texts of the Upaniṣads are really very difficult to comprehend, mainly because they do not give us a systematic account of their teachings in terms intelligible to us. They all belong to a prehistoric age and their style is so peculiar that it must have been intelligible to the contemporaries of that age. Though the texts are obscure to us, they cannot be dismissed as a body of meaningless propositions or generalisations. For isolated words and phrases, verses and prose passages in them are replete with rare insights into life and profound thoughts about questions with which we are preoccupied and on which we are unable to throw sufficient light. This is the crux of the matter. We cannot set aside the Upaniṣads, because they contain words of wisdom, words that speak about the roots of human existence; nor can we use them as an effective means of unveiling all essential secrets of human life, because their general obscurity prevents us from doing so. In the circumstance Sri Aurobindo's study of the Upaniṣads is really helpful to us who are desirous of knowing whether it is possible to develop a cogent view of them.

SRI AUROBINDO'S STUDY

What does Sri Aurobindo's study say about the philosophy of the Upaniṣads? It says that Brahman is the highest reality and the creation of this world from Brahman is accomplished "by bringing into play the great fundamental principle of Māyā or Illusion."[2] By itself Māyā is an illusion. Therefore we "cannot say that it is."[3] Nor can we say "that it is not", for it is "the Mother of the Universe".[4] The universe created by Māyā is illusory, because it is nonexistent in Brahman who is beyond all causality.[5] It is therefore held that all phenomena are "distortions ... (*vikāras*) of the absolute consciousness" or Brahman.[6] Man realises his real nature when he recognises the world to be merely a *vikāra* of Brahman, makes a bold attempt to "escape from individuality"[7] and passes finally "into infinite existence"[8] or Brahman who is real. Sri Aurobindo has presented the philosophy of the Upaniṣads on the basis of two important Upaniṣads, Māṇḍūkya and Chāndogya. This is borne out by his references to two key terms — Prājña,[9] the Lord of Wisdom of the Māṇḍūkya Upaniṣad, and Vikāra,[10] the unreal product of the real earth of the Chāndogya Upaniṣad. In this respect Sri Aurobindo follows very closely the tradition established by Gauḍapāda and Śaṅkara, the two early Māyāvādins.

THE TWO UPANIṢADS

Gauḍapāda takes all consciousness and all unconsciousness to be Māyā. When the Māṇḍūkya defines the pure Ātman to be beyond consciousness and unconsciousness (*na prajñam na aprajñam*),[11] he thinks that the Ātman is taught to be beyond Māyā. The Upaniṣad says that Viśva and Taijasa are characterised by consciousness, the former by the consciousness of the external and the latter by the consciousness of the internal. This means that the two are under the influence of Māyā. Again the Upaniṣad says that Prājña is characterised by the massed or sleep consciousness. This also means that He is subject to the action of Māyā. In other words, the world associated with the triple Ātman is affirmed to be an illusory creation of Māyā. The topic of the triple Ātman is mentioned by Sri Aurobindo as that of the triple Brahman in his study (section 6). It seems that under this topic he wanted to show how the world was brought into existence in three successive stages by Māyā. But somehow he did not carry his discussion beyond the point of Prājña. And the topic came to an abrupt end. An important point to be borne in mind is Sri Aurobindo's words about the three states of Viśva, Taijasa and Prājña. He says that they are the "three states of dream"[12] i.e. the three states of illusion. This proves that he has completely accepted Gauḍapāda's interpretation of the triple Ātman and the pure Ātman.

The word *vikāraḥ* occurs in the Chāndogya Upaniṣad (6-1-4). It refers to the product of the original clay (*mṛttikā*). As *vikāraḥ* is qualified by *nāmadheyam vācārambhaṇam,* Śaṅkara thinks that it refers to a distortion or an unreal product of the original clay[13] (*vikārabhūtonāmadheyoanṛtātmakaḥ*).[14] From this he concludes that the world, which is a product of Brahman, is an unreal creation of Māyā. When Sri Aurobindo uses the word *vikāraḥ* in the sense of distortion, the sense he has given to it is certainly due to the influence of Śaṅkara.

THE POSITIVE AND SYNTHETIC TEACHING

A reader quite familiar with the main works of Sri Aurobindo, especially *Isha* and *Kena*, *Essays on the Gita* and *The Life Divine,* will swear that they do not uphold the theory of Māyā (the theory of cosmic Illusion) in any form. Rather they subscribe to the view that the world is a real evolution from Brahman. In *The Life Divine* there are two fairly long chapters and they both examine the position of Māyāvāda. Their verdict is that the theory is inconclusive and unsatisfactory. In one place in the above work Sri Aurobindo has made a significant remark about the Upaniṣads. He says that their teaching is both "positive and synthetic".[15] It is positive, because it does not dismiss the world as illusory; it is synthetic, because it upholds a theory of real monism according to which Brahman and the world are not opposites, a reality as opposed to an unreality, but two truths of the same Reality.

THE MĀṆḌŪKYA AND CHĀNDOGYA

Sri Aurobindo has established in *The Life Divine* that the theory of Māyā cannot be traced to the Māṇḍūkya and Chāndogya Upaniṣads, as is maintained by the Māyāvādins. According to Gauḍapāda, the Māṇḍūkya Upaniṣad is a text that favours the theory of Māyā. His Kārikās try to prove the claim through many powerful arguments. In the face of these arguments Sri Aurobindo calls attention to certain key expressions and passages in the Upaniṣad and puts them in the right perspective.

The definition of Ātman as fourfold (*ātmā catuṣpāt*) is significant. Its aim is clearly to emphasise that all four forms of Ātman are to be taken collectively and harmoniously and that it is a violence to set one against the others as if the four are separated by a dichotomous division. If we fail to take cognisance of the underlying note, we are sure to miss the intended teaching of the Upaniṣad. Sri Aurobindo seems to stand as a solitary Vedāntin who has not only recovered this important note but also placed in this way the whole Upaniṣad in its original perspective. We now understand why the definition *ātmā catuṣpāt* occurs in the very beginning of the text and not elsewhere.

There are four forms: Viśva, Taijasa, Prājña and Caturtha. The first is characterised by external or waking consciousness (*bahiṣprajñaḥ*), the second by internal or dream consciousness (*antaḥprajñaḥ*), the third by sleep or massed consciousness (*prajñānaghanaḥ*), and the fourth by superconsciousness beyond both consciousness and unconsciousness (*na prajñam na aprajñam*).[16] The four are the four real forms of the one Ātman, the Reality. When Sri Aurobindo says that "all that is is the Self seen by the Self in four states of its being",[17] the formula *ātmā catuṣpāt* becomes intelligible to us.

If this interpretation is granted, two important consequences follow. First of all, the negation implied in the words *na prajñam na aprajñam* is not an absolute negation of the three forms of Viśva, Taijasa and Prājña. They do not dismiss the three forms as the delusions of Māyā and declare the superconscient Ātman to be a state void of all forms or of Māyā which is the source of forms. On the contrary, their negation is limited, it denies merely one aspect of the three forms. They deny that their *status* is "the true status of the superconscient Reality."[18] In this sense the forms never become illusions; on the contrary, they become in their status less real than the superconscient Ātman. Secondly, there is no need for this Ātman to be devoid of the nature of the cosmos or of the power which creates the cosmos. On the other hand, it assumes the nature of the cosmos and becomes the possessor of a real Māyā which creates a real cosmos. This is the reason why the Māyā implied in the text of the Māṇḍūkya is declared to be "real"[19] by Sri Aurobindo.

There are two means by which the outer mind reaches the supreme superconscience which is the highest state of Ātman. Both the means depend on the higher states of the subliminal and the superconscient behind and beyond our waking being. The first means to get into the higher states is a trance-consciousness which appears to be a kind of sleep or dream to the outer mind. Having attained the higher states, it rises from them to the highest state. The second means to get into the higher states is not the trance-consciousness but "a spiritual awakening"[20] of the outer mind. The first means is either a dream-trance or a sleep-trance. Through the dream-trance the mind enters the subliminal. Hence the subliminal is called the Dream Self. Through the sleep-trance it reaches the superconscient. Hence the superconsicient is named the Sleep Self. When the mind uses the dream-trance or the sleep-trance, it is seized "by a sense of the unreality of the cosmic Force and its creations".[21] The second means, as we have already said, is the spiritually awakened outer mind. Under this condition it is wakeful not only to the world but also to the supreme superconsicient Ātman everywhere,[22] in the world and beyond the world. The declaration *ātmā catuṣpāt* seems to have been made from this point of view. Here there is no place for the sense of the unreality of the world. For all is the real Ātman. Therefore this "leaves no room for an illusory Māyā"[23] in the text of the Upaniṣad. This is Sri Aurobindo's conclusion.

The Chāndogya says that a name is created by the language (*nāmadheyam vācārambhaṇam*) i.e. a word is created by a system of words. It was created by the system because it was implicit in that system. As the two belong to the same kind, namely, word (*vāk*), the language is the right means of knowing the name. This is the relation between the two, the name and the language. Keeping this point in view, the Upaniṣad asserts *vikāro nāmadheyam vācārambhaṇam*. From this parallelism between *vikāraḥ* and *nāmadheyam vācārambhaṇam* it is easy to know how *vikāraḥ* is related to *mṛttikā*. The *vikāraḥ* is a modification of the *mṛttikā* because it was implicit in that *mṛttikā*. As they belong to the same kind, namely, earth (*mṛd*), the *mṛttikā* is the right means (*satyam*) of knowing the *vikāraḥ*. This is to know all made of clay (*sarvammṛnmayam*) by means of knowing a clod of clay (*ekena mṛtpiṇḍena*). The original theory of Vedānta says that all effect is a modification of the cause in which it was implicit, and both the effect and the cause belong to the same category of reality (*sat*). This theory is known as *pariṇāmavāda*.

Śaṅkara's reading of *nāmadheyam vācārambhaṇam* as *nāmadheyoanṛtātmakaḥ* (the name is of the nature of unreality) gives *vikāraḥ* the sense of unreality (*na vastvasti*).[24] It amounts to making *vikāraḥ* not a modification of the cause but a projection of an unreality by Māyā. This is against the original theory of Vedānta which says that the effect is *real* like the cause. As a true Vedāntin, Sri Aurobindo has abandoned the above reading of *vācārambhaṇaśruti* and explained it in accordance with the original theory of transformation (*pariṇāmavāda*).

Let us take the substance of earth (*mṛttikā*) and the pot (*vikāraḥ*) and note how the two are related by Sri Aurobindo. The relation between the two is not that of a reality and an unreality, but of an original and non-manifest to a resultant and manifested reality.[25] The substance of earth is an original reality, because it is the original non-manifest condition of the pot; the pot is a resultant reality, because it is a result determined by the manifested condition of the substance. A passage from reality to reality is more rational, harmonious and intelligible than from reality to unreality. Hence Sri Aurobindo asks us to view both the original earth and the pot to be two realities of two connected levels. In this view the pot is surely a reality, because it is "made out of the substance of earth which is real".[26] Sri Aurobindo's elucidation of the example of earth is obviously a restatement of the Vedāntic theory of transformation. As to this view there cannot be any doubt.

THE TWO THEORIES OF EVOLUTIONISM AND ILLUSIONISM

We may speak of two theories of creation, evolutionism (*pariṇāma-vāda*) and illusionism (*māyāvāda*). The first says that the effect evolves through a transformation of the original cause, whereas the second holds that the effect is an illusory appearance of the real cause. In *Philosophy of the Upanishads* Sri Aurobindo's position is that of an illusionist who says that the Upaniṣads deal with the illusory appearance of the world from Brahman. In *The Life Divine* his position on the Upaniṣads is that of an evolutionist who says that they teach of the world coming into existence through an evolutionary transformation of Brahman.

A comparative study of his position on the Upaniṣads, as corroborated by *Philosophy of the Upanishads* on the one hand and *The Life Divine* on the other, shows very clearly that he is both an illusionist and an evolutionist. As the two texts belong to two different dates — the first is of an earlier date and the second is of a later date, it is easily established that he was originally an illusionist and that he gave up this earlier position and assumed another position as an evolutionist. Whatever is the merit of this conclusion reached on the basis of the comparison between the two texts, it is a conjecture that needs to be corroborated by appropriate evidences from Sri Aurobindo's life.

THE TWO EXPERIENCES

Sri Aurobindo had a wonderful inner life and witnessed a series of inner changes that took him to unimaginable heights of spiritual wisdom. His first spiritual experience occurred when he was in Baroda in the year 1908.

There was a yogin by name Vishnu Bhaskara Lele who was a native of Maharashtra and who was known to Sri Aurobindo's brother Barindra. Not much was known about him except that he was a yogin and had some spiritual powers. He was a Bhakta and not favourable to Advaita Vedānta. In January 1908 Sri Aurobindo was in Baroda in the house of a Baroda Sardar by name Mazumdar who was well known to him. On being told about Lele by Barindra Sri Aurobindo consented to meet the yogin and take guidance from him. This was the circumstance under which he had his first major self-experience.

Sri Aurobindo has narrated how his meeting with Lele has led to "a decisive experience of liberation and Nirvana."[27] His narration runs as follows.

> ... I was induced to meet a man without fame whom I did not know, a Bhakta with a limited mind but with some experience and evocative power. We sat together and I followed with an absolute fidelity what he instructed me to do, not myself in the least understanding where he was leading me or where I was myself going. The first result was a series of tremendously powerful experiences and radical changes of consciousness which he had never intended — for they were Adwaitic and Vedantic and he was against Adwaita Vedanta — and which were quite contrary to my own ideas, for they made me see with a stupendous intensity the world as a cinematograpic play of vacant forms in the impersonal universality of the Absolute Brahman.[28]

Now and then Sri Aurobindo returns to this important event and gives his observations on his experience. One such observation is given in the third person. It is this:

> After three years of spiritual effort with only minor results he was shown by a Yogi the way to silence his mind. This he succeeded in doing entirely in two or three days by following the method shown. There was an entire silence of thought and feeling and all the ordinary movements of consciousness except the perception and recognition of things around without any accompanying concept or other reaction. The sense of ego disappeared and ... the perception which remained saw all things as utterly unreal; this sense of unreality was overwhelming and universal.[29]

Another observation of Sri Aurobindo goes thus:

> It threw me suddenly into a condition above and without thought, unstained by any mental or vital movement; there

> was no ego, no real world — only when one looked through the immobile senses, something perceived or bore upon its sheer silence a world of empty forms, materialised shadows without true substance. There was ... just absolutely That, featureless, relationless, sheer, indescribable, unthinkable, absolute, yet supremely real and solely real.[30]

A glance at these extracts tells us three important things about Sri Aurobindo's experience. First of all, his experience conforms to that of an individual who is known by the title of "a knower of Brahman" (*brahmavid*); second, it is of the absolute and featureless Brahman; and third, as Brahman is the sole reality, the world is seen by him as a play of empty forms, forms without true substance. From these it is clear that Sri Aurobindo has reached the status of a typical Māyāvadin who lives by the formula: Brahman is real and the world is an illusion (*brahma satyam jaganmithyā*). (This is the essence of Advaita.)

As we have already noted, this event happened somewhere in January 1908. In May of the same year Sri Aurobindo was arrested and taken to Alipore Jail in connection with a bomb case thrust upon him by the Police Department. This was known as the Alipore Bomb Case. He remained there for a year till he was acquitted in May 1909 by the Sessions Court at Alipore. When he went to the jail, he had two books with him, the Gītā and the Upaniṣads. He spent almost all his time in reading and meditation. Immediately after his release from the jail Sri Aurobindo delivered a speech in *Uttarpara*, West Bengal, in the last week of May 1909. It is a beautiful statement where he describes how in the jail God revealed his presence in all men and things and prepared him for His work. This is his vivid description.

> It seemed to me that He spoke to me ... and said, "The bonds you had not strength to break, I have broken for you, because ... I have another thing for you to do and it is for that I have brought you here, to teach you what you could not learn for yourself and to train you for my work." ... His strength ... entered into me. I looked at the jail that secluded me from men and it was no longer by its high walls that I was imprisoned; no, it was Vasudeva who surrounded me. I walked under the branches of the tree in front of my cell,

> but it was not the tree, I knew it was Vasudeva, it was Sri Krishna whom I saw standing there and holding over me His shade. I looked at the bars of my cell, the very grating that did duty for a door and again I saw Vasudeva. It was Narayana who was guarding and standing sentry over me. Or I lay on the coarse blankets that were given me for a couch and felt the arms of Sri Krishna around me, the arms of my Friend and Lover. ... I looked at the prisoners in the jail, the thieves, the murderers, the swindlers, and as I looked at them. I saw Vasudeva, it was Narayana whom I found in these darkened souls and misused bodies. ...
>
> When the case opened in the lower court and we were brought before the Magistrate I was followed by the same insight. ... I looked and it was not the Magistrate whom I saw, it was Vasudeva, it was Narayana who was sitting there on the bench. I looked at the Prosecuting Counsel and it was not the Counsel for the prosecution that I saw; it was Sri Krishna who sat there, it was my Lover and Friend who sat there and smiled. "Now do you fear?" He said, "I am in all men and I overrule their actions and their words. ... The case itself is only a means for my work and nothing more".[31]

An examination of these words tells us an important thing. In Baroda the reality of Brahman beyond the world was revealed to Sri Aurobindo. In this experience the world was found by him to be empty i.e. without reality. But in the second the world was seen by him to be not empty but occupied by Brahman himself.

From the subsequent developments that occurred in Pondicherry it is clear that Sri Aurobindo's second experience is to grow into a more and more complex and comprehensive phenomenon and receive a complete statement in *The Life Divine*. As a result, he is to understand the whole significance of the immanent Brahman in the world. Rather he is to see clearly the kind of work to which he is appointed by God: he is to call upon the highest transcendent Brahman (*parātparam*)[32] to descend into the world and unfold here all the hidden powers of the immanent Brahman (*antaryāmin*).

The relevant point to be noted here is that though in the beginning Sri Aurobindo saw the world to be illusory, the world became real when he saw afterwards that Brahman has entered into that world as its Inhabitant or when he realised that the world is not only an evolution from Brahman but also a suitable place for habitation and further evolution by Brahman. Thus Sri Aurobindo was an illusionist in the beginning and became an evolutionist when the previous circumstances changed. This is what the evidences say of him.

That Sri Aurobindo is not an illusionist now is confirmed by his own words. When he speaks about himself in a letter written from Pondicherry, he says, "I am not a Mayavadin."[33] He seems to clarify his position thus: "There were reasons for considering me to be a Mayavadin in the beginning of my life, but those reasons, however overwhelming and valid they were, do not exist now. Therefore I assert that I am not a Mayavadin." His original words do tell us about his real position as a Vedāntist.

CONCLUSION

Philosophy of the Upanishads does not tell us about Sri Aurobindo's real position on the subject. It deals with a subject which he has abandoned long ago — the philosophy of Illusionism or Māyāvāda as developed from the Upaniṣads, particularly from the Chāndogya and Māṇḍūkya. This is evident from his work *The Life Divine.* It is also evident from the same work that he has developed a completely opposite view of Illusionism from the Upaniṣads. His real view on them is that they teach not only of the evolution of the world from the highest Brahman but also of the evolution of the immanent Brahman in the world.[34]

NOTES

1. Sri Aurobindo, *The Upanishads* (1972) (hereafter TU), p.1.
2. Ibid., p.23.
3. Ibid., p.26.
4. Ibid.
5. Ibid., p.25.
6. Ibid., p.17.

7. Ibid., p.44.
8. Ibid.
9. Ibid., p.49.
10. Ibid., p.17.
11. Māṇḍūkya Upaniṣad, Mantra 7.
12. TU, p.47.
13. Śaṅkara, *Chāndogya Upaniṣad Bhāṣya*, 6-1-4.
14. Śaṅkara, *Muṇḍaka Upaniṣad Bhāṣya*, 2-1-3.
15. Sri Aurobindo, *The Life Divine* (2001) (hereafter LD), p.41.
16. Māṇḍūkya Upaniṣad, Mantra 7.
17. LD, p.468.
18. LD, p.469.
19. Ibid.
20. LD, p.471.
21. Ibid.
22. Ibid.
23. LD, p.470.
24. Śaṅkara, *Chāndogya Upaniṣad Bhāṣya*, 6-1-4.
25. LD, p.475.
26. Ibid.
27. Sri Aurobindo, *On Himself* (1972) (hereafter OH), p.353.
28. OH, p.79.
29. OH, pp.85-86.
30. OH, p.101.
31. Sri Aurobindo, *Uttarpara Speech* (2006), pp.4 to 7.
32. Muṇḍaka Upaniṣad, 3-2-8.
33. OH, p.373.
34. Generally, there are two classes of readers, common men, who are not conversant with the main works of Sri Aurobindo but who want from him a general introduction to the Upaniṣads, and students, who are in the course of learning the history of Indian Philosophy and who are desirous of reading a concise book on the Upaniṣads. On seeing the title of the work under discussion they are attracted by it and plunge themselves into the work in an effort to master the subject as correctly as possible. Eventually, what they get from it is the philosophy of the Illusionism of the Upaniṣads. They do not know that Sri Aurobindo upheld this view for a while and gave it up afterwards. They are to be told that this is not his real view.

    They must be made to understand that *Philosophy of the Upanishads* is an early study of some of the Upaniṣads where Sri Aurobindo discusses the nature of the illusory Māyā in two separate sections (4 and 5) and tells us that the world is of the nature of dream or illusion.

He wrote it when he was an illusionist for a little while. His own real position on the Upaniṣads can be gathered from his major works *Isha* (1924) and *Kena* (1970), *Essays on the Gita* (1949) and *The Life Divine* (1943). In this connection *The Foundations of Indian Culture* (1959), another work by Sri Aurobindo, is also useful, but it does not give a sufficient introduction to the Upaniṣads. For its own subject is much wider than their metaphysics. A study of the Upaniṣads from the standpoint of Sri Aurobindo is a desideratum.

30

An Answer to the Critics

I was a Senior Fellow of *Indian Council of Philosophical Research*, New Delhi for three years from 2000. At the end of the second year I submitted my report on the study of the Upaniṣads and requested the Council to extend the fellowship for one more year. So the Council appointed two scholars to review my work and make suitable recommendations. They recommended that the fellowship be extended from 2001 to 2002. However, they had raised formidable objections to my thesis on the Upaniṣads.

Two of the objections are very important. (i) The textual meaning of the Upaniṣads is relative to the interpreter, for he cannot study them "with a mind which is tabula raza". As the text has no independent teaching except what the interpreter puts into it, the scholar's search for the textual meaning of the Upaniṣads is bound to end as a projection of his own mind into the text under study. (ii) The scholar's research is "coloured by anti-advaitin bias," for he is "out to vanquish his advaitin adversary". He rejects the advaitin's interpretation to be wrong because the latter has read into the text his own ideas. This means that the text is to be discriminated from the ideas projected by the advaitin. How does the scholar discriminate the text from the ideas of the advaitin? He accomplishes the task by giving his own interpretation to the text. He thus commits the same mistake for which the advaitin is held responsible. From this it is clear that the scholar's attempt is wrong. In spite of the objections the study is still relevant and views the original text to be more important than the commentary. For the text is a valuable source of knowledge.

(i) To argue that the textual meaning of the Upaniṣads is relative to and not independent of the interpreter, is to reduce the original text to a collection of mere words and declare that it has no message of its own. This amounts to abandoning all conventions of words and making the very presence of the text an incomprehensible creation. If we grant for the sake of argument that such a text could exist, we cannot explain why they are repeatedly studied and interpreted by scholars. If what they discover from the text is their own mind projected into it, their labour is wasted and they get nothing from the study. This is subjectivism culminating from pessimism. They are undesirable consequences and both of them are to be avoided by a constructive use of mind.

It is true that the text cannot be studied with a mind which is tabula raza. It can be studied only when the mind has a perspective. But it is absolutely necessary that the perspective should not be derived from an external source. What is needed is therefore a perspective based on the key words, phrases, and passages of the original text. The evidences provided by them must be indisputable and make the perspective truly founded on the text. On the other hand, if the perspective is preconceived and not derived from the original text, then the resulting interpretation will be biased.

A good interpretation has three important features: (a) all original ideas of the text attain to a highest degree of harmony; (b) all its original words, phrases, and passages are understood in their natural or primary sense; and (c) the original source of the method of explication is the text itself. Such an interpretation is considered to be most authentic and not touched by the projections of the interpreter. It supposes that the original text has a message intended to be conveyed through its words.

(ii) The allegation is that the interpretations put on the original texts of the Upaniṣads by advaitins are rejected. They are rejected not because they are given by *advaitins* but because they go against the authority of the Upaniṣads. No commentator is greater than that authority. He must uphold and not deny it under any circumstance.

Let us take an example. There is a text in the Bṛhadāraṇyaka Upaniṣad which speaks about the illusory nature of duality (*yatra dvaitam iva bhavati tad itara itaram jighrati etc.*).[1] Here the text deals with the duality of sense and object. The two are divided from each other. The sense regards itself as other (*itaraḥ*) and the object is regarded by it as other (*itaram*). When all become modifications of Ātman (*sarvam ātmaivābhūt*),[2] the two give up their duality which is illusory and become two forms of Ātman, Ātman who senses and Ātman who is sensed. In other words, Ātman (object) is sensed by Ātman (sense). This change into the forms of Ātman by the sense and the object is the whole basis of all questions raised by the Upaniṣad — what and by what (*tat kena kaṃ*). Can Ātman beyond his modifications be sensed by our senses? It is impossible, because the original Ātman cannot be measured by his modifications; he is greater than all his modifications. This is conveyed by the words — the knower cannot be known (*vijñātāram kena vijānīyāt*).[3]

However, from the words *sarvam ātmaivābhūt* advaitins point out that the senses and the objects have gone out of existence and there is nothing but Ātman (*na tu paramārthata ātmavyatirekeṇāsti kiñcit*).[4] This contradicts the concluding words of the Upaniṣad which speak of the existence of both Ātman (*taṃ*) and other things such as the senses and the objects (*idaṃ sarvaṃ*). Hence the interpretation given by the advaitins is rejected. Their right to interpret the text is not denied; what is denied is the right to contradict by anyone the authority of the Upaniṣads which is superior to all commentators.

Another example may be cited. The Muṇḍaka Upaniṣad (1-1-5) makes a distinction between lower knowledge (*aparā vidyā*) and higher knowledge (*parā vidyā*). The lower is about the Vedas and the Vedāṅgas, whereas the higher is about the attainment of the Imperishable (*tadakṣaram*).[5] There are two important questions to be answered — (1) What do the Vedas and Vedāṅgas teach and why is the teaching called lower? (2) Why is the attainment of the Imperishable called higher and what is the means of the attainment? The distinction made by the Upaniṣad will not be intelligible if the two questions are not rightly answered.

In answer to the two questions Śaṅkara says thus — (1) The Vedas teach merely the words of the Mantras for they are an assemblage of words (*śabdarāśiḥ*);[6] they are called lower because they do not produce the higher knowledge of the Imperishable; (2) the attainment of the Imperishable is called higher because the Imperishable is known by a higher means. And the Upaniṣads are the higher means of knowing the Imperishable.

If we carefully study the answers, we find that the original text is contradicted at many points. First, the Muṇḍaka Upaniṣad does not think that the Vedas are an assemblage of words. For now and then the Upaniṣads themselves quote the authority of the Vedas in support of their teachings (*tad etad ṛcā abhyuktam*)[7]. Secondly, as this proves that there is no basic difference between the Vedas and the Upaniṣads, the distinction made between lower *vidyā* and higher *vidyā* disappears. This compels the original text to speak about an illogical distinction. Thirdly, though the connection of the Vedas with the Vedāṅgas is viewed to be important by the text, it is completely ignored by the commentator. In view of these inherent defects we are forced to reject Śaṅkara's interpretation. The real point at issue is that he is not faithful to the sense of the original text viz. the Muṇḍaka Upaniṣad.

A third example may be given. It is from the chapter on *The Śāstra and the Brahmasūtra*. Śaṅkara has given two interpretations to *sūtra* 1-1-3. The first interpretation given by him is rejected. Because it goes against the *sūtra* 1-1-4 where the author of the *sūtras*, Bādarāyaṇa, has clearly asserted that *śāstra* is the source from which Brahman is known. The business of a commentator is to explain only what is stated by the author and not express his personal views about the *sūtra* under discussion. From this it is clear that Śaṅkara's first interpretation is set aside not because it is given by an advaitin but because he is not free to give that interpretation. As a commentator, he is bound by the views of Bādarāyaṇa. Though the present example is from a *smṛti* text, Śaṅkara's mistake is the same as in the previous examples — disregard of the authority of the original text.

There is a fourth example. In Chapter 19 the theory of superimposition is rejected not because it is offered by the advaitin but because the conscious assumption of the status of Brahman by That (*aham brahmāsmi*)[8] is misinterpreted as the cessation of superimposition of ignorance on Brahman (*adhyāropaṇanivṛttiḥ*)[9].

The charge that the advaitin is considered to be an adversary is absolutely baseless and inadmissible. Śaṅkara is the first and foremost commentator of the Upaniṣads. So we have to repeatedly refer to his works. And the reference is inevitable.

NOTES

1. Bṛhadāraṇyaka Upaniṣad (hereafter Bṛ. Up.), 2-4-14.
2. Ibid.
3. Ibid.
4. Śaṅkara, *Bṛhadāraṇyaka Upaniṣad Bhāṣya* (hereafter Bṛ. Up. B.), 2-4-14.
5. Muṇḍaka Upaniṣad (hereafter M. Up.), 1-1-5.
6. Śaṅkara, *Muṇḍaka Upaniṣad Bhāṣya*, 1-1-5.
7. M. Up., 3-2-10.
8. Bṛ. Up., 1-4-10.
9. Bṛ. Up. B., 1-4-10.

Appendix

N. Jayashanmugam

Having distinguished himself as a bright student of Philosophy in the graduate and the post-graduate courses of study, he stood first in the B.A. and M.A. Examinations conducted by Annamalai University. He was a recipient of UGC PG scholarship for two years (1958-1960). He received his Degree of Doctorate in Philosophy from the same University for his thesis on Sri Aurobindo. He taught Philosophy at Annamalai University and later at Sri Aurobindo International Centre of Education, Pondicherry.

Influenced by the writings of Sri Aurobindo, he began in the year 1990 a close study of the original texts of the Upaniṣads. In 2000 *Indian Council of Philosophical Research,* New Delhi, awarded him a Senior Fellowship to complete the study under the project title *Upaniṣads*: *A Study in Their Own Light.*

He has participated in several National Seminars held in Pondicherry, Chennai, and New Delhi. He has also delivered Endowment Lectures at the invitation of the Pondicherry and Madras Universities. His fields of study are: (i) Sri Aurobindo; and (ii) the Upaniṣads.

He is self-appointed to an important task and the task is to unfold the unique teachings of the Upaniṣads. He has developed his own method of study and placed the original texts in an entirely new perspective. email : njayashanmugam@gmail.com

Bibliography

Adidevananda, Swami, *Brahma-Sūtras* (*Śrī Bhāṣya*) (Part II) (Part I by Swami Vireswarananda), Calcutta, Advaita Ashrama, 1998.

Bhattacharya, Vidhusekhara, *The Āgamaśāstra of Gauḍapāda*, New Delhi, Motilal Banasidass, 1989.

Brahmananda, Swami, *The Supreme Knowledge Revealed Through Vidyās in the Upaniṣads*, Himalayas, The Divine Life Society, 1990.

Comans, Michael, *Extracting the Essence of the Śruti*, New Delhi, Motilal Banarsidass, 1996.

Deussen, Paul, *The Philosophy of the Upaniṣads*, Tr. A. S. Geden, New Delhi, Motilal Banarsidass, 1999.

Gajendragadkar, P. B., *The Ten Classical Upaniṣads*, Vol. I, Bombay, Bharatiya Vidya Bhavan, 1981.

Gambhirananda, Swami, *Eight Upaniṣads*, 2 vols., Calcutta, Advaita Ashrama. 1988.

——, *Śvetāśvatara Upaniṣad*, Calcutta, Advaita Ashrama, 1995.

——, *Brahma- Sūtra-Bhāṣya of Śaṅkarācārya*, Calcutta, Advaita Ashrama, 1972.

Hume, R. E., *The Thirteen Principal Upaniṣads*, London, Oxford University Press, 1958.

Kapali Sastry, T. V., *Lights on the Upaniṣads*, Pondicherry, Sri Aurobindo Ashram, 1947.

Krisna Warrier, A. G., *Śrīmad Bhagavad Gītā Bhāṣya of Śrī Śaṅkarācārya*, Madras, Sri Ramakrishna Math, 1983.

Madhavananda, Swami, *The Bṛhadāraṇyaka Upaniṣad with the Commentary of Śaṅkarācārya*, Calcutta, Advaita Ashrama. 1965.

Mahadevan, T. M. P., *Gauḍapāda — A Study in Early Advaita*, Madras, University of Madras, 1952.

——, *The Pañcadaśī of Bhārtitīrtha Vidyāraṇya*, Madras, University of Madras, 1969.

Nikhilananda, Swami, *The Upaniṣads*, 4 vols., London, Phoenix House, 1951.

Radhakrishnan, S., *The Principal Upaniṣads*, London, George Allen and Unwin, 1958.

Raghavachar, S. S., *Śrī Rāmānuja on the Gītā*, Mangalore, Sri Ramakrishna Ashrama, 1969.

——, *Vedārtha-Saṅgaraha of Śrī Rāmānujācārya*, Mangalore, Sri Ramakrishna Ashrama, 1968.

——, *Śrī Rāmānuja on the Upaniṣads*, Madras, Rangacharya Memorial Trust, 1972.

Satchidanandendra Saraswati, Swami, *How to Recognize the Method of Vedanta*, Holenarsipur, Adhyatma Prakasha Karyalaya, 1995.

Satya Prakash Singh, *The Philosophy of Dīrghatamas*, New Delhi, Shree Publishing House, 1990.

Sen Gupta, Anima, *Kaṭha Upaniṣad*: Samkhya Point of View, 1967.

Sethna, K. D., *Māṇḍūkya Upaniṣad*, The Integral Life Foundation, USA, 1995.

Sri Aurobindo, *The Life Divine*, Pondicherry, Sri Aurobindo Ashram, 2001.

——, *Essays on the Gita*, Pondicherry, Sri Aurobindo Ashram, 1970.

——, *Hymns to the Mystic Fire*, Pondicherry, Sri Aurobindo Ashram, 1988.

——, *The Secret of the Veda*, Pondicherry, Sri Aurobindo Ashram, 1971.

——, *Isha*, Pondicherry, Sri Aurobindo Ashram, 1924.

——, *Kena*, Pondicherry, Sri Aurobindo Ashram, 1970.

——, *The Upaniṣads*, Pondicherry, Sri Aurobindo Ashram, 1972.

Srinivasa Chari, S. M., *The Philsophy of the Vedāntasūtra*, New Delhi, Munshiram Manoharlal, 1998.

——, *The Philosophy of the Upaniṣads*, New Delhi, Munshiram Manoharlal, 2002.

Swahananda, Swami, *Pañcadaśī*, Madras, Sri Ramakrishna Math, 1967.

——, *Chāndogya Upaniṣad*, Madras, Sri Ramakrishna Math, 1956.

SANSKRIT TEXT

Īśādidaśopaniṣadaḥ (Ten Principal Upaniṣads with Śāṅkarabhāṣya), New Delhi, Motilal Banarsidass, 2000.

Index

Āditya 222, 223

Ascetics 10, 11, 16-22, 26-29, 31, 91, 92, 98, 103-105, 118, 119, 121, 122, 124, 125, 140

Aśvins 258, 259, 261- 263, 269- 271, 281- 283

Ātman 60, 70, 78, 98, 108-113, 133, 134, 140, 141, 143-146, 153-157, 159-162, 164-170, 172-176, 178, 181-196, 199, 205-207, 213, 214, 218, 241, 242, 245-252, 254-259, 264-269, 271, 272 274-278, 280, 281, 283-289, 294, 295, 298, 300, 302-310, 314, 315, 317, 318, 322, 325, 326-332, 337-346, 348-353, 359-367, 404, 405

Bādarāyaṇa 380, 381, 406

Brahman 6-11, 13, 14, 19-22, 25, 27-29, 31-36, 42, 45-47, 49, 55, 61, 82-87, 89-105, 116, 117, 122, 123, 127, 132-135, 138, 140-145, 151, 155-161, 180, 182, 196-199, 202, 204-207, 216, 218, 228-232, 234-239, 244, 246, 250, 259, 288, 295, 296, 314, 318, 319-324, 332, 337, 338, 340, 341, 352, 353, 380-383, 388-393, 396-400, 406

Bṛhadāraṇyaka Upaniṣad 7, 8, 195, 196, 228, 234, 239, 241, 242, 244, 245, 247, 254, 270, 273, 274, 287, 289, 294, 305, 307, 308, 312, 341, 346, 348, 352, 355, 361-363, 365, 367, 380-382, 384, 386, 388

Chāndogya Upaniṣad 7, 196, 202, 206, 224-226, 245, 248, 254, 296, 316, 341, 342, 353

Dadhyaṅ 258, 259, 261-263, 269-271, 278, 280-283, 286

Death 6, 12, 14, 16, 21, 27, 28, 32-34, 37, 41, 45, 47-51, 54, 55, 58, 71, 72, 74, 75, 78, 80, 241-246, 248-252, 341-343, 350

Desire 151, 153, 156, 157, 305, 307-309, 320, 322, 323, 325-328, 330, 348-350, 353, 363-365

Dīrghatamas 137, 139, 141, 144, 156, 157

Enjoyment 39, 40, 42, 49, 50, 53-54, 110, 304, 307, 366

Fulfilment 89, 93, 94, 98-102, 104, 119, 157-160, 254, 263, 270, 271, 273, 279-283, 286, 287, 289, 350-352, 355, 359

Gauḍapāda 164-166, 169, 170, 172-174, 176-178, 181-184, 186, 187, 191

Gītā 14, 15, 22, 370-372, 374-377

God 1-4, 9, 15-21, 26-28, 36-38, 50, 53, 54, 57-65, 84, 85, 87, 89, 90, 99, 101, 363, 364, 366

Gods 92, 95-102, 105, 242, 243, 245, 246, 248

Immortality 32-34, 45, 47-53, 55, 82-86, 91, 94, 151, 152, 154, 156-160, 244-246, 248, 302, 305, 309, 310, 343, 345, 346, 348, 350, 352, 353

Indra 96, 97, 100, 101

Īśa Upaniṣad 6, 12, 15, 16, 18, 22, 25, 38, 39, 56, 61, 62, 65, 66, 68, 69, 71, 73, 75, 77-79, 82, 84-86, 90-92, 98, 116-119, 121-125, 161, 181, 195, 213, 214, 225, 226, 244, 287, 297, 338, 340, 346, 361, 362, 367, 368, 392

Kaṭha Upaniṣad 108, 109, 113, 205, 213, 300, 303, 317, 319, 341, 344, 351, 362

Kena Upaniṣad 82, 85, 86, 90, 92, 98, 103, 318, 337, 351, 362

Mahad Bhūta 275, 383, 386

Madhu Brāhmaṇa 254, 258, 260, 263, 268-273, 278, 283-288

Madhu Vidyā 254, 258, 263, 270, 272, 278-286

Mahādevan, T.M.P. 293-301

Maitreyī Brāhmaṇa 254, 255, 257, 258, 260, 263, 264, 268, 269, 272, 273, 278, 288

Māṇḍūkya Upaniṣad 164, 168, 169, 172, 173, 175, 182, 184, 186-188, 190, 193-195, 199, 315, 338, 339, 362

Māyā 141-148, 204-208, 210, 214, 293, 299, 300, 391-394

Muṇḍaka Upaniṣad 65, 115-119, 121, 123-125, 127-131, 133-135, 139, 141, 144-146, 151-156, 157-162, 169, 206,

207, 210, 216, 218, 224, 250, 298, 304, 305, 312, 319, 321-325, 331, 332, 338, 346, 350-352, 354, 355, 362, 363, 365

Negation 188, 196-198, 309

Possessions 1, 3, 153, 302, 307-309, 366, 367

Renunciation 2, 118, 153, 157, 158, 348-350

Śaṅkara 128-130, 132, 133, 164, 172, 229-231, 234-236, 238, 239, 254, 256-261, 266-269, 272, 280, 283, 285, 286, 380-383, 385, 388, 391, 392, 405, 406

Śvetāśvatara Upaniṣad 115, 124, 125, 139, 141, 143-147, 298, 299

Sri Aurobindo 14, 15, 18, 25, 65, 71-74, 77, 79, 80, 94, 101, 119, 139, 159, 160, 198, 260, 262, 269, 272, 273, , 390-400

Superimposition 230, 231, 234-237, 239, 406

Toṭaka 224, 225

Uddālaka 202, 204, 208, 210, 212, 214, 218-220

Veda 127-132, 137-139, 141, 144, 145, 312-316, 318, 324, 328, 329, 352, 354, 355, 405, 406

Vedānta 137-139, 312, 324, 331, 353, 354, 363, 368, 377, 395, 397

Vidyāraṇya 202, 203, 206-212

Works 1-3, 59-62, 65, 151-154, 156-160, 162, 302, 304-307, 309, 321-325, 328, 330-332, 363-365, 367

Yājñavalkya 246-249, 251, 255, 264, 267, 274, 278, 281, 308, 309, 326-328, 349, 350, 365, 366

Yoga 108, 111, 113, 312, 313, 316-330, 332, 359, 362, 363, 367

ANCIENT INDIAN TRADITION AND MYTHOLOGY

Mahāpurāṇas *Translated into English*
Gen. Ed. Dr. G.C. TRIPATHI
Founder Eds. LATE J.L. SHASTRI and LATE G.P. BHATT

PUBLISHED VOLUMES

Vols. 1-4	ŚIVA PURĀṆA *Tr.* J.L. Shastri
Vols. 5-6	LIṄGA PURĀṆA *Tr.* J.L. Shastri
Vols. 7-11	BHĀGAVATA PURĀṆA *Tr.* G.V. Tagare
Vols. 12-14	GARUḌA PURĀṆA *Tr.* J.L. Shastri
Vols. 15-19	NĀRADA PURĀṆA *Tr.* G.V. Tagare
Vols. 20-21	KŪRMA PURĀṆA *Tr.* G.V. Tagare
Vols. 22-26	BRAHMĀṆḌA PURĀṆA *Tr.* G.V. Tagare
Vols. 27-30	AGNI PURĀṆA *Tr.* N. Gangadharan
Vols. 31-32	VARĀHA PURĀṆA *Tr.* S. Venkitasubramonia Iyer
Vols. 33-36	BRAHMA PURĀṆA *Tr.* J.L. Shastri
Vols. 37-38	VĀYU PURĀṆA *Tr.* G.V. Tagare
Vols. 39-48	PADMA PURĀṆA *Tr.* N.A. Deshpande
Vols. 49-71	SKANDA PURĀṆA *Ed.* G.P. Bhatt, *Tr. & Annot.* Shridhar Balooni & Pratosh Panda
Vols. 72-73	VĀMANA PURĀṆA *Tr. & Annot.* R.S. Shiva Ganesha Murthy
Vols. 74-76	GAṆEŚA PURĀṆA *Tr. & Annot.* Greg Bailey
Vols. 77-82	BRAHMA-VAIVARTA PURĀṆA *Tr. & Annot.* G.P. Bhatt

PURĀṆAS UNDER PREPARATION

Viṣṇu Purāṇa • Harivamśa Purāṇa • Bhaviṣya Purāṇa • Matsya Purāṇa • Devī Bhāgavata Purāṇa • Kālika Purāṇa • Mārkaṇḍeya Purāṇa • Viṣṇudharmottara Purāṇa

HINDU TRADITION SERIES

The Hindu Tradition Series aims to bring together books of the highest academic standard that critically interrogate Hindu tradition in the widest sense. Its focus is on cultural and religious history, including relevant political and social developments. The interaction with other traditions, whether originally from inside or outside the Indian subcontinent, will figure prominently among its volumes.

1. **The Mahābhārata and Greek Mythology** — FERNANDO WULFF ALONSO [978-81-208-3791-1]
2. **Viraha-Bhakti :** The Early History of Kṛṣṇa Devotion — FRIEDHELM HARDY [978-81-208-3616-1]
3. **Classical Hindu Mythology** : A Reader in the Sanskrit Purāṇas — Ed. and Tr. by CORNELLA DIMMITT and J.A.B. VAN BUTTENAN [978-81-208-3972-4]
4. **Mythology of Brahma** — GREG BAILEY
5. **India and the Hellenistic World**— KLAUS KARTTUNEN
6. **The Śrīvaiṣṇava Hagiography of Parakāla and other Papers** — FRIEDHELM HARDY

INDIA'S SANSKRIT EPIC
Text and Tradition

The Series builds on the Poona and Baroda critical editions of the Sanskrit epics, the Mahabharata and the Ramayana respectively. Its subtitle "Texts And Traditions" leans toward the textual, as the Series will invite and seek to attract volumes that address and work from the monumental texts presented in the two critical editions, in the Mahabharata's case including the Harivamsa, and on the relation between the reconstituted critical edition texts and later Sanskrit texts of the Mahabharata and Ramayana textual traditions. Studies that are critical of the critical editions themselves will, however, also be considered, as the works that study the relation between the Sanskrit texts and vernacular Mahabharata and Ramayana texts and traditions.

1. **Carried Meaning in the Mahābhārata** — DAN RUDMAN
2. **Authenticity and the Problem of the Beginning in the Mahābhārata** — VISHWA ADLURI
3. **On the Southern Recension of the Mahābhārata :** Brahman Migrations, and Brahmi Paleography — T.P. MAHADEVAN

A HISTORY OF INDIAN LITERATURE
(3 Volumes)

MAURICE WINTERNITZ

ISBN: 978-81-208-0263-6 (Set)

The present English translation is based on the original German work and has been revised in the light of further researches on the subject by different scholars in India and elsewhere.

Volume I : Introduction, Veda, Epics, Puranas and Tantras—Tr. *V.S. Sarma*

This is divided into two sections. Section I relates to Veda (the Four Saṃhitās), Brāhmaṇas, Āraṇyakas, Upaniṣads, Vedāṅgas and the literature of the Ritual. Section II relates to the study of two great Epics of India—the Rāmāyaṇa and the Mahābhārata. It carries out a general survey of the Purāṇic literature, and provides ample information about the Tantras too.

[ISBN:978-81-208-0264-3]

Volume II : Buddhist and Jaina Literature—Tr. *V.S. Sarma*

It contains two sections viz. Section III and Section IV relating to Buddhism and Jainism literature respectively.

[ISBN: 978-81-208-0265-0]

Volume III (2 Pts. in One) Pt. I : Classical Sanskrit Literature

Pt. II : Scientific Literature—Tr. *S. Jha*

It covers the history of Classical Sanskrit literature and the Scientific literature with its characteristics, grammar, lexicography, philosophy, dharmaśāstra, architecture, saṅgītaśāstra, kāmaśāstra, āyurveda, astronomy, astrology and mathematics and also has an appendix.

[ISBN: 978-81-208-0056-4]